Agile Database
Techniques
Effective Strategies for the
Agile Software Developer

Agile Database
Techniques
Effective Strategies for the
Agile Software Developer

Scott W. Ambler

Wiley Publishing, Inc.

Vice President and Publisher: Joseph B. Wikert
Executive Editor: Robert M. Elliott
Development Editor: James H. Russell
Editorial Manager: Kathryn A. Malm
Senior Production Editor: Angela Smith
Text Design & Composition: Wiley Composition Services

Library of Congress Cataloging-in-Publication Data:

ISBN: 0-471-20283-5

Printed in the United States of America

10 9 8 7 6 5 4 3 2 1

To my parents, Bill and Loreen.
Thanks muchly.

Contents

Foreword by Jon Kern

"Got database?" *Then get agile!*

The agile movement was given shape in the shadows of 11,000-foot peaks of Snowbird, Utah, in February 2001. Ever since, people and pundits alike have been talking and practicing agility. Many development groups, tired of the failed promise of heavyweight processes and death marches towards uncertain goals in uncertain timeframes, are finding comfort in a "human-readable" set of development philosophies and principles.

Scott Ambler has a strong voice in the agile community, founding the Agile Modeling Forum in February 2001. To all who "know" Scott, it is clear that he is passionate about helping development teams succeed for their stakeholders and, ultimately, their customers.

There are many resources that address object modeling, agile techniques, UML (Unified Modeling Language), language-specific intricacies, database design, SQL, and so on. Many good books present information on how to develop a good object-oriented application. Likewise, there are excellent tomes on techniques for developing and tuning databases. It is less likely that you will run across books that describe an evolutionary, agile approach to data-oriented development.

In this book, Scott addresses this key area of application development — the database. He extends the reach of agile techniques across the application team, from developer to database architect, demonstrating that agile techniques are no longer the sole domain of the development folks. The DBA can also apply the same principles to the database — developing incrementally and iteratively, just as developers do with their code base. Now, DBAs will be able to understand the agile methodologies as applied to data-oriented development. They will gain insight and learn how to fit into the larger team, how to leverage their extensive experience with a given DBMS, and how to effectively — and efficiently — support the team's persistence needs. Even if you work on a small team without "designated" DBAs, this book will be very helpful for its

*With apologies to the National Dairy Council

insights into the critical techniques for addressing the common persistence problems facing all development teams.

For those of us who have had the pleasure of introducing development teams to object-oriented methodologies, the data-modeling aspect is *always* an interesting topic. On the one hand, good object models look a lot like well-formed entity-relationship diagrams (if yours don't, well, get mentored on object modeling!) and many object modelers drive the database design from their class diagrams. On the other hand, some database experts will insist the world revolves around the database (especially where legacy databases have been driving the business for the last decade). Both positions have merit — yet neither is entirely correct. Scott presents a give-and-take, evolutionary methodology that establishes balance within the team. He points out that real-world applications often have more than one option for addressing data concerns throughout the development iterations.

Most modern development methodologies are iterative in nature and require an evolutionary approach. Most hard-core data modelers may be more familiar with a waterfall approach with big, up-front design. This can sometimes cause friction within the team and result in turf warfare. This book will teach the developer about database basics and teach the DBA the needed skills to be a member of an agile development project. Effectively intertwining agile object development and agile database development can only help teams in their quest for success.

I wish I had a book like this eight years ago when I was developing my first major thin-client, object-oriented application with a data management layer and all the associated other ilks that come along for the ride. *You* will be able to avoid many of the lessons from the school of "hard knocks" by using this book. If you have ever considered "dirty flags," two-phase commits in a distributed environment, or the struggle between "who" is in charge of referential integrity (the database or the objects), then you will benefit greatly from this work. And, if you aren't sure what these terms mean, then you *really* must consider this book!

Because almost every (business) application-development project confronts the need for data storage, this book will be an invaluable resource to most development teams. You'll want to be sure to have enough copies for both your development *and* database folks. Developers enhance their skills by learning about agile database techniques, and DBAs learn how to orient their database development techniques along more agile lines — more effectively supporting the development effort. In short, everybody stands to win. So grab a stimulating cup of something, study up, and then let the collaboration begin!

Jon Kern
Coauthor, *Agile Manifesto*

Foreword by Douglas K. Barry

I want everyone reading this foreword to turn immediately to Chapter 23 of this book. Look at the table containing recommendations on how to become more agile. Do the entries in the table make you feel a little uncomfortable? Good. Do you think these recommendations are unnecessary? Why is that? Take my advice: You really need to do what Scott is suggesting. These are the first steps you can take to improve the chances you will have a successful project. And they may just be very uncomfortable steps to take.

Some mental discomfort is good for people who want to make a change. There is no question that change is needed in how we build (or fail to build) our software systems. This includes our databases. If all we do is what we find to be comfortable, then there is little chance for change.

To me, Scott is suggesting in Chapter 23 that it is good to stand in the other people's shoes for a while. *Really* stand. Talking with other people and expressing empathy for their situation is good, but not good enough. Actually trying to do another person's job is a very different experience.

I know, because I have stood in many people's shoes. Early in my career, I was a data-modeling guru at a large corporation. Then, I got involved in software design and had to deal with other people's database designs. After that, I was the CIO of a startup database company. That was followed by many years in database-related standards development. At the same time, I started helping people to understand what is likely to be the best architecture for their needs — which is what I am currently doing. Let me tell you, it has been an education, and I have often felt uncomfortable. But I think I am better off for it. Based on my experience, it appears that Scott is showing you a good way to start on your own path.

Throughout this book, Scott includes practical suggestions for using agile techniques in database development. You might not always agree, but it will possibly challenge your thinking. And that is good as well.

Scott also offers common-sense design suggestions for developing a database and for the mapping of data between different types of systems. These suggestions are important, and you do not always find them in the basic modeling texts.

The uncommon suggestions for becoming agile and the common-sense design suggestions make this a good, all-around book for someone looking to go beyond a basic modeling text. You will find workable, real-world advice here.

Douglas K. Barry
Founder and Principal, Barry & Associates, Inc.
(www.barryandassociates.com)

Acknowledgments

I'd like to thank the following for their ideas and, more importantly, for their skepticisms: Dave Astels, Philippe Back, Francois Beauregard, Graham Berrisford, Charles Betz, Chris Britton, Steven Brown, Steve Cohen, Mike Colbert, Warren Cotton, Dale Emery, Neal Fishman, Adam Geras, Steven Gordon, Jason Gorman, Michael M. Gorman, David C. Hay, Michael Haynes, Mats Helander, Daniel Honig, Ron Jeffries, Jon Kern, Jan Emil Larsen, Kevin Light, Floyd Marinescu, Les Munday, John Nalbone, Pan Wei Ng, Paul Oldfield, Oscar Pearce, Chris Roffler, Dave Rooney, John Roth, Adrian Rutter, Yonn M. Samuels, Dwight W. Seeley, Paul Tiseo, Jason P. Tryon, Patrick Vanhuyse, Micheal Vizdos, Michael Vorburger, Sebastian Ware, David Waters, Gary Williams, Dawn M. Wolthuis, and Michael Zimmer.

I'd also like to thank my editors at John Wiley & Sons, Inc., including James H. Russell, Angela Smith, Terri Hudson, Kathryn A. Malm, and Robert M. Elliott.

Introduction

An Agile Introduction: This is a really good book. Buy it. Read it. Spread the word.

Since the early 1990s, I've been working with both object and relational database (RDB) technologies to build business applications, and since the mid-1990s I've done a fair bit of writing on the subject. These writings have appeared in *Software Development* (www.sdmagazine.com), in several of my books (in particular *Building Object Applications That Work* and *The Object Primer*), and on my personal Web site (www.ambysoft .com). The two white papers at my site, one on mapping objects to RDBs and the other describing the design of a persistence layer, have proven to be incredibly popular, with several hundred thousand downloads over the years. The persistence layer paper has even been used as the basis for several open source products. Although it's been very rewarding for me to share my ideas through these writings, I never took the time to collect this work in one place, nor have I written everything that I have to say about the topic. This book rectifies this situation.

As a consultant, I've worked with object and data professionals, their related technologies, and of course their techniques. In doing so, I've worked in traditional environments that take a near-serial approach to development as well as more modern environments that take an agile and evolutionary approach to development. Over time, I've worked on many different project teams in various roles. Data-oriented issues were important, and sometimes even critical, to the success of each project. Although traditional project teams seemed to have a handle on how to deal with data issues the more agile ones often struggled — in part because the data professionals in those organizations preferred to take a serial approach and in part because the object developers didn't appreciate the importance of data-oriented issues. Being an ex-data-specialist (oh no, my horrible secret is out!) and being experienced in object technology, I often found ways for the two groups to work together. My experience was that data professionals were often overly focused on data to the exclusion of the wide variety of challenges faced by object developers and similarly object developers had little or no data-related experience. So, I would help the two groups find ways to work together, to mentor them in each other's techniques, and to help them overcome what is known as the object-relational impedance mismatch. For these two groups to work together effectively, they each need to understand and appreciate what the other group is focused on, and I would even call into question the wisdom of having separate groups to begin with. This book describes the skills that both data professionals and object professionals require in order to build modern-day software.

As a methodologist I have actively tried to find ways to develop software effectively, and over the years have run the gambit from prescriptive approaches such as my work with process patterns (www.ambysoft.com/processPatternsPage.html) and the Enterprise Unified Process (EUP) (www.enterpriseunifiedprocess.info) to agile approaches such as Agile Modeling (AM) (www.agilemodeling.com) and now agile database techniques. In part, this book is an extension of AM to help describe how data professionals can take an evolutionary (iterative and incremental) approach to development. Although many people within the data community are adamantly opposed to evolutionary approaches, interestingly enough I've often found that those opposed to it have never actually tried it; the reality is that agile software development is real and here to stay. For data professionals to remain relevant, they must be prepared to work in an agile manner, otherwise project teams will very likely find ways to work around them (I suspect you see this sort of thing happen within your organization all of the time). My experience, on actual projects, is that you can in fact be very successful by taking an agile approach to data-oriented activities if you choose to do so. Many people will tell you that it won't work, but all they're really saying is that they either can't make it work or they don't want to. This book describes numerous, proven techniques that support evolutionary data-oriented development.

When I first started writing this book, I intended its focus to be on the agile data (AD) method (www.agiledata.org). This method, summarized in Chapter 1, describes how data professionals and application developers can work together effectively on agile projects. It also describes how enterprise professionals, such as enterprise architects and data administrators, can support agile development teams effectively. Because I was taking an iterative and incremental approach to the development of the book, I quickly realized that the real value lay in detailed development techniques instead of yet another methodology. So I refocused.

The Audience for This Book

Who is the audience for this book? The simple answer is anyone who is part of, or at least interacting with, an agile software-development team. The more complicated answer is:

Agile/extreme programmers.   Chances are pretty good that the software that you're building manipulates data: therefore, you'll need to adopt many of the techniques described in this book.

Database administrators.   This book describes how you can succeed working on an agile software-development team. Read it from cover to cover.

Data administrators.   You'll need to support more and more agile development teams as times goes on, and therefore you need to understand how they work and why they work this way. This book will provide the insight that you require to help these teams be effective.

Architects.   Agile, evolutionary development is quickly becoming the norm in most organizations. This book describes techniques that you can adopt to work effectively on these teams.

Team leads/coaches/managers.   To lead an agile software-development team effectively, you must understand the techniques that your team uses, why they apply those techniques, and the implications of doing so. This book not only describes these techniques but also discusses their trade-offs, enabling you to help your team make intelligent decisions.

Why the Focus on Agile DBAs?

Although most of the skills that I describe in this book are applicable to both application developers and database administrators (DBAs), I choose to present them from the point of view of an agile DBA. An agile DBA focuses on data-oriented issues, including traditional database administration as well as any application development involving data. Agile DBAs will also collaborate with enterprise professionals to ensure that the efforts of the project team reflect enterprise realities. The important thing is that they do this work in an agile manner. The role of agile DBA can be held by several people on your project, can be shared on a rotating basis by several people, or can be held by a single person. Although the skillset of an agile DBA can seem formidable, and it is, you'll find that you can gain these skills over time by working with others who already have skills that you're missing, by training, and by simply trying them out for yourself.

An Overview

This book is organized into four parts. The first part sets the foundation by describing the fundamental skills and philosophies that all IT professionals require to be effective at data-oriented activities. The second part describes techniques that enable evolutionary database development, showing that it is possible to take an iterative and incremental approach to data-oriented development. The third part provides an overview of detailed implementation techniques for effectively using object technology, relational database technology, and XML (Extensible Markup Language) technology together. The fourth part wraps up with a discussion of how to successfully adopt the concepts described in this book.

Part I

A significant problem in the IT industry is that most data books do not cover object-oriented development issues, and most object books seem to ignore data issues. This needs to stop. Part I describes the fundamental skills and knowledge that everyone on an agile project team should have. This includes the basics of object orientation, relational databases, the object-relational impedance mismatch, data modeling, and how to deal with legacy data issues. Without this common base of knowledge it is very difficult for application developers and data professionals to work together effectively.

Part II

Part II focuses on how to take an evolutionary approach to data. This section sets the foundation for a model-driven development (MDD) approach, or more accurately, an agile model-driven development (AMDD) approach where your application code and database schemas are based on agile models. This isn't the only way to work; you may decide to take a test-driven development (TDD) approach instead, or better yet, combine it with AMDD. Both methods support evolutionary development but because MDD is very common within the data community, I suspect that developers will gravitate more towards an AMDD approach rather than a TDD approach. However, some agile developers, particularly extreme programmers, prefer TDD over AMDD. Luckily, the two approaches work very well together, so it really doesn't matter which you choose. The implication is that TDD will become more important to data professionals in the coming years. This part also describes database refactoring, an evolutionary technique that enables you to improve your database design in small steps. In many ways, database refactoring is normalization after the fact. Chapters describing mapping objects to relational databases, performance tuning, database encapsulation, and supporting tools are included in this part because they enable evolutionary development.

Part III

Part III focuses on implementation techniques and strategies such as concurrency control, security access control, finding objects in relational databases, referential integrity, and the effective use of XML. An important observation is that many of these topics are traditionally thought of as data issues, but as you'll see there is far more to them than this — it isn't a black-and-white world.

Part IV

Part IV describes strategies for adopting agile database techniques. This chapter provides advice for individuals who want to become agile software developers and for organizations that want to adopt agile techniques.

About the Author

Scott W. Ambler is a senior consultant with Ronin International, Inc. (www.ronin-intl.com), a firm specializing in helping organizations to adopt new software-development techniques. Scott is a senior contributing editor with *Software Development* (www.sdmagazine.com) and the (co)author of numerous books, including *Agile Modeling, Mastering EJB,* Second Edition, and *The Object Primer*. In his spare time Scott is an avid photographer and martial artist, studying karate, tai chi, and yoga. Scott lives just north of Toronto, Canada, although he travels all around the world to work with clients (as far as he's concerned the more exotic the locale the better).

Setting the Foundation

This part describes fundamental skills and knowledge that everyone on an agile project team should have. Why should you invest your time reading these chapters? Without this common base of knowledge it is very difficult for application developers and data professionals to work together effectively. A significant problem in the IT industry is that most data books do not cover object-oriented development issues and most object books seem to ignore data issues. Furthermore, leading agile books have all but ignored data and enterprise issues until now. I think it's time that we all decide to start investing the time to learn about the wide range of issues that we commonly face on a daily business. Although you may feel that you have a very good understanding of one or more of these topics my advice is to skim the chapters describing your areas of expertise because I suspect I've presented many new insights on these "old topics".

Chapter 1: The Agile Data Method.   Explores how application developers, database administrators (DBAs), enterprise architects, and data administrators can work together effectively in an agile environment.

Chapter 2: From Use Cases to Databases — Real-World UML.   Object technology is the norm for modern projects; therefore, it is critical for everyone to understand the basics of object orientation and the Unified Modeling Language (UML) 2.x (including UML data modeling).

Chapter 3: Data Modeling 101.   Data modeling is a fundamental skill that all software professionals, including object professionals, require if they wish to store data effectively.

Chapter 4: Data Normalization.   Normalization is a collection of design strategies that ensure data is stored in one place and one place only, promoting the design of highly cohesive and loosely coupled data schemas.

Chapter 5: Class Normalization.   The concepts of normalization can be applied to object schemas, a complementary technique for designing patterns and programming idioms.

Chapter 6: Relational Database Technology, Like It or Not.   Relational databases (RDBs) have been the dominant technology for persisting business objects and will likely remain so; therefore, you need to understand the technology.

Chapter 7: The Object-Relational Impedance Mismatch.   Object technology and relational technology are based on different paradigms, presenting a technical impedance mismatch that must be overcome. Worse yet is the cultural mismatch between object professionals and data professionals, which must also be bridged.

Chapter 8: Legacy Databases — Everything You Need to Know But Are Afraid to Deal With.   Virtually every project team finds that it needs to work with legacy data sources, and when doing so quickly discovers serious data quality, database design, and data architecture problems that it needs to overcome.

The Agile Data Method

*It is possible to take an agile approach to data-oriented development.
The first step is to choose to work this way.*

Data is clearly an important aspect of software-based systems — something we've all known for decades — and yet many organizations still struggle with their approach to data-oriented issues within their software processes.

The goal of the agile data (AD) method is to define strategies that enable IT professionals to work together effectively on the data aspects of software systems. This isn't to say that AD is a "one size fits all" methodology. Instead, consider AD as a collection of philosophies that will enable software developers within your organization to work together effectively when it comes to the data aspects of software-based systems. Although the focus of this book is proven techniques for agile software development, it's critical to define an underlying methodological foundation.

In this chapter, I help you understand the AD method by exploring the following topics:

- Why working together is currently difficult
- The agile movement
- The philosophies of agile data
- Agile data in a nutshell
- Does agile data address our problems?

Why Working Together Is Currently Hard

In many organizations, the relationship between data professionals and developers is often less than ideal. Yes, there are some organizations where these two communities work together quite well, but there are always tensions — some healthy tension exists between groups, and from these your organization can benefit, but when the tension isn't healthy these differences often lead to conflicts. The challenges that data professionals and developers must overcome can include:

Different visions and priorities.   Developers are often focused on the specific needs of a single project and often strive to work as much as possible in isolation from the rest of the organization. Database administrators (DBAs) focus on the database(s) that they are responsible for, often "protecting" the databases by minimizing changes to them. Data administrators and data architects focus on the overall data needs of the enterprise, sometimes to the virtual exclusion of the immediate needs of project teams. Clearly, the scope of each group is different, their priorities are different, and the issues that the groups deal with are different. To make matters worse, your project stakeholders, including direct users all the way up to senior management, have varying priorities and visions as well.

Overspecialization of roles.   Specialists have a tendency to become too narrowly focused; they can work so hard to know everything there is to know about a small slice of software development that they can become oblivious of everything else. For example, it's quite common to find senior Java developers that have never heard about data normalization (discussed in Chapter 4), or even understand why you would want to do such a thing, and data architects who can't read a Unified Modeling Language (UML) state chart diagram (discussed in Chapter 2). Because these roles are overly specialized, the people in those roles often have difficulties relating to others. At the other end of the spectrum are generalists who understand the big picture but don't have any concrete skills to offer a development team. We need to find the sweet spot between these two extremes. An underlying philosophy of *Agile Modeling* (Ambler 2002a) is that software developers should have a general understanding of the overall software process *and* have one or more specialties. Because agile modelers are generalists, they understand the broad range of issues pertinent to the "software game" and yet they still have specific, valuable skills to offer to their team.

Process impedance mismatch.   One of the few things that processes such as the Unified Process (Kruchten 2000; Ambler 2001b), Extreme Programming (XP) (Beck 2000), Scrum (Beedle and Schwaber 2001), DSDM (Stapleton 1997), Crystal Clear (Cockburn 2001b), feature-driven development (FDD) (Palmer and Felsing 2002), and Agile Modeling (AM) have in common is that they all work in an evolutionary (iterative and incremental) manner. Unfortunately, many within the data community still view software development as a serial or near-serial process. Clearly, there is an impedance mismatch here, indicating that the data community needs to rethink its approach. You will see in Part II of this book that it is possible to take an evolutionary approach to data, a change that will require cultural and organizational adjustments to succeed.

Technology impedance mismatch. Developers work with objects and components, whereas data professionals work with databases and files. Software-engineering principles form the underlying foundational paradigm for objects and components, whereas set theory forms the underlying foundational paradigm for relational databases (by far the most popular database technology). Because the underlying paradigms are different, the technologies don't work together perfectly, and an impedance mismatch exists. This mismatch can be overcome, although doing so requires a significant skillset (this topic is covered in Chapter 7).

Ossified management. The technology and techniques used by software developers change rapidly, a fact that we all know very well. As people progress up the corporate hierarchy, they deal less with technology and more with people issues, the end result being that many managers have lost their technical edge. The implication is that management's previous development experiences, on which they base technical decisions, may no longer be applicable. We experienced this when we moved from procedural to object-oriented technologies — what may have been a good decision on a COBOL project often proves to be the kiss of death to a Java project. We're clearly seeing this problem once again as we move to agile software processes. Management needs to change with the times.

Organizational challenges. Common problems, such as poor communication or politics among individuals and groups, hurt the data aspects of software development just as badly as they hurt other efforts, by preventing everyone from working together effectively.

Poor documentation. Most documentation seems to be at one of the following extremes: little or no documentation or overly complex documentation that nobody reads. Mutually agreed-to development standards and guidelines, legacy system documentation, legacy database documentation, and enterprise models can be valuable resources when written well. Chapter 10 presents agile strategies for writing documentation.

Ineffective architectural efforts. Most organizations face significant challenges when it comes to enterprise architecture, the most common of which being that they don't know where to start. Biased enterprise architectures that overly focus on one view of the enterprise lead to architectures that do not adequately address the real needs of an organization. As the Zachman Framework (ZIFA 2002; Hay 2003) indicates, there are many potential views that you want to consider. These views are data/structure, function/process, network, people, time, and motivation. Ivory tower architectures — those formulated by teams that have removed themselves from the day-to-day realities of project teams — look good on paper but unfortunately fail in practice. Furthermore, developers need to accept that their efforts must reflect and conform to the constraints imposed on them by their organization's environment.

Ineffective development guidelines. Many organizations struggle to come to a collection of development guidelines that all software developers will work to. There are a large number of causes for this, including people not understanding the need to follow such guidelines, people unwilling to follow someone else's guidelines, overly complex guidelines, overly simplistic guidelines, a "one size fits all" attitude that leads to inappropriate guidelines for a specific platform, and an unwillingness to evolve guidelines over time. When you have an effective collection of guidelines available to you, and (this is key) *everyone understands and applies them appropriately*, you can dramatically improve the productivity of your software development efforts.

Ineffective modeling efforts.   This is often the result of several of the previously identified problems. People focused on a specific aspect of development will often produce models that wonderfully reflect the priorities of that narrow view but fail to take into account the realities of other views. An enterprise data model may present an excellent vision of the data required by an organization, but an enterprise model that reflects the data, functional, usage, and technical requirements of an organization is likely to be far more useful. A UML class diagram may reflect the needs of a single project, but if it doesn't reflect the realities of the legacy data sources that it will access then it is of little value in practice. Modelers, and software developers in general, need to work together and look at the full picture to be truly effective.

Detecting That You Have a Problem

It is very easy for organizations to deny that they have a problem. It can be very difficult for senior management to detect problems until it's too late because the bad news that they need to hear is filtered out long before it gets to them. Similarly, it can be difficult for people elsewhere in the organization to detect problems — perhaps everything is going quite well in their opinion — unfortunately the value system that they're using to judge the situation isn't ideal, making them blind to the problems that they are causing.

As a consultant I have the privilege of working in a wide range of organizations, and it seems to me that about one in ten organizations is reasonably successful with its approach to data-oriented activities, about six in ten think they're doing well but really aren't, and the remaining three in ten know that they have a problem but don't know what to do about it. It doesn't have to be this way.

So how do you know you've got a problem? Enterprise data professionals, including both data architects and data administrators, will be frustrated by the fact that project developers on project teams ignore their advice, standards, guidelines, and enterprise models. Worse yet, application developers often don't even know about these people and things in the first place. Developers will be frustrated by what they perceive (often rightfully so) to be the glacial pace of enterprise data professionals to make or authorize seemingly simple changes. DBAs often find themselves stuck in between these two warring factions, trying to get their work done, while struggling to keep the peace. If one or more of these problems is common within your organization you've got a problem.

The following is a list of potential symptoms that may indicate that your organization has one or more challenges that the agile data method may help you address:

- People are significantly frustrated with the efforts, or lack thereof, of one or more groups.

- Software is not being developed, or if it is it is taking far too long or is much too expensive.

- Finger pointing occurs such that you hear things like "the data administrators are holding up progress" or "the developers aren't following corporate guidelines." Worse yet, the finger pointer typically doesn't perceive that he or she is also part of the problem.

- Political issues are given higher priority than working together to develop, maintain, and support software-based systems.

- Ongoing feuds exist between people and groups. Phrases that start with "you always" and "you never" are good indicators of this.

- Well-known problems within your organization are not being addressed. Furthermore, suggestions for improvements appear to be ignored, nothing happens, and no reason for rejection is provided.

- People are working excessively long hours with little or no reward.

- Decisions affecting teams — in particular project teams — are made in an apparently arbitrary and arrogant fashion.

We need to find a way to work together effectively. There are clear differences between the data and development communities as well as between the project and enterprise communities. The fact that we're talking about different communities is also part of the problem, arguably one of the root causes. You have a fundamental decision to make: Should you use these differences as an excuse to exacerbate existing problems within your organization or should you revel in these differences and find a way to take advantage of them? I prefer the latter approach. My experience is that the values and principles of the agile movement form the basis for an effective approach to working together.

The Agile Movement

To address the challenges faced by software developers an initial group of 17 methodologists formed the Agile Software Development Alliance (www.agilealliance.org), often referred to simply as the Agile Alliance, in February 2001. An interesting thing about this group is that the members all came from different backgrounds, and yet they were able to come to an agreement on issues that methodologists typically don't agree upon (Fowler 2001a). This group of people defined a manifesto for encouraging better ways of developing software, and then, based on that manifesto, formulated a collection of principles that defines the criteria for agile software development processes such as AM.

The Manifesto for Agile Software Development

The manifesto (Agile Alliance 2001a) is defined by four simple value statements — the important thing to understand is that while you should value the concepts on the right-hand side, you should value the things on the *left-hand side* even more. A good way to think about the manifesto is that it defines preferences, not alternatives, encouraging a focus on certain areas but not eliminating others. The Agile Alliance values are as follows:

Individuals and interactions **over processes and tools.**   Teams of people build software systems, and to do that they need to work together effectively — teams include but are not limited to programmers, testers, project managers, modelers, and customers. Who do you think would develop a better system: five software developers with their own tools working together in a single room or five low-skilled "hamburger flippers" with a well-defined process, the most sophisticated tools available, and the best offices money could buy? If the project were reasonably complex, my money would be on the software developers, wouldn't yours? The point is that the most important factors that you need to consider are the people and how they work together; if you don't get that right the best tools and processes won't be of any use. Tools and processes are important, don't get me wrong, it's just that they're not as important as working together effectively. Remember the old adage, *a fool with a tool is still a fool*. This can be difficult for management to accept because they often want to believe that people and time, or men and months, are interchangeable (Brooks 1995).

Working software **over comprehensive documentation.**   When you ask a user whether he or she would want a fifty-page document describing what you intend to build or the actual software itself, what do you think that person will pick? My guess is that 99 times out of 100, the user will choose working software, assuming of course that he or she expects that you can actually deliver. If that is the case, doesn't it make more sense to work so that you produce software quickly and often, giving your users what they prefer? Furthermore, I suspect that users will have a significantly easier time understanding any software that you produce than complex technical diagrams describing its internal workings or describing an abstraction of its usage. Documentation has its place, written properly, it is a valuable guide for people's understanding of how and why a system is built and how to work with the system. However, never forget that the primary goal of software development is to create software, not documents — otherwise, it would be called documentation development wouldn't it?

Customer collaboration **over contract negotiation.**   Only your customer can tell you what they want. No, they likely do not have the skills to exactly specify the system. No, they likely won't get it right at first. Yes, they'll likely change their minds. Working together with your customers is hard, but that's the reality of the job. Having a contract with your customers is important, but, while having an understanding of everyone's rights and responsibilities may form the foundation of that contract, a contract isn't a substitute for communication. Successful developers work closely with their customers, they invest the effort to discover what their customers need, and they educate their customers along the way.

Responding to change **over following a plan.**   People change their priorities for a variety of reasons. As work progresses on your system, your project stakeholders' understanding of the problem domain and of what you're building changes. The business environment changes. Technology changes over time and *not* always for the better. Change is a reality of software development, a reality that your software process must reflect. There is nothing wrong with having a project plan; in fact, I would be worried about any project that didn't have one, but a project plan must be malleable; that is, there must be room to change it as your situation changes; otherwise, your plan quickly becomes irrelevant.

The interesting thing about these value statements is that almost everyone will instantly agree to them, and yet rarely do people adhere to them in practice. Senior management always claims that its employees are the most important aspect of the organization, and yet often they follow ISO-9000-compliant processes and treat their staff as replaceable assets. Even worse, management often refuses to provide sufficient resources to comply with the processes that they insist project teams follow — the bottom line: management needs to eat its own dog food. Everyone will readily agree that the creation of software is the fundamental goal of software development, yet many people still insist on spending months producing documentation describing what the software is and how it is going to be built instead of simply rolling up their sleeves and building it. You get the idea — people often say one thing and do another. This has to stop now. Agile modelers do what they say and say what they do.

The Principles for Agile Software Development

To help define agile software development, the members of the Agile Alliance refined the philosophies captured in their manifesto into a collection of 12 principles (Agile Alliance 2001b) that methodologies, including agile data (AD), should conform to. These principles are:

- Our highest priority is to satisfy the customer through early and continuous delivery of valuable software.

- Welcome changing requirements, even late in development. Agile processes harness change for the customer's competitive advantage.

- Deliver working software frequently, from a couple of weeks to a couple of months, with a preference for the shorter time scale.

- Business people and developers must work together daily throughout the project.

- Build projects around motivated individuals. Give them the environment and support they need, and trust them to get the job done.

- The most efficient and effective method of conveying information to and within a development team is face-to-face conversation.

- Working software is the primary measure of progress.

- Agile processes promote sustainable development. The sponsors, developers, and users should be able to maintain a constant pace indefinitely.

- Continuous attention to technical excellence and good design enhances agility.

- Simplicity — the art of maximizing the amount of work not done — is essential.

- The best architectures, requirements, and designs emerge from self-organizing teams.

- At regular intervals, the team reflects on how to become more effective and then tunes and adjusts its behavior accordingly.

Stop for a moment and think about these principles. Is this the way that your software projects actually work? Is this the way that you think projects should work? Reread the principles again. Are they radical and impossible goals as some people would claim? Are they meaningless motherhood and apple pie statements? Or are they simply common sense? My belief is that these principles form a foundation of common sense upon which you can base successful software-development efforts, a foundation that can be used to direct the data-oriented efforts of software developers.

The Philosophies of Agile Data

First and foremost, the agile data method subscribes to the values and principles of the Agile Alliance. Although this advice is a very good start, it needs to be extended with philosophies that reflect the realities faced by data professionals. The philosophies of agile data are:

Data.   Data is one of several important aspects of software-based systems. Most, if not all, applications are based on moving, utilizing, or otherwise manipulating some kind of data, after all.

Enterprise issues.   Development teams must consider and act appropriately regarding enterprise issues. Their applications must fit into the greater scheme of things by conforming to the common enterprise architecture (or at least to the future agreed-upon architecture), by following common development standards, and by reusing existing legacy assets wherever possible.

Enterprise groups.   Enterprise groups exist to nurture enterprise assets and to support other groups, such as development teams, within your organization. These enterprise groups should act in an agile manner that reflects the expectations of their customers and the ways in which their customers work.

Every project is unique.   Each development project is unique, requiring a flexible approach tailored to its needs. One software process does not fit all, and therefore the relative importance of data varies based on the nature of the problem being addressed.

Teamwork.   Software developers must work together effectively, actively striving to overcome the challenges that make it difficult to do so.

Sweet spot.   You should actively strive to find the "sweet spot" for any issue, avoiding the black and white extremes to find the gray that works best for your overall situation.

Interestingly, most of these philosophies aren't specific to data; instead, they are applicable to software-development efforts in general. As the first principle implies, you need to look at the overall picture and not just data; therefore, data-specific principles very likely won't serve you very well. Heresy? No. Just common sense.

Agile Data in a Nutshell

The best way to understand the AD method is to explore its four roles — agile DBA, application developer, enterprise administrator, and enterprise architect — and how they interact with each other. The first two roles, the focus of this book, are project-level development roles. The second two roles, which are featured prominently throughout the book due to their importance, are enterprise-level support roles. An agile software developer can take on one or more of these roles, although his or her focus will very likely be on one or both of the project-level roles.

Let's explore each role in greater detail.

Agile DBAs

An *agile DBA* (Schuh 2001) is anyone who is actively involved with the creation and evolution of the data aspects of one or more applications. The responsibilities of this role include, but are not limited to, the responsibilities typically associated with the traditional roles of database programmers, database administrators (DBAs), data testers, data modelers, business analysts, project managers, and deployment engineers. This is the type of role that a DBA within a small organization typically finds himself or herself in: a sort of "data jack of all trades."

The primary customers of agile DBAs are application developers, although enterprise administrators and enterprise architects are very close seconds. When agile DBAs are asked to support the business community, their primary customers will also include direct end users and their managers. This is particularly true when agile DBAs support applications that are data focused, in particular reporting applications.

An agile DBA will work closely with application developers, typically supporting a single larger team or several smaller teams as the case may be. Agile DBAs can often be responsible for several data sources (for example, databases, files, XML structures, and so on) or at least be coresponsible for them. For example, if two development teams access the same database and each of them has its own agile DBA, those two people will then need to work together to evolve that database over time. This is slightly different from Schuh's original vision of an agile DBA — his focus was on how a DBA can be effective on a single team, whereas the AD method looks at the entire enterprise. The important thing is that you work in a manner appropriate to your environment.

The biggest potential change for traditional DBAs in becoming an agile DBA is that they will need to learn to work in an evolutionary manner. Modern development processes such as the Unified Process (UP) or Extreme Programming (XP) don't provide detailed requirements up front nor do they focus on detailed models (and certainly not detailed data models up front). Instead they evolve their models over time to reflect their changing understanding of the problem domain as well as the changing requirements of their stakeholders. Some project teams may choose to work in a more serial manner, they may even choose to produce a detailed conceptual data model early in the project's life cycle, but those teams will be few and far between (although you will be expected to support them too). Agile DBAs will need to communicate the constraints imposed by legacy data sources (discussed in Chapter 8), working with application developers to understand those constraints and work appropriately.

Agile DBAs will evolve their legacy data schemas over time, applying common database refactorings (discussed in Chapter 12) as appropriate and working with new tools to evolve and migrate their data schemas over time. This is a difficult but necessary task. Agile DBAs will also need to work with application developers to model their data needs, working with UML-based artifacts such as class diagrams with some project teams and conceptual data models with other teams. Agile DBAs will work with application developers to write and test database code such as stored procedures, data-oriented code within applications that interacts with their data sources, and even aid in mapping the application schema to the data schema. Performance tuning (discussed in Chapter 15), both of the database and mappings to the database, is an important aspect of the job.

Agile DBAs commonly work with enterprise administrators, who are responsible for maintaining and evolving the corporate meta data describing the enterprise and the corporate development standards and guidelines. Agile DBAs will use this information and follow the standards and guidelines, as well as provide valuable feedback. Agile DBAs will also interact with enterprise administrators and other agile DBAs to evolve the various enterprise data sources over time, including critical meta data.

Agile DBAs also work with enterprise architects to ensure that their work fits into the overall picture and to help evolve the enterprise architecture over time.

Much of the material presented in this book is presented from the point of view of agile DBAs and application developers. I wrote it this way to remain both as consistent and as simple as possible.

Application Developers

For the sake of the agile data method an *application developer* is anyone who is actively involved with the creation and evolution of the nondata aspects of a software application (remember, any given person could take on several roles). The primary focus of an application developer is on the single system or product line that he or she is assigned to. The responsibilities of this role can include the responsibilities traditionally associated with the "traditional roles" of programmers, modelers, testers, team leads, business analysts, project managers, and deployment engineers.

As noted earlier, application developers work very closely with agile DBAs who are responsible for working on the data aspects of one or more applications. The primary customers of application developers include the potential users of their system, their managers, and the operations and support group(s) within their organization. Secondary customers include other project stakeholders such as senior management, enterprise administrators, and enterprise architects.

It is important for application developers to recognize that although their primary focus is fulfilling the current needs of direct project stakeholders, their project exists within the larger scope of the organization. This philosophy reflects AM's (discussed in Chapter 10) principles *Software Is Your Primary Goal* and *Enabling The Next Effort Is Your Secondary Goal* — in this case part of the next effort is ensuring that your project conforms to the overall enterprise vision. Application developers are best served by recognizing that they are working on one project of many within their organization, that many projects came before theirs, that many projects will come after theirs, and that, therefore, they need to work with people in the other roles to ensure that they do the right thing.

Application developers will adopt and follow agile software development processes such as FDD, DSDM, and XP. When it comes to modeling and documentation, they are likely to enhance these processes with the principles and practices of AM. All three of these processes, being agile, implore developers to work closely with their project stakeholders. An implication is that developers are responsible for helping to educate their stakeholders, including both users and managers, in the basics of software development to help them make more informed decisions when it comes to technology.

An organization's legacy systems, including legacy data sources (discussed in Chapter 8), will constrain the efforts of application developers. These systems will often be very difficult to evolve, and if they can evolve it will often happen very slowly. Luckily, agile DBAs will be able to help application developers deal with the realities imposed upon them by legacy data sources, but they will need to work with enterprise administrators and more so with enterprise architects to ensure that their efforts reflect the long-term needs of your organization. Like agile DBAs, application developers will also need to recognize that they need to follow their organization's development practices, including the guidelines and standards supported by enterprise administrators. Application developers are expected to provide feedback regarding the standards and guidelines; everyone in the organization should do so and be prepared to work with the enterprise administrators to develop guidelines for development environments that are new to the organization.

Application developers also need to work closely with enterprise architects to ensure that their project takes advantage of existing enterprise resources and fits properly into the overall enterprise vision. The enterprise architects should be able to provide this guidance and will work with your team to architect and even build your system. Furthermore, application developers should expect to be mentored in "senior" skills such as architecture and modeling. This approach makes it easy for your team to support enterprise efforts and helps keep the enterprise architects grounded because they quickly discover whether their architecture actually works in practice.

Enterprise Administrators

An *enterprise administrator* is anyone who is actively involved in identifying, documenting, evolving, protecting, and eventually retiring corporate IT assets. These assets include corporate data, corporate development standards/guidelines, and reusable software such as components, frameworks, and services. The responsibilities of this role potentially include, but are not limited to, the responsibilities associated with traditional roles of data administrators, network administrators, reuse engineers, and software process specialists. Enterprise administrators work closely with enterprise architects, although their primary customer teams are senior management and project teams. In many ways enterprise administrators are the "keepers of the corporate gates," supporting project teams, while at the same time guiding them to ensure that the long-term vision of the enterprise is fulfilled. An important goal is to guard and improve the quality of corporate assets, including but not limited to data. Good enterprise administrators are generalists with one or more specialties, one of which could be data administration, who understand a wide range of issues pertinent to the enterprise.

Enterprise administrators recognize that there is more to this job than data administration and will work in an evolutionary manner when supporting agile software-development teams. This is because enterprise administrators work closely with agile DBAs, and to a lesser extent application developers, who work in this manner. Enterprise administrators work with agile DBAs to ensure that their databases reflect the overall needs and direction of the enterprise. Enterprise administrators will find ways to communicate the importance of their role to agile DBAs and application developers, and the best way to do this is to focus on things that will make them more effective in their jobs — few people refuse a helping hand. Trying to impose your will through onerous processes or management edicts very likely won't work.

Enterprise administrators work with both agile DBAs and application developers to ensure that these folks understand the corporate standards and guidelines that they should follow. However, their role is to support the standards and guidelines, not enforce them. A good rule of thumb is that if you need to act as the "standards police," then you have lost the battle. Furthermore, this failure is very likely your fault because you didn't communicate the standards well, didn't gain support, or tried to enforce unrealistic guidelines. If the standards and guidelines make sense, they're written well, and they're easy to conform to, data and application developers will be willing to follow them. However, when this is not the case, when the standards and guidelines aren't appropriate or place an inordinate burden on projects, enterprise administrators should expect pushback. Yes, some individuals may chaff at following standards and guidelines but that's something that project coaches/managers will need to deal with.

When pushback occurs, an enterprise administrator works with the project team(s) to explore and address the problem. They are prepared to evolve the standards and guidelines over time to reflect lessons learned and the changing realities of the organization. One size will not fit all — your relational database naming conventions may be very different from your Java naming conventions and that's okay because those are two different environments with two different sets of priorities.

Enterprise administrators work closely with enterprise architects to communicate the constraints imposed by the current environment to the architects. More importantly, the enterprise administrators need to understand the future direction envisioned by the enterprise architects to ensure that their efforts support the long-term direction of the organization.

Enterprise Architects

An *enterprise architect* is anyone who is actively involved in the creation, evolution, and support/communication of the enterprise architecture. The architecture will often be described as a collection of models. These models describe a wide variety of views, one of which may be data oriented, although network/hardware views, business process views, usage views, and organizational structure views (to name a few) are equally as valuable. The responsibilities of this role includes, but is not limited to, the responsibilities associated with the traditional roles of enterprise data architects, enterprise process architects, enterprise network architects, and so on.

As with the role of enterprise administrator, the role of enterprise architect has a greater scope than just that of dealing with data — instead they look at the entire enterprise picture. The enterprise architect's main job is to look into the future, to attempt to identify a direction in which the organization is going, and hence to determine how its IT infrastructure needs to evolve. Enterprise architects are naturally constrained by the current situation the organization finds itself in, its environment, and its ability to evolve. Enterprise architects work closely with enterprise administrators to ensure that they understand the current environment and to communicate their vision for the future. The primary customers of enterprise architects are the organization's senior management, including both IT management and business management, whom they work with to evolve the enterprise vision. The project teams are also primary customers because their work should reflect the overall enterprise architecture and because they provide critical feedback to that architecture.

Enterprise architects focus on a wide variety of architectural issues, data being only one of them. Their main goal is to develop and then support enterprise architectural models. It isn't sufficient for an enterprise architect to produce good models, he or she must evangelize those models, work with development teams, and educate senior management in the implications of the architecture of system-related issues in general. In addition to the CIO and CTO of your organization, your enterprise architects are likely to have the most visibility with senior management; therefore, they need to be prepared to aid senior management to make strategic decisions.

Enterprise architects work with agile DBAs and with application developers. The most important thing that enterprise architects can do is to "walk the talk" and roll up their sleeves and get actively involved with the project. This will earn the respect of the developers, dramatically increasing the chance that they'll actually understand and follow the vision of the enterprise architecture. The advantage of this approach is that it provides immediate and concrete feedback as to whether the architecture actually works and provides valuable insights for how the architecture needs to evolve.

Enterprise architects need to be prepared to work in an iterative and incremental manner. They are ill advised to try to create an all-encompassing set of enterprise models up front. Instead, create an initial, high-level architecture, and then work closely with one or more development teams to make sure that it works. AM includes a practice called *Model In Small Increments* that is based on the premise that the longer you model without receiving concrete feedback, such at that provided by an actual project, the greater the chance that your model doesn't reflect the real-world needs of your organization. Agile enterprise architects avoid ivory-tower architectures this way. An agile approach to enterprise architecture is described at the following Web page: www.agiledata.org/essays/enterpriseArchitecture.html.

Agile Software Developers

An underlying assumption of the AD method is that your organization wants to take an agile approach to software development. Agile software development reflects a shift of mindset, a new way of thinking. To succeed at the AD method, people in the four roles described earlier must have this mindset, a mindset that is characterized by the following traits:

Teamwork. Agile software developers recognize the importance of working together effectively with others and will act accordingly. They have the humility to respect and appreciate the views and abilities of others; without this humility, they are unlikely to willingly choose to collaborate with others. A critical implication is that everyone is going to have to rethink the way that they work and be willing to change for the greater good. The attitude that "my group is the center of the universe and everyone has to conform to our vision and follow our process" doesn't work well.

Common, effective processes. Agile software developers actively seek to define an overall approach that everyone agrees to. My experience is that processes imposed from the top are very likely to fail because all it takes is one group to reject the process and "go rogue." A better process-improvement strategy is to organically grow a workable software process that reflects the needs of everyone involved. Because software developers are intelligent people with valuable skills, you are likely to find that a collection of principles that everyone agrees to is often the most important part of an effective process. In the case of the AD method these are the values and principles of agile software development as well as the AD philosophies.

Co-location. Agile software developers are willing to co-locate with others as needed. You might need to give up your comfortable cubicle or office for a while to work in a shared team space, or even have someone share your office to work with you on a project. This reflects the fact that communication and collaboration are critical to your success; you are much more effective working with others than you are working alone.

Generalizing specialists. Agile software developers are generalists with one or more specialties. The implication is that everyone needs to have a wide range of skills and be willing to work with others to improve upon existing skills and to learn new ones. (Chapter 23 explores this concept in greater detail.)

Process flexibility. Agile software developers are also prepared to tailor their approach to meet the needs of the projects they are involved with. For example, a project team working on a reporting database may very well take a different approach than one working on an online application written in Java or C#. No single approach suits all situations.

Sufficient documentation. Agile software developers recognize that documentation is a necessity in their jobs, something they can be very effective at if they choose. For example, enterprise architects recognize that the goal of enterprise modeling is to produce effective models that meet the needs of their audience, not to produce reams of documentation. They recognize that many traditional architectural efforts fail because developers are not willing to invest the time to wade through the documentation to learn the architecture. Application developers realize that system documentation is required to support future enhancement efforts and agile DBAs realize that documentation is required that describes the data sources that they support. Agile software developers will take an agile approach to documentation (discussed in Chapter 10) and produce well-written and concise documents that are just barely good enough.

Does Agile Data Solve Our Problems?

An important question to ask is whether the philosophies and suggested cultural changes discussed in this book address the problems that organizations face when it comes to the data aspects of software development. The following list shows that this in fact is the case, discussing each of the potential problems mentioned earlier in the chapter and the solution suggested by the AD method.

Different visions and priorities.   Agile data implores software developers to work together and to understand and respect the viewpoints of their coworkers.

Overspecialization of roles.   Agile data asks software developers to find the "sweet spot" between the extremes of being a generalist and being a specialist, ideally by becoming a generalist with one or more specialties.

Process impedance mismatch.   Agile data makes it clear that enterprise and data professionals must to be prepared to work following an incremental and iterative approach, the norm for most modern development and the defacto standard for agile software development. It also makes it apparent that application developers must recognize that the existing environment, and future vision for the organization, places constraints on their efforts.

Technology impedance mismatch.   Agile data requires that software developers work together closely, learning from each other as they do so. Agile DBAs have the skills to map the application schema to the data schema, to write data-oriented code, and to performance tune their work.

Ossified management.   Agile data asks enterprise architects to work with senior management and educate them in the realities of modern software development. Similarly, application developers should work with and help educate all levels of management.

Organizational challenges.   Agile data requires software developers to work with one another and with your project stakeholders, to respect them, and to actively strive to work together effectively.

Poor documentation.   Agile data directs software developers to follow the principles of Agile Documentation (discussed in Chapter 10).

Ineffective architectural efforts.   Agile data advises enterprise architects to take a multiview/model approach to architecture and to actively work on a project team to support and prove that their architecture works. The feedback from these efforts should then be reflected in future iterations of the architecture.

Ineffective development guidelines.   Agile data implores enterprise administrators to write clear, effective, and applicable standards and guidelines and to be prepared to act on feedback from the development teams.

Ineffective modeling efforts.   Agile data directs software developers to follow the principles and practices of the AM methodology (discussed in Chapter 10).

Summary

The heart of the agile data method is its philosophies and the changes that those philosophies imply for the way that software developers approach their jobs. The first step is to recognize that you have a problem; many organizations have a serious problem with respect to how their application developers and data professionals work together on one level, as well as how project team members work together with enterprise team members on another level. However, it isn't enough for the agile data method to merely present a collection of philosophies, it must also describe real-world, proven techniques that software developers can apply on the job. You should consider these techniques, select the ones that sound like they'll benefit you, tailor them, and apply them appropriately within your environment. Software developers can work together effectively, but they must choose to do so.

CHAPTER 2

From Use Cases to Databases — Real-World UML

The shift to agile software development techniques is equivalent to the shift to the object-oriented paradigm.

The prevalence of programming languages such as Java, C++, Object Pascal, C#, and Visual Basic make it incredibly clear that object-oriented technology has become the approach of choice for new development projects. Agile software developers, be they application developers or agile DBAs, must have an understanding of object orientation if they are to be effective on modern software projects. This includes understanding basic concepts such as inheritance, polymorphism, and object persistence. Furthermore, they must have experience with the industry-standard Unified Modeling Language (UML). A good starting point is to understand what I consider to be the core UML diagrams — use-case diagrams, sequence diagrams, and class diagrams — although, as I argue in Chapter 10, you must be willing to learn more models over time.

One of the advantages of working closely with other software developers is that you learn new skills from them, and the most effective developers will learn and adapt fundamental concepts from other disciplines. An example is *class normalization*, the object-oriented version of *data normalization*, which is a collection of simple rules for reducing coupling and increasing cohesion within your object designs (data normalization and class normalization are the topics of Chapters 4 and 5, respectively).

This chapter is aimed at agile DBAs who want to gain a basic understanding of the object paradigm, allowing them to understand where application developers are coming from. The primary goal of this chapter is to provide agile DBAs with a sufficient understanding of objects to provide a basis from which to communicate with application developers. Everyone on a project team must share a common base of knowledge if they are to understand and work with their colleagues effectively. Similarly, other chapters in Part I provide an overview of fundamental data concepts, such as relational database technology and data modeling, that application developers need to learn so that they understand where agile DBAs are coming from. This chapter presents:

- An overview of fundamental object-oriented concepts and techniques
- An introduction to the Unified Modeling Language (UML)
- A profile for data modeling using UML notation

An Overview of Object-Oriented Concepts

Agile software developers, including agile DBAs, need to be familiar with the basic concepts of object-orientation. The *object-oriented* (OO) *paradigm* is a development strategy based on the concept that systems should be built from a collection of reusable components called *objects*. Instead of separating data and functionality, as is done in the structured paradigm, objects encompass both. Although the object-oriented paradigm sounds similar to the structured paradigm, it is actually quite different. A common mistake that many experienced developers make is to assume that they have been "doing objects" all along just because they have been applying similar software-engineering principles. To succeed with the OO paradigm you must recognize how the OO approach is different from the structured approach.

Consider the design of an information system for an order-entry system. Taking the structured approach, you would define the layout of a database and the design of a program to access that data. In the database, there would be information about customers, orders, order items, and items. The program would allow users to make orders, search for items, define shipping instructions, and so on. The program would access and update the database, in effect supporting the day-to-day business of the company.

Now, consider the university information system from an object-oriented perspective. In the real world, there are customers, orders, order items, and items. All of these things would be considered objects. In the real world, customers know things (they have names, addresses, telephone numbers, and so on), and they do things (make orders, search for items, and pay invoices). From a systems perspective orders also know things (the date they were created, the applicable taxes, and so on), and they do things (calculate totals and calculate taxes). Similarly, order items know things (the type and number of items ordered) and should be able to do things too (such as tell you their subtotal). Items also know things (their unit price and current stock level) and should be able to do things (calculate their shipping volume).

To implement this system, we would define a collection of *classes* (a class is a generic representation of similar objects; that is, a class is to objects as tables are to rows) that interact with each other. For example, we would have *Customer*, *Order*, *OrderItem*, and *Item* classes. The collection of these classes would make up our application, which would include both the functionality (the program) and the data.

The OO approach results in a completely different view of what an application is all about. Rather than having a program that accesses a database, we have an application that exists in what is called an *object space*. The object space is where both the program and the data for the application logically reside. However, many people will choose to persist their data in relational databases, mapping their classes to the data tables within the database (see Chapter 14). The implication is that when you start to bring physical implementation issues into account, such as the need to persist objects, that there is a significant need for application developers and agile DBAs to work together effectively.

To understand OO you need to understand common object terminology. The critical terms to understand are summarized in Table 2.1, and you can find a much more detailed explanation of these terms in *The Object Primer* (Ambler 2001a). Some of these concepts you will have seen before, and some of them you haven't. Many OO concepts, such as encapsulation, coupling, and cohesion come from software engineering. These concepts are important because they underpin good OO design. The main point is that you do not want to deceive yourself — just because you have seen some of these concepts before doesn't mean you were using OO, it just means you were using good design techniques. Although good design is a big part of OO, there is still a lot more to it than that.

Agile DBAs need to understand the terms presented in Table 2.1 because the application developers whom you work with will use these terms, and many others, on a regular basis. To communicate effectively with application developers, you must understand their vocabulary and they must understand yours. Another important aspect of learning the basics of OO is to understand each of the diagrams of UML — you don't need to become a UML expert, but you do need to know the basics.

Table 2.1   Common Object-Oriented Terms

TERM	DESCRIPTION
Abstract class	A class that does not have objects instantiated from it.
Abstraction	The identification of the essential characteristics of an item.
Aggregation	Represents "is part of" or "contains" relationships between two classes or components.
Aggregation hierarchy	A set of classes that are related through aggregation.
Association	Objects are related to (associated with) other objects.
Attribute	Something that a class knows (data/information).
Class	A software abstraction of similar objects, and a template from which objects are created.
Cohesion	The degree to which the aspects of an encapsulated unit (such as a component or a class) are related to one another.
Composition	A strong form of aggregation in which the "whole" object is completely responsible for its parts, and each "part" object is only associated to the one "whole" object.

(continued)

Table 2.1   *(continued)*

TERM	DESCRIPTION
Concrete class	A class that has objects instantiated from it.
Coupling	The degree of dependence between two items.
Encapsulation	The grouping of related concepts into one item, such as a class or component.
Information hiding	The restriction of external access to attributes.
Inheritance	Represents "is a," "is like," and "is a kind of" relationships. When class "B" inherits from class "A," it automatically has all of the attributes and operations that "A" implements (or inherits from other classes).
Inheritance hierarchy	A set of classes that are related through inheritance.
Instance	An object is an instance of a class.
Instantiate	We instantiate (create) objects from classes.
Interface	The definition of a collection of one or more operation signatures that defines a cohesive set of behaviors.
Message	Either a request for information or a request to perform an action.
Messaging	In order to collaborate, classes send messages to each other.
Multiple inheritance	When a class directly inherits from more than one class.
Multiplicity	A UML concept combining the data-modeling concepts of cardinality (how many) and optionality.
Object	A person, place, thing, event, concept, screen, or report.
Object schema	The structure of your object-oriented software.
Object space	Main memory plus all available storage space on the network, including persistent storage such as a relational database.
Operation	Something a class does (similar to a function in structured programming).
Override	Sometimes you need to override (redefine) attributes and/or methods in subclasses.
Pattern	A reusable solution to a common problem, taking relevant forces into account.
Persistence	The issue of how objects are permanently stored.
Persistent object	An object that is saved to permanent storage.

Table 2.1   *(continued)*

TERM	DESCRIPTION
Polymorphism	Different objects can respond to the same message in different ways, enabling objects to interact with one another without knowing their exact type.
Single inheritance	When a class directly inherits from only one class.
Stereotype	Denotes a common usage of a modeling element.
Subclass	If class "B" inherits from class "A," we say that "B" is a subclass of "A."
Superclass	If class "B" inherits from class "A," we say that "A" is a superclass of "B."
Transient object	An object that is not saved to permanent storage.

An Introduction to the Unified Modeling Language (UML)

The goal of this section is to provide you with a basic overview of UML; it is not to teach you the details of each individual technique nor how to create each type of diagram. To present a consistent set of examples I work through a simple order entry system.

TIP Fowler and Scott's (1999) *UML Distilled* is your best bet if you're looking for a brief overview of the UML. Craig Larman's (2002) *Applying UML and Patterns* is likely the best book available if you're looking for a detailed tutorial on UML. *The Object Primer* (Ambler 2001a) is a good "in between" solution that describes the entire object development life cycle, covering non-UML models (data models, change cases, essential models, and so on) and non-modeling topics. If you want a comprehensive book, check out Tom Pender's (2003) *UML Bible*. The URL www.agilemodeling.com/artifacts/index.htm leads to a wide variety of model overviews.

TIP Start simple when learning UML. You don't need to learn the entire UML notation available to you (and believe me there's a lot), only the notation that you'll use in practice. The examples presented in this section use the core UML, and there is one for each UML diagram. As you look at each diagram focus on learning the core notation first, and then later focus in on the other notation as necessary.

Core UML Diagrams

The following sections describe what I consider to be the three core UML diagrams for developing business software: UML use-case diagrams, UML sequence diagrams, and UML class diagrams. These are the diagrams that you will see used the most in practice: use-case diagrams to provide an overview of usage requirements, sequence diagrams to analyze the use cases and map to your classes, and class diagrams to explore the structure of your object-oriented software (what I like to refer to as your *object schema*). These three diagrams will cover 80 percent of your object-modeling needs when building a business application using object technology.

Use Case Diagrams

According to the UML specification a *use-case diagram* is "a diagram that shows the relationships among actors and use cases within a system." Use-case diagrams are often used to:

- Provide an overview of all or part of the usage requirements for a system or organization in the form of an essential (Constantine and Lockwood 1999) model or a business model (Rational Corporation 2001).

- Communicate the scope of a development project.

- Model the analysis of your usage requirements in the form of a system use-case model (Cockburn 2001; Ambler 2001a).

Figure 2.1 depicts a simple use-case diagram that depicts several use cases, actors, their associations, and an optional system boundary box. A *use case*, which is represented in diagrams as a horizontal ellipse, is a sequence of actions that provides a measurable value to an *actor*. An actor, which is represented in diagrams as a stick figure, is defined as a person, organization, or external system that plays a role in one or more interactions with your system. Use-case diagrams illustrate associations between actors and use cases, a relationship exists whenever an actor is involved in an interaction that is described by a use case. Associations between actors and use cases are modeled as lines connecting them to one another, with an optional arrowhead on one end of the line indicating the direction of the initial invocation of the relationship. Associations also exist between use cases in system use-case models and are depicted using dashed lines with the UML stereotypes of <<extend>> or <<include>>. It is also possible to model inheritance between use cases, as you can see *Ship International Order* inherits from *Ship Order*. The rectangle around the use cases is called the *system boundary box*, and as the name suggests, it delimits the scope of your system. Anything within the box is implemented by your system; anything outside of the box isn't.

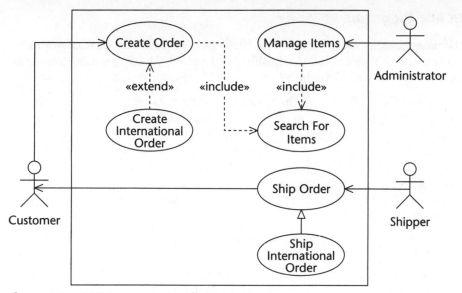

Figure 2.1   A UML 2.x use-case diagram.

A use-case model comprises one or more use-case diagrams and any supporting documentation such as use-case specifications and actor definitions. Within most use-case models the use-case specifications tend to be the primary artifact with use-case diagrams filling a supporting role as the "gluc" that keeps the requirements model together. Use-case models should be developed from the point of view of your project stakeholders and not from the (often technical) point of view of developers.

Although Extreme Programming (XP) projects will work with user stories and acceptance test cases as their primary requirements artifacts, it is still valuable for XP developers to have a grasp of use-case modeling. First, the initial requirements for your project may have been defined via use cases. This can happen when a project starts out following another process, perhaps the Rational Unified Process (RUP), only to decide part way through to take an XP approach instead. Second, you may find yourself working with developers who understand use cases very well but who are new to user stories — if you understand both, you'll be able to relate user stories to them more easily.

Sequence Diagrams

UML Sequence diagrams are a dynamic modeling technique, as are UML communication/collaboration diagrams and, arguably, UML activity diagrams. UML sequence diagrams are typically used to:

Validate and flesh out the logic of a usage scenario. A usage scenario is exactly what its name indicates — the description of a potential way that your system is used. The logic of a usage scenario may be part of a use case, perhaps an alternate course; one entire pass through a use case, such as the logic described by the basic course of action or a portion of the basic course of action plus one or more alternate scenarios; or a pass through the logic contained in several use cases, for example a customer places an order and then cancels another order made earlier in the day.

Explore your design. Sequence diagrams provide a way for you to visually step through the invocation of the operations defined by your classes.

To detect bottlenecks within an object-oriented design. Message flow analysis can give you an idea of where you need to change your design to distribute the load within your system, a feature automated by some CASE tools.

To indicate complex classes in your application. This implies that you may need to draw state chart diagrams for them.

For example, Figure 2.2 models a portion of the basic course of action for the "Create Order" use case. The boxes across the top of the diagram represent classifiers or their instances, typically use cases, objects, classes, or actors. Because you can send messages to both objects and classes (objects respond to messages through the invocation of an operation, and classes do so through the invocation of static operations), it makes sense to include both on sequence diagrams. Because actors initiate and take an active part in usage scenarios they are also included in sequence diagrams. Objects have labels in the standard UML format "name: ClassName," where name is optional (objects that have not been given a name on the diagram are called anonymous objects). Classes have labels in the format ClassName, for example *SecurityLogon* and *OrderCreator*, and actors have names in the format Actor Name, for example *Online Customer* — both common naming conventions (Ambler 2003).

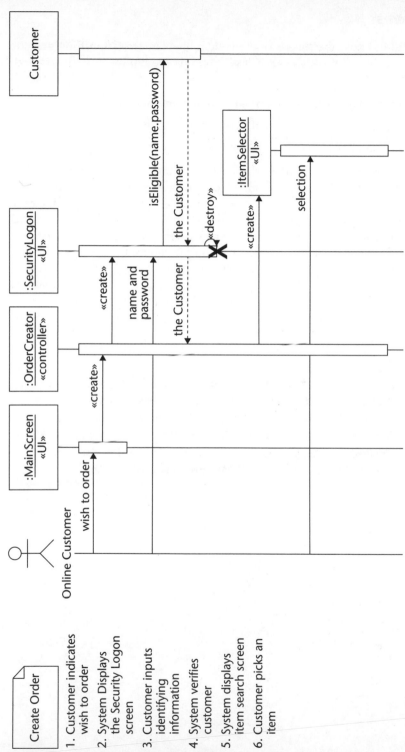

Figure 2.2 A UML 2.*x* sequence diagram.

Class Diagrams

UML class diagrams show the classes of the system, their interrelationships, and the operations and attributes of the classes. Class diagrams are typically used, although not all at once, to:

- Explore domain concepts in the form of a domain model
- Analyze requirements in the form of a conceptual/analysis model
- Depict the detailed design of object-oriented or object-based software

A class model comprises one or more class diagrams and the supporting specifications that describe model elements, including classes, relationships between classes, and interfaces. Figure 2.3 depicts an example of an analysis-level UML class diagram. Classes are shown as boxes with three sections — the top for the name of the class, the middle for the attributes, and the bottom for the operations. Associations between classes are depicted as lines between classes. Associations should include multiplicity indicators at each end, for example 0..1 representing "zero or one" and 1..* representing "one or more." Associations may have roles indicated, for example the mentors association, a recursive relation that professor objects have with other professor objects, indicates the roles of advisor and associate. A design class model would show greater detail. For example, it is common to see the visibility and type of attributes depicted on design class diagrams as well as full operation signatures.

TIP What happens if you're not developing business applications, are there different core diagrams? Yes. For real-time or embedded systems, the core diagrams are typically UML state chart diagrams, UML communication/ collaboration diagrams (or UML sequence diagrams, depending on your team's preference), and UML class diagrams. For architectural efforts, the core diagrams are often UML deployment and UML component diagrams.

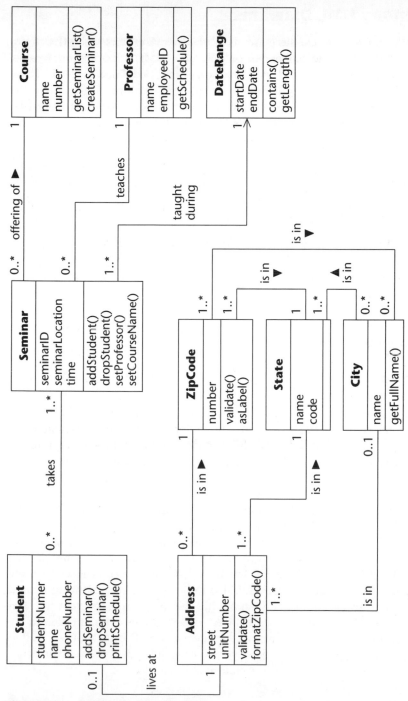

Figure 2.3 A UML 2.x class diagram.

Supplementary UML Diagrams

In addition to the core diagrams, there are also five other diagrams — UML activity diagrams, UML communication/collaboration diagrams, UML component diagrams, UML deployment diagrams, and UML state chart diagrams — defined by UML. These diagrams are still valuable in the right situations, but they aren't used as much as the core diagrams. All agile software developers should learn how to work with these diagrams at some point in their careers, but they likely aren't the first model types that you'll learn.

Activity Diagrams

UML activity diagrams are the object-oriented equivalent of flowcharts and data-flow diagrams (DFDs) from the structured development model (Gane and Sarson 1979). In UML 1.*x*, UML activity diagrams were a specialization of UML state chart diagrams, although in UML 2.*x* they are full-fledged artifacts. UML activity diagrams are used to explore the logic of:

- A complex operation
- A complex business rule
- A single use case
- Several use cases
- A business process
- Software processes

Figure 2.4 depicts a UML activity diagram, showing the logic of how someone logs on to the system and creates an order. The filled circle represents the starting point of the activity diagram, effectively a placeholder, and the filled circle with a border represents the ending point. The rounded rectangles represent processes or activities that are performed. The activities in this diagram map reasonably closely to use cases, although activities can also be much finer grained — I could have chosen to document the logic of a method instead of a high-level business process. The diamonds represent decision points; although in this example the decision point had only two possible outcomes, it could just as easily had many more. The arrows represent transitions between activities, modeling the flow order between the various activities. The text on the arrows represent conditions that must be fulfilled to proceed along the transition and are always described using the format [condition]. The thick bars represent the start and end of potentially parallel processes — after you are successfully enrolled in the university, you must attend the mandatory overview presentation as well as enroll in at least one seminar and pay at least some of your tuition. It is possible to exit an activity in several ways, as you see with the *Log on to System* activity.

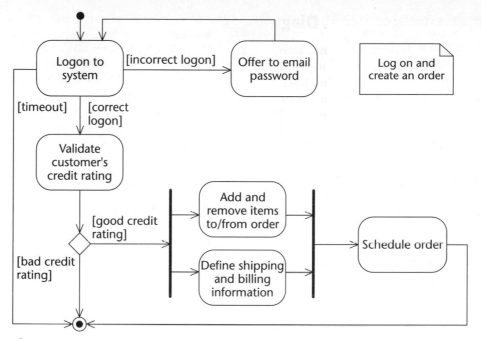

Figure 2.4 A UML 2.x activity diagram.

This activity diagram is interesting because it potentially cuts across the logic of several use cases — at least one for logging on to the system and another for creating an order. This is a good thing use-case models do not communicate the time ordering of processes well. For example, although the use-case diagram presented in Figure 2.1 gives you a very good idea as to the type of functionality this system performs, it offers no definitive answer as to the order that these use cases might occur in. The activity diagram in Figure 2.4, however, does. Each UML diagram has its strengths and weaknesses, so remember to follow Agile Modeling's practice *Apply the Right Artifact(s)* and use each one appropriately.

Communication/Collaboration Diagrams

UML communication diagrams, formerly called collaboration diagrams, (like UML sequence diagrams) are used to explore the dynamic nature of your software. Communication diagrams show the message flow between objects in an OO application, and also imply the basic associations (relationships) between classes. Communication diagrams are often used to:

- Provide a bird's-eye view of a collection of collaborating objects, particularly within a real-time environment.

- Allocate functionality to classes by exploring the behavioral aspects of a system.

■ Model the logic of the implementation of a complex operation, particularly one that interacts with a large number of other objects.

■ Explore the roles that objects take within a system, as well as the different relationships they are involved with when in those roles.

Figure 2.5 presents a simplified communication diagram for creating an order invoice. The rectangles represent the various objects involved that make up the application, and the lines between the classes represent the relationships (associations, aggregation, composition, dependencies, or inheritance) between them. The same notation for classes and objects used on UML sequence diagrams are used on UML communication diagrams, an example of the consistency of the UML. The details of your associations, such as their multiplicities, are not modeled as this information is contained on your UML class diagrams. Messages are depicted as a labeled arrow that indicates the direction of the message, using a notation similar to that used on sequence diagrams. You may optionally indicate the sequence number in which the message is sent (for example, 2.1), indicate an optional return value, and indicate the method name and the parameters (if any) passed to it.

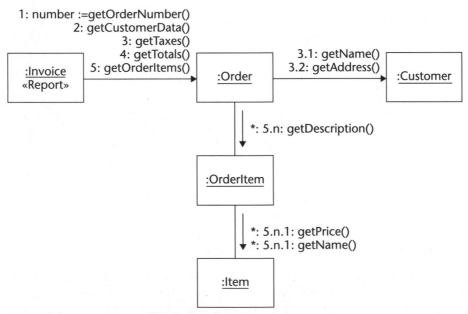

Figure 2.5   A UML 2.x collaboration diagram.

In Figure 2.5 you see that the *Invoice* class collaborates with the order object to obtain the information needed to display its information. It first invokes the getter method to obtain the number of the order, you know that this is the first message invoked because its sequence number is one. The next thing that happens is the request for customer data to the order object. To fulfill this responsibility the order collaborates with its corresponding customer object. Notice how I chose to indicate the return value in the description of the first message but not the second: A good rule of thumb is that if it is obvious what the return value is, then you should not clutter your diagram by indicating the return value. I broke this rule to provide an example of how to model return values. Also notice the numbering scheme that I used. It is clear that the invocation of getPrice() and getName() on the item object is the result of invoking getDescription() on the order item object. To display the list of order items that appear on the order, the order object loops through the instances of *OrderItem* to get the appropriate information. This is indicated with the *: notation in front of the message name.

Component Diagrams

Component-based development (CBD) and object-oriented development go hand in hand, and it is generally recognized that object technology is the preferred foundation from which to build components. UML includes a component diagram that shows the dependencies among software components, including the classifiers that specify them such as implementation classes, and the artifacts that implement them such as source code files, binary code files, executable files, scripts and tables.

UML component diagrams, along with UML activity diagrams, are arguably one of the "forgotten" UML diagrams. Few books invest much time discussing them; I suspect the primary reason for this is because many methodologists appear to relegate them to low-level design diagrams for specifying the configuration of your software. UML component diagrams become much more useful when used as architectural-level artifacts, either to model your technical infrastructure or your business/domain architecture (Ambler 1998, Herzum and Sims 2000).

Figure 2.6 depicts a business architecture component model for the order entry system. The UML 2.*x* notation for components is a rectangle with a <<Component>> stereotype (or as you see in the diagram a stereotype depicting the 1.*x* component shape). Components implement one or more interfaces, modeled using the same "lollipop" notation that UML class diagrams use. Components have dependencies on the interfaces of other components, modeled using the standard UML dependency notation. The diagram shows two UI components, perhaps implemented as a collection of JavaServer Pages (JSPs) or as Visual Basic graphical user interface (GUI) screens, that interact with several large-scale business/domain components such as *Customer* and *Catalog*. These components would encapsulate many business classes; for example, complex components could be built from several hundred classes. The classes within these business components, in turn, interact with infrastructure components for basic services such as security, messaging, and persistence.

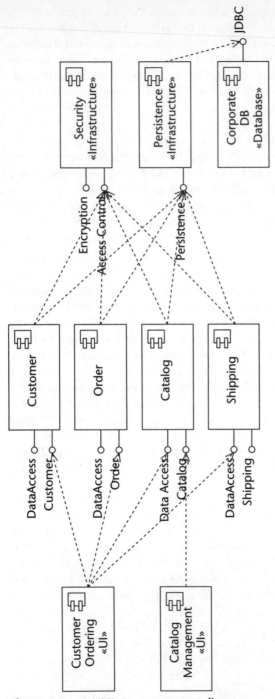

Figure 2.6 A UML 2.x component diagram.

Deployment Diagrams

A UML deployment diagram depicts a static view of the runtime configuration of hardware nodes and the software components that run on those nodes. UML deployment diagrams show the hardware for your system, the software that is installed on that hardware, and the middleware used to connect the disparate machines to one another. You create a deployment model to:

- Explore the issues involved with installing your system in production.
- Explore the dependencies that your system has with other systems that are currently in, or planned for, your production environment.
- Depict a major deployment configuration of a business application.
- Design the hardware and software configuration of an embedded system.
- Depict the hardware/network infrastructure of an organization.

Figure 2.7 depicts a UML deployment diagram for the customer order application. The three-dimensional boxes represent nodes such as computers or switches and connections between nodes are represented with simple lines. As you would expect software components, interfaces, and dependencies are indicated using the standard UML notations. Stereotypes indicate that the connection between the browser and the application server uses the Internet's standard HTTP protocol and that Java's Remote Method Invocation (RMI) protocol is used across the connection between the application server and the data server. As you might expect, the components have the same type of stereotypes that they do on the UML component diagram in Figure 2.6.

State Chart Diagrams

UML state chart diagrams depict the dynamic behavior of an entity based on its response to events, showing how the entity reacts to various events, depending on the current state that it is in. Create a UML state chart diagram to:

- Explore the complex behavior of a class, actor, subsystem, or component.
- Model real-time systems.

Figure 2.8 presents an example state chart diagram for the *Order* class. The rounded rectangles represent states: You see that instances of *Order* can be in the *Definition*, *Scheduled*, *Shipping*, and *Shipped* states. An object starts in an initial state, represented by the closed circle, and can end up in a final state, represented by the bordered circle. The arrows represent transitions, progressions from one state to another. For example, when an order is in the *Scheduled* state, it can either be reopened for update, marked for shipping, or canceled. Transitions can also have guards on them, conditions that must be true for the transition to be triggered. An example of a guard is shown on the transition from the *Shipping* to the *Fulfilled* states — this transition only occurs if no more items need to be shipped. The UML notation for this is in the format [guard description]. It is also possible to indicate the invocation of methods on your transition, for example notifyCustomer() is invoked on the above mentioned transition. Operations can also be invoked while an object is in a given state, as you can see in the *Shipping* state.

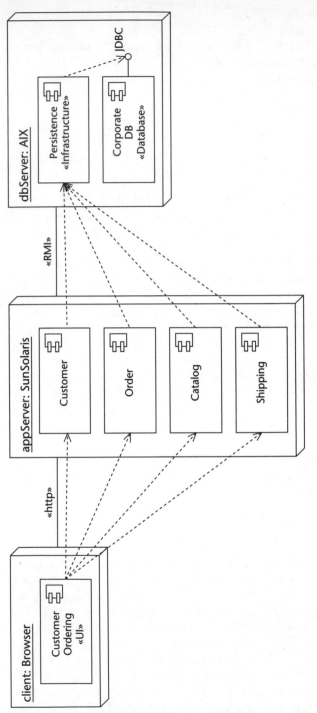

Figure 2.7 A UML 2.x deployment diagram.

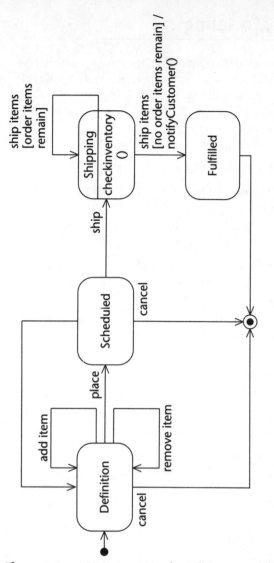

Figure 2.8   A UML 2.x state chart diagram.

A UML Profile for Data Modeling

This section summarizes the UML data-modeling notation that I apply in this book. The notation is defined as a profile for UML class diagrams. In this profile, I follow the philosophy of separating *core notation* — specifically the roughly 20 percent of the notation that you are likely to use in practice — from supplementary notation that isn't as common although still needed in some situations.

So why does the UML need a data-modeling profile? For several reasons:

- Object developers need to model how their data will be persisted.

- There currently is no industry standard for data modeling notation (there are several common notations, however).

- Tool vendors need guidance as to how to implement this type of model in their tools, otherwise we will have interoperability problems between tools.

- A data-modeling profile would help to bring data modeling onto the radar scopes of the multitude of writers who limit themselves to UML (which makes you wonder whether they actually build software).

- For object developers and data professionals to communicate with one another effectively they need a common ground, a UML data-modeling profile could help with this.

This profile is discussed in detail in the following sections, which are organized by usage and present answers to common "How do I model XYZ?" questions in priority order. These questions are:

- How do I indicate the type of model or storage mechanism?

- How do I model tables, entities, and views?

- How do I model relationships?

- How do I model data attributes and columns?

- How do I model keys?

- How do I model constraints and triggers?

- How do I model stored procedures?

- How do I model sections within a database?

- How do I model everything else?

NOTE The notation presented here isn't perfect but I truly believe that it's the best source available to you today. Nor is this profile complete — for the most part it focuses on the physical modeling of a relational database, although it does cover other aspects of data modeling as needed. This profile also strays into style issues, something UML profiles usually don't do, issues that in my opinion are critical to successful modeling (Ambler 2003).

NOTE At the time of this writing I don't have the benefit of simply adopting an industry standard, something that Agile Modeling (AM)'s *Apply Modeling Standards* practice advises, so I'm forced to present my own solution here. The Unified Modeling Language (UML) does not yet cover data modeling, even though persistence-related issues are clearly an important aspect of an object-oriented software project. For several years, I have argued that UML needs a data model (Ambler 1997, Ambler 1997b, Ambler 2001a, Ambler 2002a) and have vacillated between various ways that it should be done. Other methodologists have argued the same (Naiburg and Maksimchuk 2001, Rational Corporation 2000, Muller 1999) because they too recognize the clear need for a data-modeling profile. Unfortunately, we have all developed slightly different modeling notations, a problem that the Object Management Group (OMG) may choose to address in a future version of UML. Until then, ongoing work on this profile is posted at www.agiledata.org/essays/umlDataModeling Profile.html. Who knows? Perhaps this profile will become a "grass roots" defacto standard.

Indicating the Type of Model or Storage Mechanism

The type of model should be indicated either using the appropriate stereotype listed in Table 2.2 or simply as free-form text in a UML note. In the case of a physical data model, the type of storage mechanism should be indicated with one of the stereotypes listed in Table 2.3.

Table 2.2   Stereotypes to Indicate Model Types (Core Notation)

STEREOTYPE	MODEL TYPE
<<Class Model>>	Object-oriented or object-relational model
<<Conceptual Data Model>>	Conceptual data model
<<Logical Data Model>>	Logical data model (LDM)
<<Physical Data Model>>	Physical data model (PDM)

Table 2.3 Stereotypes for Various Persistent Storage Mechanisms
(Supplementary Notation)

STEREOTYPE	STORAGE MECHANISM TYPE
<<File>>	File
<<Hierarchical Database>>	Hierarchical database
<<Object-Oriented Database>>	Object-oriented database (OODB)
<<Object-Relational Database>>	Object-relational database (ORDB)
<<Network Database>>	Network database
<<Relational Database>>	Relational database (RDB)
<<XML Database>>	XML database

Modeling Tables, Entities, and Views

Tables, entities, and views are all modeled using class boxes, as you see in Figure 2.9 and Figure 2.10, and the appropriate stereotypes are listed in Table 2.4. Class boxes that appear on conceptual and logical data models are by definition entities, so the stereotype is optional. Similarly, on a physical data model for a relational database, it is assumed that any class box without a stereotype is a table. In Figure 2.10, you see that views have dependencies on the table structures.

Indices, shown in Figure 2.10, are also modeled using class boxes. They are optionally dependent either on the table for which they are an index or on the actual columns that make up the index (this is more accurate, although it can be more complex to depict when the index implements a composite key). In the model, you see that IEmployee1 is dependent on the Employee_POID column, whereas IEmployee2 is dependent on just the table, requiring you to list the columns for the index when you follow this style. As you can see, the notation used for IEmployee2 is wordier but less clumsy — if you're going to model indices this should be your preference with respect to style issues. IEmployee3, like IEmployee1, is dependent on a single column, in this case Social_Security_Number.

TIP *Don't model indices.* The existence of an index is implied by the fact that you have indicated the primary key column(s) and any alternate key columns — in relational databases keys are implemented via indices. By also modeling the indices you unnecessarily clutter your diagrams.

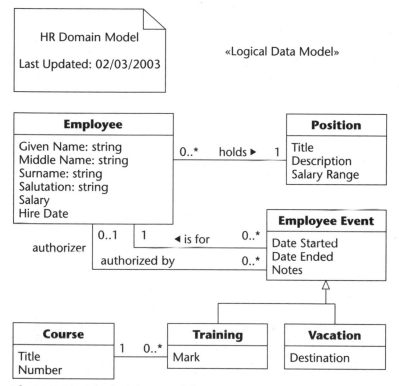

Figure 2.9   A logical data model.

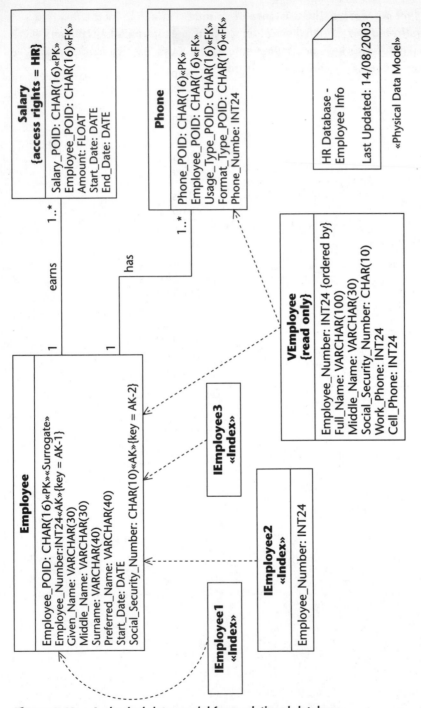

Figure 2.10   A physical data model for a relational database.

Table 2.4   Stereotypes for Classes

STEREOTYPE	DIAGRAM TYPE	CORE NOTATION	APPLICATION
<<Aggregate>>	Physical	No	Apply this to aggregate tables used to store denormalized data (often for reporting purposes).
<<Associative Table>>	Physical	Yes	Apply this to associative tables in a PDM for a relational database.
<<Entity>>	Logical, Conceptual	No	This is optional notation that is implied by the model type.
<<Index>>	Physical	No	Apply this when you are modeling an index that implements a table key within a relational database. Doing so indicates a dependency from the index to the table or to the key column(s) that the index implements.
<<Lookup Table>>	Physical	No	Apply this to relational tables that are used for simple lookup lists.
<<Stored Procedures>>	Physical	Yes	Apply this to a class that contains only the operation signatures for the stored procedures of the database.
<<Table>>	Physical	No	Optional notation that is implied by the model type.
<<View>>	Physical	Yes	Apply this when you are modeling a view to a table. Indicate a dependency to each table involved in the definition of the view.

Modeling Relationships

Relationships are modeled using the notation for associations as you can see in Figure 2.9 and Figure 2.10. Standard multiplicity (e.g. 0..1, 1..*, and 2..5) notation may be applied, as can roles. Table 2.5 lists the potential stereotypes that you may apply to relationships, some of which have a common visual representation as well as a textual one.

Table 2.5   Stereotypes for Associations

STEREOTYPE	VISUAL STEREOTYPE	DIAGRAM TYPE	CORE NOTATION	APPLICATION
<<Aggregation>>	Hollow diamond: ◇——— Aggregation	All	No	Indicates an aggregation relationship between two entities. Note that aggregation is no longer supported in UML 2.0 so this notation should be avoided.
<<Composition>>	Filled diamond: ◆——— Composition	All	No	Indicates a composition relationship between two entities.
<<Dependency>>	Dashed line with open arrowhead: <---------- Dependency	Physical	Yes	Indicates a dependency of a view or index on the schema of a table.
<<Identifying>>	None	Physical	No	Indicates an identifying relationship between two dependent tables (the child table cannot exist without the parent table).
<<Non-Identifying>>	None	Physical	No	Indicates a nonidentifying relationship between two independent tables.
<<Subtype>>	Inheritance arrow: ▽——— Subtyping	All	Yes	Indicates subtype/supertype or inheritance relationships between two entities.
<<Uni-directional>>	Open arrowhead: ←——— Unidirectional	All	No	Indicates that the relationship between two entities should only be traversed in a single direction.

NOTE The notation for qualifiers shouldn't be used. Although it would be a valid option to model foreign keys, in practice this often proves confusing when a single table is involved in many relationships.

Modeling Data Attributes and Columns

Data attributes on conceptual and logical data models, as well as columns on physical data models, are modeled using the standard attribute notation. Modeling the type of an attribute on a conceptual or logical data model is optional, although in practice this is often done. Stylistically, if the model is being used to model data requirements then the type should be indicated only when it is an actual requirement. For example, if a customer number must be alphanumeric, then indicate it as such; otherwise, if it is optional how this attribute is implemented, do not indicate the type.

Constraints, such as a column being not null, should be modeled using normal UML constraints.

Derived data, the result of denormalization, should be preceded by the standard "/" symbol.

NOTE The notation for visibility shouldn't be used — the assumption is that the data is publicly accessible. Although visibility symbols could be used to indicate the need to indicate access control, this is better done using constraints because access control issues are often very complex.

Modeling Keys

In my opinion, the modeling of keys is the most complicated issue addressed by this profile. This is done for several reasons:

- An entity can have several candidate keys, each of which may be a composite.
- A table can have a primary key and several alternate keys, each of which can be a composite.
- The order in which the columns appear in table keys can be important.
- Traditional data models typically don't have a good way of distinguishing which key an attribute or column is a part of; this information is often left for supporting documentation.

As you can see in Figure 2.11, the notation for indicating keys can get quite complex. Minimally, you should mark the attribute or column with one of the stereotypes in Table 2.6.

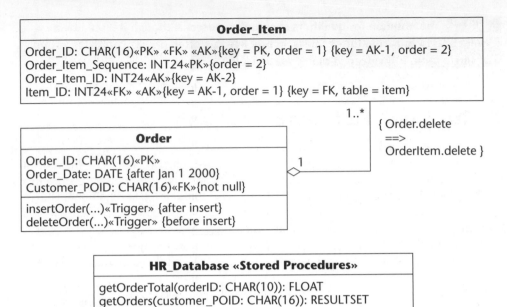

Order_Item

Order_ID: CHAR(16)«PK» «FK» «AK»{key = PK, order = 1} {key = AK-1, order = 2}
Order_Item_Sequence: INT24«PK»{order = 2}
Order_Item_ID: INT24«AK»{key = AK-2}
Item_ID: INT24«FK» «AK»{key = AK-1, order = 1} {key = FK, table = item}

1..*   { Order.delete
            ==>
            OrderItem.delete }

Order

Order_ID: CHAR(16)«PK»
Order_Date: DATE {after Jan 1 2000}
Customer_POID: CHAR(16)«FK»{not null}

insertOrder(...)«Trigger» {after insert}
deleteOrder(...)«Trigger» {before insert}

1

HR_Database «Stored Procedures»

getOrderTotal(orderID: CHAR(10)): FLOAT
getOrders(customer_POID: CHAR(16)): RESULTSET

Figure 2.11   Modeling constraints and behavior in a physical data model.

NOTE Although I would normally prefer stereotypes such as <<Primary Key>> over <<PK>>, I chose the abbreviated version because it reflects existing norms within the data community for indicating keys. Furthermore, because some columns can be involved with several keys the longer form of the stereotype would become cumbersome. Finally, this is also the stereotype suggested by Rational Corporation (2000).

Table 2.6   Stereotypes for Modeling Keys

STEREOTYPE	DIAGRAM TYPE	CORE NOTATION	APPLICATION
<<AK>>	Physical	No	Indicates that a column is part of an alternate key, also known as a secondary key, for a table.
<<Auto Generated>>	Physical	No	Indicates that the column value is automatically generated by the database.

(continued)

Table 2.6   *(continued)*

STEREOTYPE	DIAGRAM TYPE	CORE NOTATION	APPLICATION
<<CK>>	Conceptual, Logical	Yes	Indicates that an attribute is part of a candidate key for an entity.
<<FK>>	Physical	Yes	Indicates that a column is part of a foreign key to another table.
<<Natural>>	All	No	Indicates that an attribute or column is part of a natural key.
<<PK>>	Physical	Yes	Indicates that a column is part of a primary key for a table.
<<Surrogate>>	Physical	No	Indicates that a column is a surrogate key.

You can optionally model the detailed information pertaining to keys using UML named values (described in Table 2.7). For example, in Figure 2.11 you see that:

- The Order_ID column is the first element of the primary key.
- Order_Item_Sequence is the second element of the primary key.
- Order_ID is part of several keys: therefore, I needed to indicate additional information where appropriate. For example, Order_ID is the second element of the first alternate key.
- Because Order_Item_Sequence is part of a single key, I didn't need to indicate the order.
- Item_ID is the first element of the first alternate key.
- Item_ID is also a foreign key to the Item table.

In Figure 2.10 I indicated that Employee_POID is a surrogate key to provide an example of how to do this (had it been a natural key, I would have applied the stereotype <<Natural>> instead).

TIP I generally prefer to indicate whether a key is autogenerated, natural, or surrogate In the documentation instead of on the diagrams — this is an option for you although in my opinion this sort of information adds too much clutter.

Table 2.7   Named Values for Modeling Keys (Supplementary Notation)

VALUE	APPLICATION	EXAMPLES
key	Indicates which candidate or alternate key an attribute/column belongs to. When the column is part of several keys (for example if it is part of two different foreign keys), then you need to indicate which one you are referring to. In the second example, the column is part of the third alternate key.	key = FK key = AK-3
order	Indicates the order of appearance in which an attribute appears when it is part of a composite key. In the example the column would be the fourth column in the key.	order = 4
table	Indicates the table that a foreign key refers to. This is optional because it can often be inferred from the diagram.	table = Customer

Modeling Constraints and Triggers

Most constraints (domains, columns, tables, and databases) can be modeled using the UML's Object Constraint Language (OCL) where appropriate. Examples of this are depicted in Figure 2.11, a domain constraint on the Order_Date is defined indicating that it must be later than January 1, 2000. A column constraint is also defined, the Customer_POID column must not be null. Table and database constraints, not shown, could be modeled the same way. For example, Figure 2.11 depicts how a referential integrity (RI) constraint can be modeled between two tables using OCL notation. Notice that when an order is deleted the order items should also be deleted. Although this is implied by the fact that there is an aggregation relationship between the two tables, the constraint makes this explicit. However, too many RI constraints can quickly clutter your diagrams; therefore, supporting documentation for your database design might be a better option for this information — remember AM's *Depict Models Simply* practice.

In Figure 2.10 the *Salary* table includes an access control constraint, only people in the Human Resources (HR) department are allowed to access this information. Other examples in this diagram include the read-only constraint on the *VEmployee* view and the ordered by constraint on Employee_Number in this view.

Triggers are modeled using the notation for operations. In Figure 2.11 you see that the stereotype of <<Trigger>> was applied and value of "after insert" and "before delete" were modeled to show when the triggers would be fired.

Modeling Stored Procedures

Stored procedures should be modeled using a single class with the stereotype <<Stored Procedures>>, as shown in Figure 2.11. This class lists the operation signatures of the stored procedures using the standard UML notation for operation signatures. Stylistically, the name of this class should either be the database or the name of the package within the database.

> **NOTE** Although it is standard UML practice for stereotypes to be singular, in this case the plural form makes the most sense. The other alternative is to apply the stereotype <<Stored Procedure>> to each individual operation signature, something that would unnecessarily clutter the diagram.

Modeling Sections within a Database

Many database-management systems provide the ability to segregate your database into sections. In Oracle, these sections are called tablespaces, and other vendors call them partitions or data areas. Regardless of the term, you should use a standard UML package with a stereotype that reflects the terminology used by your database vendor (for example, <<Tablespace>>, <<Partition>>, and so on).

Modeling Everything Else

There is far more to data modeling than what is covered by this profile. The approach that I've taken is to identify the type of information that you are likely to include on your diagrams, but this is only a subset of the information that you are likely to gather as you're modeling. For example, logical data attribute information and descriptions of relationships can be important aspects of logical data models. Similarly, replication info (for example, which tables get replicated, how often, and so on), sizing information (average number of rows, growth rate, and so forth), and archiving information can be critical aspects of your physical data model. Complex business rules are applicable to all types of models. Although this information is important, in my opinion it does not belong on your diagrams but instead in your documentation. Follow AM's practice of *Depict Models Simply* by keeping this sort of information out of your diagrams.

Summary

This chapter presented a very brief overview of object-orientation (OO), the Unified Modeling Language (UML), and a proposed profile for data modeling using the UML. The goal of this chapter is to help provide all agile developers with a common language, in this case the language of OO and the UML, which they can communicate with each other. As Alistair Cockburn (2002) likes to say, software development is a communication game. It's incredibly hard to communicate effectively without a common language.

CHAPTER 3

Data Modeling 101

*Software development is a lot like swimming;
it is very dangerous to do it alone.*

My personal philosophy is that every IT professional should have a basic understanding of data modeling. They don't need to be experts at data modeling, but they should be prepared to be involved in the creation of such a model, be able to read an existing data model, understand when and when not to create a data model, and appreciate fundamental data design techniques. At the same time, data modeling skills alone are not enough to be successful in this day and age — as I argued in Chapter 1, you need to be a generalizing specialist with a wide range of skills.

This chapter presents an overview of fundamental data modeling skills that all developers should have, skills that can be applied to both traditional projects that take a serial approach and on agile projects that take an evolutionary approach. The primary audience for this chapter is application developers who need to gain an understanding of some of the critical activities performed by an agile DBA. This understanding should lead to an appreciation of what agile DBAs do and why they do them, and it should help to bridge the communication gap between these two roles. To achieve these goals, this chapter covers the following topics:

- The role of the agile DBA
- What is data modeling?
- How to model data
- How to become better at data modeling

The Role of the Agile DBA

Although you wouldn't think it, data modeling can be one of the most challenging tasks that an agile DBA can be involved with on an agile software-development project. The approach to data modeling will often be at the center of any controversy between the agile software developers and the traditional data professionals within your organization. Agile software developers will lean toward an evolutionary approach, where data modeling is just one of many activities, and traditional data professionals will often lean toward a "big design up front (BDUF)" approach, where data models are the primary artifacts, if not *the* artifacts. This problem results from a combination of the cultural impedance mismatch described in Chapter 7 and "normal" political maneuvering within an organization. As a result, agile DBAs often find that navigating the political waters is an important part of their data modeling efforts.

Additionally, when it comes to data modeling, agile DBAs will:

- Mentor application developers in fundamental data modeling techniques.

- Mentor experienced enterprise architects and administrators in evolutionary data modeling techniques.

- Ensure that the team follows data modeling standards and conventions.

- Develop and evolve the data model(s), in an evolutionary (iterative and incremental) manner, to meet the needs of the project team.

- Keep the database schema(s) in sync with the physical data model(s).

What Is Data Modeling?

Data modeling is the act of exploring data-oriented structures. Like other modeling artifacts, data models can be used for a variety of purposes, from high-level conceptual models to physical data models. From the point of view of an object-oriented developer, data modeling is conceptually similar to class modeling. With data modeling you identify data entities, whereas with class modeling you identify classes. Data attributes are assigned to data entities just as you would assign attributes and operations to classes. There are associations between entities, similar to the associations between classes — relationships, inheritance, composition, and aggregation are all applicable concepts in data modeling.

Data modeling is different from class modeling because it focuses solely on data — class models allow you to explore both the behavior and data aspects of your domain, but with a data model you can only explore data issues. Because of this focus data modelers have a tendency to be much better at getting the data "right" than object modelers.

How Are Data Models Used in Practice?

Although methodology issues are covered at the end of this chapter, right now we need to discuss how data models can be used in practice to better understand them. You are likely to see three basic styles of data model:

Conceptual data models. These models, sometimes called domain models, are typically used to explore domain concepts with project stakeholders. Conceptual data models are often created as the precursor to logical data models (LDMs) or as alternatives to LDMs.

Logical data models (LDMs). LDMs are used to explore the domain concepts, and their relationships, of your problem domain. This can be done for the scope of a single project or for your entire enterprise. LDMs depict the logical data entities, typically referred to simply as data entities, the data attributes describing those entities, and the relationships between the entities.

Physical data models (PDMs). PDMs are used to design the internal schema of a database, depicting the data tables, the data columns of those tables, and the relationships between the tables. The focus of this chapter is on physical modeling.

TIP Data models aren't the only structural models. Although the focus of this chapter is data modeling, there are often alternatives to data-oriented artifacts (see Agile Modeling's *Multiple Models* principle described in Chapter 10). For example, when it comes to conceptual modeling, ORM diagrams aren't your only option: in addition to LDMs it is quite common for people to create UML class diagrams and even Class Responsibility Collaborator (CRC) cards instead. In fact, my experience is that in some situations CRC cards are superior to ORM diagrams because it is very easy to get project stakeholders actively involved in the creation of the model. Instead of a traditional, analyst-led drawing session, you can instead facilitate stakeholders through the creation of CRC cards (Ambler 2001a).

Although LDMs and PDMs sound very similar, and they in fact are, the level of detail that they model can be significantly different. This is because the goals for each diagram are different — you can use an LDM to explore domain concepts with your stakeholders and the PDM to define your database design. Figure 3.1 presents a simple LDM and Figure 3.2 a simple PDM, both modeling the concept of customers and addresses as well as the relationship between them. Both diagrams apply the Barker (1990) notation, which is summarized in Figure 3.4. The LDM depicts the two business entities, in this case *Customer* and *Address*, their logical attributes, and the relationship between the two entities. Notice how implementation details are not shown.

The PDM shows greater detail than the LDM, including an associative table required to implement the association as well as the keys needed to maintain the relationships. PDMs should also reflect your organization's database naming standards, in this case an abbreviation of the entity name is appended to each column name and an abbreviation for "Number" was consistently introduced. A PDM should also indicate the data types for the columns, such as *integer* and *char(5)*. Although Figure 3.2 does not show them, lookup tables for how the address is used as well as for states and countries are implied by the attributes *ADDR_USAGE_CODE*, *STATE_CODE*, and *COUNTRY_CODE*.

An important observation about Figures 3.1 and 3.2 is that I'm not slavishly following Barker's approach to naming relationships. For example, between *Customer* and *Address* there really should be two names "Each CUSTOMER may be located in one or more ADDRESSES" and "Each ADDRESS may be the site of one or more CUSTOMERS."Although these names explicitly define the relationship I personally think that they're visual noise that clutter the diagram. I prefer simple names such as "has" and then trust my readers to interpret the name in each direction. I'll only add more information where it's needed, in this case I think that it isn't. However, a significant advantage of describing the names the way that Barker suggests is that it's a good test to see if you actually understand the relationship – if you can't name it then you likely don't understand it.

Data models can be used effectively at both the enterprise level and at the project level. Enterprise architects will often create one or more high-level LDMs that depict the data structures that support your enterprise, models typically referred to as enterprise data models or enterprise information models. An enterprise data model is one of several critical views that your organization's enterprise architects may choose to maintain and support — other views may explore your network/hardware infrastructure, your organization structure, your software infrastructure, and your business processes (to name a few). Enterprise data models provide information that a project team can use both as a set of constraints and to provide important insights into the structure of their system.

Project teams will typically create LDMs as a primary analysis artifact when their implementation environment is predominantly procedural in nature, for example when they are using structured COBOL as an implementation language. LDMs are also a good choice when a project is data-oriented in nature, perhaps a data warehouse or reporting system is being developed. However, in my experience LDMs are often a poor choice when a project team is using object-oriented or component-based technologies (because they'd rather work with object and component models) or simply when the project is not data-oriented in nature (for example, you're building embedded software). As Agile Modeling (AM) advises, follow the practice *Apply The Right Artifact(s)*. Or, as your grandfather likely advised you, use the right tool for the job.

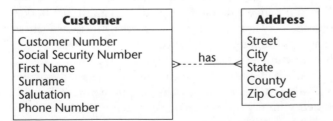

Figure 3.1   A simple logical data model (Barker notation).

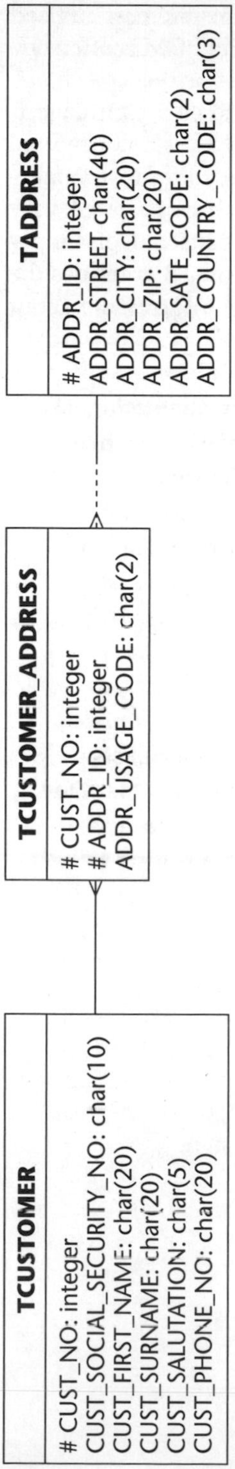

Figure 3.2 A simple physical data model (Barker notation).

When a relational database is used for data storage, project teams are best advised to create a PDM to model its internal schema. My experience is that a PDM is often one of the critical design artifacts for business-application-development projects.

Halpin (2001) points out that many data professionals prefer to create an Object-Role Model (ORM), as depicted in Figure 3.3, instead of an LDM for a conceptual model. The advantage is that the notation is very simple, something your project stakeholders can quickly grasp; the disadvantage is that the models become large very quickly. ORMs enable you to first explore actual data examples instead of simply jumping to a potentially incorrect abstraction — for example, Figure 3.3 examines the relationship between customers and addresses in detail. For more information about ORM, visit www.orm.net.

TIP Expanding your modeling skills enables you to reduce documentation. My experience is that people will capture information in the best place that they know. As a result, I typically discard ORMs after I'm finished with them. I sometimes use ORMs to explore the domain with project stakeholders but later replace them with a more traditional artifact such as an LDM, a class diagram, or even a PDM. As a "generalizing specialist" (Ambler 2003b), someone with one or more specialties who also strives to gain general skills and knowledge, this is an easy decision for me to make; I know that this information that I've just "discarded" will be captured in another artifact — a model, the tests, or even the code — that I understand. Specialists who only understand a limited number of artifacts and therefore "hand off" their work to other specialists don't have this option. Not only are they tempted to keep the artifacts that they create but also to invest even more time to enhance the artifacts. Therefore, I typically find that generalizing specialists are more likely than specialists to travel light.

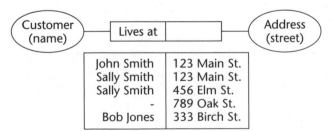

Figure 3.3   A simple object-role model.

Notation 101: How to Read Data Models

Figure 3.4 presents a summary of the syntax of four common data modeling notations: Information Engineering (IE), Barker, IDEFX1, and the Unified Modeling Language (UML). This diagram isn't meant to be comprehensive, instead its goal is to provide a basic overview. Furthermore, for the sake of brevity I wasn't able to depict the highly detailed approach to relationship naming that Barker suggests. A brief discussion of each notation can be found in the following list. Chapter 2 gives you more detailed information on UML, and for more information on IE, Barker, and IDEFX1, I highly suggest David Hay's (1999) paper "A Comparison of Data Modeling Techniques," which can be found at www.essentialstrategies.com/publications/modeling/compare.htm.

IE. The IE notation (Finkelstein 1989) is simple and easy to read, and is well suited for high-level logical and enterprise data modeling. The only drawback of this notation, arguably an advantage, is that it does not support the identification of attributes of an entity. The assumption is that the attributes will be modeled with another diagram or simply described in the supporting documentation.

Barker. Barker is one of the more popular notations, being supported by Oracle's toolset, and is well suited for all types of data models. The only real drawback (although, granted, no notation is perfect) is that its approach to subtyping can become clunky with hierarchies that go several levels deep.

IDEFX1. This notation is overly complex. It was originally intended for physical modeling but has been misapplied for logical modeling as well. Although popular within some U.S. government agencies, particularly the Department of Defense (DoD), this notation has been all but abandoned by everyone else. Avoid using it if you can.

UML. This is not yet an official data modeling notation. Although several suggestions for a data modeling profile for the UML exist, including Naiburg and Maksimchuk's (2001) and my own (Chapter 2), none are complete, and more importantly they are not "official" UML yet. Having said that, considering the popularity of UML, the other data-oriented efforts of the Object Management Group (OMG), and the lack of a notational standard within the data community, it is only a matter of time until a UML data modeling notation is accepted within the software industry.

Quotation	Information Engineering	Barker Notation	IDEFX1	UML
Multiplicities:				
Zero or one				0..1
One only				1
Zero or more				0..*
One or more				1..*
Specific range	N/A	N/A	N/A	3..7
Attributes:				
Names	N/A	Attribute Name: Type	attribute-name: Type	attributeName: Type
Primary key/unique identifier	N/A	# Attribute Name	attribute-name	attributeName «PK» {order#}
Foreign key	N/A	N/A	attribute-name (FK)	attributName «FK» {to=tablename}
Associations:				
Labels	Customer owns accessed by Account	Customer owns accessed by Account	Customer owns accessed by Account	Customer owns Account
Quantity roles	N/A	N/A	N/A	Customer owner
Subtyping	Subtype is a Super Type	Super Type Sub Type	Sub Type attr. Super Type	Subtype Super Type
Aggregation	Part is part of Whole	Part part of Whole	Part is part of Whole	Part Whole
Composition	Part is part of Whole	Part part of Whole	Part is part of Whole	Part Whole
Constraint	Person Customer Employee	N/A	N/A	Person {or} Customer Employee
Exclusive Or (XOR) Constraint	Item Product Service	Item Product Service	N/A	Item {xor} Product Service

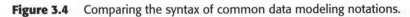

Figure 3.4   Comparing the syntax of common data modeling notations.

How to Model Data

Now that you've seen how data models can be used and have been introduced to common notations, the next step is to learn how to model data. As pointed out earlier, the focus is on physical data models although most of these skills are applicable to conceptual and logical modeling as well. When you are data modeling, the following tasks are performed in an iterative manner:

- Identify entity types
- Identify attributes
- Apply naming conventions
- Identify relationships
- Apply data model patterns
- Assign keys

TIP **Very good practical books about data modeling include *Joe Celko's Data & Databases* (Celko 1999) and *Data Modeling for Information Professionals* (Schmidt 1998) because they both focus on practical issues with data modeling. *The Data Modeling Handbook* (Reingruber and Gregory 1994) and *Data Model Patterns* (Hay 1996) are both excellent resources once you've mastered the fundamentals. *An Introduction to Database Systems* (Date 2001) is a good academic treatise for anyone wishing to become a data specialist.**

Identify Data Entities

An entity type is similar conceptually to object-orientation's concept of a class — an entity type represents a collection of similar entities. An entity type could represent a collection of people, places, things, events, or concepts. Examples of entity types in an order entry system would include *Customer*, *Address*, *Order*, *Item*, and *Tax*. If you were performing class modeling, you would expect to discover classes with the exact same names. However, the difference between a class and an entity type is that classes have both data and behavior, whereas entity types just have data.

Ideally an entity type should be "normal", the data modeling world's version of cohesive. A normal entity type depicts one concept, just as a cohesive class models one concept. For example, customer and order are clearly two different concepts; therefore, it makes sense to model them as separate entities. (Data normalization is described further in Chapter 4.)

Identify Attributes

Each entity type will have one or more data attributes. For example, in Figure 3.1 you saw that *Customer* has attributes such as *First Name* and *Surname* and in Figure 3.2 that the *TCUSTOMER* table had corresponding data columns *CUST_FIRST_NAME* and *CUST_SURNAME* (a column is the implementation of a data attribute within a relational database).

Attributes should also be cohesive from the point of view of your domain, something that is often a judgment call. In Figure 3.1, I decided that I wanted to model the fact that people had both first and last names instead of just a name (for example, "Scott" and "Ambler" versus "Scott Ambler"), whereas I did not distinguish between the sections of an American zip code (for example, 90210-1234-5678). Getting the level of detail right can have a significant impact on your development and maintenance efforts. Refactoring a single data column into several columns can be quite difficult (database refactoring is described in detail in Chapter 12), although overspecifying an attribute (for example, having three attributes for zip code when you only needed one) can result in overbuilding your system and cause you to incur greater development and maintenance costs than you actually needed.

Apply Data-Naming Conventions

Your organization should have standards and guidelines applicable to data modeling, something you should be able to obtain from your enterprise administrators (if they don't exist you should lobby to have some put in place). These guidelines should include naming conventions for all types of data modeling, the logical naming conventions should be focused on human readability, whereas the physical naming conventions will reflect technical considerations. You can clearly see that different naming conventions were applied in Figures 3.1 and 3.2.

Agile Modeling (AM), which I discuss in Chapter 10, includes the *Apply Modeling Standards* practice. The basic idea is that developers should agree to and follow a common set of modeling standards on a software project. Just as there is value in following common coding conventions (clean code that follows your chosen coding guidelines is easier to understand and evolve than code that doesn't), there is similar value in following common modeling conventions.

Identifying Relationships

In the real world, entities have relationships with other entities. For example, customers *place* orders, customers *live at* addresses, and line items *are part of* orders. *Place*, *live at*, and *are part of* are all terms that define relationships between entities. The relationships between entities are conceptually identical to the relationships (associations) between objects.

Figure 3.5 depicts a partial LDM for an online ordering system. The first thing to notice is the various styles applied to relationship names and roles — different relationships require different approaches. For example, the relationship between *Customer* and *Order* has two names, *places* and *is placed by*, whereas the relationship between *Customer* and *Address* has one. In this example, having a second name on the relationship, the idea being that you want to specify how to read the relationship in each direction, is redundant — you're better off to find a clear wording for a single relationship name, decreasing the clutter on your diagram. Similarly, you will often find that by specifying the roles that an entity plays in a relationship will often negate the need to give the relationship a name (although some CASE tools may inadvertently force you to do this). For example, the role of *billing address* and the label *billed to* are clearly redundant; you really only need one. As an example, the role *part of* that *Line Item* has in its relationship with *Order* is sufficiently obvious without a relationship name.

You also need to identify the cardinality and optionality of a relationship (the UML combines the concepts of optionality and cardinality into the single concept of multiplicity). Cardinality represents the concept of "how many," whereas optionality represents the concept of "whether you must have something." For example, it is not enough to know that customers place orders. How many orders can a customer place? None, one, or several? Furthermore, relationships are two-way streets: not only do customers place orders, but orders are placed by customers. This leads to questions such as: How many customers can be enrolled in any given order and is it possible to have an order with no customer involved? Figure 3.5 shows that customers place one or more orders and that any given order is placed by one customer and one customer only. It also shows that a customer lives at one or more addresses and that any given address has zero or more customers living at it.

Although UML distinguishes between different types of relationships — associations, inheritance, aggregation, composition, and dependency — data modelers often aren't as concerned with this issue as much as object modelers are. Subtyping, one application of inheritance, is often found in data models, an example of which is the *is a* relationship between *Item* and its two subtypes *Service* and *Product*. Aggregation and composition are much less common and typically must be implied from the data model, as you see with the *part of* role that *Line Item* takes with *Order*. UML dependencies are typically a software construct and therefore wouldn't appear on a data model, unless of course it was a very highly detailed physical model that showed how views, triggers, or stored procedures depended on the schema of one or more tables.

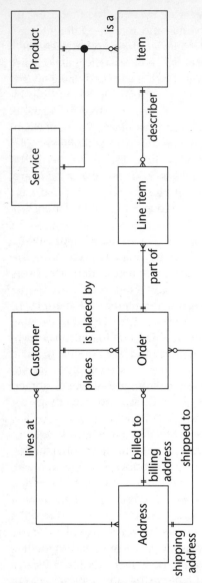

Figure 3.5   A logical data model (Information Engineering notation).

Apply Data Model Patterns

Some data modelers will apply common data model patterns. David Hay's (1996) book *Data Model Patterns* is the best reference on the subject, just as object-oriented developers will apply analysis patterns (Fowler 1997; Ambler 1997) and design patterns (Gamma et al. 1995). Data model patterns are conceptually closest to analysis patterns because they describe solutions to common domain issues. Hay's book is a very good reference for anyone involved in analysis-level modeling, even when you're taking an object approach instead of a data approach, because his patterns model business structures from a wide variety of business domains.

Assign Keys

First, some terminology. A key is one or more data attributes that uniquely identify an entity. A key that is made up of two or more attributes is called a *composite key*. A key that is formed of attributes that already exist in the real world is called a *natural key*. For example, U.S. citizens are issued a Social Security number (SSN) that is unique to them. SSN could be used as a natural key, assuming that privacy laws allow it, for a Person entity (assuming that the scope of your organization is limited to the United States). An entity type in a logical data model will have zero or more *candidate keys,* also referred to simply as *unique identifiers*. For example, if we only interact with American citizens then SSN is one candidate key for the *Person* data entity and the combination of name and phone number (assuming the combination is unique) is potentially a second candidate key. Both of these keys are called candidate keys because they are candidates chosen to be the *primary key*, an *alternate key* (also known as a *secondary key*), or perhaps not even a key at all, within a physical data model. A primary key is the preferred key for an entity type, whereas an alternate key (also known as a secondary key) is an alternate way to access rows within a table. In a physical database a key would be formed of one or more table columns whose value(s) uniquely identify a row within a relational table.

Figure 3.6 presents an alternate design to that presented in Figure 3.2; in this case, a different naming convention was adopted and the model itself is more extensive. In Figure 3.6, the *Customer* table has the *CustomerNumber* column as its primary key and *SocialSecurityNumber* as an alternate key. This indicates that the preferred way to access customer information is through the value of a person's customer number, although your software can get at the same information if it has the person's Social Security number. The *CustomerHasAddress* table has a composite primary key, the combination of *CustomerNumber* and *AddressID*. A *foreign key* is one or more attributes in a data entity that represent a key, either primary or secondary, in another data entity. Foreign keys are used to maintain relationships between rows. For example, the relationships between rows in the *CustomerHasAddress* table and the *Customer* table are maintained by the *CustomerNumber* column within the *CustomerHasAddress* table. The interesting thing about the *CustomerNumber* column is the fact that it is part of the primary key for *CustomerHasAddress* as well as the foreign key to the *Customer* table. Similarly, the *AddressID* column is part of the primary key of *CustomerHasAddress* as well as a foreign key to the *Address* table to maintain the relationship with rows of *Address*.

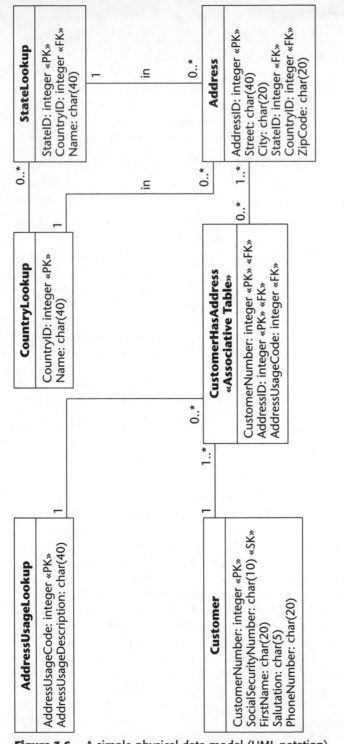

Figure 3.6   A simple physical data model (UML notation).

TIP The only type of key that you model on conceptual and logical data models is candidate keys, if you choose to model them at all. Candidate keys are generally not modeled on physical models, instead primary, alternate, and foreign keys are.

There are two strategies for assigning keys to tables. The first is to simply use a natural key, one or more existing data attributes that are unique to the business concept. For the *Customer* table, there were two candidate keys, in this case *CustomerNumber* and *SocialSecurityNumber*. The second strategy is to introduce a new column to be used as a key. This new column is called a surrogate key, a key that has no business meaning, an example of which is the *AddressID* column of the *Address* table in Figure 3.6. Addresses don't have an "easy" natural key because you would need to use all of the columns of the *Address* table to form a key for itself; therefore, introducing a surrogate key is a much better option in this case. The primary advantage of natural keys is that they exist already, you don't need to introduce a new "unnatural" value to your data schema. However, the primary disadvantage of natural keys is that because they have business meaning it is possible that they may need to change if your business requirements change. For example, if your users decide to make *CustomerNumber* alphanumeric instead of numeric, then in addition to updating the schema for the *Customer* table (which is unavoidable), you would have to change every single table where *CustomerNumber* is used as a foreign key. If the *Customer* table instead used a surrogate key, then the change would have been localized to just the *Customer* table itself (*CustomerNumber* in this case would just be a nonkey column of the table). If you needed to make a similar change to your surrogate key strategy, perhaps adding a couple of extra digits to your key values because you've run out of values, then you would have the exact same problem. This points out the need to set a workable surrogate key strategy. There are several common options:

Key values assigned by the database. Most of the leading database vendors — companies such as Oracle, Sybase, and Informix — implement a surrogate key strategy called incremental keys. The basic idea is to maintain a counter within the database server, writing the current value to a hidden system table to maintain consistency, and then assign a value to newly created table rows. Every time a row is created the counter is incremented and that value is assigned as the key value for that row. The implementation strategies vary from vendor to vendor, sometimes the values assigned are unique across all tables, whereas sometimes values are unique only within a single table, but the general concept is the same.

MAX() + 1. A common strategy is to use an integer column, start the value for the first record at 1, then for a new row set the value to the maximum value in this column plus one, using the SQL MAX function. Although this approach is simple it suffers from performance problems with large tables and only guarantees a unique key value within the table. You potentially have problems when you delete the row with the greatest key value because you will now "reuse" its key value for the next inserted row.

Universally unique identifiers (UUIDs).   UUIDs are 128-bit values that are created from a hash of the ID of your Ethernet card, or an equivalent software representation, and the current datetime of your computer system. The algorithm for doing this is defined by the Open Software Foundation (www.opengroup.org).

Globally unique identifiers (GUIDs).   GUIDs are a Microsoft standard that extend UUIDs, following the same strategy if an Ethernet card exists, and if not then they hash a software ID and the current datetime to produce a value that is guaranteed unique to the machine that creates it.

High-low strategy.   The basic idea is that your key value, often called a persistent object identifier (POID) or simply an object identified (OID), has in two logical parts: A unique HIGH value that you obtain from a defined source and an n-digit LOW value that your application assigns itself. Each time that a HIGH value is obtained, the LOW value will be set to zero. For example, if the application that you're running requests a value for HIGH, it will be assigned the value 1701. Assuming that n (the number of digits for LOW) is four, then all persistent object identifiers that the application assigns to objects will be a combination of 17010000, 17010001, 17010002, and so on until 17019999. At this point, a new value for HIGH is obtained, LOW is reset to zero, and you continue again. If another application requests a value for HIGH immediately after you, it will be given the value of 1702, and the OIDs that will be assigned to objects that it creates will be 17020000, 17020001, and so on. As you can see, as long as HIGH is unique, then all POID values will be unique. An implementation of a HIGH-LOW generator can be found at www.theserverside.com.

TIP   I advise that you prefer surrogate keys, but be realistic. The fundamental issue is that keys are a significant source of coupling within a relational schema, and as a result they are difficult to change. The implication is that you want to avoid keys with business meaning because business meaning changes. However, at the same time, you need to remember that some data is commonly accessed by unique identifiers, for example customers via their customer number, American employees via their Social Security number (SSN), and states via their state code (for example, CA for California). In these cases you may want to use the natural key instead of a surrogate key such as a UUID or POID. Or you may simply want to support alternate keys. Keys are one of the religious issues within the data community. Some people prefer all natural keys whereas others prefer all surrogate keys. Both "camps" are extremists in my opinion. You are much better advised to find the sweet spot for your environment and use a combination of natural and surrogate keys as appropriate.

How can you be effective at assigning keys? Consider the following tips:

Avoid "smart" keys.   A "smart" key is one that contains one or more subparts that provide meaning. For example, the first two digits of a U.S. zip code indicate the state that the zip code is in. The first problem with smart keys is that they have business meaning. The second problem is that their use often becomes convoluted over time. For example some large states have several codes, California has zip codes beginning with 90 and 91, making queries based on state codes more complex. Third, they often increase the chance that the strategy will need to be expanded. Considering that zip codes are nine digits in length (the following four digits are used at the discretion of owners of buildings uniquely identified by zip codes), it's far less likely that you'd run out of nine-digit numbers before running out of two-digit codes assigned to individual states.

Consider assigning natural keys for simple "lookup" tables. A lookup table is one that is used to relate codes to detailed information. For example, you might have a lookup table listing color codes to the names of colors. For example the code 127 represents "Tulip Yellow." Simple lookup tables typically consist of a code column and a description/name column, whereas complex lookup tables consist of a code column and several informational columns.

Natural keys don't always work for lookup tables. Another example of a lookup table is one that contains a row for each state, province, or territory in North America. For example there would be a row for California, a U.S. state, and for Ontario, a Canadian province. The primary goal of this table is to provide an official list of these geographical entities, a list that is reasonably static over time (the last change to it would have been in the late 1990s when the Northwest Territories, a territory of Canada, was split into Nunavut and the Northwest Territories). A valid natural key for this table would be the state code, a unique two-character code — for example, CA for California and ON for Ontario. Unfortunately this approach doesn't work because Canadian government decided to keep the same state code, NW, for the two territories.

Your applications must still support "natural key searches." If you choose to take a surrogate key approach to your database design keep in mind that your applications must continue to support searches on the domain columns that still uniquely identify rows. For example, your *Customer* table may have a *Customer_POID* column used as a surrogate key as well as a *Customer_Number* column and a *Social_Security_Number* column. You would likely need to support searches based on both the customer number and the Social Security number. (Searching is discussed in detail in Chapter 18.)

How to Become Better at Modeling Data

How do you improve your data modeling skills? Practice, practice, practice. Whenever you get a chance, you should work closely with agile DBAs, volunteer to model data with them, and ask them questions as the work progresses. Agile DBAs will be following the AM practice *Model With Others* and so should welcome the assistance as well as the questions — one of the best ways to really learn your craft is to have someone ask "Why are you doing it that way?" You should be able to learn physical data modeling skills from agile DBAs, and often logical data modeling skills as well.

Similarly, you should take the opportunity to work with the enterprise architects within your organization. Chapter 1 argues they should be taking an active role on your project, mentoring your project team in the enterprise architecture (if any), mentoring you in modeling and architectural skills, and aiding in your team's modeling and development efforts. Once again, volunteer to work with them and ask questions when you are doing so. Enterprise architects will be able to teach you conceptual and logical data modeling skills as well as instill and an appreciation for enterprise issues.

You also need to do some reading. Although this chapter is a good start, it is only a brief introduction. I listed several good books earlier in the chapter although a better approach is to simply ask the agile DBAs that you work with what they think you should read.

Summary

All professional software developers should understand the fundamentals of data modeling. In this chapter, you saw that data models can be used to explore the conceptual problem domain, to explore the logical data structures that support your problem domain, and to design your database schema. Although you have alternatives for conceptual and logical modeling, in my experience data models are best suited for physical data modeling (particularly when you're using relational database technology).

Data modeling is a valuable skill to have and has been since the 1970s. Data modeling provides a common framework within which you can work with agile DBAs, and may even prove to be the initial skill that enables you to make a career transition into becoming a full-fledged agile DBA.

CHAPTER 4

Data Normalization

Normalization produces highly cohesive and loosely coupled data schemas.
Denormalization improves performance. Make the trade-offs wisely.

Data normalization is a process in which data attributes within a data model are organized to increase the cohesion of entity types and to reduce the coupling between
entity types. The goal of data normalization is to reduce, or even eliminate, data redundancy. This is an important consideration for application developers because it is
incredibly difficult to store objects in a relational database if a data attribute is stored in
several places.

To explore the techniques of data normalization, this chapter addresses the following topics:

- The first three normal forms
- Why data normalization?
- The role of the agile DBA
- First normal form (1NF)
- Second normal form (2NF)
- Third normal form (3NF)
- Beyond 3NF

Why Data Normalization?

The advantage of having a highly normalized data schema is that information is stored in one place and one place only, reducing the possibility of inconsistent data. Furthermore, highly normalized data schemas in general are closer conceptually to object-oriented schemas because the object-oriented goals of promoting high cohesion and loose coupling between classes results in similar solutions (at least from a data point of view). This generally makes it easier to map your objects to your data schema.

Unfortunately, normalization usually comes at a performance cost. With the data schema of Figure 4.1 all the data for a single order is stored in one row (assuming orders of up to nine order items), making it very easy to access. With the data schema of Figure 4.1, you could quickly determine the total amount of an order by reading the single row from the *Order0NF* table. To do so with the data schema in Figure 4.5, you would need to read data from a row in the *Order* table, data from all the rows from the *OrderItem* table for that order, and data from the corresponding rows in the *Item* table for each order item. For this query, the data schema of Figure 4.1 very likely provides better performance. Performance tuning, including denormalization, is covered in Chapter 15.

The Role of the Agile DBA

When it comes to data normalization agile DBAs must be prepared to mentor their coworkers in this technique and to help them apply data normalization techniques where appropriate. This includes helping developers to:

Normalize operational databases.   Operational databases, also called operational data stores (ODSs), are where your application typically saves its data. The more normalized a database is, the easier this task becomes. This is different from reporting databases, described in Chapter 21, which are often denormalized to support a wide variety of reports.

Take an evolutionary approach to normalization.   Although normalization is often applied within the scope of a near-serial process the fact is that you can apply the rules of normalization within an evolutionary process as well. You can normalize very small sections of a data model at a time, as I will show in this chapter. Evolutionary development is covered in Part II of this book.

Denormalize for performance.   It is quite common to denormalize data schemas to improve the performance of a database. Techniques for performance tuning are described in Chapter 15.

The Rules of Data Normalization

Table 4.1 summarizes the three most common normalization rules that describe how to put entity types into a series of increasing levels of normalization. Higher levels of data normalization (Date 2000) are beyond the scope of this book — the important thing is

```
┌─────────────────────────────────────┐
│              OrderONF               │
├─────────────────────────────────────┤
│ OrderId: integer <<PK>>             │
│ DateOrdered: date                   │
│ DateFulfilled: date                 │
│ Payment1Amount: currency            │
│ Payment1Type: char(4)               │
│ Payment1Description: char(40)       │
│ Payment2Amount: currency            │
│ Payment2Type: char(4)               │
│ Payment2Description: char(40)       │
│ TaxFederal: currency                │
│ TaxState: currency                  │
│ TaxLocal: currency                  │
│ SubtotalBeforeTax: currency         │
│ ShipToName: char(45)                │
│ ShipToStreet: char(40)              │
│ ShipToCity: char(20)                │
│ ShipToState: char(20)               │
│ ShipToCountry: char(20)             │
│ ShipToZipCode: char(20)             │
│ ShipToPhone: char(20)               │
│ BillToName: char(45)                │
│ BillToStreet: char(40)              │
│ BillToCity: char(20)                │
│ BillToState: char(20)               │
│ BillToCountry: char(20)             │
│ BillToZipCode: char(20)             │
│ BillToPhone: char(20)               │
│ ItemName1: char(40)                 │
│ NumberOrdered1: integer             │
│ InitialItemPrice1: currency         │
│ TotalPriceExtended1: currency       │
│ ItemName2: char(40)                 │
│ NumberOrdered2: integer             │
│ InitialItemPrice2: currency         │
│ TotalPriceExtended2: currency       │
│ . . .                               │
│ ItemName9: char(40)                 │
│ NumberOrdered9: integer             │
│ InitialItemPrice9: currency         │
│ TotalPriceExtended9: currency       │
└─────────────────────────────────────┘
```

Figure 4.1 An initial data schema for order (UML notation).

to remember that you want to store data in one place and one place only. With respect to terminology, a data schema is considered to be at the level of normalization of its least normalized entity type. For example, if all of your entity types are at second normal form (2NF) or higher, then we say that your data schema is at 2NF.

Data normalization rules are typically applied to physical data models although there is nothing stops you from applying them to conceptual and logical models as well. However, the goal of conceptual modeling is to facilitate understanding of the domain between you and your stakeholders, and the act of applying design-oriented

Table 4.1   First Three Data Normalization Rules

LEVEL	RULE
First normal form (1NF)	An entity type is in 1NF when it contains no repeating groups of data.
Second normal form (2NF)	An entity type is in 2NF when it is in 1NF *and* when all of its nonkey attributes are fully dependent on its primary key.
Third normal form (3NF)	An entity type is in 3NF when it is in 2NF *and* when all of its attributes are directly dependent on the primary key.

rules that your stakeholders may not understand will likely defeat that purpose. Normalization of logical models is a matter of preference.

First Normal Form (1NF)

An entity type is in first normal form (1NF) when it contains no repeating groups of data. For example, in Figure 4.1 you see that there are several repeating attributes in the data *Order0NF* table (semantically each column is in fact unique in a relational table; however, logically you see that the same groups of data attributes do in fact repeat) — the ordered item information repeats nine times and the contact information is repeated twice, once for shipping information and once for billing information. Although this initial version of orders could work, what happens when an order has more than nine order items? Do you create additional order records for them? What about the vast majority of orders that only have one or two items? Do we really want to waste all that storage space in the database for the empty fields? Likely not. Furthermore, do you want to write the code required to process the nine copies of item information, even if it is only to marshal it back and forth between the appropriate number of objects? Once again, likely not.

Figure 4.2 presents a reworked data schema where the order schema is put into first normal form. The introduction of the *OrderItem1NF* table enables us to have many, or a few, order items associated with an order, increasing the flexibility of our schema while reducing storage requirements for small orders (the majority of our business). The *ContactInformation1NF* table offers a similar benefit, when an order is shipped and billed to the same person (once again the majority of cases), you could use the same contact information record in the database, to reduce data redundancy. *OrderPayment1NF* was introduced to enable customers to make several payments against an order — *Order0NF* could accept up to two payments, the type being something like "MC" and the description "MasterCard Payment." although with the new approach far more than two payments could be supported. Multiple payments are accepted only when the total of an order is large enough that a customer must pay via more than one approach, perhaps paying some by check and some by credit card.

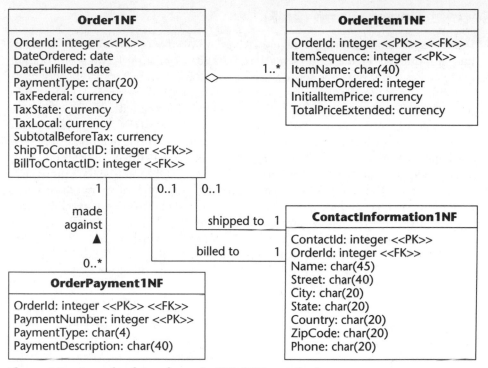

Figure 4.2 An order data schema in 1NF (UML notation).

An important thing to notice is the application of primary and foreign keys in the new solution. *Order1NF* has kept *OrderID*, the original key of *Order0NF*, as its primary key. To maintain the relationship back to *Order1NF*, the *OrderItem1NF* table includes the *OrderID* column within its schema, which is why it has the stereotype <<FK>>. When a new table is introduced into a schema, in this case *OrderItem1NF*, as the result of first normalization efforts, it is common to use the primary key of the original table (*Order0NF*) as part of the primary key of the new table. Because *OrderID* is not unique for order items, you can have several order items on an order, the column *ItemSequence* was added to form a composite primary key for the *OrderItem1NF* table. A different approach to keys was taken with the *ContactInformation1NF* table. The column *ContactID*, a surrogate key that has no business meaning, was made the primary key — *OrderID* is needed as a foreign key to maintain the relationship back to *Order1NF*. A good rule of thumb is that if the tables are highly related to one another (there is an aggregation relationship between *Order1NF* and *OrderItem1NF*), then it is likely that it makes sense to include the primary key of the original table as part of the primary key of the new table. If the two tables are not as strongly related (there is merely a relationship between *Order1NF* and *ContactInformation1NF*), then a surrogate key may make more sense; however, because each row of *ContactInformation1NF* is associated with only one row of *Order1NF*, keeping *OrderID* as the key would be a valid (and easier) approach to take.

Second Normal Form (2NF)

Although the solution presented in Figure 4.2 has improved over that of Figure 4.1, it can be further improved. Figure 4.3 presents the data schema of Figure 4.2 in second normal form (2NF). An entity type is in second normal form (2NF) when it is in 1NF and when every nonkey attribute (that is, any attribute that is not part of the primary key) is fully dependent on the primary key. This was definitely not the case with the *OrderItem1NF* table; therefore, we need to introduce the new table *Item2NF*. The problem with *OrderItem1NF* is that item information, such as the name and price of an item, does not depend upon an order for that item. For example, if Bob orders three widgets and Doug orders five widgets, the facts that the item is called a "widget" and that the unit price is $19.95 is constant. This information depends on the concept of an item, not the concept of an order for an item, and therefore should not be stored in the order items table — for this reason, the *Item2NF* table was introduced. *OrderItem2NF* retained the *TotalPriceExtended* column, a calculated value that is the number of items ordered multiplied by the price of the item. The value of the *SubtotalBeforeTax* column within the *Order2NF* table is the total of the values of the total price extended for each of its order items.

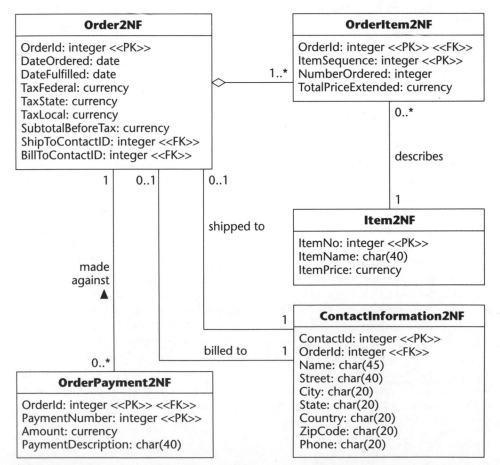

Figure 4.3   An order in 2NF (UML notation).

Third Normal Form (3NF)

An entity type is in *third normal form (3NF)* when it is in 2NF and when all of its attributes are directly dependent on the primary key. A better way to word this rule might be that the attributes of an entity type must depend on all portions of the primary key; therefore, 3NF is an issue only for tables with composite keys. In this case, there is a problem with the *OrderPayment2NF* table, the payment type description (such as "Mastercard" or "Check") depends only on the payment type, not on the combination of the order ID and the payment type. To resolve this problem the *PaymentType3NF* table was introduced, as shown in Figure 4.4, containing a description of the payment type as well as a unique identifier for each payment type.

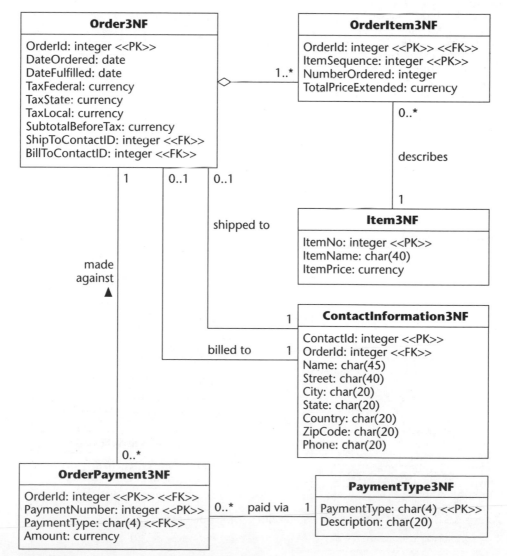

Figure 4.4   An order in 3NF (UML notation).

Beyond 3NF

The data schema of Figure 4.4 can still be improved upon, at least from the point of view of data redundancy, by removing attributes that can be calculated or derived from other ones. In this case, we could remove the *SubtotalBeforeTax* column within the *Order3NF* table and the *TotalPriceExtended* column of *OrderItem3NF*, as you see in Figure 4.5. The point is that although the first three rules of normalization are important to understand, they're only a very good start. Further forms are normalization are described in *An Introduction to Database Systems* (Date 2000).

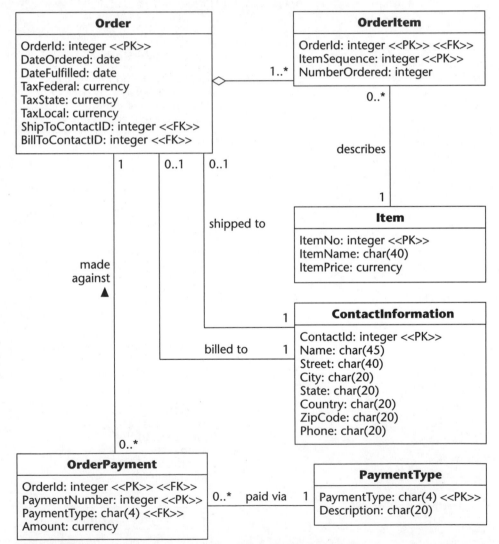

Figure 4.5 An order without calculated values (UML notation).

Summary

This chapter provided an overview of the first three rules of data normalization, showing you how to apply them in practice. The first rule of data normalization motivates you to introduce a new table for repeating information. The second rule of normalization motivates you to improve the cohesion of tables by ensuring that data columns depend on the key to that table. Finally, the third rule of normalization motivates you to introduce tables for data that only depend on a portion of a composite (multicolumn) key. How do you remember these rules? Through a clever play on words: a data attribute will depend upon the key, the whole key, and nothing but the key so help me Codd. (E. F. Codd is considered to be the "father" of relational databases.)

CHAPTER 5

Class Normalization

Good designs are highly cohesive and loosely coupled. The more ways that you have to reach this goal the better.

In Chapter 4, you saw that data normalization is a technique by which you organize data in such a way as to reduce and even eliminate data redundancy, effectively increasing the cohesiveness of your data schema. Can the rules of data normalization be applied to object schemas? Yes, but you need to modify them a bit. The rules of data normalization aren't ideal for objects because they only address data and not behavior. You need to consider both when normalizing an object schema. Class normalization (Ambler 1997) is a process by which you reorganize the structure of your object schema in such a way as to increase the cohesion of classes while minimizing the coupling between them.

To explore the techniques associated with class normalization, the following topics are discussed in this chapter:

- How does class normalization relate to other object-oriented design practices?
- The role of the agile DBA
- First object normal form (1ONF)
- Second object normal form (2ONF)
- Third object normal form (3ONF)
- Beyond 3ONF

How Does Class Normalization Relate to Other Object Design Practices?

Fundamentally class normalization is a technique for improving the quality of your object schemas. The exact same thing can be said of the application of common design pattern, such as those defined by the "Gang of Four (GoF)" in *Design Patterns* (Gamma et. al. 1995). Design patterns are known solutions to common problems, examples of which include the *Strategy* pattern for implementing a collection of related algorithms and the *Singleton* pattern for implementing a class that only has one instance. The application of common design patterns will often result in a highly normalized object schema, although the overzealous application of design patterns can result in you overbuilding your software unnecessarily. As Agile Modeling (AM) suggests (Chapter 10), you should follow the practice the *Apply Patterns Gently* approach and ease into a design pattern over time. In my opinion, the most important benefit of class normalization over design patterns is that the concept is familiar to data professionals and thus provides a bridge for them to help learn object techniques (at least that's been my experience). Another common approach to improving object schemas is refactoring (Fowler 1999), an approach overviewed in Chapter 12. Refactoring is a disciplined way to restructure code by applying small changes to your code to improve its design. Refactoring enables you to evolve your design slowly over time. Class normalization and refactoring fit together quite well — as you're normalizing your classes you will effectively be applying many known refactorings to your object schema. A fundamental difference between class normalization and refactoring is that class normalization is typically performed to your class models, whereas refactorings are applied to your source code.

Do you need to understand all three techniques? Yes. It is always beneficial to have several techniques in your intellectual toolkit. What would you think of a carpenter with only one type of saw, one type of hammer, and one type of screwdriver? My guess would be that he or she wouldn't be as effective as one with a selection of tools. The same thing can be said of agile software developers.

The Role of the Agile DBA

Class normalization is an important technique for agile DBAs, as well as application developers, to have in their intellectual toolbox. Be prepared to work with your teammates to apply these design rules.

The Rules of Class Normalization

The rules of class normalization are summarized in Table 5.1 and are discussed further in the following sections.

Table 5.1   Class Normalization Rules

LEVEL	RULE
First object normal form (1ONF)	A class is in first object normal form (1ONF) when specific behavior required by an attribute that is actually a collection of similar attributes is encapsulated within its own class.
Second object normal form (2ONF)	A class is in second object normal form (2ONF) when it is in first object normal form (1ONF) *and* when "shared" behavior required by more than one instance of the class is encapsulated within its own class(es).
Third object normal form (3ONF)	A class is in third object normal form (3ONF) when it is in second object normal form *and* when it encapsulates only one set of cohesive behavior.

First Object Normal Form (1ONF)

A class is in first object normal form (1ONF) when specific behavior required by an attribute that is actually a collection of similar attributes is encapsulated within its own class. An object schema is in 1ONF when all of its classes are in 1ONF.

Consider the class *Student* in Figure 5.1. You can see that it implements the behavior for adding and dropping students to and from seminars. The attribute *seminars* is a collection of seminar information, perhaps implemented as an array of arrays, that is used to track what seminars a student is assigned to. The operation *addSeminar()* enrolls the student into another seminar, whereas *dropSeminar()* removes the student from one. The operation *printSchedule()* produces a list of all the seminars the student is enrolled in so that the student can have a printed schedule. The operations *setProfessor()* and *setCourseName()* make the appropriate changes to data within the *seminars* collection. This design is clearly not very cohesive — this single class is implementing functionality that is appropriate to several concepts.

Student
studentNumber
name
address
phoneNumber
seminars
addSeminar()
dropSeminar()
printSchedule()
setProfessor()
setCourseName()
getSeminarLength()

Figure 5.1   The Student class in 0ONF.

Figure 5.2 depicts the object schema in 1ONF. *Seminar* was introduced, with both the data and the functionality required to keep track of when and where a seminar is taught, as well as who teaches it and what course it is. It also implements the functionality needed to add students to the seminar and drop students from the seminar. By encapsulating this behavior in *Seminar*, you have increased the cohesion of the design — *Student* now does student kinds of things and *Seminar* does seminar types of things. In the schema of Figure 5.1 *Student* did both.

It should be clear that 1ONF is simply the object equivalent of data's first normal form (1NF) as discussed in Chapter 4 — with 1NF you remove repeating groups of data from a data entity, and with 1ONF you remove repeating groups of behavior from a class.

Second Object Normal Form (2ONF)

A class is in second object normal form (2ONF) when it is in first object normal form (1ONF) and when "shared" behavior required by more than one instance of the class is encapsulated within its own class(es). An object schema is in 2ONF when all of its classes are in 2ONF.

Consider *Seminar* in Figure 5.2. It implements the behavior of maintaining both information about the course that is being taught in the seminar and about the professor teaching that course. Although this approach would work, it unfortunately doesn't work very well. When the name of a course changes you'd have to change the course name for every seminar of that course. That's a lot of work. Figure 5.3 depicts the object schema in 2ONF. To improve the design of *Seminar*, we have introduced two new classes, *Course* and *Professor*, which encapsulate the appropriate behavior needed to implement course objects and professor objects. As before, notice how easy it is to introduce new functionality to our application. *Course* now has methods to list the seminars that it is being taught in (needed for scheduling purposes) and to create new seminars because popular courses often need to have additional seminars added at the last moment to meet student demand. The *Professor* class now has the ability to produce a teaching schedule so that the real-world person has the information needed to manage his or her time.

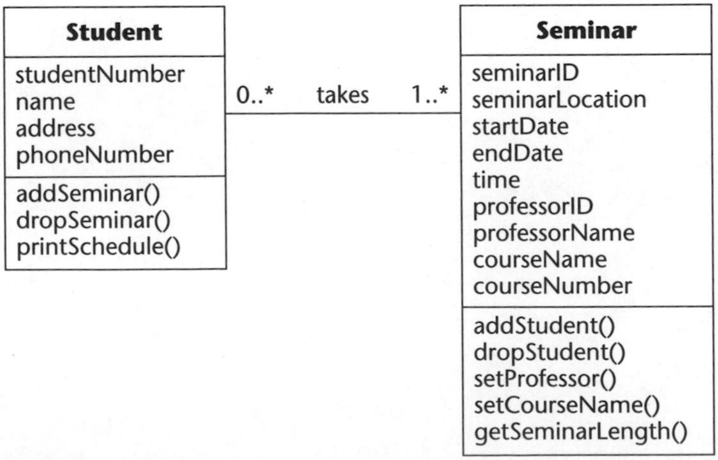

Student				**Seminar**
studentNumber name address phoneNumber	0..*	takes	1..*	seminarID seminarLocation startDate endDate time professorID professorName courseName courseNumber
addSeminar() dropSeminar() printSchedule()				addStudent() dropStudent() setProfessor() setCourseName() getSeminarLength()

Figure 5.2   The object schema in 1ONF.

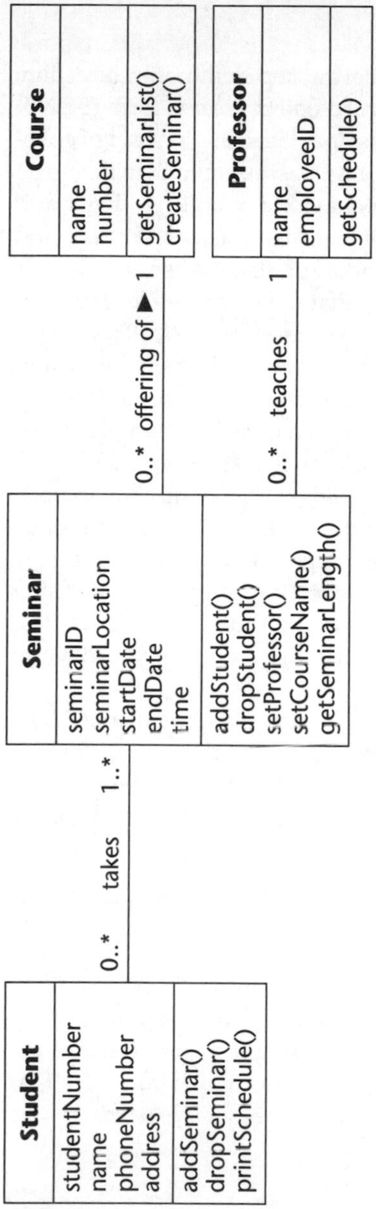

Student

studentNumber
name
phoneNumber
address

addSeminar()
dropSeminar()
printSchedule()

0..*   takes   1..*

Seminar

seminarID
seminarLocation
startDate
endDate
time

addStudent()
dropStudent()
setProfessor()
setCourseName()
getSeminarLength()

0..*   offering of ▶ 1

Course

name
number

getSeminarList()
createSeminar()

0..*   teaches   1

Professor

name
employeeID

getSchedule()

Figure 5.3   The object schema in 2ONF.

Third Object Normal Form (3ONF)

Although putting the object schema in 2ONF is definitely a step in the right direction, we can still improve the design further. A class is in third object normal form (3ONF) when it is in second object normal form and when it encapsulates only one set of cohesive behavior. An object schema is in 3ONF when all of its classes are in 3ONF.

In Figure 5.3 the *Student* class encapsulates the behavior for both students and addresses. The first step would be to refactor *Student* into two classes, *Student* and *Address*. This would make the design more cohesive and more flexible because there is a very good chance that students aren't the only things that have addresses. However, this isn't enough because *Address* still needs to be normalized. Specifically, there is behavior that is associated only with zip codes, formatting, and validation. For example, based on the zip code it should be possible to determine whether or not the city and state of an address are valid. This realization leads to the class diagram presented in Figure 5.4, which implements addresses as four distinct classes: *Address*, *ZipCode*, *City*, and *State*. The advantage of this approach is twofold — first of all the zip code functionality is implemented in one place, increasing the cohesiveness of the model. Second, by making zip codes, cities, and states their own separate classes, you can now easily group addresses, based on various criteria, for reporting purposes, increasing the flexibility of the application. The main drawback is that to build a single address you have to build it from four distinct objects, increasing the code that you have to write, test, and maintain.

You're still not done, because the *Seminar* class of Figure 5.3 implements "date range" behavior — it has a start date and an end date, and it calculates the difference between the two dates. Because this sort of behavior forms a cohesive whole, and because it is more than likely needed in other places, it makes sense to introduce the class *DateRange*, as shown in Figure 5.4.

Beyond 3ONF

Good object-oriented designs are loosely coupled and highly cohesive. The first three rules of class normalization describe common ways to rework your designs to help ensure this. However, you can achieve these same goals through refactoring and the proper application of design patterns. My advice is to apply normalization rules first to get your design most of the way there, then apply other techniques as needed.

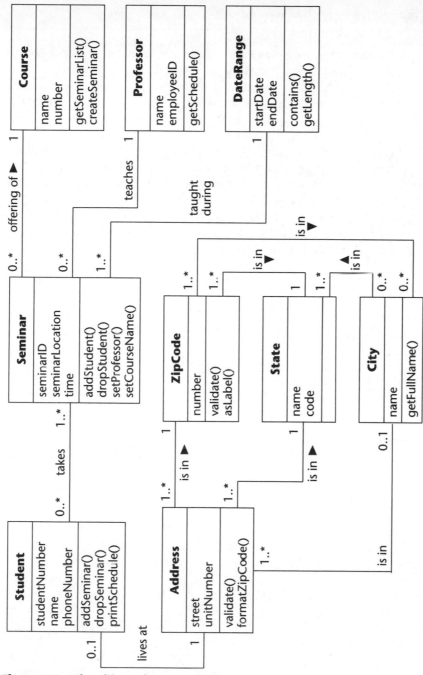

Figure 5.4 The object schema in 3ONF.

Summary

This chapter presented an object-oriented design technique called class normalization, the OO equivalent of data normalization. To put a class into first object normal form (1ONF), you refactor repeating data structures into their own class. A class is in second object normal form (2ONF) when "shared" behavior required by several entities is encapsulated within its own class. A class is in third object normal form (3ONF) when it implements a single, cohesive set of behaviors.

Although the techniques of class normalization aren't yet as popular as refactoring or the application of design patterns, I believe that they are important because they provide a very good bridge between the object and data paradigms. The rules of class normalization provide advice that effective object designers have been doing for years, so there is really nothing new in that respect. More importantly, they describe basic object design techniques in a manner that data professionals can readily understand, helping to improve the communication within your project team.

Relational Database Technology, Like It or Not

Sometimes you need to accept the devil that you know.

A *relational database* is a persistent storage mechanism that enables you to both store data and optionally implement functionality. The goal of this chapter is to provide an overview of relational database (RDB) technology and to explore the issues applicable to its use in modern organizations. RDBs are used to store the information required by applications built using procedural technologies such as COBOL or FORTRAN, object technologies such as Java and C#, and component-based technologies such as Visual Basic. Because RDBs are the dominant persistent storage technology, it is critical that all software professionals understand at least the basics of RDBs, the challenges surrounding the technology, and when it is appropriate to use RDBs.

In this chapter, I discuss the following topics:

- Relational database technology
- Simple features of relational databases
- Advanced features of relational databases
- Coupling: your greatest enemy
- Additional challenges of relational databases
- Encapsulation: your greatest ally
- Beyond relational databases: you actually have a choice

Relational Database Technology

Let's begin with an overview of some common terminology. Relational databases store data in tables. Tables are organized into columns, and each column stores one type of data (integer, real number, character strings, date, and so on). The data for a single "instance" of a table is stored as a row. For example, the *Customer* table could have columns such as *CustomerNumber*, *FirstName*, and *Surname*, and a row within that table might look something like {1701, "James", "Kirk"}. Tables typically have keys; a *key* is one or more columns that uniquely identify a row within the table. In the case of the *Customer* table, the key would be *CustomerNumber*.

To improve access time to a data table, you define an index on the table. An *index* provides a quick way to look up data based on one or more columns in the table, just like the index of a book enables you to find specific information quickly.

Simple Features of Relational Databases

The most common use of relational databases is to implement simple *CRUD* — create, read, update, and delete — functionality. For example, an application could:

- *Create* a new order and insert it into your database.
- *Read* an existing order and work with the data.
- *Update* the database with the new information.
- *Delete* an existing order (if a customer has canceled it, for example).

The vast majority of your interaction with an RDB will likely be to implement basic CRUD functionality.

The easiest way to manipulate a database is to submit Structured Query Language (SQL) statements to it. The following code depicts a simple data model using the proposed UML data-modeling notation described in Chapter 2. (Data modeling is described in Chapter 3.)

```
INSERT INTO Seminar
    (SEMINAR_ID, COURSE_ID, OVERSEER_ID, SEMINAR_NUMBER)
VALUES
    (74656, 1234, 'THX0001138', 2)
```

To create a row in the Seminar table, you would issue an INSERT statement, an example of which is shown in the preceding code.

```
SELECT * FROM Seminar
WHERE SEMINAR_ID = 1701
```

Similarly, the following shows an example of how to read a row by issuing a SELECT statement:

```
SELECT * FROM Seminar
WHERE SEMINAR_ID = 1701
```

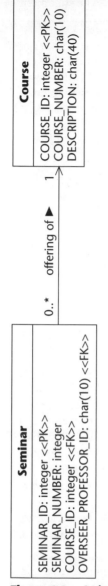

Figure 6.1   A simple UML data model.

The following code shows how to update an existing row via an UPDATE statement:

```
UPDATE Seminar
    SET OVERSEER_ID = 'NCC0001701', SEMINAR_NUMBER = 3
WHERE SEMINAR_ID = 1701
```

Finally, the following code shows how to delete a row with a DELETE statement:

```
DELETE FROM Seminar
WHERE SEMINAR_ID > 1701
AND OVERSEER_ID = 'THX0001138'
```

All four of these examples were adapted, as well as the data model, from *The Object Primer* Second Edition (Ambler 2001a). A very good resource for learning SQL is *SQL Queries for Mere Mortals* by Michael J. Hernandez and John L. Viescas (Hernandez and Viescas 2000).

Advanced Features of Relational Databases

There are several advanced features of relational databases that developers learn once they've familiarized themselves with basic CRUD functionality. Each of these features is so important, and often so complex, that they require their own chapters to cover them properly. So for now, I will introduce you to the concepts and will cover the details in Part III, which include:

Object storage.   To store an object in a relational database you need to *flatten* it — create a data representation of the object — because relational databases only store data. To retrieve the object you would read the data from the database and then create the object — often referred to as *restoring* the object — based on that data. Although storing objects in a relational database sounds like a simple thing to achieve, practice has shown that it isn't. This is due to the *object-relational impedance mismatch*, the fact that relational database technology and object technology are based on different underlying theories, a topic discussed in Chapter 7. To store objects successfully in relational databases, you need to learn how to map your object schema to your relational database schema, a subject covered in detail in Chapter 14.

Implementing behavior within the database.   Behavior is implemented in a relational database via stored procedures and/or stored functions that can be invoked internally within the database and often by external applications. Stored functions and procedures are operations that run within an RDB, the difference being what the operation can return and whether it can be invoked in a query. The differences aren't important for our purposes so the term *stored procedure* will be used to refer to both stored functions and stored procedures. In the past, stored procedures were written in a proprietary language, such as Oracle's PL/SQL, although Java is quickly becoming the language of choice for database programming. A stored procedure typically runs some SQL code, massages the data, and then hands back a response in the form of zero or more records, a response code, or a database error message.

Concurrency control.   Consider an airline reservation system. There is a flight with one seat left on it, and two people are trying to reserve that seat at the same time. Both people check the flight status and are told that a seat is still available. Both enter their payment information and click the reservation button at the same time. What should happen? If the system is working properly only one person should be given a seat and the other should be told that there is no longer one available. Concurrency control is what makes this happen. Concurrency control must be implemented throughout your object source code and within your database, something that is discussed in detail in Chapter 17.

Transaction control.   A transaction is a collection of actions on your database — such as the saving of, retrieval of, or deletion of data — which form a work unit. A *flat transaction* takes an "all-or-nothing" approach, where all the actions must either succeed or be rolled back (canceled). A *nested transaction* takes an approach where some of the actions are transactions in their own right. These subtransactions are committed once successful and are not rolled back if the larger transaction fails. Transactions may be short-lived, running in thousandths of a second, or long-lived, taking hours, days, weeks, or even months to complete. Transaction control is discussed in Chapter 17.

Enforcing referential integrity.   Referential integrity (RI) is the assurance that a reference from one entity to another entity is valid. For example, if a customer references an address, that address must exist. If the address is deleted, all references to it must also be removed or your system must not allow the deletion. Contrary to popular belief, RI isn't just a database issue, it's an issue for your entire system. A customer is implemented as an object within a Java application and as one or more records in your database — addresses are also implemented as objects and as rows. To delete an address, you must remove the address object from memory, any direct or indirect references to it (an indirect reference to an address would include a customer object knowing the value of the *AddressID*, the primary key of the address in the database), the address row(s) from your database, and any references to it (via foreign keys) in your database. To complicate matters, if you have a farm of application servers that address object could exist simultaneously on several machines. Furthermore, if you have other applications accessing your database, then it is possible that they too have representations of the address in their memory as well. Worse yet, if the address is stored in several places (for example, different databases) you should also consider taking this into account. Strategies for implementing referential integrity are described in Chapter 19.

Table 6.1 describes the common technical features found in relational database products, possible ways that developers will use them, and the potential drawbacks associated with their use.

Database cursors.   A database cursor is effectively a handle to the results of a SQL query, enabling you to move forward and backward through the result set one or more records at a time. Benefits include accessing large results sets in smaller portions enables your application to display initial results earlier, increasing response time. Performance is improved when a portion of a result set is required because less data is transmitted across the network. Potential drawbacks include application developers needing to understand that the underlying data can change between the times that data records are accessed via the cursor; previously retrieved records may have been deleted, records may have been inserted into previously retrieved portions of the result set, or previously retrieved records may have been modified. Not all cursors are created equal. Some cursors only allow forward scrolling. Cursors are a resource drain on the database because they are memory intensive.

Java.   Most database vendors support a Java VM within the database. Potential benefits include the development of relatively platform-independent behavior in the database, development of data-intensive behavior that results in a relatively small return value, encapsulation of database access to support security access control to information, and implementation of shared behavior required by many applications. Potential drawbacks include different versions of VMs on the application server and the database server, which increases the complexity of development, and that behavior implemented in the database can easily become a bottleneck.

Triggers.   A trigger is a procedure that is run either before or after an action (such as a create, update, or delete) is performed on a row in a database table. Potential benefits include enforce referential integrity (see Chapter 19 for details) within your database. These types of triggers can often be automatically generated by your data modeling or database-administration tool. Often a lowest common denominator for implementing referential integrity constraints. Perform handcrafted audit logging. Potential drawbacks include the fact that handcrafted, or hand-modified, triggers can be difficult to maintain and will increase your dependency on your database vendor. Triggers are typically implemented in a proprietary language, requiring an extra skillset on your team. Because triggers are automatically invoked, they can be very dangerous (such as "uncontrolled" cascading deletions resulting from chained delete triggers). Behavior implemented in the database can easily become a bottleneck if your database doesn't scale well.

Coupling: Your Greatest Enemy

Coupling is a measure of the degree of dependence between two items — the more highly coupled two things are, the greater the chance that a change in one will require a change in another. Coupling is the root of all evil when it comes to software development, and the more things that your database schema is coupled to, the harder it will be to maintain and to evolve your software. Relational database schemas can be coupled to:

Your application source code.   When you change your database schema, you must also change the source code within your application that accesses the changed portion of the schema. Figure 6.2 depicts the best-case scenario — when it is only your application code that is coupled to your database schema. This situation is traditionally referred to as a stovepipe. These situations do exist and are often referred to as standalone applications, stovepipe systems, or greenfield projects. Count yourself lucky if this is your situation because it is very rare in practice.

Other application source code.   Figure 6.3 depicts the worst-case scenario for relational databases — a wide variety of software systems are coupled to your database schema, a situation that is quite common with existing production databases. It is quite common to find that in addition to the application that your team is currently working on other applications, some of which you know about and some of which you don't, are also coupled to your database. Perhaps an online system reads from and writes to your database. Perhaps a manager has written a spreadsheet, unbeknownst to you, that reads data from your database that she uses to summarize information critical to her job.

Data load source code.   Data loads from other sources, such as government-provided tax tables or your own test data, are often coupled to your database schema.

Data extract source code.   There may be data extraction scripts or programs that read data from your database, perhaps to produce an XML data file or simply so your data can be loaded into another database.

Persistence frameworks/layers.   A persistence framework encapsulates the logic for mapping application classes to persistent storage sources such as your database. When you refactor your database schema, you will need to update the meta data, or the source code as the case may be, which describes the mappings.

Itself.   Coupling exists within your database. A single column is coupled to any stored procedure that references it, other tables that use the column as a foreign key, any view that references the column, and so on. A simple change could result in several changes throughout your database.

Data migration scripts.   Changes to your database schema will require changes to your data migration scripts.

Test code.   Testing code includes any source code that puts your database into a known state, that performs transactions that affect your database, and that reads the results from the database to compare it against expected results. Clearly, this code may need to be updated to reflect any database schema changes that you make.

Documentation.   Some of the most important documentation that you are likely to keep pertains to your physical database schema, including, but not limited to, physical data models and descriptive meta data (see Chapter 14). When your database schema changes, the documentation describing it will also need to change. Although Agile Modeling (AM) implores you to *Update Only When It Hurts*, because your documentation doesn't have to be perfectly in synch with your schema at all times, the reality is that you will need to update your docs at some point.

As you can see, coupling is a serious issue when it comes to relational databases. To make matters worse the concept of coupling is virtually ignored within database theory circles. Although most database theory books will cover data normalization in excruciating detail, I argue that normalization (Chapter 4) is the data community's way of addressing cohesion. My experience is that coupling becomes a serious issue only when you start to consider behavioral issues (for example, code), something that traditional database theory chooses not to address. This is another reason to follow AM's *Multiple Models* principle and look beyond data (Ambler 2002a).

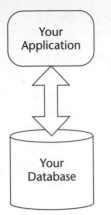

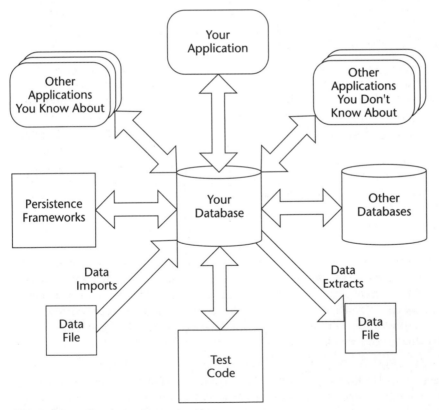

Figure 6.2   The best-case scenario.

Figure 6.3   The worst-case scenario.

Additional Challenges with Relational Databases

Coupling isn't the only challenge that you face with relational databases, although it is clearly an important one. Other issues that you will face include:

Performance issues are difficult to predict.   When you are working with a shared database, as in the situation implied in Figure 6.3, you may find that the performance characteristics of your database are hard to predict because each application accesses the database in its own unique way. For example, perhaps one legacy application updates information pertaining to items for sale sporadically throughout the month, enabling a human operator to add new items or update existing ones, an activity that doesn't really affect your application's performance in a meaningful way. However, this same application also performs batch loads of items available for sale via other companies that you have partnered with, items that you want to carry on your Web site as soon as they are available. These batch loads can take several minutes, during which period the *Item* table is under heavy load and thus your online application is potentially affected.

Data integrity is difficult to ensure with shared databases.   Because no single application has control over the data, it is very difficult to be sure that all applications are operating under the same business principles. For example, your application may consider an order as fulfilled once it has been shipped and a payment has been received. The original legacy application that is still in use by your customer support representatives to take orders over the phone may consider an order fulfilled once it has been shipped, the payment received, and the payment deposited into your bank account. A slight difference in the way that a fundamental business rule has been implemented may have serious business implications for any application that accesses the shared databases. Less subtly, imagine what would happen if your online order-taking application calculates the total for an order and stores it in the order table, whereas the legacy application calculates the subtotals only for order items but does not total the order. When the order fulfillment application sees an order with no total it calculates the total, and appropriate taxes, whereas if a total already exists it uses the existing figure. If a customer makes an order online and then calls back a few hours later and has one of your customer service representatives modify the existing order, perhaps to add several items to it, the order total is no longer current because it has not been updated properly. Referential integrity issues such as this are covered in detail in Chapter 19.

Operational databases require different design strategies than reporting databases.   The schemas of operational databases reflect the operational needs of the applications that access them, often resulting in a reasonably normalized schema with some portions of it denormalized for performance reasons. Reporting databases, on the other hand, are typically highly denormalized with significant data redundancy within them to support a wide range of reporting needs. Data normalization techniques are described in Chapter 4 and denormalization techniques in Chapter 15.

Every technology has its strengths and weaknesses, and relational database technology is not an exception to this rule. Luckily there are ways that you can mitigate some of these challenges, and encapsulation is an important technique for doing so.

Encapsulation: Your Greatest Ally

Encapsulation is a design issue that deals with how functionality is compartmentalized within a system. You should not have to know how something is implemented to be able to use it. The implication of encapsulation is that you can build anything anyway you want, and then you can later change the implementation and it will not affect other components within the system (as long as the interface to that component did not change).

People often say that encapsulation is the act of painting the box black – you are defining how something is going to be done, but you are not telling the rest of the world how you're going to do it. For example, consider your bank. How do they keep track of your account information, on a mainframe, a mini, or a PC? What database do they use? What operating system? It doesn't matter to you because the bank has encapsulated the way in which they perform account services. You just walk up to a teller and perform whatever transactions you wish.

By encapsulating access to a database, perhaps through something as simple as data access objects or through something as complex as a persistence framework, you can reduce the coupling that your database is involved with. Chapter 13 compares and contrasts various encapsulation strategies that you have available to you. For now, assume that it is possible to hide the details of your database schema from the majority of the developers within your organization, while at the same time giving them access to your database. Some people, often just the agile DBA(s) responsible for supporting the database, will need to understand and work with the underlying schema to maintain and evolve the encapsulation strategy.

One advantage of encapsulating access to your database is that it enables application programmers to focus on the business problem itself. Assume that you're doing something simple such as creating data access objects that implement the SQL code to access your database schema. The application's programmers will work with these data access classes, not the database. This enables your agile DBA to evolve the database schema as needed, perhaps via database refactorings (Chapter 14), and all he or she needs to worry about is keeping the data access classes up to date. This reveals a second advantage to this approach — it provides greater freedom for agile DBAs to do their job.

Figure 6.4 depicts the concept of encapsulating access to your database, showing how the best-case scenario in Figure 6.2 and the worst-case scenario in Figure 6.3 would likely change. In the best-case scenario, your business source code interacts with the data access objects, which in turn interact with the database. The primary advantage is that all data-related code is in one place, making it easier to modify whenever database schema changes occur or to support performance-related changes. It's interesting to note that the business code that your application programmers are writing would still be coupled to the data access objects. Therefore, they'd need to change their code whenever the interface of a data access object changed. You'll never get away from coupling. However, from the point of view of the application programmer, this is a much easier change to detect and act on. With the database encapsulation strategy in place, the application programmers are only dealing with program source code (for example, Java) and not program source code plus SQL code.

Things aren't quite so ideal for the worst-case scenario. Although it is possible that all applications could take advantage of your encapsulation strategy, the reality is that only a subset will be able to. Platform incompatibility can be an issue in any of the following scenarios, just for example:

- Your data access objects are written in Java but some legacy applications are written using technologies that can't easily access Java.

- You've chosen not to rework some of your legacy applications to use the database encapsulation strategy.

- Some applications already have an encapsulation strategy in place (if so, you might want to consider reusing the existing strategy instead of building your own).

- You want to use technologies, such as a bulk load facility, that require direct access to the database schema.

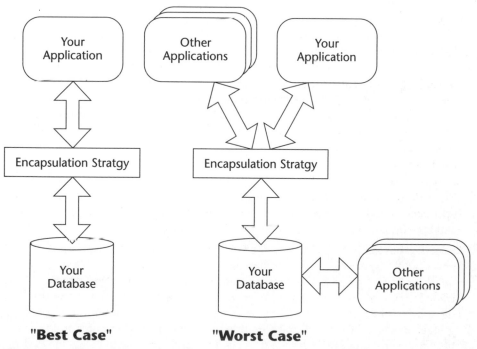

"Best Case"   **"Worst Case"**

Figure 6.4   The scenarios revisited.

The point is that a portion of your organization's application will be able to take advantage of your encapsulation strategy and a portion won't. There is still a benefit to an encapsulation strategy: you are reducing coupling and therefore reducing your development costs and maintenance burden, but unfortunately the problem is that you aren't fully realizing the benefits of encapsulation.

Another advantage of encapsulating access to a database is that it gives you a common place, in addition to the database itself, to implement data-oriented business rules.

Beyond Relational Databases: You Actually Have a Choice

Because there are some clear problems with relational database technology, you may decide to use another technology. Yes, RDBs are the most commonly used type of persistence mechanism but they are not the only option available to you. Your options are as follows:

Object/relational databases.   Object/relational databases (ORDBs), also known as object/relational database management systems (ORDBMSs), add new object storage capabilities to relational databases. ORDBs, add new facilities to integrate management of traditional fielded data, complex objects such as time-series and geospatial data, and diverse binary media such as audio, video, images, and (sometimes) Java applets. ORDBs basically add to RDBs features such as defined data types; for example, you could define a data type called *SurfaceAddress* that has all of the attributes and behaviors of an address, as well as the ability to navigate objects. This is in addition to an RDB's ability to join tables. By implementing objects within the database, an ORDB can execute complex analytical and data manipulation operations to search and transform multimedia and other complex objects. ORDBs support the robust transaction and data-management features of RDBs and at the same time offer a limited form of the flexibility of object-oriented databases. Because of ORDBs relational foundation, database administrators work with familiar tabular structures and data definition languages (DDLs) and programmers access them via familiar approaches such as SQL3, JDBC (Java Database Connectivity), and proprietary call interfaces.

Object databases.   Object databases (ODBs), also known as object-oriented databases (OODBs) or object-oriented database management systems (OODBMSs), nearly seamlessly add database/persistence functionality to object programming languages. In other words, full-fledged objects are implemented in the database. They bring much more than persistent storage of programming language objects: ODBs extend the semantics of Java to provide full-featured database programming capability via new class libraries specific to the ODB vendor, while retaining native language compatibility. A major benefit of this approach is the unification of the application and database development into a seamless model. As a result, applications require less code and use more natural persistence modeling, and code bases are easier to maintain. Object-oriented developers can write complete database applications with a modest amount of additional effort without the need to marshal their objects into flattened data structures for storage. As a result, you forgo the marshalling overhead inherent with other persistence mechanism technologies (such as RDBs). This one-to-one mapping of application objects to database objects provides higher performance management of objects and enables better management of the complex interrelationships between objects.

XML databases.   Native XML databases store information as XML documents following one of two approaches: First, a native XML database will either store a modified form of the entire XML document in the file system, perhaps in a compressed or preparsed binary form. Second, a native XML database may opt to map the structure of the document to the database, for example mapping the Document Object Model (DOM) to internal structures such as Elements, Attributes, and Text — exactly what is mapped depends on the database. The most important difference between these approaches, from the point of view of an application developer, is the way they are accessed: with the first approach the only interface to the data is XML and related technologies such as XPath (a language design specifically for addressing parts of an XML document, visit www.w3.org for details) or the DOM. With the second approach the database should be accessible via standard technologies such as JDBC. The important thing to understand about native XML databases is that they work with the internal structures of the XML documents, but they don't store them as a binary large object (BLOB) in the database.

Flat files.   Flat files, such as .txt or. CSV (comma separated value) files, are commonly used to store data. A single file can be used to store one type of data structure, such as customer information or sales transaction information, or through a coding and formatting strategy of the structures of several types of data structures. One approach to flat file organization is either to have data values separated by a predefined character, such as a comma or tag such as </FirstName> in an XML document. Another common approach is to delimit data values by size — the first 20 characters of the row represent the first name of the customer, the next 20 characters represent the surname, and so on.

Hierarchical databases.   Hierarchical databases link data structures together like a family tree such that each record type has only one owner; for example, an order is owned by only one customer. Hierarchical structures were widely used in the first mainframe database management systems and are still a very common source of data in many large organizations. Hierarchical databases fell out of favor with the advent of relational databases due to their lack of flexibility because it wouldn't easily support data access outside the original design of the data structure. For example, in the customer-order schema, you could only access an order through a customer, you couldn't easily find all the orders that included the sale of an item because the hierarchical database schema isn't designed to handle that.

Prevalence layer.   Klaus Wuestefeld defines prevalence as "transparent persistence, fault-tolerance and load-balancing of the execution of the business logic of an information system through the use of state snapshots as well as command and query queuing or logging." A prevalence layer is effectively a simple persistence framework that serializes objects and writes them to log files. From the point of view of developers, all objects are cached in memory, and the persistence of the objects is truly treated as a background task that the developers don't need to worry about.

Table 6.1 presents a comparison of the various types of persistence mechanisms and provides references to vendors where applicable. Table 6.2 presents suggestions for when you might use each type of technology. Large organizations will find that they are using several types of persistence mechanisms and will even install the products of several different vendors. Not only do you have a choice, but you might be forced to work with a wide range of databases whether you want to or not.

Table 6.1   Comparing Types of Persistence Mechanisms

MECHANISM	ADVANTAGES	DISADVANTAGES	COMMON PRODUCTS
Flat File	• Supports a simple approach to persistence • Good solution for smaller systems • Most development languages have built-in support for file streams • No licensing costs	Ad hoc access difficult	N/A
Hierarchical Database	Supports transaction-oriented applications	Not in common use for development of new applications	• IBM's ISAM (www.ibm.com) • IBM's VSAM (www.ibm.com)
Object Databases	• "Pure" approach to persisting objects • Existing vendors have survived the market shakeout and are likely here to stay • Excellent option for an application-specific database (for example, the best-case scenario of Figure 6.2) when object-technology is used	• Not well accepted in the market place • No single dominant vendor • DefinedStandards, such as Object Query Language (OQL), are still evolving	• Computer Associate's Jasmine (www.ca.com) • Versant Developer Suite (www.versant.com) • Object Design's ObjectStore (www.object design.com)

Table 6.1   *(continued)*

MECHANISM	ADVANTAGES	DISADVANTAGES	COMMON PRODUCTS
	• Provides uniformity of approach toward application and data storage • Facilitates refactoring (Chapter 14) because everything is an object		• Objectivity/DB (www.objectivity .com) Poet (www .poet.com)
Object/Relational Databases	• Relational vendors are slowly adopting object-relational features • Less of an impedance mismatch with objects	• Not well accepted in the market place • No single dominant vendor • Emerging standards, such as SQL3, are not yet widely adopted • Small experience base	• Cloudscape (www.ibm.com) • Cincom UniSQL (www.cincom .com) • Relational vendors listed above
Prevalence Layer	• Transparent persistence of objects • Performance (sometimes several orders of magnitude over relational databases) • Simplicity	• Emerging technology • Significant RAM required on server	Prevayler (www.prevayler .org)
Relational Databases	• Mature technology • Dominate the persistence mechanism market • Several well-established vendors • Standards, such as SQL and JDBC, well defined and accepted • Significant experience base of developers	• Object-relational impedance mismatch (Chapter 7) can be a significant problem • Mapping objects to relational databases can be a difficult skill to learn (see Chapter 14)	• Oracle (www .oracle.com) • Sybase (www .sybase.com) • IBM DB2 (www .ibm.com) • Microsoft SqlServer (www .microsoft.com)

(continued)

Table 6.1 *(continued)*

MECHANISM	ADVANTAGES	DISADVANTAGES	COMMON PRODUCTS
XML Databases	• Native support for persisting XML data structures (not just as a BLOB) • For XML-intensive applications it removes the need for marshalling between XML structures and the database structure	• Emerging technology • Standards, for example, the XML equivalent of SQL, are not yet in place for XML data access • Not well-suited for transactional systems	• OpenLink Software's Virtuoso (www.openlinksw.com) • Software AG's Tamino (www.softwareag.com) • X-Hive/DB (www.x-hive.com)

Table 6.2 Potential Applications for Types of Persistence Mechanisms

MECHANISM	POTENTIAL APPLICATIONS
Flat Files	• Simple applications, particularly those with a "read all the information, manipulate it for a while, and save it to disk" paradigm such as word processors or spreadsheets, where a relational database would be gross overkill • Persistence of configuration information • Sharing of information with other systems Audit logging/reporting
Hierarchical Databases	• Transaction-oriented applications • Common source of legacy data
Object Databases	• Complex, highly interrelated data structures (for example, CAD/CAM parts inventory) • Complex and low-volume transactions (for example, Computer-Aided Design/Computer-Aided Manufacturing (CAD/CAM), Geographical Information Systems (GIS) applications) • Simple, high-volume transactions (for example, point of sale systems) • Single-application, or single application family, software products
Object/Relational Databases	• Complex, highly interrelated data structures (for example, CAD/CAM parts inventory) • Complex and low-volume transactions (for example, CAD/CAM, GIS applications) • Simple, high-volume transactions (for example, point of sale systems) • Single-application, or single application family, software products

Table 6.2   *(continued)*

MECHANISM	POTENTIAL APPLICATIONS
Prevalence Layer	• Complex object structures • Single-application, or single application family, software products
Relational Databases	• High-volume applications • Transaction-oriented applications • Simple-to-intermediate complexity of data • Data-intensive applications • Shared, operational database • Reporting database
XML Databases	Ideally suited for XML-intensive applications such as enterprise integration portals or online reporting facilities

Summary

Relational database technology isn't perfect, no technology is. The reason why I have spent so much effort discussing the drawbacks of this technology is that it is important that you understand what it is that you're working with. Many writers will focus on the benefits of relational databases, and there are clearly many benefits, but ignore the drawbacks. Other writers will focus on academic issues such as the concept that there is no "true relational database" that fulfills all of E. F. Codd's original 12 features, not to mention the more finely defined features of his later writings. That's an interesting issue to discuss over beer but I prefer to focus on the practical issues that developers face day to day when working with this technology.

Coupling is a serious issue for all IT professionals, including both application developers and agile DBAs. Encapsulating access to your database can help to alleviate the problems of coupling but it is only a partial solution. It is also important to recognize that relational databases are only one of several choices that you have available to you to persist your data. Nonrelational approaches are viable solutions for some situations and should be given appropriate consideration. Having said this, my assumption throughout the rest of this book is that you will be working with relational databases to make your data persistent.

CHAPTER 7

The Object-Relational Impedance Mismatch

The differences make us stronger, as long as they don't divide us in the process.

Object-oriented technologies support the creation of applications out of classes that implement both data and behavior. Relational technologies support the storage of data in tables and the manipulation of that data via a data manipulation language (DML). The Structured Query Language (SQL) is the traditional DML implementation language although some relational databases now internally support objects as well, a trend that will only grow stronger over time. It is clear that object technologies and relational technologies are in common use in most organizations, that both are here to stay for a while, and that both are being used together to build complex software-based systems. It is also clear that the fit between the two technologies isn't perfect; in the early 1990s, the difference between the two approaches was labeled the *object-relational impedance mismatch*, (or the *impedance mismatch* for short), a term that is still in common use today.

Much of the conversation about the impedance mismatch focuses on the technical differences between object and relational technologies, and rightfully so because there are significant differences. Unfortunately, there has been less attention spent on the cultural differences between the object-oriented community and the data community. These differences are often revealed when object professionals and data professionals argue with each other regarding the approach that should be taken by a project team.

This chapter explores:

- The role of the agile DBA
- The technological impedance mismatch
- Deceptive similarities
- Subtle differences

- The cultural impedance mismatch
- Strategies for overcoming the impedance mismatch

The Role of the Agile DBA

On the technical side, it is the job of an agile DBA to work with application developers to make object and relational technologies work together. On the cultural side, agile DBAs will often find themselves in the role of mediator, typically between agile software developers and traditional data professionals. In short, agile DBAs act as bridges between both the object and data worlds and between the agile and traditional worlds.

The Technological Impedance Mismatch

Why does a technological impedance mismatch exist? The object-oriented paradigm is based on proven software engineering principles. The relational paradigm, however, is based on proven mathematical principles. Because the underlying paradigms are different, the two technologies do not work together seamlessly.

The impedance mismatch becomes apparent when you look at the preferred approach to access: With the object paradigm you traverse objects via their relationships, whereas with the relational paradigm you join rows of tables. This fundamental difference results in a nonideal combination of object and relational technologies, although when have you ever used two different things together without a few hitches?

Why is this a problem? The greater the mismatch between your object and data schemas, the more code you will need to write, test, and maintain to resolve the mismatch. Furthermore, your code is likely to run slower due to the greater complexity required to coordinate the differing schemas.

To succeed using objects and relational databases together you need to understand both paradigms and their differences, and then make intelligent trade-offs based on that knowledge. Chapter 6 provided an overview of relational databases, and Chapter 3 described the basics of data modeling, together providing you with sufficient background to understand the relational paradigm. Similarly, Chapter 2 provided an overview of object orientation and UML, explaining the basics of the object-oriented paradigm. Until you understand both paradigms and gain real-world experience working in both technologies, it will be very difficult to see past the deceptive similarities between the two.

Deceptive Similarities

Figure 7.1 depicts a physical data model (PDM) using the UML data-modeling notation described in Chapter 2. Figure 7.2 depicts a UML class diagram. On the surface they look like very similar diagrams, and when you only look at the surface, in fact they are. It's how you arrive at the two diagrams that can be very different.

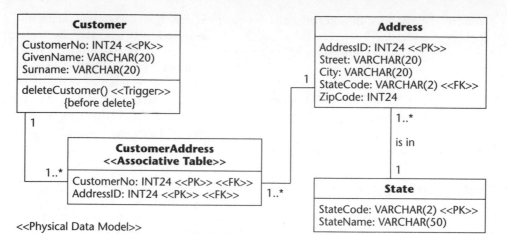

<<Physical Data Model>>

Figure 7.1 A physical data model (UML notation).

Let's consider the deceptive similarities between the two diagrams. Both diagrams depict structure, the PDM shows four database tables and the relationships between them, whereas the UML class diagram shows four classes and their corresponding relationships. Both diagrams depict data: the PDM shows the columns within the tables, and the class model shows the attributes of the classes. Both diagrams also depict behavior; for example, the *Customer* table of Figure 7.1 includes a delete trigger and the *Customer* class of Figure 7.2 includes two operations. The two diagrams also use similar notations, something that I did on purpose to make matters worse.

I think you can see how easy it is for an experienced data professional to claim that a class model is merely a data model with behavior. Another common mistake is to assume that a class model is simply the combination of a data model and a process model. The reality is that a class model depicts structure, and within that structure data and behavior are both depicted. Business processes, such as those depicted by a data flow diagram (DFD) or perhaps a use-case model, are not shown on class models. Class models can be very deceptive in this regard, particularly if you haven't spent a lot of time working with object technology.

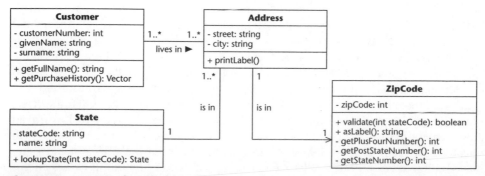

Figure 7.2 A UML class diagram.

You can also see how an experienced object-oriented developer can claim that a data model is merely a subset of a class model. Both of these attitudes are a mistake, because they provide a false justification for not learning more about the other technique. What is worse is that these attitudes are prevalent in much of the literature on the subject. People who write about data techniques rarely delve into object techniques, other than perhaps to claim that object developers need to learn more about data modeling (a philosophy that I adhere to). Object writers are just as bad, often claiming that you merely need to apply a handful of stereotypes to a UML class model if you want to model data. Chapter 2 shows that there is a little more to it than that.

Subtle Differences

Agile software developers realize that there are subtle differences between data modeling and class modeling. First, an address is implemented as a single table in Figure 7.1 but as two classes, *Address* and *ZipCode*, in Figure 7.2. The *ZipCode* class was created to encapsulate the logic of validating a zip code number and formatting it appropriately for mailing labels. For example, you can determine if a zip code is in a given state by looking at its first two digits. To prepare it for printing on a label, hyphens should be inserted in the appropriate places. The bottom line is that the *ZipCode* class encapsulates cohesive behavior. However, in the PDM of Figure 7.1 this behavior isn't relevant, therefore a zip code can map to a single column in the *Address* table. It's interesting to note that in this case two dissimilar classes will map to one table (the basics of mapping objects to relational databases is covered in Chapter 14).

Differences in your modeling approaches will result in subtle differences between the object schema and the data schema:

- Modelers create different structures in class models, which take into account both data and behavior, than in data models, which only consider data.

- Data normalization (Chapter 4) encompasses different strategies than class normalization (Chapter 5).

- The application of data analysis patterns (Hay 1996) as opposed to object-oriented analysis patterns (Fowler 1997, Ambler 1997) and design patterns (Gamma et. al. 1995) results in differences.

There are differences in the types of relationships that each model supports, with class diagrams being slightly more robust than physical data models for relational databases. For example, you see that there is a many-to-many relationship between Customer and Address in Figure 7.2, a relationship that was resolved in Figure 7.1 via the *CustomerAddress* associative table. Object technology supports this type of relationship but relational databases do not, which is why the associative table was introduced.

Consider the relationship between *Address* and *ZipCode* in Figure 7.2. On the surface, it looks like it has been modeled wrong, but I argue that it hasn't. In the real world, an address can be in several zip codes, for example very large warehouses. A zip code will typically have zero or more addresses in it, a new subdivision may not have any houses built in it yet but could have been assigned a zip code. The multiplicities on this association are clearly wrong, if you assume that our goal was to model reality. However, our goal was to model the requirements for the system, not reality. The requirements don't necessitate that we traverse the relationship in both directions; hence it's unidirectional. We don't have to deal with large warehouses so our object doesn't have to support addresses with several zip codes. We choose to indicate a multiplicity of 1 beside *Address*, allowing us to have several *ZipCode* objects representing the same concept, for example the 90210 zip code, in memory at once. We don't need to traverse from *ZipCode* to *Address* so why bother to write the extra code to ensure that we only have one representation in memory at a time? Do the simplest thing possible.

Figure 7.2 also depicts a unidirectional association between *Address* and *ZipCode*, something that relational databases do not natively support. Relationships are implemented via foreign keys in relational databases, effectively allowing for a join in either direction. For example, you could write SQL code to join the *State* table with the *Address* table to obtain the name of the state for an address. Or you could join the *Address* table with the *State* table to define a list of all the addresses in a single state. To my knowledge, you never see any writings within the data community discussing the directionality of joins like this because it really isn't an issue. However, directionality is an important issue in class models. Figure 7.3 depicts a fully attributed class model that includes the scaffolding code and data required to implement associations. For example, the *Customer* class implements a vector (Java is the implementation language) named *addresses* in which it stores references to *Address* objects. It also implements getAddresses() and setAddresses() accessor operations and addAddress() and removeAddress() operations to maintain the association with *Address*. *Address* implements similar data and operations to maintain the association in the other direction. You also see that *Address* implements similar things to generate the association that it has with *ZipCode*, but that *ZipCode* doesn't need to implement similar code because the association is unidirectional. Therefore, there is less code to write, test, and maintain — so unidirectional associations can be very good things.

Another advantage is that the code will truly reflect the requirements, something that the maintenance developers in the future will appreciate. Part of maintenance is the removal of functionality that is no longer required. When you overbuild your software, it becomes very difficult to determine what portions of a system are actually needed, even if comprehensive documentation exists, and therefore it makes the maintenance effort that much harder.

Figure 7.3 also hints at a schism within the object community. It is common practice to not show keys on class diagrams (Ambler 2003), for example there aren't any shown on Figure 7.2. However, the reality is that when you are using a relational database to store your objects, each object must maintain enough information to be able to successfully write itself, and the relationships it is involved with, back out to the database. This is something that I call "shadow information," which you can see has been added in Figure 7.3 in the form of attributes with implementation visibility (no visibility symbol is shown). For example, the *Address* class now includes the attribute *addressID*, which corresponds to *AddressID* in the *Address* table (the attributes customers, state, and *zipCode* are required to maintain the relationships to the *Customer*, *State*, and *ZipCode* classes, respectively).

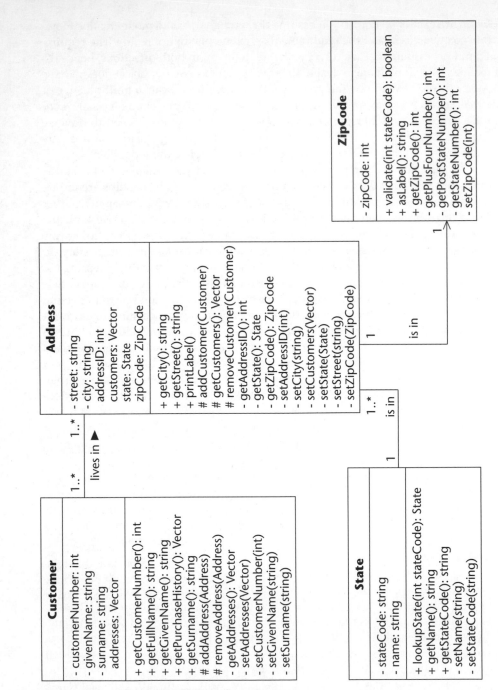

Figure 7.3 Fully attributed UML class diagram.

The schism is that the object community has a tendency to underestimate the importance of object persistence. Symptoms of this problem include:

- The lack of an official data model in the UML (see Chapter 2).

- The practice of not modeling keys on class diagrams.

- The misguided belief that you can model the persistent aspects of your system by applying a few stereotypes to a UML class diagram.

- Many popular object-oriented analysis and design (OOA&D) books spend little or no time discussing object persistence issues.

Yet in reality, object developers discover that they need to spend significant portions of their time making their object persistent, perhaps because they've run into performance problems after improper mappings (Chapter 14) or because they've discovered that they didn't take legacy data constraints (Chapter 8) into account in their design. My experience is that persistence is a significant blind spot for many object developers, one that promotes the cultural impedance mismatch discussed in the next section.

You can see that there are deceptive similarities and subtle differences between data models and class models. To be effective using object and relational technologies together, you need to understand this and act accordingly. A very common mistake is to think that you've done this before, that the types of models are basically the same thing. On the surface they are, but that's only the surface.

The Cultural Impedance Mismatch

The cultural impedance mismatch, something that I call the "object-data divide" (Ambler 2000a, Ambler 2000b), refers to the politics between the object community and the data community. These often consist of the dysfunctional politics between the two communities that occur within software organizations and even the software industry itself — problems that the agile data (AD) method strives to overcome. Symptoms of the object-data divide include object developers that claim relational technology either shouldn't or can't be used to store objects and data professionals that claim that object/component models must be driven by data models. Like most prejudices, neither of these beliefs are even remotely based on fact: in Chapter 6 you saw that relational databases are used to store a wide range of data, including the data representing objects, and in Chapter 9 you will see are several ways to approach development in addition to a data-driven approach.

To understand why our industry suffers from the object-data divide you need to consider the history of object technology. Object technology was first introduced in the late 1960s and adopted by the business community in the late 1980s and early 1990s — even now many organizations are just starting to use it for mission-critical software. As with most other new technologies, there was spectacular hype surrounding objects at the start:

Everything is an object.

Object technology is a silver bullet that solves all of our problems.

Objects are easier to understand and to work with.

Object technology is the only thing that you'll ever need.

In time reality prevailed and these claims were seen for what they were, wishful thinking at best. Unfortunately, one bit of hype did serious damage, the idea that the pure approach supported by objectbases would quickly eclipse the "questionable" use of relational technologies. This mistaken belief, combined with the findings of several significant research studies that showed that object techniques and structured techniques (for example, SQL) don't mix well in practice, led many within the object community to proclaim that objects and relational databases shouldn't be used together.

At the same time, the data community was coming into its own. Already important in the traditional mainframe world, data modelers found their role in the two-tier client server world (the dominant technology at the time for new application development) to be equally critical. Development in both of these worlds worked similarly: the data professionals would develop the data schema and the application developers would write their program code. This worked because there wasn't a lot of conceptual overlap between the two tasks — data models showed the data entities and their relationships whereas the application/process models showed how the application worked with the data. From the point of view of data professionals, very little had changed in their world. Then object technology came along. Some data professionals quickly recognized that the object paradigm was a completely new way to develop software; I was among them, and joined the growing object crowd. Unfortunately, many data professionals either believed the object paradigm to be another fad doomed to fail or merely another programming technology and therefore remained content with what they perceived to be the status quo.

Unfortunately both communities got it wrong. Objectbases never proved to be more than a niche technology, to the dismay of object purists, whereas relational databases have effectively become the defacto standard for storing data. Furthermore, the studies of the late 80s and early 90s actually showed that you shouldn't use structured models for object implementation languages such as C++ or Smalltalk, or object models for structured implementation languages such as COBOL or BASIC. Neither addressed the idea of melding object and structured modeling techniques. In fact, practice has shown that it is reasonably straightforward to map objects to relational databases (see Chapter 14).

To the dismay of data professionals, object modeling techniques, particularly those of the Unified Modeling Language (UML), are significantly more robust than data modeling techniques and are arguably a superset of data modeling (Muller 1999). The object approach had superceded the data approach, in fact there was such a significant conceptual overlap that many data professionals mistakenly believed that class diagrams were merely data models with operations added in because they hadn't recognized the subtle differences. What they didn't realize was that the complexity of modeling behavior requires more than just class diagrams — there is a reason why the UML defines a collection of diagrams — and that their focus on data alone was too narrow for the needs of modern application development. Object techniques proved to work well in practice — not only isn't object technology a fad, but it has become the dominant development platform, and the status quo has changed to the point that most modern development methodologies devote more than a few pages to data modeling (to their detriment).

The object-data divide produces dire consequences:

IT project teams fail to produce software on time and on budget. Granted, there are many factors affecting this problem, but there is little hope if your staff is unable to effectively work together.

The technical impedance mismatch is exacerbated. When object modelers and your data modelers do not work together, you risk having a significant mismatch between your object schema and your data schema.

Data models often prove to be poor drivers for object models. A common mistake that organizations make is to take a data-driven approach to development even on object-oriented projects, often for the simple reason that this is the way that they know how to work. They think this approach works because they have been fooled by the deceptive similarities between data models and class diagrams, not realizing the implications of the subtle differences. With an evolutionary approach to development (discussed in Part II) you discover that you iterate between different types of models, you don't let one blindly drive another.

Increased staff turnover. The political infighting resulting from the object-data divide typically leads to the frustration of everyone involved, application developers and data professionals alike, leading to higher-than-average staff turnover.

Summary

Object and relational technologies are real and are both here to stay. Unfortunately, the two technologies differ, these differences being referred to as "the object-relational impedance mismatch." In this chapter you learned that there are two aspects to the impedance mismatch: technical and cultural.

The technical mismatch can be overcome by ensuring that project team members, including both application developers and agile DBAs, understand the basics of both technologies. Furthermore, you should actively try to reduce the coupling that your database schema is involved with by encapsulating access to your database(s) as best you can (Chapter 13), by designing your database well (Chapter 3), and by keeping the design clean through database refactoring (Chapter 12).

Overcoming the cultural impedance mismatch is much more difficult. Everyone needs to recognize that the problem exists and needs to be overcome. Object and data professionals have different skills, different backgrounds, different philosophies, and different ways that they prefer to work. Instead of finding ways to work together that takes advantages of these differences, many software shops instead have chosen to erect communication and political barriers between the two groups of professionals. These barriers must be removed, something that the adoption of the agile data (AD) method can help with. An important first step is to recognize that different projects require different approaches, that one "process size" does not fit all (see Chapter 9), and to manage accordingly. It isn't sufficient for the data group to be right, or the application group to be right, they need to be right together. In short: stop playing political games and instead find ways to work together.

CHAPTER 8

Legacy Databases —
Everything You Need to Know
But Are Afraid to Deal With

What is the difference between a data architect and a terrorist?
You can negotiate with a terrorist.
David C. Hay

Sometimes you are in a position to develop your data schema from scratch when you are developing a new system using object-oriented technologies. If so, consider yourself among the lucky few because the vast majority of developers are often forced to tolerate one or more existing legacy data designs. Worse yet, it is often presumed that these data sources cannot be improved because of the corresponding changes that would be required to the legacy applications that currently access them. The problems presented by legacy data sources are often too difficult to fix immediately, therefore you have to learn to work around them.

The goal of this chapter is to introduce both application developers and agile DBAs to the realities of working with legacy data. For our purposes, any computer artifact, including, but not limited to, data and software, is considered to be a legacy asset once it is deployed and in production. For example, the C# application and its XML database that you deployed last week are now considered to be legacy assets even though they are the built from the most modern technologies within your organization. A legacy data source is any file, database, or software asset (such as a Web service or business application) that supplies or produces data and that has already been deployed. For the sake of brevity we will only focus on the data aspects of legacy software assets.

The topics covered in this chapter are:

- The role of the agile DBA
- Sources of legacy data
- Common problems encountered when working with legacy data

- Strategies for working with legacy data
- Data integration technologies

The Role of the Agile DBA

The tasks that an agile DBA performs with respect to working with legacy data (depicted in Figure 8.1) are as follows:

Identify legacy data sources.   Your organization's enterprise professionals, including both enterprise administrators and enterprise architects, should have knowledge of legacy data sources. This is particularly true of enterprise administrators because they are responsible for supporting and evolving these data sources over time. A good agile DBA will have a general knowledge of what data sources exist, and more importantly will work with the enterprise professionals to identify the right data. It isn't enough to know that customer data is stored in 17 places; a good agile DBA will know (or determine) the differences between the 17 sources and will be able to identify the best source(s) for the team.

Obtain access to the legacy data.   Agile DBAs will work with the owner(s) of the legacy data to obtain access to both the data and to the documentation, if any, describing it. Ideally the agile DBA will already have a good working relationship with these people; otherwise, he or she will need to begin building one. It is often the unofficial relationships between people, instead of the official lines of reporting within an organization, that smooth the way to obtaining access to both the legacy data as well as the corresponding documentation. You may discover that no documentation exists, or that it is out of date, and, therefore, you will need to work with the owners to ensure that it is put in place. The documentation describing a legacy data source is effectively a contract model, an Agile Modeling (AM) concept as described in Chapter 10.

Develop data converters with the application developers.   Legacy data commonly suffers from serious data-quality and data-design problems, as described below. As a result, agile DBAs will need to work with the application developers to write one or more data converters to access the legacy data, putting it into a format that either the database or the application requires. You may need to convert in both directions, sharing your updated data with the original source.

Mentor application developers in legacy data.   Most application developers will not understand the legacy data sources, the problems with the data, or the implications of those problems. Agile DBAs will need to work closely with application programmers to transfer the skills and knowledge that are required to work effectively with the legacy data.

Submit change requests to the legacy system owners. Agile DBAs may find opportunities to improve the quality of the legacy data source, although if they are not the owner of that data source then they are not in a position to fix the problem. Therefore, they will want to submit change requests to the owner(s), either through a formal change request process or informally in an appropriate manner (in conversation, via an email, or whatever), in the hope that the problem will be resolved in the future.

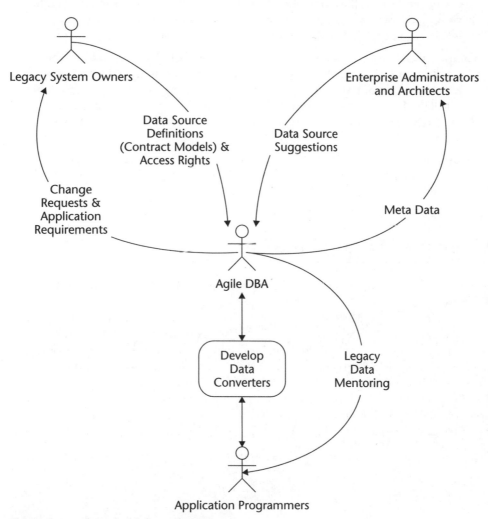

Figure 8.1 The role of the agile DBA.

Evolve meta data with enterprise administrators.   In some cases, your team will find itself working with legacy data sources that are well documented. Sometimes, the contract models supplied by the legacy system owners will be supported by detailed meta data, including logical data definitions, maintained by your organization's enterprise administrators. At other times, you will discover that the legacy data sources are not yet mapped to organization-level meta data or that they are partially mapped. In these cases, agile DBAs may find themselves working with the enterprise administrators and legacy system owners to define and evolve the relevant meta data. Although it is important for you to support efforts such as this, remember that your first priority is your project team — don't allow this to needlessly affect your project schedule.

Communicate application requirements.   You will often communicate your application requirements to the legacy system owners to give them a better understanding of the changing needs within your organization. This communication will often consist of simple conversations because the legacy system owners likely do not have the time, nor the interest, to read your requirements artifacts.

Avoid known data quality, design, and architecture problems.   This chapter describes a wide range of common problems with legacy data sources, problems that agile DBAs will help their project team to avoid in their work.

Sources of Legacy Data

Where does legacy data come from? Virtually everywhere. Figure 8.2 shows that there are many sources from which you may obtain legacy data. This includes existing relational databases, as well as hierarchical, network, object, XML, dimensional databases, and object/relational databases. Files, such as XML documents, or "flat files," such as configuration files and comma-delimited text files, are also common sources of legacy data. Software, including legacy applications that have been wrapped (perhaps via CORBA [Common Object Request Broker Architecture]) and legacy services such as Web services or CICS (complex instruction set computer) transactions, can also provide access to existing information. The point is that there is often far more to gaining access to legacy data than simply writing an SQL query against an existing relational database.

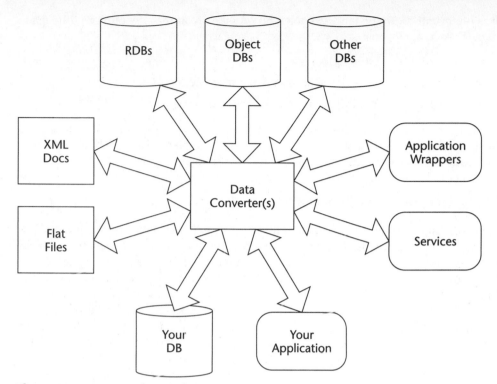

Figure 8.2 Common legacy data sources.

Understanding Common Problems with Legacy Data

The need to work with legacy data constrains a development team. Following are the major problems that legacy data can cause:

- It reduces the team's flexibility because they cannot easily manipulate the source data schema to reflect the needs of their object schema (see Chapter 14).

- Legacy data often doesn't provide the full range of information required by the team because the data does not reflect their new requirements.

- Legacy data is often constrained itself by the other applications that work with it; constraints that are then put on the team.

- Legacy data is often difficult to work with because of a combination of quality, design, architecture, and political issues.

It is important to understand the potential problems you may encounter with legacy data for several reasons:

- You will know what to look for
- You will have strategies to address known problems
- You can avoid making the same mistakes in your own work

There are three technical issues to be concerned with when dealing with legacy data, including data quality challenges, database design problems, data architecture problems, and one nontechnical issue: process-related challenges.

Data Quality Challenges

Table 8.1 lists the most common data-quality problems that you may encounter. The third column summarizes the potential impact on your application code if the problem is not resolved, and the fourth column lists potential database refactorings (see Chapter 12 and the Appendix) that you could apply to resolve the problem. It is important to understand that any given data source may suffer from several of these problems, and sometimes a single data column/field may even experience several problems.

Agile DBAs will work with application programmers to identify the data needs of the functionality they are currently working on, to then identify potential sources for that data, and in the case of legacy data to help them access that data. Part of the job of accessing the data is to help application developers to transform and cleanse the data to make it usable. Agile DBAs will be aware of the potential problems summarized in Table 8.1 and will work closely with the application programmers to overcome the challenges.

Database Design Problems

The second type of problems with legacy data sources that agile DBAs need to be aware of is fundamental design problems. Existing data designs, or even new data designs, are rarely perfect and often suffer from significant challenges. Table 8.2 summarizes common data design problems you will likely discover. These design problems may be the result of poor database design in the first place, perhaps the designers did not have a very good understanding of data modeling (Chapter 3). Sometimes the initial design of a data source was very good but over time the quality degraded as ill-advised schema changes were made, something referred to as schema entropy.

Once again, the agile DBA will need to work closely with application programmers to overcome these problems. Their past experience dealing with similar design problems, as well as their personal relationship with the owners of the legacy data source(s), will prove to be a valuable asset to the project team.

Table 8.1   Typical Quality Problems with Legacy Data

PROBLEM	EXAMPLE	POTENTIAL IMPACT ON YOUR APPLICATION	POTENTIAL DATABASE REFACTORINGS
A single column is used for several purposes.	Additional information for an inventory item is stored in the *Notes* column. Additional information will be one or more of a lengthy description of the item, storage requirements, or safety requirements when handling the item.	• One or more attributes of your objects may need to be mapped to this field, requiring a complex parsing algorithm to determine the proper usage of the column. • Your objects may be forced to implement a similar attribute instead of implementing several attributes as your design originally described.	• Split Column (to *Notes*)
The purpose of a column is determined by the value of one or more other columns.	If the value of *DateType* is 17, then *PersonDate* represents the date of birth of the person. If the value is 84, then *PersonDate* is the person's date of graduation from high school. If the value is between 35 and 48, then it is the date the person entered high school.	• A potentially complex mapping is required to work with the value stored in the column.	• Remove Unused Column (to remove *DateType*) • Split Column (to *PersonDate*)
There are inconsistent data values.	The *AgeInYears* column for a person contains the value negative 3. Or the *AgeInYears* column contains 7, although the *BirthDate* is August 14, 1967 and the current date is October 10, 2001.	• Your application will need to implement validation code to ensure that the base data values are correct. • Strategies to replace incorrect values may need to be defined and implemented. • An error-handling strategy will need to be developed to deal with bad data, see "Strategies for Working with Legacy Data" later in this chapter.	• Introduce Trigger(s) for Calculated Column (between *BirthDate* and *AgeInYears*) • Remove Redundant Column (to *AgeInYears*)

(continued)

Table 8.1 *(continued)*

PROBLEM	EXAMPLE	POTENTIAL IMPACT ON YOUR APPLICATION	POTENTIAL DATABASE REFACTORINGS
There is inconsistent/incorrect data formatting.	The name of a person is stored in one table in the format "Firstname Surname," yet in another table as "Surname, Firstname."	• Parsing code will be required to both retrieve and store the data as appropriate.	• Introduce Common Format
There is missing data.	The date of birth of a person has not been recorded in some records.	• See strategies for dealing with inconsistent data values.	• N/A
Columns are missing.	You need the middle name of a person but a column for it does not exist.	• You may need to add the column to the existing legacy schema. • You might need to do without the data. • Identify a default value until the data is available. • An alternate source for the data may need to be found.	• N/A
There are additional columns.	The Social Security number for a person is stored in the database, and you don't need it.	• If the columns are required for other applications, you may be required to implement them in your objects to ensure that the other applications can use the data your application generates. • You may need to write the appropriate default value to the database when inserting a new record. • For database updates, you may need to read the original value and then write it back out again.	• Introduce Default Value to a Column • Remove Redundant Column

Table 8.1 (continued)

PROBLEM	EXAMPLE	POTENTIAL IMPACT ON YOUR APPLICATION	POTENTIAL DATABASE REFACTORINGS
Multiple sources exist for the same data.	Customer information is stored in three separate legacy databases or customer name is stored in several tables within the same database.	• Identify a single source for your information and use only that. • Be prepared to access multiple sources for the same information. • Identify rules for choosing a preferred source when you discover the same information is stored in several places.	• N/A
Important entities, attributes, and relationships are hidden and floating in text fields.	A notes text field contains the information ("Clark and Lois Kent, Daily Planet Publications").	• Develop code to parse the information from the fields. • Do without the information.	• Replace Blob With Table • Split Column
Data values that stray from their field descriptions and business rules.	The maiden name column is being used to store a person's fabric preference for clothing.	• You need to update the documentation to reflect the actual usage. • Developers that took the documentation at face value may need to update their code. • Data analysis should be performed to determine the exact usage in case different applications are using the field for different purposes.	• Split Column

(continued)

Table 8.1 *(continued)*

PROBLEM	EXAMPLE	POTENTIAL IMPACT ON YOUR APPLICATION	POTENTIAL DATABASE REFACTORINGS
Various key strategies exist for the same type of entity.	One table stores customer information using SSN as the key, another uses the client ID as the key, and another uses a surrogate key.	• You need to be prepared to access similar data via several strategies, implying the need for similar finder operations in some classes. • Some attributes of an object may be immutable; that is, their value cannot be changed, because they represent part of a key in your relational database.	• Consolidate Key Strategy For Entity
Unrealized relationships exist between data records.	A customer has a primary home and a summer home, both of which are recorded in your database, but there is no relationship stored in the database regarding this fact.	• Data may be inadvertently replicated, eventually a new address record is inadvertently created (and the relationship now defined) for the summer home even though one already exists. • Additional code may need to be developed to detect potential problems. Procedures for handling the problems will also be required.	• Introduce Explicit Relationship
One attribute is stored in several fields.	The *Person* class requires a single name field whereas it is stored in the columns *FirstName* and *Surname* in your database.	• Potentially complex parsing code may be required to retrieve and then save the data.	• Combine Columns Representing a Single Concept

Table 8.1 (continued)

PROBLEM	EXAMPLE	POTENTIAL IMPACT ON YOUR APPLICATION	POTENTIAL DATABASE REFACTORINGS
There is inconsistent use of special characters.	A date uses hyphens to separate the year, month, and day, whereas a numerical value stored as a string uses hyphens to indicate negative numbers.	• Complexity of parsing code increases. • Additional documentation is required indicating character usage.	• Introduce Common Format
Different data types exist for similar columns.	A customer ID is stored as a number in one table and a string in another.	• You may need to decide how you want the data to be handled by your objects and then transform it to/from your data source(s) as appropriate. • If foreign keys have a different type than the original data they represent then table joins, and hence any SQL embedded in your objects, become more difficult.	• Apply Standard Types to Similar Data
Different levels of detail exist.	An object requires the total sales for the month, but your database stores individual totals for each order, or an object requires the weight of individual components of an item, such as the doors and engine of a car, but your database only records the aggregate weight.	• Potentially complex mapping code may be required to resolve the various levels of detail.	• Introduce Calculated Column • Replace Column

(continued)

Table 8.1 *(continued)*

PROBLEM	EXAMPLE	POTENTIAL IMPACT ON YOUR APPLICATION	POTENTIAL DATABASE REFACTORINGS
Different modes of operation exist.	Some data is a read-only snapshot of information, whereas other data is read-write.	• The design of your objects must reflect the nature of the data they are mapped to. Objects may be based on read-only data and therefore you cannot update or delete them.	• Separate Read-Only Data
Varying timeliness of data	The Customer data is current, Address data is one day out of date, and the data pertaining to countries and states is accurate to the end of the previous quarter because you purchase that information from an external source.	• Your application must reflect, and potentially report, the timeliness of the information that they are based on.	• Separate Data Based on Timeliness
Varying default values exist.	Your object uses a default of Green for a given value yet another application has been using Yellow, resulting in a preponderance (in the opinion of your users) of yellow values stored in the database.	• You may need to negotiate a new default value with your users. • You may not be allowed to store your default value (that is, Green may be an illegal value in the database).	• Introduce Default Value to a Column
Various representations of data exist.	The day of the week is stored as T, Tues, 2, and Tuesday in four separate columns.	• Translation code that goes back and forth between a common value that your object(s) use will need to be developed.	• Apply Standard Codes • Apply Standard Types to Similar Data

Table 8.2 Database Design Problems

PROBLEM	EXAMPLE(S)	IMPLICATIONS
A database encapsulation scheme exists, but it's difficult to use.	• Access to the database is provided only through stored procedures, for example to create a new customer you must invoke a specified stored procedure. • Access to views on the database is permitted; direct table access is denied. • The database must be accessed via an API (application programming interface) implemented by a C or COBOL wrapper that in turn accesses the database directly. • The database must be accessed via predefined data classes/objects, often because of underlying data quality problems.	• The encapsulation scheme must be made to look like a data source that your objects can work with. • The encapsulation scheme may increase the response time of database access if it is not well built. • The individual components of the encapsulation scheme may not be able to be included as a step in a transaction.
Naming conventions are inconsistent.	• Your database(s) may follow different naming conventions from one another and likely do not follow common coding naming conventions.	• Team members will need to understand all relevant naming conventions. • Political pressure may be put on your team to follow corporate data-naming conventions that are inappropriate for use with your objects. Instead follow data-naming conventions in your database and object-naming conventions in your application source code.

(continued)

Table 8.2 Database Design Problems

PROBLEM	EXAMPLE(S)	IMPLICATIONS
There is inadequate documentation.	• The documentation for your database is sparse, nonexistent, or out of date.	• A significant legacy data analysis effort will be required to determine the proper usage of each table, column, and stored procedure within your database.
Original design goals are at odds with current project needs.	• The legacy database was built for internal use by data entry clerks to capture customer orders in batch mode, whereas you are building a 24/7 order entry application to be deployed over the Internet. • Your application considers phone numbers to be full-fledged entities, whereas the database stores them as a column of the *Customer* table.	• A new database may need to be created with a data conversion/replication facility put in place between the various data sources.
An inconsistent key strategy exists.	• Your database uses natural keys for some tables, surrogate keys in others, and different strategies for surrogates keys when they are used.	• Developers must understand and then appropriately code support for the various key strategies for their objects. • Key generation code increases in complexity to support the various strategies. • Additional source code to validate that natural keys are in fact unique will be required. • Relationship management code increases in complexity because it needs to support a wide range of keys.

Data Architecture Problems

Agile DBAs need to be aware of the problems with the data architecture within your enterprise, information that they will often gain through discussions with enterprise architects. These problems typically result from project teams not conforming to an enterprise architectural vision, often because such a vision seldom exists. Or perhaps the project team simply wasn't aware of data architectural issues. Table 8.3 summarizes some of the potential data architecture problems that you may discover (Ulrich 2002). A common implication of these architecture problems is that you need to put an effective data-access approach in place such as introducing a staging database or a robust data encapsulation strategy. Staging databases are discussed in the "Introduce a Staging Database For Complex Data Access" section later in this chapter, and encapsulation strategies are covered in Chapter 13.

Process Mistakes

The technical challenges associated with legacy data are bad enough, but unfortunately nontechnical ones often overshadow them. The most difficult aspect of software development is to get people to work together effectively, and dealing with legacy data is no exception. Organizations will often hobble development teams because they are unable, or unwilling, to define and then work toward an effective vision. When it comes to working with legacy data there are several common process-oriented mistakes that I have seen organizations make:

Working with legacy data when you don't need to.   Many applications can in fact work quite well as standalone systems; they don't need to share data with other systems. Yes, in an ideal world every system that you build would work with a common database, or set of databases, and there wouldn't be any concerns about redundant data. It isn't an ideal world. Sometimes, it is easier to live with redundant data than it is to work with existing legacy data. Remember AM's advice (Chapter 10) to *Maximize Stakeholder Investment*, and choose the most effective strategy available to you — sometimes that means you'll build a standalone system even when you don't want to.

Data design drives your object model.   When you have to work with them, legacy data schemas are clearly a constraint on the design of any new application. But that doesn't mean that the existing data schema needs to drive the design of your application. Do you really want to make the existing mess any bigger than it needs to be? Shouldn't the requirements for your application drive its design instead? Chapter 9 argues that you should always strive to take the most appropriate approach to building a system, sometimes a data-driven approach is your best bet but very often it isn't.

Legacy data issues overshadow everything else.   As the first philosophy of the agile data method points out, data is clearly an important aspect of any system but it is only one of many. Allowing one issue to dominate your project, or even your organization, is simply poor management.

Table 8.3 Data Architecture Problems

PROBLEM	EXAMPLE	IMPLICATION(S)
Applications are responsible for data cleansing.	Known data quality problems are addressed through data cleansing code in all of the applications that access it.	• Your team will likely need to take the same approach. • You may be able to reuse some of the data cleansing code. • Database refactoring (Chapter 12) should be considered to evolve the database schema.
Different database paradigms exist.	Some of your data is stored in a relational database (for example, Sybase), some in a hierarchical database (for example, IMS), some in a network database (for example, IDMS), and some in an object database (for example, Versant).	• An effective data access approach is required.
Different hardware platforms exist.	Data is stored on mainframes, mid-tier servers, desktop computers, and hand-held devices.	• An effective data access approach is required.
Different storage devices exist.	Some of your data is stored in an online database supporting direct access, whereas other data is stored on magnetic tape.	• An effective data access approach is required.
Fragmented data sources exist.	Basic name and address data for customers is stored in one database, preference information in another, and order history in yet another.	• An effective data access approach is required.
Inaccessible data exists.	Data pertaining to corporate customers is stored in a standalone database that is not connected to your corporate network.	• The agile DBA will need to negotiate access to the data. • The application team may need to do without some data. • A new application-specific database may need to be introduced.

Table 8.3 *(continued)*

PROBLEM	EXAMPLE	IMPLICATION(S)
Inconsistent semantics exist.	Employee start date indicates the day that the person started working within the company in one database, the date they started working in their current division in another, and the date that they started working in their current position in another.	• In the short term, the inconsistencies may need to be accepted by the team or a single definition chosen and any data not conforming to that definition is ignored. • In the long term, the proper semantics should be defined and the databases refactored where appropriate.
The architecture is inflexible.	All mission-critical data must be stored on the mainframe. Furthermore, changes to the mainframe database schema must go through an arduous change control process.	• The application team may need to accept the inflexible architecture. • The application team may choose to introduce their own application-specific database for some or all data. • In the long term, the inflexibility should be addressed.
There is a lack of event notification.	Your application needs to know when customer data is changed by other applications, but these applications only update their own data sources, and the changes are fed into a shared database in batch at night.	• Your team may need to introduce a way to accept and reject incoming changes from other applications. • You may need to introduce an event notification architecture that other teams can reuse.
Redundant data sources exist.	Customer data is stored in 17 databases.	• An effective data access approach is required.

(continued)

Table 8.3 *(continued)*

PROBLEM	EXAMPLE	IMPLICATION(S)
Security is inefficient.	Users require a separate logon ID for each of the eight major platforms within your organization.	• A complex approach to security may need to be supported by the application team. • The application team may choose to forgo accessing some databases. • In the long term, your enterprise architects and enterprise administrators should rework the security scheme.
Security is lacking.	With the exception of a subset of human resources-related data (for example, salary), users have unfettered access to all data within your organization. No sort of audit logging is performed to record who makes changes to the source data.	• In the short term, the application team should implement, as best they can, the level of security required by their stakeholders. • In the long term, your enterprise architects and enterprise administrators should rework the security scheme.
The timeliness of data sources varies.	Customer data is updated by a daily batch job that runs at 4 A.M., inventory information is updated several times throughout the day, and orders are placed in real time.	• Effective data access approach required. • In the long term, your enterprise architects should strive to move to a 24/7 (near) real-time environment.

Application developers ignore legacy data issues.   As I pointed out earlier, legacy data schemas are an important constraint on your application design, one that you ignore at your peril. Working with legacy data can be very difficult, but it isn't going to get any easier by sticking your head in the sand.

You choose to not (eventually) fix the legacy data source.   Instead of fixing a legacy data schema, perhaps via database refactoring (Chapter 12), some organizations instead choose to leave the data schema alone and encapsulate it with data-translation code which applications then work with. Although this is a step in the right direction, it is only one of several steps (see below). You are effectively giving up when you choose not to fix a legacy data schema, a strategy that will only lead to failure in the long run.

Politics.   Data is a critical resource. Smart politicians know that anyone who controls access to a critical resource can wield significant power within an organization. Therefore the owners of legacy data may be unwilling to grant your application team access to the data, the documentation describing the data, or both. They may even insist on building any data access/conversion code themselves, which is a good thing if they're able to work to your schedule, but unfortunately this is seldom the case. The owners of a legacy data source can easily put your project at risk if they choose to do so, something that underlines the importance of agile DBAs building a good working relationship with them.

You don't see the software forest for the legacy data trees.   Do not allow legacy data access/conversion efforts to take on a life of their own. Agile software developers will stay focused on fulfilling the highest priority requirements of their project's stakeholders, and part of doing so may entail obtaining access to some legacy data. In other words, agile software developers will take an iterative and incremental approach to accessing and converting legacy data, they don't do it simply for the sake of doing it.

You don't put contract models in place.   AM implores you to put contract models in place describing integration points with other systems. Any time your system accesses a legacy data source, you effectively have an integration point that you should describe with permanent documentation. This style of documentation is referred to as a contract model because there is an implicit contract between you and the owner of the legacy data — they won't change the data schema without negotiating the change with you. Adopting the philosophy of putting contract models in place is important to the long-term success of your application because it reduces maintenance risk to your team.

Agile DBAs understand these nontechnical issues associated with legacy data and are prepared to work through them. This is why it is critical for an agile DBA to have a good working relationship with the owners of the legacy data, with developers, and with enterprise administrators — the better your relationship, the easier it will be to deal with any problems that arise. However, it isn't sufficient for agile DBAs to understand the potential problems with legacy data, they must also understand potential strategies for addressing the problems.

Strategies for Working with Legacy Data

My assumption in this section is that your project needs to access one or more sources of legacy data but that it is not responsible for an organization-wide data conversion effort, for example, you are not working on an enterprise application integration (EAI) project. That isn't to say that the advice presented below couldn't be modified for such a situation. However, because the focus of this book is on philosophies and techniques that agile DBAs and application developers can apply when developing business applications, this section will remain consistent with that vision.

> **TIP** I highly recommend that you check out Michael Feathers' (2002) paper "Working Effectively with Legacy Code," which provides some interesting insights into the issues surrounding the refactoring of legacy systems. Although he deals with code and not data, his ideas are definitely complementary to those presented here.

Try to Avoid Working with Legacy Data

The simplest solution is to not work with legacy data at all. If you can avoid working with legacy data, and therefore avoid the constraints that it places on you, then do so. Table 8.4 summarizes strategies that your team may try to apply in order to avoid working with legacy data, or to at least avoid a complex conversion effort. The strategies are presented in order from the simplest to the most complex.

> **CAUTION** Taking the big design up front (BDUF) approach to development forces legacy schemas on you. That is, in cases such as when your database schema is created early in the life of your project, you are effectively inflicting a legacy schema on yourself. Don't do this.

Develop a Data-Error-Handling Strategy

It should be clear by now that you are very likely to discover quality problems with the source data. When this happens, you will want to apply one or more of the following strategies for handling the error:

Convert the faulty data.   Apply one or more of the strategies described below to fix the problem, if possible.

Drop the faulty data.   When faulty data cannot be fixed, you may decide to simply ignore it and continue working without it. This is the simplest approach available to you but does not address the underlying problem(s) with the data.

Log the error.   A simple approach for addressing the actual problem(s) is to record the error in an audit log that is then shared with the appropriate people, typically the legacy data owners and potentially even enterprise administrators.

Fix the source data.   This requires write access to the source data, as well as the trust of the legacy data owners. Another access point is through integration with a system that can make the update.

Work Iteratively and Incrementally

Agile software developers work in an iterative and incremental manner. It is possible for data professionals to also work in this manner but that they must choose to do so. Agile developers will not attempt to write the data access/conversion code in one fell swoop. Instead, they will write only the data-oriented code that they require for the business requirements that they are currently working on. Therefore their data-oriented code will grow and evolve in an iterative and incremental fashion, just as the code for the rest of the application evolves.

Working with legacy data, and in particular converting it into a cleaner and more usable design, is often viewed by traditional developers as a large and onerous task. They're partially right — it is an onerous task — but it doesn't have to be a large one; instead you can break the problem up into smaller portions and tackle each one at a time. It's like the old adage "How do you eat an elephant? One bite at a time." Chapter 12 describes database refactoring, a technique for improving the design of a database schema in such a manner.

Yes, many data professionals are more comfortable taking a serial approach to development but this is simply not an option for modern development efforts. Choose to try new ways to work.

Prefer Read-Only Legacy Data Access

It can be exceptionally difficult to address many of the data-quality problems summarized in Table 8.1 and the database-design problems of Table 8.2 when you simply have to read the data. My experience is that it is often an order of magnitude harder to support both reading from and writing to a legacy data source as compared to just reading from it. For example, say both legacy data value X and value Y both map to "fixed" value A. If your application needs to update the legacy value, what should A be written back as, X or Y? The fundamental issue is that to support both read and write data access you need to define conversion rules for each direction. Writing data to a legacy data source entails greater risk than simply reading it because when you write data you must preserve its semantics — semantics that you may not fully comprehend without extensive analysis of the other systems that also write to that database. The implication is that it is clearly to your advantage to avoid updating legacy data sources whenever possible.

Table 8.4 Strategies for Avoiding Legacy Data Access/Conversions

STRATEGY	ADVANTAGES	DISADVANTAGES
Create your own, stand-alone database.	• Most flexible approach from the point of view of developers because you can create a database schema that reflects your actual needs.	• Likely does not fit in well with your enterprise architecture. • Likely to require double input on the part of your stakeholders — they will have to input the same data into existing legacy systems as well as your new system.
Reprioritize/drop functionality that requires legacy data access. Your stakeholders may decide to forgo some functionality that requires legacy data access when they realize the cost of achieving that access.	• Your development effort is greatly simplified. • For functionality that is reprioritized, another data conversion effort might address the data that you require in the meantime.	• It is rare to have only one or two requirements that depend on legacy data access. • You may simply be putting off a high-risk effort to a later date.

(continued)

Table 8.4 *(continued)*

STRATEGY	ADVANTAGES	DISADVANTAGES
Accept legacy data as is. Your team chooses to directly access the data without a conversion effort.	• Your objects work with the legacy data sources. • No data conversion code is required.	• Significant redesign and coding of your objects is likely required for this to work. The burden has simply shifted to the application code. • The actual problem, a poor database design, is not addressed and will continue to affect future projects. • May not be feasible depending on the extent of the mismatch between the legacy database design and the requirements for your application. • Performance is likely to be significantly affected because of mapping problems (see Chapter 14). • The use of a persistence layer/framework (see Chapter 13) is likely not an option if the mappings between your objects and the legacy data schema are too complex.
Refactor the legacy data source. The legacy system owners improve the quality of the legacy data source, allowing your team to work with high-quality legacy data.	• You have a clean database design to work with. • Your database schema can be redesigned to reflect the current needs of your organization as well as modern object-oriented and component-based technologies.	• This may not occur in time for your project team. • This is very difficult to achieve in practice. • Legacy applications will need to be updated to reflect the new data schema. • Database refactoring is a continuous process, requiring a cultural change among the data professionals within your organization. It is not a one-time-only effort.

Encapsulate Legacy Data Access

As Chapter 13 discusses in detail, you want to encapsulate access to databases. This is true for the database(s) you are responsible for, and it is true of legacy data sources. By encapsulating database access, you reduce coupling with a database and thus increase its maintainability and flexibility. You also reduce the burden on your application developers; they only need to know how to work with the encapsulation strategy and not with all of the individual data sources. Encapsulating access to a legacy data source is highly desirable because you do not want to couple your application code to data-oriented code that will need to evolve as the legacy data sources evolve. This can be particularly true when you need to support both read and write access to legacy data sources and/or when multiple data sources exist.

Introduce Data Adapters for Simple Legacy Access

In simple situations, you have to work with one legacy data source, you only need a subset of the data, and the data is relatively clean. In this case, your best option is to introduce a class that accesses the legacy data. For example, assume that you need access to customer data stored in a legacy database. The data that you currently require is stored in two different tables, there are several minor problems with the quality of the data, and there is one relatively complicated data quality issue. You decide to create a class called *CustomerDataAdapter* that encapsulates all of the functionality to work with this legacy data. This class would include the code necessary to read the data, and write it as well if required. It would also implement the functionality required to convert the legacy data into something usable by your business classes, and back again if need be. When a customer object requires data it requests it via *CustomerDataAdapter*, obtaining the data it needs at the time. If another type of business class required legacy data, for example the *Order* class, then you would implement an *OrderDataAdapter* to do this — one data adapter class per business class.

This is basically the data equivalent of the *Adapter* design pattern (Gamma et. al. 1995), something I guess should be called the *Data Adapter* pattern. There are several advantages to this approach:

- All of the data access code for a business entity is implemented in a single class.

- You have complete control over how the legacy data is accessed; you simply have to code it.

- As the data needs for the business class changes, due to new requirements, you can easily change the data-oriented code because it's in one place.

- The code can easily be refactored to work as part of a more comprehensive data-conversion strategy at some point in the future, perhaps to fill a staging database (see the next section).

There are also several disadvantages:

- You will potentially have a large number of data adapter classes, one for each business class, to implement and maintain.

- Your business classes may need to maintain information about the legacy keys (see Chapter 3), information often referred to as "shadow information" required as part of your mapping effort (see Chapter 14), in order for your data adapter to access the legacy data.

- It can be difficult to take advantage of commercial tools that are architected for full-fledged data conversion efforts.

Introduce a Staging Database for Complex Data Access

As your project progresses, you may discover that the data adapter approach isn't sufficient. Perhaps your application requires better performance that can only be achieved through a batch approach to converting the legacy data. Perhaps there is another data-conversion effort in progress within your organization that you want to take advantage of, one that is based on introducing a new database schema. Perhaps your legacy data needs are so complex that it becomes clear to you that a new approach is needed.

Figure 8.3 depicts the concept of a staging database, a database that is introduced for the sole purpose of providing easy access to legacy data. The idea is that data converters are written, perhaps by refactoring your data adapters, to access the data of a single legacy data source, cleanse the data, and finally write it into the staging database. If the legacy data needs to be updated, then similar code needs to be written to support conversion in the opposite direction. The main advantage of this approach is that legacy data problems can be addressed without your application even being aware of them — from the point of view of your application it's working with nice, clean legacy data. The main disadvantage is the additional complexity inherent in the approach.

There are several issues that you need to decide upon when introducing a legacy database.

- Is the staging database a physically separate database or is it a virtual database that is simply implemented as a different set of tables within your application database? This decision will be driven by your organization's architecture standards and the abilities of your database technology (sometimes it's significantly easier to have a single database).

- In the case of two physical databases, does your application code directly work with both the staging database and your own database (if any)? If so, the complexity of your database encapsulation strategy (Chapter 13) increases because it needs to work with two databases. If not, then you will need to develop a strategy for moving data between the two databases.

- You need to determine the "database of record" for critical information. The database of record is the database that is considered the official source for information. This very likely was the legacy database(s) that you're accessing

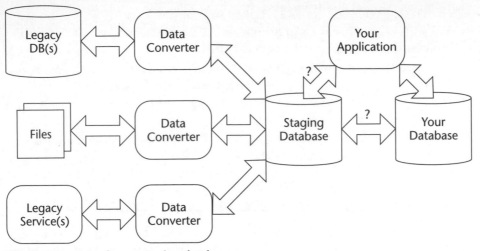

Figure 8.3   Introduce a staging database.

and very likely this will remain the case for as long as those databases exist. This issue is important whenever you store information in several places — in this case, the legacy source(s), the staging database, and your application database — because the data may not always be referentially consistent (see Chapter 19).

TIP Convert the data once. That is, strive to write you data conversion code so that it detects whether a legacy data record has already been converted; if so, then it should skip that record and continue to the next. To do this successfully you need a way to compare the time of last update of the legacy data with the time that it was last converted.

Adopt Existing Tools

Your organization may have existing tools and facilities in place that you can use to access legacy data. For example, you may have a corporate license for one or more Extract-Transform-Load (ETL) tools that are typically used for large-scale data conversion projects. Perhaps other application teams have already written data adapters or data converters that your team can reuse. In short, follow AM's practice of *Reuse Existing Resources* whenever possible.

Data Integration Technologies

There are several important technologies available to you for integrating legacy data sources. My goal here is to make you aware that they exist. These technologies include:

Service-based technology. This is a programmatic approach to data access where a common business transaction is implemented as a single function call. Examples include Web services, remote procedure calls (RPCs), and CICS transactions. The basic idea is that a client invokes the service, the service is performed, and the result returned. Services can be used to wrap access to legacy data sources via the Data Adapter pattern to implement an interface to the data source that can be invoked by a wide range of applications.

Consolidated database(s). This is a data-oriented solution where the legacy data sources are converted and then combined into one or more databases. This is effectively the staging database concept taken one step further — the staging database becomes the source of record for the data, and the individual legacy sources are removed over time.

Messaging-based approaches. This is a programmatic approach where access to the legacy data is wrapped, and then the wrappers are invoked via a common messaging platform. I explore various wrapping techniques in *Building Object Applications That Work* (Ambler 1997). Requests for data are sent to a messaging system, perhaps IBM's MQSeries product (www.ibm.com) or Tibco's Active-Enterprise (www.tibco.com), and the responses are returned to the caller via the messaging system when available. Provided that the wrappers have been written the messaging system provides a common interface to legacy data for application programmers.

Common Warehouse Metamodel (CWM). The CWM is a specification defined by the Object Management Group (www.omg.org) that describes meta data interchange among data-warehousing, business-intelligence, knowledge-management, and portal technologies. This specification is important to integration efforts because it provides a standard for the exchange of descriptive information regarding data sources. This standard enables developers to programmatically determine the nature of a data source (something commonly called reflection) and potentially simplifies your enterprise administrators' meta data-management efforts.

Extensible Markup Language (XML). XML is a common format used to share data in a platform-independent manner. XML is discussed in detail in Chapter 22.

When choosing data-integration technologies for your project, the most important thing that an agile DBA can do is to work with your enterprise architects and administrators to ensure that your team's choices reflect the long-term architectural vision for your organization. Ideally this vision is well known already. However, when you are working with new technologies or when your organization is in the process of defining the vision, you may discover that you need to work with enterprise personnel closely to get this right.

Summary

Working with legacy data is a common, and often very frustrating, reality of software development. There are often a wide variety of problems with the legacy data, including data quality, data design, data architecture, and political/process-related issues. This chapter explored these problems in detail, giving you the background that you require to begin dealing with them effectively.

You were also introduced to a collection of strategies and technologies for working with legacy data. The first one is to avoid working with it if possible. Why needlessly suffer problems? You saw that working iteratively and incrementally is a viable approach for dealing with legacy data. The hardest part is choosing to work this way. Technical solutions were also identified, including the development of data adapters and staging databases.

Working with legacy data is a difficult task, one that I don't wish on anyone. Unfortunately, we all have to do it, so it's better to accept this fact, gain the skills that we need to succeed, and then get on with the work. This chapter has laid the foundation from which to gain the skills that you require to do so.

Two

Evolutionary Database Development

This part describes how to take an evolutionary (iterative and incremental) approach to data-oriented development. You likely need to read all the material in this part. The best approach is to start with Chapter 9 for an overview and then read the rest of the chapters in the order that makes the most sense to you. Experienced agile modelers might choose to skip Chapter 10. Developers experienced with database encapsulation, mapping objects, and performance tuning may choose to skim these chapters but should expect to discover several new ideas that they haven't considered before. The bottom line is that the "let's create a data model early in the life cycle, baseline it, and then force developers to follow a strict change-management process" is no longer acceptable (if it ever was) — data professionals need to change their approach and this part describes techniques for doing exactly that.

Chapter 9: Vive L' Évolution. This chapter argues that agile software development is real and here to stay, that data is an important aspect of most systems, and that all agile methodologies take an evolutionary approach to development. Therefore, if data professionals wish to remain relevant, they must embrace evolutionary development.

Chapter 10: Agile Model-Driven Development (AMDD). Agile Modeling (AM) is a chaordic collection of practices for the effective development of models and documents. AM defines a streamlined approach to evolutionary modeling for agile developers.

Chapter 11: Test-Driven Development (TDD).   Test-driven development (TDD) is a development approach whereby developers add a test before they add new functional code. This minimizes the feedback loop, while providing developers with the confidence to proceed in small, evolutionary steps.

Chapter 12: Database Refactoring.   A database refactoring is a small change to a database schema that improves its design. The process of database refactoring enables you to evolve your data schema in step with the evolution of the systems that access that data.

Chapter 13: Database Encapsulation Strategies.   Encapsulating access to data sources enables developers to evolve both the data schema and their application schemas independently of one another.

Chapter 14: Mapping Objects to Relational Databases.   When working with object and relational technologies, you must map your object schema to your database schema, evolving it over time as your two schemas evolve.

Chapter 15: Performance Tuning.   The need to ensure sufficient system performance is often a primary motivator of evolutionary changes late in the life cycle for traditional projects. On agile projects, it motivates changes almost from the beginning.

Chapter 16: Tools for Evolutionary Database Development.   There is a quickly emerging collection of tools, many of which are available for free, that support agile database techniques.

CHAPTER 9

Vive L' Évolution

Agile software development is evolutionary, not serial. Deal with it.

Would you use the same methodology to create a Web page describing your family and the embedded software for a NASA space probe? Of course not. Would you take the same approach with a team of six people that you would with a team of 600 people? Once again, likely not. Different situations obviously call for different approaches, and in the two situations I've described this is clearly true.

Unfortunately, many people struggle when the differences aren't so clear. Should you follow the same process for a building an *n*-tiered Web application as you would for a data warehouse? Should you follow the same process for building an online version of your customer ordering system that you successfully followed 10 years ago when you built the existing system that your internal customer service representatives now use? The answer to both questions is no. An *n*-tiered application requires a different set of primary artifacts than a data warehouse — different technologies are best modeled and built using different techniques. The requirements for an online customer ordering system aren't clear, as you may have noticed from the wide variety of e-commerce strategies in the past few years, when compared to your internal system built years ago. The implication is that the near-serial process that you followed years ago, a process that is very likely resistant to change, isn't up to the dynamic nature of today's environment.

In this chapter, I discuss:

- The need for methodological flexibility

- Why you should beware of data-oriented BDUF

- Evolutionary development on a project

- The "natural order of things" and evolutionary development

The Need for Methodological Flexibility

As an example of the need to be flexible with methodological requirements, imagine this situation: Senior management within your company has decided to adopt the ICONIX methodology (Rosenberg and Scott 1999) as the official software process that all development teams will follow from now on. The ICONIX methodology is based on the idea that you'll iteratively and incrementally identify requirements via use cases, analyze those use cases with robustness diagrams, and then design your software using UML sequence diagrams and UML class diagrams. The class diagram is then used to develop your physical database schema and code. Figure 9.1 depicts this process, the large arrows representing the main flow of work and the small arrows representing iterative feedback. ICONIX is well suited for project teams that build business applications using object- or component-based technologies.

ICONIX sounds great, doesn't it? Perhaps to your Java developers, but what about the people working on your data-warehousing project? A data-warehousing project would be better served by a data-oriented approach along the lines of the one depicted in Figure 9.2. How successful do you think a data-warehousing project would be if you forced the developers to follow ICONIX? Now, let's turn it around; how successful do you think an n-tiered Java project would be if you forced the data-oriented approach of Figure 9.2 on those responsible for it? Not as successful as they could have been, certainly. Yet, surprisingly enough, this is exactly what many organizations do. They desperately want to find a "one size fits all" approach to software development, presumably for consistency and ease of management, but in doing so they put the projects at risk. Just as you need to use the right tool for a job you need to follow the right process for a software development project.

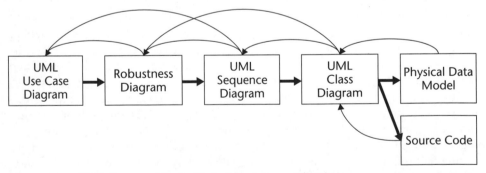

Figure 9.1   Modeling an object-oriented business application.

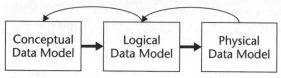

Figure 9.2 Modeling a data warehouse.

To succeed at software development, you need to be flexible in your choice of software-development methodology. There are several reasons why it is important to be so:

Different technologies require different techniques. Object-oriented methodologies are best suited for projects using object-oriented technologies, whereas data-oriented methodologies are best suited for data-oriented applications.

Every individual is unique. People are not replaceable parts. Each person has a different background, different preferences for the way in which they work, and different cognitive styles (for example, are they visual or nonvisual thinkers?). An approach that works incredibly well for you might be difficult for me to grasp, and vice versa.

Every team is unique. Because teams are made up of unique individuals, each team requires a unique way to work in order to maximize its potential. Several teams could follow ICONIX but each will need its own version tailored to meet their exact needs.

Your external needs vary. Some projects must conform to government regulations. Some projects are highly dependent on suppliers, such as technology vendors or software-development outsourcers, and therefore must tune their processes to reflect the ways that their suppliers need to work. Many projects are affected by neither of these issues.

Project categories vary. An online system used by your customers will be built in a different manner than an internal application used by a junior account, which will be built differently than an internally used data warehouse. Similarly, the building of a new "Greenfield" application will be different from the refurbishment of an existing, legacy application. Different types of projects require different approaches because each category has different priorities and goals.

Beware of Data-Oriented BDUF

A common approach within traditional organizations is what I like to call a data-oriented *big design up front* (BDUF) approach. This strategy is based on two concepts:

- Your primary modeling artifacts are conceptual, logical, and physical data models. Data is a critical asset and therefore should be a primary driver of your development efforts.

- You need to develop and baseline these models early in your project. The goal is to think through the major issues at the beginning of the project and thereby prevent any "surprises" later in the project. This will enable you to proceed in parallel; that is, the data group can focus on data-oriented activities and the development team can build the application. Many organizations will go so far as to insist on having the physical data model in place before coding starts to provide a point of commonality — the database — between the groups. A change-management process is put in place to allow changes to be made to the primary artifacts (the data models).

Unfortunately, many data professionals believe that you need to get your data models "mostly right" reasonably early in a project. This misconception is often the result of:

Prevailing organizational culture.   Many organizations still follow a traditional, near-serial software process based on a BDUF approach to modeling. Because they haven't made the shift to agile software development yet, they haven't come to the realization that they need to change their mindset. An interesting observation is that slow-moving organizations want to freeze everything and that faster organizations don't — perhaps the reason why your organization takes so long to get anything done is your penchant for BDUF?

Prevailing professional culture.   The data community is just beginning to assess agile techniques and has not yet had a chance to absorb the evolutionary mindset of agile developers. Agile software development is new; for the most part it's coming out of the object community, and until this book, very little attention has been given to agile database techniques. Worse yet, many within the data community are still struggling with object-orientation, let alone agility.

Lack of experience with evolutionary techniques.   Many data professionals haven't had the opportunity to try an evolutionary approach, and because they haven't seen it with their own eyes they are justifiably skeptical (but that doesn't mean you should go into a state of denial either). If you don't yet have experience with evolutionary data modeling, you can at least read about the experiences of others. Fowler and Sadalage (2003) describe their efforts on a multisite, 100+ person project that followed a collection of techniques very similar to those described in this book.

Prescriptive processes.   Many organizations have well-defined, prescriptive processes in place that make it difficult to change your data models once they've been accepted. The need to review and baseline models dramatically slows you down, and the need to "accept" a model indicates a command-and-control mindset; this is very likely hampering your efforts. Agile Modeling (AM)'s practices of *Model with Others*, *Active Stakeholder Participation*, and *Collective Ownership* go a long way to removing the need for reviews. When all you know is a prescriptive process, it's very difficult to imagine that another, significantly faster and more effective way is possible.

Lack of supporting tools.   Tools are generally behind methods, although with the open source movement and recent consolidations among development tool vendors we're starting to see very good progress. Chapter 16 describes the current state of tools for evolutionary data-oriented development.

There are several serious problems with a data-oriented DBUF approach to development:

One size does not fit all.   This approach assumes that a data-oriented process works well for all types of projects, which we saw in the previous section is not true.

It isn't just about data.   Although this approach deals with data quite effectively, it is blind to many other important development issues. When I build a system, not only do I have to worry about data issues but I also have to worry about user interface design, the way my users work with the system, business rules, hardware architecture, middleware, reusable components, object structure, and object collaborations, which are also important issues (among many). A data-oriented approach is too narrowly focused to meet today's needs.

You can't think everything through at the start.   Have you ever decorated a living room? Perhaps you decided to think things through first by sketching out a design; after all, who wants to move furniture around needlessly or purchase things that don't match one another? So, did you redecorate your living room according to plan, step back to look at it, and say, "Yep, that's perfect"? Chances are good that you, or your spouse, really said something like, "Perhaps the couch would look better over here as long as we angle the television this way and . . . ." The point is that if you can't think through the design of a living room up front, what makes you think that you can think through the design of a software-based system, which is many orders of magnitude more complex? The BDUF approach, even with a "change management" process in place, simply isn't realistic.

It doesn't easily support change.   When you go through the effort of thinking everything through up front, of reviewing and accepting the models, then splitting the work off to several teams working in parallel, the last thing you want is for the models to change. Therefore, you put a change-management process in place that makes it difficult to change the shared data models. You force people to submit change requests, you review the change requests, you perform an impact analysis of the change requests, then maybe sometime later you'll actually make the change. Sounds more like a change prevention process to me.

It doesn't support close interpersonal interactions.   Software development is a communication game (Cockburn 2002), yet when you have several groups working in parallel on "their own things," you're effectively erecting barriers to communication. Having a separate group of data specialists working on the data and another group of application specialists working on the code may seem like a good idea but it actually increases the risk to your project. This is because these people aren't working together as closely as possible, thus making it likely that they will either repeat the work of each other or even worse do work that contradicts the efforts of one another. Attending meetings with one another, reviewing the work of each other, sharing documents via email doesn't hold a candle to working side by side. Are you really trying to make software development more efficient by assigning work to different groups or are you merely reinforcing the political power bases of the managers of those groups?

Data-oriented BDUF is a viable way to build software. But it's certainly not agile, and it certainly doesn't reflect the realities of most modern application-development efforts. It might have worked for you 20 years ago, although I doubt it was your best option back then either (I was naively working like this in the 1980s, by the way), but it isn't appropriate now. It is time to rethink your approach to data-oriented development and adopt evolutionary techniques.

Evolutionary Development on a Project

Evolutionary development is an iterative and incremental approach to software development. Instead of creating a comprehensive artifact, such as a requirements specification, that you review and accept before creating a comprehensive design model (and so on), you instead evolve the critical development artifacts over time in an iterative manner. Instead of building and then delivering your system in a single "big bang" release, you instead deliver it incrementally over time. In short, evolutionary development is new to many existing data professionals, and many traditional programmers as well.

I have three very important observations to share with you:

Modern software processes take an evolutionary approach to development. Consider the leading software processes: Extreme Programming (XP) (Beck 2000), Feature-Driven Development (FDD) (Palmer and Felsing 2002), the Rational Unified Process (RUP) (Kruchten 2000), Dynamic Systems Development Method (DSDM) (Stapleton 2003), and Scrum (Beedle and Schwaber 2001). What do they have in common? They're all iterative and incremental. Every single one of them takes an evolutionary approach to development. The only popular methodology that does not take an evolutionary approach to development is IEEE 12207 (www.ieee.org) and at the time of this writing the IEEE is in the process of defining a "standard" evolutionary life cycle. The writing is on the wall, like it or not.

Most leading processes are agile.   With the exception of IEEE 12207 and the RUP all of these software processes are agile. Yes, it is possible to instantiate an agile version of the RUP (I've even been involved with a few) but my experience is that it rarely occurs in practice.

Data is still important.   I also argued in Chapter 1 that data is a critical aspect of most business applications, a belief that is captured in the first philosophy of the agile data (AD) method.

The implication is that if data professionals are to remain relevant, they also need to take an evolutionary approach to development. Is this possible? Absolutely, but they have to choose to work this way. Figure 9.3 depicts a high-level overview of the relationships among critical development techniques. Instead of showing them in the near-serial style of Figures 9.1 and 9.2, the diagram instead shows a collection of fully connected activities. It is interesting to note that there is no starting point, nor is there an ending point, instead you iterate back and forth between activities as required. Furthermore, this diagram isn't complete. For example, it doesn't include activities for project management, acceptance testing, or installation to name a few. My focus for now is on data-oriented development activities.

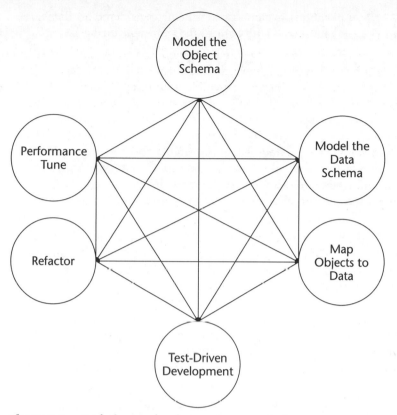

Figure 9.3   Evolutionary development on a project.

How does the process of Figure 9.3 work? Let's work through it a task at a time:

Modeling.   There are two modeling-oriented activities, object modeling and data modeling, both of which would naturally be supported by normalization techniques. Neither object modeling nor data modeling is agile by itself; it's how you apply these techniques that counts. Chapter 10 describes AM and how models can be used to drive your development efforts in an agile manner, something I like to call Agile Modeling-Driven Development (AMDD).

Mapping.   Because you're using object technology and relational databases (RDBs) together, you need to understand how to overcome the impedance mismatch between the two. That's what mapping (described in Chapter 14) is all about. Because you are developing your object and data schemas in an evolutionary manner, you will clearly need to evolve your mappings over time. Similarly, difficulties in mapping may motivate changes to either your object or data schemas, perhaps even to both at once.

Test-driven development (TDD).   TDD is an approach where you write a new test, you watch it fail, then you write the little bit of functional code required to ensure that the test is passed. You then proceed iteratively, as Chapter 11 describes, programming in an evolutionary manner. TDD is a very common approach for agile application developers and is being considered for database development. TDD dovetails well with both AMDD and refactoring.

Refactoring.   A code refactoring is a small improvement to your source code that improves its design without adding new functionality. A database refactoring, the topic of Chapter 12, is a small improvement to your database schema that doesn't change its functional or informational semantics. Database refactoring, like code refactoring, enables you to evolve your design over time to help you to meet the new needs of your stakeholders. Database refactoring is made significantly easier when access to a database is encapsulated and good tools are utilized. When you refactor your code design you are effectively evolving your object schema, and when you refactor your database design you effectively evolve your data schema; therefore refactoring may motivate changes to your corresponding models.

Performance tuning.   Because modern systems use several technologies, including both object technology and RDBs, developers must be prepared to tune both these technologies and the interactions between them. Because you're delivering working software incrementally — perhaps monthly, weekly, or even daily — you must tune system performance (see Chapter 15) on an ongoing basis. The implication is that performance tuning may motivate changes to your object schema, your data schema, or to your mappings between the two. Furthermore, changes to any of these things may have a performance impact on your system, which in turn could motivate an iterative change to another aspect of your system. It's all interconnected.

Let's consider a typical scenario. Your project has been organized into two-week long "iterations." At the beginning of the iteration, your team pulls two-week's worth of work from the top of your requirements stack, effectively giving you the highest-priority functionality to work on. You divvy up the work between your teammates, perhaps forming pairs as you would on an XP team project or feature teams as you would on an FDD team, and begin to work. Each subteam will explore the requirement they are working on in greater detail, creating new (or evolving existing) object-oriented models as appropriate. For example, an FDD team will have an object-oriented domain model that they evolve throughout the project, whereas an XP team may have a collection of CRC cards that they work with. They'll also evolve their data model(s) or maybe just update data definition language (DDL) scripts that they use to refactor the database schema. They'll implement their code, hopefully taking a TDD approach, and refactor both the code and database schema as needed. They may discover that they need to do some more modeling to think through some complicated issues, then they'll go back to implementation. The team will update their models, code, and mappings as part of their overall performance-tuning efforts while this is happening.

The important thing to understand is that they're quickly iterating back and forth between these tasks as required. The models, code, tests, and mappings all evolve together. With an evolutionary approach to development your models, including data-oriented ones, are developed over time. There is no "requirements phase" or "design phase"; instead modeling is performed as needed throughout your project in a continuous manner.

The "Natural Order" of Things and Evolutionary Development

Although evolutionary development may seem chaotic, and to people not familiar with it then it very likely is, but the reality is that in fact it's chaordic (Hock 2000). Chaordic is a word coined by Dee Hock to represent the idea that order can come from seeming chaos. The process of Figure 9.3 certainly appears chaotic, yet many people are building great software by taking this type of approach. How does it work? People still do things in an intelligent order, albeit taking much smaller steps doing so.

For example, on a project using object technology and relational databases together, a good strategy is to do analysis/domain/conceptual modeling before design-object modeling, which in turn leads to physical-data-design modeling, then mapping the two models, then refactoring them in conjunction with performance tuning. This is the overall order, something that Figures 9.1 and 9.2 imply with their big arrows, yet you still iterate back and forth as needed.

Let's go at it from a slightly different point of view. Figure 9.4 depicts a high-level process diagram for evolutionary development that makes data-oriented activities a little more explicit. First, notice how the arrows are two-way, implying that you iterate back and forth between activities. Second, as with Figure 9.3, there is no starting point. Although you may choose to start with your enterprise model, then do some conceptual modeling, then let your conceptual model drive your object and data schemas, this doesn't have to be the case. Depending on the nature of your project, you could start with a project-level conceptual model (you may not have an enterprise model) or you may start first with traditional object modeling activities such as use-case modeling. It doesn't really matter because agile software developers will iterate to another activity as required. Third, notice how I use the term "enterprise structural modeling" and not "enterprise data modeling" — many organizations are choosing to use UML class models or even UML component models (Herzum and Sims 2000; Atkinson et. al. 2002) instead of data models for structural modeling. One of my biggest beefs with the Zachman Framework (ZIFA 2002; Hay 2003) is that its first column, labeled "Data," biases you toward data-oriented artifacts, whereas "Structure" would be more inclusive. Regardless of the type of artifacts you choose, the same fundamental goals are being achieved, albeit by different means. An advantage of occasionally referring to an enterprise model during your project-level efforts, or better yet working closely with an enterprise architect, is that it provides a good opportunity to see if your system reflects the needs of the enterprise (or it indicates that the enterprise model is in need of updating). Fourth, I've combined the notions of conceptual and domain modeling into one model because they're often commingled anyway (if they're done at all).

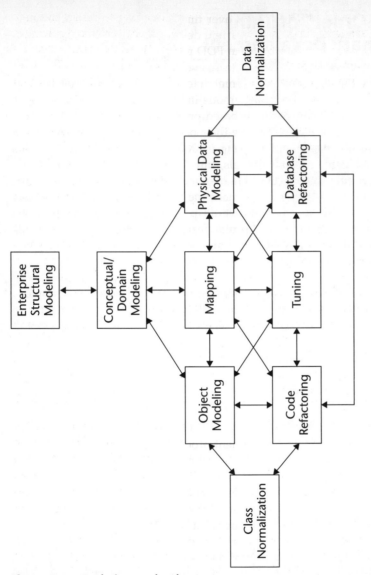

Figure 9.4 Evolutionary development.

The basic idea is that your models evolve over time, changing to reflect the new requirements that you are working on in the current development iteration (typically a period ranging from one to several weeks). An FDD project typically starts by developing an initial object domain model that the team evolves over time as they work on features. This is something that Stephen Palmer refers to as the JEDI (just enough design initially) approach — they do enough modeling to get the lay of the land and then iteratively add content and refinement based on the features. An XP team will very likely forgo this step and instead evolve their object and data schemas as they work on user stories. There's nothing stopping an XP team from developing other models, including conceptual/domain models, but it's not an explicit part of the process. Each new requirement may motivate one or more changes to your models, code, and other development artifacts. You'll make these changes, test them, fix things as required, integrate your work into the overall project, and iterate as required. Because agile requirements are typically granular, features can often be implemented in several hours and user stories in a couple of hours or days, and you are able to safely and quickly evolve your development artifacts to meet the current needs of your project stakeholders.

The secret is to adopt AM's *Model with a Purpose* principle — once a model has fulfilled its purpose, for the moment, stop working on it and move on to something else. Your models don't have to be perfect; they don't have to be complete; they just need to be barely good enough.

Summary

In this chapter, you saw that evolutionary approaches to software development are not only supported by leading software-development processes, they are in fact the norm for agile processes. You also learned that there are some significant problems with the near-serial, BDUF approaches favored by many traditional data professionals. Most importantly, you discovered that it is possible to take an evolutionary approach to data-oriented development activities, techniques that are described in greater detail in following chapters. The bottom line is that if you want to work with an agile team, you need to be prepared to work in an evolutionary manner. It is a choice to work in this way, just as it's a choice to not do so. Agile software developers embrace change and therefore decide to work in an evolutionary manner.

CHAPTER 10

Agile Model-Driven Development (AMDD)

Models and documents don't need to be perfect,
they just need to be barely good enough.

Modeling and documentation are an important part of any software developer's job. Developers may choose to create a wide range of requirements models, architectural models, and design models for their systems. Agile DBAs may choose to create both logical and physical data models in the course of their work. Enterprise architects will also create a wide variety of models to describe an organization's environments and so will enterprise administrators. Modeling and documentation are critical aspects of the jobs of all agile software developers; therefore, it makes sense to ask how you can be effective creating them. Luckily there is an answer: Agile Modeling (AM).

NOTE This chapter provides a brief discussion of agile modeling; for more in-depth coverage of AM, see my companion book *Agile Modeling: Effective Practices for Extreme Programming and the Unified Process* (Ambler 2002a).

In this chapter, we will explore:

- The role of the agile DBA
- What is Agile Modeling?
- When is a model agile?
- What is Agile Model-Driven Development (AMDD)?
- Agile documentation

The Role of the Agile DBA

Agile DBAs apply the values, principles, and practices of AM to evolve their understanding of both the problem domain and of the solution space. They work closely with their teammates, creating models with them and learning new modeling techniques from them. They will create agile models to work through complicated issues or to communicate their work to others.

What Is Agile Modeling?

Agile Modeling (AM) is a practice-based methodology for effective modeling and documentation of software-based systems. The AM methodology is a collection of practices, guided by principles and values, that is meant to be applied by software professionals on a day-to-day basis.

AM is not a prescriptive process; that is, it does not define detailed procedures for how to create a given type of model, but instead provides advice for how to be effective as a modeler. AM is *chaordic* (Hock 2000) in that it blends the "chaos" of simple modeling practices with the "order" inherent in software modeling artifacts. AM is not about less modeling; in fact, many developers will find that they are doing more modeling than they did before being introduced to AM. AM is "touchy-feely"; that is, it's not a bunch of hard-and-fast rules — think of AM as an art, not a science.

An *agile modeler* is anyone who models following the AM methodology, applying AM's practices in accordance with its principles and values.

AM has three main goals:

- To define and show how to put into practice a collection of values, principles, and practices pertaining to effective, light-weight modeling. What makes AM a catalyst for improvement isn't the modeling techniques themselves — such as use-case models, class models, data models, or user-interface models — but how they are applied.

- To address the issue of how to apply modeling techniques on software projects, taking an agile approach such as Extreme Programming (XP). Sometimes it is significantly more productive for a developer to draw some bubbles and lines to think through an idea, or to compare several different approaches to solving a problem, than it is to simply start writing code. This is the danger in being too code-centric — sometimes a quick sketch can help you avoid significant reworking when you are coding.

- To address how you can improve your modeling activities by following a "near-agile" approach to software development, and in particular using project teams that have adopted an instantiation of the Unified Process such as the Rational Unified Process (RUP) (Kruchten 2000) or the Enterprise Unified Process (EUP) (Ambler 2001b). Although you must be following an agile software process to truly be agile modeling, you may still adopt and benefit from many of AM's practices on nonagile projects.

AM Values

The values of AM provide a philosophical foundation upon which its principles are based, providing the primary motivation for the method. AM's values include those of XP and extends it with a fifth one, humility. Briefly, those values are:

Communication.   It is critical to have effective communication within your development team as well as with and between all project stakeholders.

Simplicity.   Strive to develop the simplest solution possible that meets all of your needs.

Feedback.   Obtain feedback regarding your efforts often and early.

Courage.   Have the courage to make and stick to your decisions.

Humility.   Have the humility to admit that you may not know everything, that others have value to add to your project efforts.

AM Principles

The principles of AM flesh out the philosophical foundation defined by its values. You use AM's principles to guide your application of its practices. The principles are:

Assume simplicity.   As you develop, you should assume that the simplest solution is the best solution.

Content is more important than representation.   Any given model could have several ways to represent it. For example, a UI specification could be created using Post-it notes on a large sheet of paper (an essential or low-fidelity prototype), as a sketch on paper or a whiteboard, as a "traditional" prototype built using a prototyping tool or programming language, or as a formal document including both a visual representation and a textual description of the UI.

Embrace change.   Accept the fact that change happens. Revel in it, for change is one of the things that make software development exciting.

Enabling the next effort is your secondary goal.   Your project can still be considered a failure even when your team delivers a working system to your users — part of fulfilling the needs of your project stakeholders is to ensure that your system is robust enough so that it can be extended over time. As Alistair Cockburn (2002) likes to say, when you are playing the software development game, your secondary goal is to set up to play the next game.

Everyone can learn from everyone else.   Agile modelers have the humility to recognize that they can never truly master something; there is always opportunity to learn more and to extend your knowledge. They take the opportunity to work with and learn from others, to try new ways of doing things, and to reflect on what seems to work and what doesn't.

Incremental change.   To embrace change, you need to take an incremental approach to your own development efforts; that is, to change your system a small portion at a time instead of trying to get everything accomplished in one big release. You can make a big change as a series of small, incremental changes.

Know your models.   Because you have multiple models that you can apply as an agile modeler you need to know their strengths and weaknesses to be effective in their use.

Local adaptation.   It is doubtful that you will be able to apply AM "out of the box"; instead, you will need to modify it to reflect your environment, including the nature of your organization, your coworkers, your project stakeholders, and your project itself.

Maximize stakeholder investment.   Your project stakeholders are investing resources — time, money, facilities, and so on — to have software developed that meets their needs. Stakeholders deserve to invest their resources the best way possible and to not have them frittered away by your team. Furthermore, stakeholders deserve to have the final say in how those resources are invested or not invested. If it were your money, would you want it any other way?

Model with a purpose.   If you cannot identify why and for whom you are creating a model, then why are you bothering to work on it all?

Multiple models.   You have a wide range of modeling artifacts available to you (many of which are summarized in the Appendix). These artifacts include, but are not limited to, the diagrams of the Unified Modeling Language (UML), structured development artifacts such as data models, and low-tech artifacts such as essential user interface models and CRC cards (Ambler 2001a).

Open and honest communication.   People need to be free, and to *perceive* that they are free, to offer suggestions. Open and honest communication enables people to make better decisions because the information that they are basing them on is more accurate.

Quality work.   Agile developers understand that they should invest the effort to make permanent artifacts, such as source code, user documentation, and technical system documentation of sufficient quality.

Rapid feedback.   Feedback is one of the five values of AM, and because the time between an action and the feedback on that action is critical, agile modelers prefer rapid feedback over delayed feedback whenever possible.

Software is your primary goal.   The primary goal of software development is to produce high-quality software that meets the needs of your project stakeholders in an effective manner.

Travel light.   Traveling light means that you create just enough models and documentation to get by.

Work with people's instincts.   As you gain experience developing software your instincts become sharper, and what your instincts are telling you subconsciously can often be an important input into your modeling efforts.

Agile Modeling Practices

To model in an agile manner, software developers will apply AM's practices appropriately. Fundamental practices include:

Active stakeholder participation.   Project success often requires a significant level of involvement by project stakeholders — senior management needs to publicly and privately support your project, operations and support staff must actively work with your project team toward making your production environment ready to accept your system, other system teams must work with yours to support integration efforts, and maintenance developers must work to become adept at the technologies and techniques used by your system.

Apply modeling standards.   Developers should agree to and follow a common set of modeling standards on a software project.

Apply patterns gently.   Effective modelers learn and then appropriately apply common architectural, design, and analysis patterns in their models. However, both Martin Fowler (2001b) and Joshua Kerievsky (2001) believe that developers should consider easing into the application of a pattern, to apply it gently.

Apply the right artifact(s).   This practice is AM's equivalent of the adage "use the right tool for the job"; in this case, you want to create the right model(s) to get the job done. Each artifact — such as a UML state chart, an essential use-case, a source code, or a data-flow diagram (DFD) — has its own specific strengths and weaknesses, and therefore is appropriate for some situations but not others.

Collective ownership.   Everyone can work on any model, and ideally any artifact on the project, if they need to.

Consider testability.   When you are modeling you should be constantly asking yourself, "How are we going to test this?" because if you can't test the software that you are building you shouldn't be building it.

Create several models in parallel.   Because each type of model has its strengths and weaknesses, no single model is sufficient for your modeling needs. By working on several at once, you can easily iterate back and forth between them and use each model for what it is best suited for.

Create simple content.   You should keep the actual content of your models — your requirements, your analysis, your architecture, or your design — as simple as you possibly can while still fulfilling the needs of your project stakeholders. The implication is that you should not add additional aspects to your models unless they are justifiable.

Depict models simply.   Use a subset of the modeling notation available to you — a simple model that shows the key features that you are trying to understand, perhaps a class model depicting the primary responsibilities of classes and the relationships between them, often proves to be sufficient.

Discard temporary models.   The vast majority of the models that you create are temporary/working models — design sketches, low-fidelity prototypes, index cards, potential architecture/design alternatives, and so on — which are models that fulfill their purpose but then no longer add value once they have done so.

Display models publicly.   This supports the principle of fostering open and honest communication on your team, because all of the current models are quickly accessible to them, as well as with your project stakeholders because you aren't hiding anything from them.

Formalize contract models.   Contract models are often required when an external group controls an information resource that your system requires, such as a database, legacy application or information service. A contract model is formalized when both parties mutually agree to it and are ready to mutually change it over time if required.

Iterate to another artifact.   Whenever you find you are having difficulties working on one artifact (perhaps you are working on a use case and find that you are struggling to describe the business logic), that's a sign that you should iterate to another artifact. By iterating to another artifact, you immediately become "unstuck" because you are making progress working on that other artifact.

Model in small increments.   With incremental development, you model a little, code a little, test a little, deliver a little, and then repeat as needed. No more big design up front (BDUF), whereby you invest weeks or even months creating models and documents.

Model to communicate.   One reason why you model is to communicate with people external to your team or to create a contract model that describes the interface with another system.

Model to understand.   The most important application of modeling is to explore the problem space, to identify and analyze the requirements for the system, or to compare and contrast potential design alternatives to identify the potentially simplest solution that meets the requirements.

Model with others.   Software development is a lot like swimming, it's very dangerous to do it alone because if you make a mistake it can be a long time before you discover it.

Prove it with code.   A model is an abstraction, one that should accurately reflect an aspect of whatever you are building. To determine if it will actually work you should validate that your model works by writing the corresponding code.

Reuse existing resources.   There is a wealth of information that agile modelers can take advantage of by reusing resources such as existing enterprise models, modeling style guidelines (Ambler 2003), and common design patterns (Gamma et. al. 1995).

Update only when it hurts.   You should update an artifact, such as a model or document, only when you absolutely need to, when not having the model updated is more painful than the effort of updating it.

Use the simplest tools.   The vast majority of models can be drawn on a whiteboard, on paper, or even the back of a napkin. Note that AM has nothing against

CASE (computer-aided software engineering) tools – if investing in a CASE tool is the most effective use of your resources, then by all means do so and then use it to the best of its ability.

When Is a Model Agile?

At its core, AM is simply a collection of techniques that reflects the principles and values shared by many experienced software developers. If there is such a thing as agile modeling, then are there also agile models? Yes. An agile model is a model that is just barely good enough. But how do you know when a model is good enough? Agile models are good enough when they exhibit the following traits:

- They fulfill their purpose and no more.
- They are understandable.
- They are sufficiently accurate.
- They are sufficiently consistent.
- They are sufficiently detailed.
- They provide positive value.
- They are as simple as possible.

An interesting implication is that an "agile model" is potentially more flexible than what many people perceive a model to be. A Class Responsibility Collaborator (CRC) model is a collection of index cards. An essential user interface prototype can be created from flip-chart paper and Post-it notes. A screen sketch or a UML class diagram can be drawn on a whiteboard. A user-interface prototype can be created using an HTML (Hypertext Markup Language) editor. A UML class diagram could be created using a drawing tool such as Visio (www.microsoft.com) or a sophisticated modeling/CASE tool such as TogetherCC (www.borland.com) that supports the generation and reverse engineering of source code. All of these models could be considered agile models if they meet the criteria listed above. The tools — index cards, paper, whiteboards, CASE — that you use to create a model don't determine whether it's agile or not, the way that you use the model does. Big difference.

What Is Agile Model-Driven Development (AMDD)?

Model-Driven Development (MDD) is an approach to software development whereby extensive models are created before source code is written. A primary example of MDD is the Object Management Group (OMG)'s Model-Driven Architecture (MDA) standard, which is based on the concept that you create formal models using sophisticated modeling tools from which code is generated (Kleppe, Warmer, & Bast 2003).

With MDD a serial approach to development is often taken. MDD is quite popular with traditionalists, although as the Rational Unified Process (RUP) (Kruchten 2000;

Ambler 2001b) shows, it is possible to take an iterative approach with MDD. Agile-Model-Driven Development (AMDD) is the agile form of MDD — instead of creating extensive models before writing source code you instead create agile models, which are just barely good enough.

Is agile MDA possible? Yes, and in its most effective form, it would simply be a sophisticated version of AMDD. As long as you're working closely with others, including your stakeholders, and focusing on delivering working software on a regular basis, then it makes sense to me. Yes, agile MDA would require a collection of complex modeling tools and developers that know how to work with them effectively. I have no doubt that this will in fact occur in a small number of situations, but I expect it to be a very small number.

Agile Documentation

Agile developers recognize that documentation is an intrinsic part of any system, the creation and maintenance of which is a "necessary evil" to some and an enjoyable task for others. Documentation is an aspect of software development that can be made agile when you choose to do so. Like agile models, agile documents are just barely good enough. A document is agile when it meets the following criteria:

Agile documents maximize stakeholder investment.   The benefit provided by an agile document is greater than the investment in its creation and maintenance, and ideally the investment made in that documentation was the best option available for those resources. In other words, documentation must at least provide positive value and ideally provides the best value possible.

Agile documents are "lean and mean."   An agile document contains just enough information to fulfill its purpose, in other words it is as simple as it can possibly be. For example, portions of an agile document could be written in point/bullet form instead of prose — you're still capturing the critical information without investing time to make it look pretty; remember, *content is more important than representation*. Agile documents will often provide references to other sources of information. When writing an agile document also remember simplicity — that the simplest documentation will be sufficient — and create simple content whenever possible. One way to keep agile documents that are lean and mean is to follow pragmatic programming's (Hunt and Thomas 2000) "DRY" — which stands for don't repeat yourself — principle. Redundant, convoluted material that repeats information again and again is tedious to deal with to say the least. Also, work with your document's audience — what is lean and mean for you may be completely insufficient for them.

Agile documents fulfill a purpose.   Agile documents are cohesive; that is, they fulfill a single, defined purpose. If you do not know why you are creating the document, or if the purpose for creating the document is questionable, then you should stop and rethink what you are doing.

Agile documents describe information that is not likely to change.   The greater the chance that information will change the less value there is in investing significant time writing external documentation about it — the information may change before you're finished writing, and it will be difficult to maintain over time. For example, your system architecture, once it has stabilized, will change slowly over time so, it's a good candidate for external documentation.

Agile documents describe "good things to know."   Agile documents capture critical information, information that is not readily obvious such as design rationale, requirements, usage procedures, or operational procedures. Agile documents do not capture obvious information.

Agile documents have a specific customer and facilitate the work efforts of that customer.   System documentation is typically written for maintenance developers, providing an overview of the system's architecture and potentially summarizing critical requirements and design decisions. User documentation often includes tutorials for using a system written in language that your users understand, whereas operations documentation describes how to run your system and is written in language that operations staff can understand. Different customers require different types of documents and very likely different writing styles. You must work closely with the customer for your documentation, or potential customer, if you want to create something that will actually meet their needs. When you don't you're at risk of creating too much documentation or unnecessary documentation and hence becoming less agile.

Agile documents are sufficiently accurate, consistent, and detailed.   Have you ever learned how to use new software by using a book describing a previous version of that software? Did you succeed? Likely. Was it a perfect situation? Likely not. Did it cover all the new features of the software? Of course not, but it still got you up and running with the software package. Were you willing to spend your own money, perhaps on the order of $30, to purchase the latest version of the book you needed? Likely not, because it wasn't worth it to you. Agile documents do not need to be perfect, they just need to be good enough.

Agile documents are sufficiently indexed.   Documentation isn't effective if you cannot easily find the information contained in it. Would you purchase a reference manual without an index or table of contents? Your indexing scheme should reflect the needs of a document's audience. Luckily, word processors include features to easily create tables of contents, and an index, and even lists of figures and tables.

The following list summarizes additional points about agile documentation from Chapter 14 of *Agile Modeling* (Ambler 2002a):

- The fundamental issue is effective communication, not documentation.
- Models are not necessarily documents, and documents are not necessarily models.
- Documentation is as much a part of the system as the source code.

- The benefit of having documentation must be greater than the cost of creating and maintaining it.

- Never trust the documentation.

- Each system has its own unique documentation needs. One size does not fit all.

- Ask whether you *need* the documentation, and why you believe you *need* the documentation, not whether you *want* it.

- The investment in system documentation is a business decision, not a technical one.

- Create documentation only when you need it — don't create documentation for the sake of documentation.

- Update documentation only when it hurts.

- The customer, not the developer, determines whether documentation is sufficient.

Summary

AM not only streamlines your modeling and documentation efforts, it is also an enabling technique for evolutionary development. The collaborative environment fostered by AM promotes communication and cooperation between everyone involved on your project. This helps to break down some of the traditional barriers between groups in your organization and to motivate all developers to learn and apply the wide range of artifacts required to create modern software — there's more to modeling than data models.

The reality is that agile software development is evolutionary in nature and your data-oriented activities are no exception. AM lays the foundation for an evolutionary approach to database development that I call Agile Model-Driven Development (AMDD). AMDD is the evolutionary alternative to traditional MDD.

Test-Driven Development (TDD)

*You can build very large and complex systems that work
without doing any modeling at all.*

Test-driven development (TDD) (Beck 2003; Astels 2003), also known as test-first programming or test-first development, is an evolutionary approach to development whereby you must first write a test that fails before you write new functional code. What is the primary goal of TDD? One view is that the goal of TDD is specification and not validation (Martin, Newkirk, and Koss 2003). In other words, it's one way to think through your design before your write your functional code. Another view is that TDD is a programming technique. As Ron Jeffries likes to say, the goal of TDD is to write clean code that works. I think that there is merit in both arguments, although I leave it for you to decide.

This chapter discusses the following topics:

- The steps of TDD
- TDD and traditional testing
- TDD and documentation
- Test-driven database development
- TDD and Agile Model-Driven Development (AMDD)
- How does TDD work?

How Does TDD Work?

A significant advantage of TDD is that it enables you to take small steps when writing software. This is a practice that I have promoted for years (Ambler 2001a; Ambler 1998a) because it is far more productive than attempting to code in large steps. For example, assume that you add some new functional code, compile, and test it. Chances are pretty good that your tests will be broken by defects that exist in the new code. It is much easier to find and then fix those defects if you've written two new lines of code than two thousand. The implication is that the faster your compiler and regression test suite, the more attractive it is to proceed in smaller and smaller steps. I generally prefer to add a few new lines of functional code, typically less than 10, before I recompile and rerun my tests.

I think Bob Martin says it well (Martin, Newkirk, and Koss 2003):

The act of writing a unit test is more an act of design than of verification. It is also more an act of documentation than of verification. The act of writing a unit test closes a remarkable number of feedback loops, the least of which is the one pertaining to verification of function.

The first reaction that many people have to agile techniques is that they're okay for small projects, perhaps involving a handful of people for several months, but that they wouldn't work for "real" projects that are much larger. That's simply not true. Beck (2003) reports working on a Smalltalk system taking a completely test-driven approach, which took 4 years and 40 person years of effort, resulting in 250,000 lines of functional code and 250,000 lines of test code. There are 4,000 tests running in under 20 minutes, with the full suite being run several times a day. Although there are larger systems out there (I've personally worked on systems where several hundred person years of effort were involved), it is clear that TDD works for good-sized systems.

The Steps of TDD

An overview of the steps of TDD is provided in the UML activity diagram in Figure 11.1. The first step is to quickly add a test, basically just enough code to fail. Next, you run your tests, often the complete test suite, although for sake of speed you may decide to run only a subset to ensure that the new test does in fact fail. You then update your functional code to make it pass the new tests. The fourth step is to run your tests again. If they fail, you need to update your functional code and retest it. Once the tests are passed, the next step is to start over (you may also want to refactor any duplication out of your design as needed).

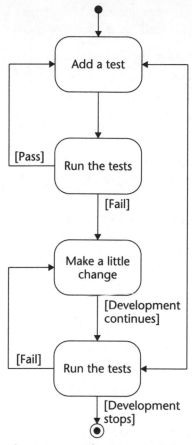

Figure 11.1   The process of TDD.

TDD completely turns traditional development around. Instead of writing functional code first and then your testing code as an afterthought, if you write it at all, you write your test code before your functional code. Furthermore, you do so in very small steps — one test and a small bit of corresponding functional code at a time. A programmer taking a TDD approach refuses to write a new function until there is first a test that is failed because that function isn't present. In fact, such a developer refuses to add even a single line of code until a test exists for it. Once the test is in place, the developer then does the work required to ensure that the test suite is now passed (your new code may break several existing tests as well as the new one). This sounds simple in principle, but when you are first learning to take a TDD approach, it proves to require great discipline because it is easy to "slip" and write functional code without first writing a new test. One of the advantages of pair programming (Williams and Kessler 2002) is that the other member of your pair helps you to stay on track.

An underlying assumption of TDD is that you have a unit-testing framework available to you. Agile software developers often use the xUnit family of open source tools, such as JUnit (www.junit.org) or VBUnit (www.vbunit.org), although commercial tools are also viable options. Without such tools, TDD is virtually impossible. Figure 11.2 presents a UML state chart diagram for how people typically work with the xUnit tools.

NOTE This diagram was suggested to me by Keith Ray whose TDD blog can be found at homepage.mac.com/keithray/blog/index.html.

Kent Beck, who popularized TDD in Extreme Programming (XP) (Beck 2000), defines two simple rules for TDD (Beck 2003). First, you should write new business code only when an automated test has failed. Second, you should eliminate any duplication that you find. Beck explains how these two simple rules generate complex individual and group behavior:

- You design organically, with the running code providing feedback between decisions.

- You write your own tests because you can't wait 20 times per day for someone else to write them for you.

- Your development environment must provide rapid response to small changes (for example, you need a fast compiler and regression test suite).

- Your designs must consist of highly cohesive, loosely coupled components (for example, your design is highly normalized) to make testing easier (this also makes evolution and maintenance of your system easier too).

For developers, the implication is that they need to learn how to write effective unit tests. Beck's experience is that good unit tests:

- Run fast (they have short setups, run times, and breakdowns).

- Run in isolation (you should be able to reorder them).

- Use data that makes them easy to read and to understand.

- Use real data (for example, copies of production data) when they need to.

- Represent one step toward your overall goal.

TIP Two really good books have been written recently about TDD. The first one is *Test Driven Development: By Example* by Kent Beck (Beck 2003) and the second is *Test Driven Development: A Practical Guide* by Dave Astels (Astels 2003). A good online resource is Brian Marick's Agile Testing home page, www.testing.com/agile/, which provides a very good collection of links. Another interesting read is Jeff Langr's white paper, "Evolution of Test and Code Via Test-First Design," which is posted at www.objectmentor.com/resources/articles/tfd.pdf.

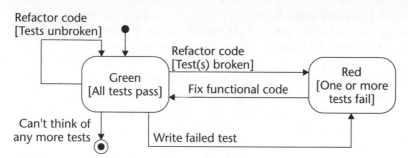

Figure 11.2 Testing via the xUnit framework.

TDD and Traditional Testing

TDD is primarily a programming technique with the side effect of ensuring that your source code is thoroughly unit tested. However, there is more to testing than this. You'll still need to consider traditional testing techniques such as functional testing, user-acceptance testing, system-integration testing, and so on. Much of this testing can also be done early in your project if you choose to do so (and you should). In fact, in XP the acceptance tests for a user story are specified by the project stakeholder(s) either before or in parallel to the code being written, giving stakeholders the confidence that the system does in fact meet their requirements.

With traditional testing a successful test finds one or more defects. It is the same with TDD; when a test fails, you have made progress because you now know that you need to resolve the problem. More importantly, you have a clear measure of success when the test no longer fails. TDD increases your confidence that your system actually meets the requirements defined for it, that your system actually works, and therefore that you can proceed with confidence.

As with traditional testing, the greater the risk profile of the system the more thorough your tests need to be. With both traditional testing and TDD you aren't striving for perfection; instead, you are testing to the importance of the system. To paraphrase Agile Modeling (AM), you should "test with a purpose" and know why you are testing something and to what level it needs to be tested. An interesting side effect of TDD is that you achieve 100 percent coverage test — every single line of code is tested — something that traditional testing doesn't guarantee (although it does recommend it). In general I think it's fairly safe to say that TDD results in significantly better code testing than do traditional techniques.

TDD and Documentation

Like it or not, most programmers don't read the written documentation for a system; instead, they prefer to work with the code. And there's nothing wrong with this. When trying to understand a class or operation, most programmers will first look for sample code that already invokes it. Well-written unit tests do exactly this — they provide a working specification of your functional code — and as a result unit tests effectively become a significant portion of your technical documentation. The implication is that the expectations of the prodocumentation crowd need to reflect this reality.

Similarly, acceptance tests can form an important part of your requirements documentation. This makes a lot of sense when you stop and think about it. Your acceptance tests define exactly what your stakeholders expect of your system; therefore, they specify your critical requirements.

Are tests sufficient documentation? Very likely not, but they do form an important part of it. For example, you are likely to find that you still need user, system overview, operations, and support documentation. You may even find that you require summary documentation providing an overview of the business process that your system supports. When you approach documentation with an open mind, I suspect that you will find that these two types of tests cover the majority of your documentation needs for developers and business stakeholders.

Test-Driven Database Development

At the time of this writing an important question being asked within the agile community is "can TDD work for data-oriented development?" When you look at the process depicted in Figure 19.1, it is important to note that none of the steps specify object-oriented programming languages, such as Java or C#, even though those are the environments TDD is typically used in. Why couldn't you write a test before making a change to your database schema? Why couldn't you make the change, run the tests, and refactor your schema as required? It seems to me that you only need to choose to work this way.

My guess is that in the near term database TDD won't work as smoothly as application TDD. The first challenge is tool support. Although unit-testing tools, such as DBUnit (www.dbunit.org), are now available they are still an emerging technology at the time of this writing. Some DBAs are improving the quality of the testing they do, but I haven't yet seen anyone take a TDD approach to database development. One challenge is that unit-testing tools are still not well accepted within the data community, although that is changing, so my expectation is that over the next few years database TDD will grow. Second, the concept of evolutionary development is new to many data professionals and as a result the motivation to take a TDD approach has yet to take hold. This issue affects the nature of the tools available to data professionals — because a serial mindset still dominates within the traditional data community, most tools do not support evolutionary development. My hope is that tool vendors will catch on to this shift in paradigm, but my expectation is that we'll need to develop open source tools instead. Third, my experience is that most people who do data-oriented work seem to prefer a model-driven, and not a test-driven approach. One cause of this is likely because a test-driven approach hasn't been widely considered until now, another reason might be that many data professionals are likely visual thinkers and therefore prefer a modeling-driven approach.

TDD and Agile Model-Driven Development (AMDD)

How does TDD compare with Model-Driven Development (MDD), or more to the point Agile Model-Driven Development (AMDD) — discussed in Chapter 10? I believe:

- TDD shortens the programming feedback loop, whereas AMDD shortens the modeling feedback loop.

- TDD provides detailed specification (tests), whereas AMDD can provide traditional specifications (data models).

- TDD promotes the development of high-quality code, whereas AMDD promotes high-quality communication with your stakeholders and other developers.

- TDD provides concrete evidence that your software works, whereas AMDD supports your team, including stakeholders, in working toward a common understanding.

- TDD "speaks" to programmers, whereas AMDD "speaks" to data professionals.

- TDD provides very finely grained concrete feedback on the order of minutes, whereas AMDD enables verbal feedback on the order minutes (concrete feedback requires developers to follow the practice *Prove It with Code* and thus becomes dependent on non-AM techniques).

- TDD helps to ensure that your design is clean by focusing on creation of operations that are callable and testable, whereas AMDD provides an opportunity to think through larger design/architectural issues before you code.

- TDD is non-visually-oriented, whereas AMDD is visually oriented.

- Both techniques are new to traditional developers and therefore may be threatening to them.

- Both techniques support evolutionary development.

Which approach should you take? The answer depends on your, and your teammates', cognitive preferences. Some people are primarily "visual thinkers," also called spatial thinkers, and they may prefer to think things through via drawing. Other people are primarily text-oriented, nonvisual, or nonspatial thinkers, who don't work well with drawings, and therefore they may prefer a TDD approach. Of course, most people land somewhere in the middle of these two extremes, and as a result they prefer to use each technique when it makes the most sense. In short, the answer is to use the two techniques together so as to gain the advantages of both.

How do you combine the two approaches? AMDD should be used to create models with your project stakeholders to help explore their requirements and then to explore those requirements sufficiently in architectural and design models (often simple sketches). TDD should be used as a critical part of your build efforts to ensure that you develop clean, working code. The end result is that you will have a high-quality, working system that meets the actual needs of your project stakeholders.

Summary

Test-driven development (TDD) is a development technique where you must first write a test that fails before you write new functional code. TDD is being quickly adopted by agile software developers for development of application source code and may soon be adopted by agile DBAs for database development. TDD should be seen as complementary to Agile Model-Driven Development (AMDD) approaches, and the two can and should be used together. TDD does not replace traditional testing; instead, it defines a proven way to ensure effective unit testing. A side effect of TDD is that the resulting tests are working examples for invoking the code, thereby providing a working specification for the code. My experience is that TDD works incredibly well in practice, and it is something that all agile software developers should consider adopting.

CHAPTER 12

Database Refactoring

That's one small step for [a] man, one giant leap for mankind.
Neil Armstrong

You learned in Chapter 1 that agile methodologies such as Extreme Programming (XP) (Beck 2000) and DSDM (Stapleton 2003) take an iterative and incremental approach to software development. Application developers on XP and DSDM projects typically forsake big design up front (BDUF) approaches in favor of emergent approaches where the design of a system evolves throughout the life of the project. On an agile development project, the final design often isn't known until the application is ready to be released. This is a very different way to work for many experienced IT professionals.

The implication is that the traditional approach of creating a (nearly) complete set of logical and physical data models up front isn't going to work — if it ever did. The main advantage of this approach is that it makes the job of the traditional database administrator (DBA) much easier: the data schema is put into place early and that's what people use. However, there are several disadvantages. First, it requires the designers to get it right early, forcing you to identify most requirements even earlier in the project, and therefore forcing your project team into taking a serial approach to development. Second, it doesn't support change easily. As your project progresses your project stakeholders understanding of what they need will evolve, motivating them to evolve their requirements. The business environment will also change during your project, once again motivating your stakeholders to evolve their requirements. In short, the traditional way of working simply doesn't work well in an agile environment. If agile DBAs are going to work on and support project teams that are following agile methodologies, they need to find techniques that support working iteratively and incrementally. My experience is that one critical technique is what I call database refactoring.

This chapter covers:

- Refactoring
- Database refactoring
- Why database refactoring is hard
- How to refactor your database
- Common database refactoring smells
- Adopting database refactoring within your organization
- Database refactoring best practices

Refactoring

Martin Fowler (1999) describes a programming technique called *refactoring*, a disciplined way to restructure code. The basic idea is that you make small changes to your code to improve your design, making it easier to understand and to modify. Refactoring enables you to evolve your code slowly over time, to take an iterative and incremental approach to programming.

A critical aspect of refactoring is that it retains the behavioral semantics of your code, at least from a black box point of view. For example, there is a very simple refactoring called *Rename Method*, perhaps from getPersons() to getPeople(). Although this change looks easy on the surface, you need to do more than just make this single change; you must also change every single invocation of this operation throughout all of your application code to invoke the new name. Once you've made these changes, you can say you've truly refactored your code because it still works as before.

It is important to understand that you do not add functionality when you are refactoring. When you refactor, you improve existing code; when you add functionality, you are adding new code. Yes, you may need to refactor your existing code before you can add new functionality. Yes, you may discover later on that you need to refactor the new code that you just added. The point to be made is that refactoring and adding new functionality are two different but complementary tasks.

Refactoring can be dangerous. Even though you're making a small change to your code, you still run the risk of introducing a defect. For example, when you are renaming getPersons() to getPeople(), it wouldn't be sufficient for you to simply read all of your Java class files into a text editor and do a global search and replace on "getPersons." What would happen if another of your Java classes also implemented an operation called getPersons(), an operation that was also invoked within your code, that you didn't want to rename? What would happen if your code was invoking getPersons() implemented by a class within a third-party library that you don't have the source code for? Even worse, what if that very same third-party class also implemented getPeople()? Suddenly, you would have introduced some very subtle bugs into your application without knowing it.

Clearly, you need to be very systematic in the way that you refactor and use tools and techniques that support this technique. Most modern integrated development environments (IDEs) now support code refactoring to some extent, which is a good start. To make refactoring work in practice, however, you also need an up-to-date regression-testing suite that you can run against your code to validate that it still works. A typical approach is to refactor your code, compile it, and run your regression tests.

TIP The book *Refactoring: Improving the Design of Existing Code* by Martin Fowler (1999) is your best starting point when it comes to refactoring. The site www.refactoring.com includes links to new writings and www.agilealliance.org includes some links to good refactoring papers as well.

Database Refactoring

In the February 2002 issue of *Software Development* (www.sdmagazine.com), I described a technique that I called data refactoring (Ambler 2002d). This article described my preliminary experiences at something that should more appropriately have been called database refactoring in hindsight — hence the new name. From this point forward I'll use the term refactoring to refer to traditional refactoring as described by Fowler to distinguish it from database refactoring.

Let's start with some definitions. A *database refactoring* is a simple change to a database schema that improves its design while retaining both its behavioral and informational semantics. For the sake of this discussion a database schema includes both structural aspects, such as table and view definitions, and functional aspects such as stored procedures and triggers. An interesting thing to note is that a database refactoring is conceptually more difficult than a code refactoring; code refactorings only need to maintain behavioral semantics, while database refactorings also must maintain informational semantics.

Database refactoring, the process, is the act of making the simple change to your database schema. One way to look at database refactoring is that it is a way to normalize your physical database schema after the fact.

There is a database refactoring (the Appendix presents a catalog of database refactorings) named *Split Column*, where you replace a single table column with two or more other columns. For example, you are working on the *Person* table in your database and discover that the *FirstDate* column is being used for two distinct purposes — when the person is a customer this column stores their birth date, and when the person is an employee it stores their hire date. Your application now needs to support people who can be both a customer and an employee, so you've got a problem. Before you can implement this new requirement, you need to fix your database schema by replacing the *FirstDate* column with *BirthDate* and *HireDate* columns. To maintain the behavioral semantics of your database schema, you need to update all source code that accesses the *FirstDate* column to now work with the two new columns. To maintain the informational semantics, you will need to write a migration script that loops through the table, determines the type, then copies the existing date into the appropriate column. Although this sounds easy, and sometimes it is, my experience is that database refactoring is incredibly difficult in practice.

Preserving Semantics

Informational semantics refers to the meaning of the information within the database from the point of view of the users of that information. To preserve the informational semantics implies that when you change the values of the data stored in a column, the clients for that information shouldn't be affected by the improvement. Similarly with respect to behavioral semantics, the goal is to keep the black box functionality the same — any source code that works with the changed aspects of your database schema must be reworked to accomplish the same functionality as before.

For example, assume that you have a *FullName* column with values such as "John Smith" and "Jones, Sally" and decide to apply *Introduce Common Format* and reformat it so that all names are stored as "Jones, Sally." You're still storing the name as a string, the same data is there, and one of the original formats is still being used, although one of the formats is no longer supported. Any application source code that cannot process the new standardized format would need to be reworked to do so. In the strict sense of the term, the semantics have in fact changed (you're no longer supporting the older data format) but from a business point of view they haven't changed — you're still successfully storing the full name of a person. In my mind, semantics boils down to your level of abstraction, and from the point of view of the users of your application(s), everything still seems to work as before. Therefore, the informational and behavioral semantics pertaining to the *FullName* column have been preserved.

What Database Refactorings Aren't

A small transformation to your schema to extend it, such as the addition of a new column or table, is not a database refactoring because the change extends your design. A large number of small changes simultaneously applied to your database schema, such as the renaming of 10 columns, would not be considered a database refactoring because this isn't a single, small change. Database refactorings are small changes to your database schema that improve its design while preserving the behavioral and informational semantics. That's it. I have no doubt that you can make those changes to your schema, and you may even follow a similar process, but they're not database refactorings.

> **NOTE** The point to take home is that a database refactoring is a simple change to a database schema that improves its design while retaining both its behavioral and informational semantics. Database refactorings do not add new features to a database.

Categories of Database Refactorings

To date, I have identified five categories of database refactorings. There are two major categories, data quality and structural, as well as three subcategories of structural refactorings. These categories are:

Data quality.   These are database refactorings that focus on improving the quality of the data within a database. Examples include *Introduce Column Constraint* and *Replace Type Code with Booleans*.

Structural.   As the name implies, these types of database refactorings change your database schema. Examples include *Rename Column* and *Separate Read-Only Data*. A database refactoring is considered "just" a structural refactoring when it doesn't fall into one of the following subcategories (architectural, performance, or referential integrity).

Architectural.   This is a kind of structural database refactoring whereby one type of database item (for example, a column or table) is refactored into another type (for example, a stored procedure or view). Examples include *Encapsulate Calculation with a Method* and *Encapsulate Table with a View*.

Performance.   This is a kind of structural database refactoring whereby the motivation behind the refactoring is to improve your database performance (performance tuning is described in detail in Chapter 15). Examples include *Introduce Calculated Data Column* and *Introduce Alternate Index*.

Referential integrity.   This is a kind of structural database refactoring where the motivation behind the refactoring is to ensure referential integrity (which is described in detail in Chapter 19). Examples include *Introduce Cascading Delete* and *Introduce Trigger(s) for Calculated Column*.

Why Database Refactoring Is Hard

Database refactoring is a difficult process because of coupling. Coupling is a measure of the degree of dependence between two items — the more highly coupled two things are, the greater the chance that a change in one will require a change in another. Coupling is the "root of all evil" when it comes to database refactoring; the more things that your database schema is coupled to, the harder it is to refactor. In Chapter 13 you'll learn that relational database schemas are potentially coupled to a wide variety of things:

- Your application source code
- Other application source code
- Data load source code

- Data extract source code
- Persistence frameworks/layers
- Your database schema
- Data migration scripts
- Test code
- Documentation

As you can see, coupling is a serious problem when it comes to database refactoring. To make matters worse, the concept of coupling is virtually ignored within database theory circles. Although most database theory books will cover data normalization in excruciating detail (in Chapter 4 I argued that normalization is the data community's way of addressing cohesion), there is often very little coverage of ways to reduce coupling. My experience is that coupling becomes a serious issue only when you start to consider behavioral issues (for example, code), something that traditional database theory chooses not to address.

Figure 12.1 depicts the best-case scenario for database refactoring — when it is only your application code that is coupled to your database schema. This situation is traditionally referred to as a *stovepipe*. These situations do exist and are often referred to as standalone applications, stovepipe systems, or greenfield projects. Count yourself lucky if this is your situation because it is very rare in practice. Figure 12.2 depicts the worst-case scenario for database refactoring efforts, where a wide variety of software systems are coupled to your database schema, a situation that is quite common with existing production databases. It is quite common to find that in addition to the application that your team is currently working on that other applications, some of which you know about and some of which you don't, are also coupled to your database. Perhaps an online system reads from and writes to your database. Perhaps a manager has written a spreadsheet, unbeknownst to you, that reads data from your database that she uses to summarize information critical to her job. These applications will potentially need to be refactored to reflect the database refactorings that you perform.

NOTE The point to take home here is that the greater the coupling of your database to external items, even within the database itself, the harder it is to refactor your database schema.

For the sake of simplicity, throughout the rest of this chapter the term "application" will refer to all external systems, databases, applications, programs, and test suites that are coupled to your database.

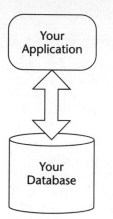

Figure 12.1 The best-case scenario.

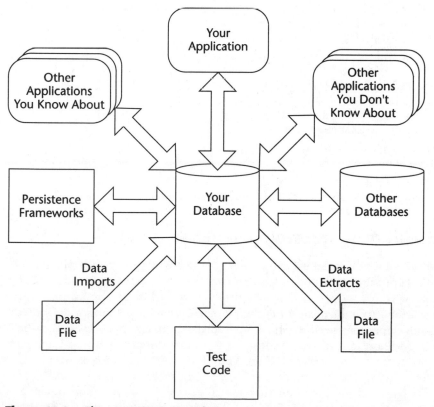

Figure 12.2 The worst-case scenario.

How to Refactor Your Database

Before I describe the steps for refactoring a database I need to address a critical issue — Does the simple situation depicted in Figure 12.1 imply that you'll do different things than the highly coupled one of Figure 12.2? Yes and no. The fundamental process itself remains the same although the difficulty of implementing individual database refactorings increases dramatically as the amount of coupling that your database is involved with increases. I have personally only attempted database refactoring in relatively simple situations in which the database was coupled at most to a handful of applications. I have yet to attempt database refactoring in situations where the legacy database was coupled to tens or hundreds of applications for the simple reason that I have yet to work in an organization with the technical and cultural environment required to support this technique. That's not to say that it's impossible, my belief is that you could build an organization from the ground up that could easily support database refactoring within a complex environment. I also believe, as I describe later in this chapter, that it is possible to evolve your environment over time to support database refactoring regardless of how high the coupling is, although I'm the first to admit that this evolution would be very difficult.

This section is written under the assumption that your technical and cultural environments are organized to support database refactoring. Although this sounds like a big assumption, and it is, I will describe what you need to do to get to the point where these environments are in fact in place. Anything less would be inappropriate.

I like to think of database refactoring as a three-step process:

1. Start in your development sandbox.

2. Implement the code in your integration sandbox(es).

3. Install the code in production.

The following sections discuss each of these steps in detail.

Step 1: Start in Your Development Sandbox

Your development sandbox is the technical environment where your software, including both your application code and database schema, is developed and unit tested. The need to refactor your database schema is typically identified by an application developer who is trying to implement a new requirement or who is fixing a defect. For example, a developer may need to extend an application to accept Canadian mailing addresses in addition to American addresses. The main difference is that Canadian addresses have postal codes such as R2D 2C3 instead of zip codes such as 90210-1234. Unfortunately the *ZipCode* column of the *SurfaceAddress* table is numeric and, therefore, will not currently support Canadian postal codes. The application developer describes the needed change to one of the agile DBA(s) on the project and the database refactoring effort begins.

To perform the database refactoring, the agile DBA and application developer will typically work through some or all of the following steps:

- Verify that a database refactoring is required.
- Choose the most appropriate database refactoring.
- Determine data cleansing needs.
- Write unit tests.
- Deprecate the original schema.
- Implement the change.
- Update the database management scripts.
- Run regression tests.
- Document the refactoring.
- Version control the work.

Verify That a Database Refactoring Is Required

The first thing that the agile DBA does is try to determine if the database refactoring is the right one and if it even needs to occur. Perhaps the required data structure does exist but the application developer is not aware of it. For example, perhaps an *InternationalSurfaceAddress* table exists that does support Canadian postal codes. Perhaps a *PostalCode* column exists in the *SurfaceAddress* table that the developer doesn't know about. Because the agile DBA should have a better knowledge of the project team's database and other corporate databases, and will know whom to contact about issues such as this, he or she will be in a good position to determine the best approach to solving this problem. Unfortunately, in this case the data does not exist elsewhere.

The second thing that the agile DBA does is internally assess the likelihood that the change is actually needed. This is usually a "gut call" based on the agile DBA's previous experience with the application developer. Does the application developer have a good reason for making the schema change? Can he explain the business requirement that the change supports and does the requirement feel right? Has this application developer suggested good changes or has he changed his mind several days later? Depending on this assessment, the agile DBA may suggest that the application developer think the change through some more or may decide to continue working with the application developer but wait for a greater period of time before actually applying the change in the project-integration environment (Step 2) if the agile DBA feels that the change will need to be reversed.

The next thing the agile DBA does is to assess the overall impact of the refactoring. In the simple situation in Figure 12.1, this is fairly straightforward because the agile DBA should have an understanding of how the application is coupled to this part of the database. When this isn't the case the agile DBA needs to work with the application developer to do so. In the complex case in Figure 12.2, the agile DBA will need to have an understanding of the overall technical infrastructure within the organization and how the other applications are coupled to the database. This is knowledge that he or she will need to build up over time by working with the enterprise architects, enterprise administrators, application developers, and even other agile DBAs. When the agile DBA isn't sure of the impact, he or she will either need to decide to make a decision at the time and go with a gut feeling or decide to advise the application developer to wait while they talk to the right people. The goal of this effort is to ensure that you do not attempt a database refactoring that you aren't likely going to be able to do — if you are going to need to update, test, and redeploy 20 other applications to make this refactoring, then it likely isn't viable for you to continue.

TIP Points to take home from this discussion include:

- Make a go/no-go decision early in the database refactoring process — only attempt refactorings that you will be able to implement in production.

- To support agile development, an agile DBA needs to be empowered to determine whether a database refactoring is viable, but be prepared to back out of that decision if enterprise administrators later deny the change.

- Agile DBAs need to support iterative and incremental development efforts by making required database schema changes in a timely manner but must balance this by ensuring that they minimize the number of unnecessary or trivial changes.

Choose the Most Appropriate Database Refactoring

An important skill that agile DBAs require is the understanding that there are typically several choices for implementing new data structures and new logic within a database. For example, in this case, you could decide to add a new column to store the postal code, you could implement a new table for this new type of address, or you could modify the existing column to accept the new type of data. In this instance, assume that you decide to apply the *Replace Column* database refactoring, a structural refactoring, to implement a new column called *PostCode* that can handle both zip codes and postal codes.

Determine Data Cleansing Needs

When you are implementing a structural database refactoring, or one of the subcategories you need to first determine if the data itself is sufficiently clean to be refactored. Depending on the quality of the existing data, you may quickly discover the need to cleanse the source data. This would require one or more separate data quality refactorings before continuing with the structural refactoring. Data-quality problems are quite common with legacy database designs that have been allowed to degrade over time. Chapter 8 explores the issues surrounding legacy databases and describes common data quality problems that you are likely to face.

To identify any relevant data quality problems, you decide to take a quick look at the values contained in the *ZipCode* column. Most of the values in the column are four-and five-digit values, both of which are valid because states such as New Jersey contain zip codes such as 08809 whereas California has 90345. However, you also discover six- and seven-digit zip codes, which are clearly not legal, and a few eight- and nine-digit codes (88091234 would be translated to 08809-1234 and similarly 903451234 to 90345-1234). Needless to say there is a problem with some of the zip codes, which you record so you can deal with it at a future date.

Write Your Unit Tests

Like code refactoring, database refactoring is enabled by the existence of a comprehensive test suite — you know you can safely change your database schema if you can easily validate that the database still works after the change. The XP community suggests that you write your tests before you write your business code, or in this case your database code. If you do not have unit tests for the part of the database that you are currently modifying, then you should write the appropriate tests now. Even if you do have a unit test suite in place, you will discover that many database refactorings, particularly structural ones, will break your tests and force you to update your testing code.

Unfortunately, unit tests do not exist for this portion of the database, a possible explanation for the existence of the data-quality problems. You need to make an architectural decision as to the best place to implement your unit tests. For example, you should clearly verify that zip codes are valid. Does this belong in your application unit tests or in your database unit tests? Checking for a valid value could be seen as a business rule issue, therefore motivating you to write a unit test for your business code, or as a simple data issue and therefore motivate you to write a database unit test. Here's my advice:

- Your primary goal is to ensure that the tests exist.
- You should try to have each test implemented once, either at the application level or at the database level but not both.
- Some unit tests will be at the application level and some at the database level, and that's okay.
- Go for the lowest common denominator — if the database is accessed by several applications then any data-related tests should appear in your database test suite, helping to ensure they're tested once.
- When you have a choice, implement the test at the level where you have the best testing tools (often at the application level). Testing tools are discussed in Chapter 16.

An important part of writing database tests is the creation of test data. You have several strategies for doing so:

Have source test data.   You can simply maintain a database instance or file filled with test data that application teams test against. Developers would need to import data from this instance to populate the databases in their sandbox, and similarly you would need to load data into your project-integration and test/QA sandboxes. These load routines would be considered another application that is coupled to your database along the lines of what is described in Figure 12.2. The implication is that you will need to refactor these load routines, and the source data itself, as you refactor your database.

Test data creation scripts.   This would effectively be a miniapplication that would clear out and then populate your database with known information. This application would need to evolve in step with your database.

Self-contained test cases.   Your individual tests can set up the data that they require. A good strategy is for an individual test to put the database into a known state, to run against that state, and then to back out any changes afterwards so as to leave the database as it was found. This approach requires discipline on the part of anyone writing unit tests but has the advantage that it simplifies your analysis efforts when the test results aren't what you expect.

These approaches to creating test data can be used alone or in combination. A significant advantage of writing creation scripts and self-contained test cases is that it is much more likely that the developers of that code will place it under configuration management (CM) control (see below). Although it is possible to put test data itself under CM control, worst case you generate an export file that you check in; this isn't a common practice and therefore may not occur as frequently as required. Choose an approach that reflects the culture of your organization.

Deprecate the Original Schema (Structural Refactorings Only)

An effective technique that Pramod Sadalage and Peter Schuh (2002) promote is a deprecation period for the original portion of the schema that you're changing. They observe that you can't simply make a structural change to your database schema instantly, that instead you need to work with both the old and the new schema in parallel for a while to provide time for the other application teams to refactor and redeploy their systems. Although this isn't really an issue right now when you're working in the developer's sandbox, it very likely will be once you promote your code into the other environments. This parallel running time is referred to as the *deprecation period*, a period that must reflect the realities of the sandboxes that you're working in. For example, when the database refactoring is being deployed in your development sandbox, the deprecation period may only be a few hours, just enough time to test that the database refactoring works. When it's in your project-integration sandbox, it may be a few days, just enough time for your teammates to update and retest their code. When it's in your test/QA and production sandboxes, the deprecation period may be several months or even several years. Once the deprecation period has expired the original schema, plus any scaffolding code that you needed to write to support the deprecated schema, needs to be removed and retested. Once that is done, your database refactoring is truly complete.

Figure 12.3 shows how this idea would work when we apply the *Replace Column* database refactoring to *ZipCode*. Notice the changes between the original schema and the schema during the deprecation period. *PostCode* has been added as a column, exactly what you would expect. The *ZipCode* column has been marked as deprecated — you know this because a removal date has been assigned to it using a UML named variable. A trigger was also introduced to keep the values contained in the two columns synchronized, the assumption being that new application code will work with *PostCode* but should not be expected to keep *ZipCode* up-to-date, and that older application code that has not been refactored to use the new schema won't know to keep *PostCode* up to date. This trigger is an example of database scaffolding code, simple and common code that is required to keep your database "glued together." This code has been assigned the same removal date as *ZipCode*.

Why don't data quality refactorings such as *Introduce Column Constraint* and *Introduce Common Format* require you to deprecate your original schema? Because they simply improve the data quality by narrowing the acceptable values within a column. As long as these values reflect the existing business rules within the applications that access them, there is no need to run parallel versions of the same data.

> **NOTE** An interesting thing to notice about Figure 12.3 is the addition of the *Country* column to *Address*. Wait a minute, there isn't an *Add Column* database refactoring in the catalog. Have we found a new type of database refactoring? No. Database refactorings are small changes to database schemas that *improve* their design, not simply *change* the design. Adding a new column is a change to the schema but not a design improvement to it. Although this is clearly a very small nuance, I believe that it's an important one.

Implement the Change

The application developer(s) and agile DBA work together to make the changes within the development sandbox. The strategy is to start each refactoring simply; by performing the refactoring within the development sandbox first, you are effectively putting yourself in the situation described in Figure 12.1. As you perform the initial database refactoring, you will also need to refactor your application code to work with the new version of the database schema.

Furthermore, at this point in time, you should perform an initial performance analysis to determine the potential impact of the change — for some refactorings, you may decide to back out at this point because of poor performance. An advantage of this approach is that the agile DBA will gain an initial feel for how the application will be affected by the refactoring, providing insight into potential changes required by other applications.

An important part of implementing the change is ensuring that the changed portion of your database schema follows your corporate database development guidelines. These guidelines should be provided and supported by your enterprise administration group, and at a minimum should address naming and documentation guidelines. In short, always remember to follow Agile Modeling's *Apply Modeling Standards* practice.

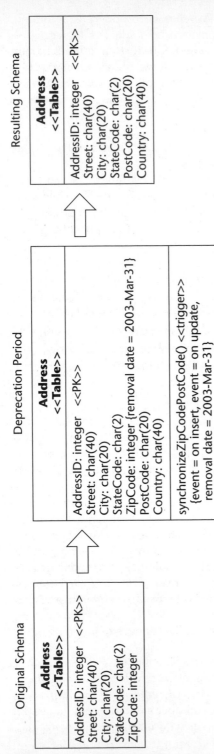

Figure 12.3   Refactoring the Address table.

Update Your Database Management Script(s)

A critical part of implementing a database refactoring is updating your database management scripts. These scripts are used to modify your database schema and should be written so that they can be applied in any of your sandboxes. Let's explore how you use each script:

Database change log.   This script contains the source code implementing all database schema changes in the order that they were applied throughout the course of a project. When you are implementing a database refactoring, you include only the immediate changes in this log. When applying the *Replace Column* database refactoring, we would include the DDL for adding the *PostCode* column and the DDL to implement the trigger(s) to maintain the values between the *PostCode* and *ZipCode* columns during the deprecation period.

Update log.   This log contains the source code for future changes to the database schema that are to be run after the deprecation period for database refactorings. In the example, this would be the source code required to remove the *ZipCode* column and the triggers we introduced.

Data migration log.   This log contains the data manipulation language (DML) to reformat or cleanse the source data throughout the course of your project. In our example, this would include any code to improve the quality of the values in the *ZipCode* column.

Run Your Regression Tests

Once the changes to your application code and database schema have been put in place, you then need to run your regression test suite. This effort should be as automated as you can make it, including the installation or generation of test data, the actual running of the tests themselves, the comparison of the actual test results with the expected results, and the resetting of the database back the way you found it. Because successful tests find problems, you will need to rework things until you get it right. A significant advantage of database refactorings' being small changes is that if your tests do in fact break you've got a pretty good idea where the problem lies — in the application code and database schema that you just changed. The larger your changes are, the more difficult it becomes to track down problems, and therefore the slower and less effective your development efforts are. You'll find that developing in small, incremental steps works incredibly well in practice.

Document the Refactoring

Because your database is a shared resource (at minimum, it is shared within your application development team if not by several application teams), the agile DBA needs to communicate the changes that have been made. At this point in time, your goal is to communicate the changes within your team; later you will need to communicate the suggested changes to all interested parties. This initial communication might be a simple update at your regular team meeting or a simple email (you may want to consider creating an internal mailing list specifically for the purpose of announcing database changes that anyone who is interested can subscribe to). Another aspect of this communication will be updating any relevant documentation. This documentation will be critical later on when you promote your changes into your test/QA sandbox and later into production because other teams need to know how the database schema has evolved. This documentation will likely be required by enterprise administrators so they can update the relevant meta data (better yet, the agile DBA should update this meta data as part of the refactoring effort). Chapter 10 presents an overview of how to write documentation in an agile manner.

If you haven't already done so, you should update the physical data model (PDM) for your database. I personally have a tendency to model the new schema in a PDM tool such as ERWin and then generate the initial DDL that I'll then modify and include in my database change scripts. There are several good modeling tools available that support this type of functionality and I find it easier than manually writing the DDL myself.

Version Control Your Work

A critical skill for agile developers is the habit of putting all of their work under configuration management (CM) control by checking it into a version-control tool. In the case of database refactoring, this includes any DDL that you've created, change scripts, data-migration scripts, test data, test cases, test-data-generation code, documentation, and models. This is in addition to the application-oriented artifacts that you would normally version — treat your database-oriented artifact the exact same way that you'd treat other development artifacts and you should be okay.

Step 2: Implement the Code in Your Integration Sandbox(es)

After several days have passed, you will be ready to implement your database refactoring within your project-integration sandbox. The reason why you need to wait to do so is to give your teammates time to refactor their own code to use the new schema. Note that on an XP team you could very well have been the person reworking the code due to XP's practice of collective ownership. On a Feature-Driven Development (FDD) team, however, because individual feature teams own their own portions of the code these other teams may be required to implement necessary changes themselves (Palmer & Felsing 2002). Each agile development methodology has its own way of doing things.

Teams that have chosen to encapsulate access to their database via the use of a persistence framework (see Chapter 13 for a discussion) will find it easier to react to database schema changes and therefore may find they can tighten up the period between implementing a database refactoring within a development sandbox and in their project-integration sandbox. This is due to the fact that the database schema is represented in meta data; therefore, many database schema changes will only require updates to the meta data and not to the actual source code.

To deploy the code into each sandbox, you will need to both build your application and run your database management scripts. The next step is to rerun your regression tests to ensure that your system still works — if not, you will need to fix it in your development environment, redeploy it, and retest it. Chapter 16 describes how you deploy code from your development sandbox into your project-integration sandbox and from there into your organization's test/QA sandbox. The goal in your project-integration sandbox is to validate that the work of everyone on your team works together, whereas your goal in the test/QA sandbox is to validate that your system works well with the other systems within your organization.

A critical part of deploying database refactorings into your test/QA sandbox (I'm using the plural now because you typically introduce several database factors into this environment at once) is communication. Long before you change your database schema, you need to communicate and negotiate the changes with the owners of all of the other applications that access your database. Your enterprise administrators will be involved in this negotiation; they may even facilitate the effort to ensure that the overall needs of your organization are met. Luckily the process that you followed in your development sandbox has made this aspect of database refactoring easier:

- The agile DBA only allowed database refactorings that can realistically be implemented — if another application team isn't going to be able to rework their code to access the new schema then you can't make the change.

- Even if it's only a brief description of each change, the documentation that the agile DBA wrote is important because it provides an overview of the changes that are about to be deployed.

- The new version physical data model (PDM), which was updated as database refactorings were implemented, serves as a focal point for the negotiations with other teams. AM would consider the PDM to be a "contract model" that your team has with the other application teams, a model that they can count on to be accurate and that they can count on being actively involved in negotiating changes to.

- It is interesting to note that AM's *Formalize Contract Models* practice can aid in your communication efforts because it provides a list of people that you need to communicate with. I discussed in Chapter 10 that a *contract model* defines an interface to an application. For example, the contract model for a relational database might be a physical data model and any supporting documentation, whereas the contract model for an XML data feed into an application might be an XML schema definition. It's called a contract model because it effectively defines a contract between you and any project teams that use the defined interface to your database. If you want to change an aspect of the interface, you must first negotiate that change, or at least at a minimum inform people of the pending change and give them time to rework their applications.

Step 3: Install the Code in Production

Installing the code in production is the hardest part of database refactoring, particularly in the complex situation in Figure 12.2. You will need to:

1. Deploy your new database schema. You will need to run your database change and your data migration logs against the existing production schema to evolve the schema, to cleanse the data, to migrate the data, and to initialize the data within any new tables.

2. Deploy all affected applications. Every application affected by the changes will potentially need to be deployed as well. If you are supporting the original schema as well as the new schema during a defined deprecation period then these applications will only need to be redeployed before the end of the deprecation period, enabling you to gradually install updated versions over time. This reduces the risk to your organization.

3. Test, test, test. You need to test both the database and the applications that access the database. All applications should have been tested in your test/QA sandbox, illustrating the need for a robust regression test suite for every application (more on this later). In production, everything needs to be retested to verify that it is operating correctly.

4. Remove the deprecated schema. Once the deprecation period has ended, the update log needs to be run to remove the remnants of the previous schema and any deprecation scaffolding code that supported it. This step may occur months, or even years, after the original deployment. It is quite common to include this step as part of a future database deployment.

5. Retest, retest, retest. If you remove the deprecated schema outside the scope of another full-fledged database deployment, then you'll need to retest the database and applications to ensure that they work.

Common Database Refactoring Smells

In *Refactoring: Improving the Design of Existing Code* (Fowler 1999), Martin Fowler likes to talk about "code smells," things that he sees in source code that often "smell" of a problem with that code. My experience is that just as there are common smells that reveal the potential need to refactor your code, there are similarly common smells pertaining to potential data refactorings. These smells include:

Multipurpose columns or tables.   Whenever something exhibits low cohesion (in other words, it is used for several purposes), you know you have a potential problem. Examples would be a table that is used to store information about people and corporations, or a column used to store either someone's birth date if that person is a customer or that person's start date as an employee. If something is being used for several purposes, it is very likely that extra code exists to ensure that the data is being used the "right way," and worse yet you are very likely constrained in the functionality that you can now support. For example, how would you store the birth date of an employee?

Redundant data.   You saw in Chapter 4 that redundant data is a serious problem in operational databases. Database refactorings can be applied to normalize your database after it has been released into production.

Large tables (many columns, many rows).   Large tables are indicative of performance problems, low cohesion, and/or redundant data.

"Smart" columns.   A "smart column" is one in which different positions within the data represent different concepts. Examples include U.S. zip codes, in which the first two digits indicate the state, and client numbers in which the first four digits indicate the client's home branch. Smart columns often prove to be bad design decisions in the long term, forcing you to make schema changes at some point.

Fear that if you change it you might break it.   This is a very good indication that you have a serious technical risk on your hands, one that will only get worse the longer you leave it. By putting a framework in place to refactor your database, including both tools and process, you will reduce this risk to your organization.

It is important to understand that these smells don't guarantee that you need to refactor your database, it is just that they are an indication that you need to look into the pertinent portion of your database.

Adopting Database Refactoring within Your Organization

Although the adoption of effective tools (discussed in Chapter 16) is an important part of enabling database refactoring, it is only the tip of the iceberg — database refactoring requires a significant cultural change within your organization. Because database refactoring is an enabling technique of the agile data method many of the cultural issues for adopting database refactoring are the same ones that you face adopting the agile data method in general. These cultural issues include a serial mindset within many data professionals, resistance to change, and political inertia. The following approach should help you to overcome these challenges:

Start simple.   Database refactoring is easiest in greenfield environments where a new application accesses a new database, and the next easiest situation is when a single application accesses a legacy database. Both of these scenarios are typified by Figure 12.1. By starting simple, you provide yourself with an environment in which you can learn the basics, once you understand the basics, you are in a much better position to tackle the situations typified by Figure 12.2.

Accept that iterative and incremental development is the norm.   Modern software development methodologies take an iterative and incremental approach to software development. This includes agile methodologies such as XP and DSDM as well as rigorous methodologies such as the Rational Unified Process

(Kruchten 2000), the Enterprise Unified Process (Ambler 2001b), and the OPEN Process (Graham, Henderson-Sellers, and Younessi 1997). Although serial development is often the preferred approach by many data professionals, unfortunately it doesn't reflect the current way that application developers work. Time to change.

Accept that there is no magic solution to get you out of your existing mess. Many IT environments are a morass of poorly designed, poorly documented, and generally inconsistent systems and databases. Even those systems that started out in good shape have degraded over time due to entropy. Life's tough. Your organization created this problem, and you're going to have to help get out of it. The problem isn't going to get better by itself; in fact, it will only get worse. It is naive to sit back and wait for a magic tool to come along that will fix everything for you; the cold reality is that you're going to have to roll up your sleeves and do a lot of hard work to get yourself out of the mess you're currently in. Database refactoring is very likely your least risky option (Table 12.1 compares and contrasts the strategies available to you).

Adopt a 100 percent regression testing policy. For database refactoring to work, and in general for iteratively and incremental development to work, you need to be effective at regression testing. To be successful at database refactoring, you need to not only be able to regression test the database itself but any application that is coupled to your database. The implication is that you require regression test suites for every single application, something you very likely do not have. Although it is unlikely that you will be allowed to stop all other development efforts for a couple of years to build a comprehensive set of tests, the reality is that you need to start somewhere. The following is a good policy:

1. Write the regression tests for your database.

2. As you need them, develop regression tests for the parts of the applications that you refactor in response to a database refactoring. Although this will slow your efforts down initially, over time this investment will pay off in increased quality and increased ability to respond to new changes.

3. Lobby for a corporate policy that requires developers to create tests for any new code that they develop and for any existing code that they update.

This policy will ensure that you build up the test suite that you need to succeed, although it will likely take several years to do so.

Try it. I have no doubt that you can create a long list of reasons why database refactoring won't work in your environment. So what? Database refactoring is very likely significantly different from what you're doing today. So what? In legacy environments, database refactoring can be very difficult. So what? It takes courage to change, and you may even fail in the attempt. So what? If you don't try, you'll never know if you can become more effective, if you can decrease development time and costs, and if you can slowly improve the quality of your data assets within your organization. Try database refactoring on a pilot project and see what happens. You will likely find that Michael Feathers' (2002) advice regarding legacy refactoring to be valuable.

Database refactoring works in practice, it isn't simply just another academic theory. For the vast majority of organizations, this is a new, "bleeding edge" technique. One of the problems with an innovative technique such as this is that you've never tried it before.

Database Refactoring Best Practices

Fowler (1999) suggests a collection of best practices for code refactoring, practices that I recast below for database refactoring:

Refactor to ease additions to your schema.   You often find that you have to add a new feature to a database, such as a new column or stored procedure. Unfortunately, you may find that the database schema does not easily support that new feature. Start by refactoring your database schema to make it easier to add the feature, and then add the feature.

Ensure that the test suite is in place.   Before you start database refactoring ensure that you have a solid suite of regressions tests for the database and all systems that access that database. These tests can be self-checking.

Take small steps.   Database refactoring changes the schema in small steps; each refactoring should be made one at a time. The advantage is that if you make a mistake it is easy to find the bug because it will likely be in the part of the schema that you just changed.

Program for people.   Any fool can create a schema that the database will understand. Good agile DBAs develop database schemas that human beings can understand.

Don't publish data models prematurely.   The more applications that are coupled to your data schema, the harder it is to change. When you first create a portion of a schema, it will very likely be in flux, evolving at first but then stabilizing over time. Therefore to reduce the number of code refactorings motivated by database refactorings, you should wait until your new schema is reasonably stable before announcing it to the world.

The need to document reflects a need to refactor.   When you find that you need to write supporting documentation to describe a table, column, or stored procedure that is a good indication that you need to refactor that portion of your schema to make it easier to understand. Perhaps a simple renaming can avoid several paragraphs of documentation. The cleaner your design, the less documentation you will require.

Test frequently.   If you have good regression test suites in place for your database and every application coupled to it, it becomes much safer for you to make a database refactoring because when you rerun the tests you'll know right away if you've broken anything.

TIP The point to carry away from this discussion is, to paraphrase Neil Armstrong, that database refactoring is "one small change for a database, one giant leap for software development practices."

Database Refactoring in the Real World

Database refactoring supports an incremental approach to the evolution of your database schema, one of the three fundamental strategies summarized in Table 12.1. Each strategy has its unique strengths and weaknesses. I suspect that many organizations, perhaps because of a serial mindset, have either tried the big-bang release approach or have been too scared to do so and have now given up. It doesn't have to be this way. Yes, it will likely take a significant effort for your organization to put the culture and technologies in place to support database refactoring across your enterprise, but in the long run this is likely far more palatable than your other alternatives.

Table 12.1   Database Evolution Strategies

STRATEGY	STRENGTHS	WEAKNESSES
Give up	Easy to accept in the short term.	• Your database schema won't get better on its own and will very likely get worse. • The magical tool that will come along and solve all of your problems won't. • New application designs will need to be bastardized to conform to your poor database schema. • It will become increasingly difficult to support new functionality.
Big-bang release	Delivers a new database schema.	• High risk approach because you need to rewrite everything and then release it at once, something your organization is not used to attempting. • Very difficult to attempt in parallel with development of new functionality. • Requires sophisticated testing infrastructure and supporting process.

Table 12.1   *(continued)*

STRATEGY	STRENGTHS	WEAKNESSES
Incremental releases	• Delivers a new database schema. • Provides a mechanism to continue to evolve your database schema as needed. • Reduces risk to your organization by defining a continuous change process. • Relatively easy to implement in parallel with development of new functionality.	• Requires sophisticated testing infrastructure and supporting process. • Organizational culture may need to change to support incremental development processes.

Summary

Database refactoring is a work in progress. Although this chapter presents the fundamentals of the process, the Appendix, which lists known database refactorings, is also a work in progress — one that I will likely follow up with a new book within a couple of years. The list isn't comprehensive nor does it provide detailed examples.

Regardless of your strategy, database evolution is difficult, something that is particularly true when your database is highly coupled to other things. Database refactoring is not a silver bullet that's going to magically solve all of your database problems. This chapter described how to successfully approach database refactoring within a simple, stovepipe environment.

CHAPTER 13

Database Encapsulation
Strategies

Coupling is your greatest enemy. Encapsulation is your greatest ally.

Encapsulation is a software-design issue that deals with how functionality is compartmentalized within a system. The main concept behind encapsulation is that you should not have to know how something is implemented to be able to use it. Some people say that encapsulation is the act of painting the box black — you are defining how something is going to be done, but you are not telling the rest of the world how you're going to do it. For example, consider your bank. Do they keep track of your account information on a mainframe, a mini, or a PC? What database do they use? What operating system? The answer is that it doesn't matter to you; the bank has encapsulated the way in which they perform account services. You just walk up to a teller and perform whatever transactions you wish.

The implication of encapsulation in terms of software development is that you can build the separate components of a given application in any way you want and then later change the implementation without affecting other system components (as long as the interface to that component did not change).

This chapter explores:

- Database encapsulation layers
- The role of the agile DBA
- Encapsulation layer architectures
- Encapsulation layer implementation strategies
- Marshaling and data validation
- Error handling

Database Encapsulation Layers

A *database encapsulation layer* hides the implementation details of your database(s), including their physical schemas, from your business code. In effect, it provides your business objects with persistence services — the ability to read data from, write data to, and delete data from data sources — without the business objects having to know anything about the database itself. Ideally, your business objects should know nothing about how they are stored; it just happens.

Database encapsulation layers aren't magic, and they aren't academic theories; database encapsulation layers are commonly used in both simple and complex applications. Database encapsulation layers are important for every agile software developer to be aware of and prepared to use.

An effective database encapsulation layer will provide several benefits:

- Reduces the coupling between your object schema and your data schema, thereby increasing your ability to evolve either one and thus better support an emergent/evolutionary approach to design. Note that your business code will still be coupled to the database-encapsulation layer. You can't completely remove the coupling, but you can dramatically reduce it.

- Implements all data-related code in one place, including the data bindings that implement the mappings between your object and data schemas, making it easier to support any database schema changes that occur or to support performance-related changes.

- Simplifies the job of application programmers. With a database-encapsulation layer in place, the application programmers only have to deal with program source code (for example, Java) and not program source code plus SQL code.

- Enables application programmers to focus on the business problem and agile DBA(s) to focus on the database. Both groups still need to work together of course, but each can focus in on its own jobs better.

- Gives you a common place, in addition to the database itself, to implement data-oriented business rules.

- Takes advantage of specific database and features, increasing application performance.

There are potentially several disadvantages of database-encapsulation layers:

- They require some kind of investment, whether that investment be money or time and effort. You either need to build, buy, or download a data-encapsulation layer.

- They often require reasonably clean mappings. A data encapsulation layer can flounder when the mappings between your object and data schemas (Chapter 14) become complex.

- They can provide too little control over database access. Some data-encapsulation strategies, such as Enterprise JavaBeans' container-managed persistence (CMP) approach (Roman, Ambler, and Jewell 2002), overencapsulate database access. For example, with CMP you have no control over when an object is saved — it's typically done automatically whenever the values of an object's attributes change even though you may want to wait before updating.

The Role of the Agile DBA

Figure 13.1 depicts the role of an agile DBA with regard to encapsulation layers. There are three main activities that an agile DBA will be involved with:

Determine encapsulation strategy. You will work with enterprise architects and application programmers to determine an appropriate encapsulation strategy. This strategy will be based on the current approach within your organization; perhaps there is a database encapsulation layer(s) in place already or at least an existing vision. You may choose to forgo a database-encapsulation strategy at this time, deciding to take a brute-force approach for now (see the section *Brute Force*), trusting that you can revisit this decision at a later date if need be.

Develop an encapsulation layer. You will work with the application programmers to implement your chosen encapsulation strategy. This could be something as simple as installing an existing layer, perhaps a commercial package that your organization has purchased, an open source software (OSS) package that you have downloaded, or a package built by another project team. You may also discover that your project team has decided to build its own solution, an effort that you may choose to be involved with because of your database expertise. You may discover that you need to mentor some application programmers in the use of the database encapsulation layer, and even in the concept of using one.

Implement database access. You will work with the application programmers on an ongoing basis to implement database access within their business objects. Depending on the implementation strategy of your layer (see the following section), this could range from helping them to write SQL code to something as simple as helping them to administer the metadata of a persistence framework.

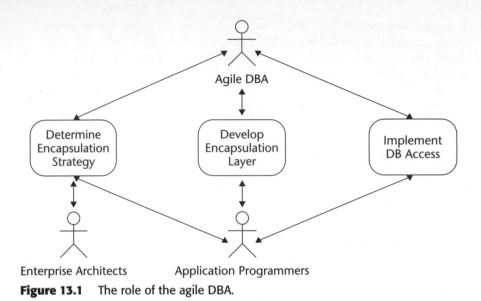

Figure 13.1   The role of the agile DBA.

Encapsulation-Layer Architectures

Figure 13.2 depicts the simplest architecture for encapsulating access to a relational database — a single application working with a single database. In this situation, there is the greatest potential for flexibility, so your team should be able to choose the implementation strategy, such as data access objects or a persistence framework, that best fits your situation. Furthermore, you should be in a position to evolve both your object schema and your database schema as you implement new requirements.

A far more realistic situation to be in is depicted in Figure 13.3, which shows a multiple-application, single-database architecture. This architecture is common in organizations that have a centralized legacy database (see Chapter 8) with which all applications work. Another realistic situation is shown in Figure 13.4, where there are multiple applications working with multiple databases. In this case, you are likely accessing both your database(s), if you have any at all, as well as one or more legacy data sources.

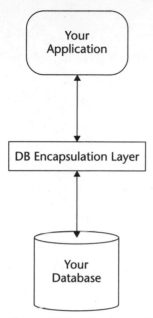

Figure 13.2   Single-application, single-database architecture.

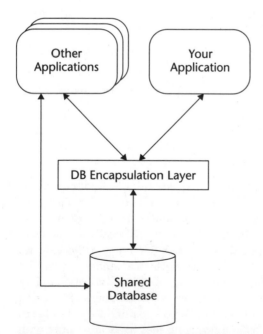

Figure 13.3   Multiapplication, single-database architecture.

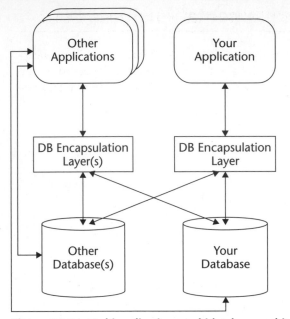

Figure 13.4   Multiapplication, multidatabase architecture.

One interesting observation about both of these diagrams is that some applications may not take advantage of the encapsulation layer(s) and will instead directly access data. There are several reasons that this may be the case:

- Your data encapsulation layer is written in a language that some legacy applications can't easily access.

- You've chosen not to rework some of your legacy applications to use the database-encapsulation layers.

- You want to use technologies, such as a bulk load facility or a reporting framework, that require direct access to the database schema. Note that this may motivate your team to sometimes go around the encapsulation layer.

The point is that some applications will be able to take advantage of your encapsulation layer(s) and some won't. There are still benefits because you are reducing coupling and therefore reducing your development costs and maintenance burden.

Figure 13.4 makes it clear that some applications have an encapsulation layer in place already. If this is the case, you might want to consider reusing the existing approach instead of developing your own. By having a single encapsulation layer that all applications use to access all data sources (where appropriate), you potentially reduce the effort it takes to evolve your database schemas via database refactoring because there is only one encapsulation layer to update. If you've purchased the encapsulation layer, you may be able to reduce overall licensing fees by dealing only with one vendor. The potential disadvantage is that the team responsible for maintaining the encapsulation layer could become a bottleneck if they are unable or unwilling to work in an agile manner.

Encapsulation-Layer Implementation Strategies

Regardless of whether you intend to purchase, build, or download a database-encapsulation layer, it's critical for both agile DBAs and application developers to understand the various implementation strategies. There are four basic strategies that you should consider using, including:

- Brute force
- Data access objects
- Persistence frameworks
- Services

In the following sections, I provide an overview of each strategy, describe how to read a single object from a database using that strategy, and discuss the development implications of taking that approach.

> **NOTE** In the following sections, I describe how to read an object from the database because it often involves the most effort. First, a query must be formulated and submitted to the database. The result set is then converted into an object, an activity called *unmarshaling*. Inserts, updates, and deletes are less interesting because they only require the formulation and submission of a query. Error handling — including the detection of error codes returned from the database, the reporting of problems to users, and the potential logging of the error — will be ignored (for now) for the sake of simplicity. Error handling is discussed at the end of this chapter.

Brute Force (the Encapsulation Strategy That Isn't One)

The brute-force approach isn't a database-encapsulation strategy; it's what you do when you don't have a database-encapsulation layer. However, it is a valid option for database access and therefore I discuss it here along with the "real" encapsulation strategies. Furthermore, the brute-force strategy is by far the most common approach because it is simple and provides programmers with complete control over how their business objects interact with the database. Because of its simplicity this is a very good approach to take at the beginning of a project when your database access requirements are fairly straightforward. As your database access needs become more complex, encapsulation strategies such as data access objects or persistence frameworks are likely to become better options.

The basic strategy behind the brute-force approach is that business objects access data sources directly, typically by submitting SQL or Object Query Language (OQL) code to the database. In Java applications, this is done via the Java Database Connectivity (JDBC) class library and via the Open Database Connectivity (ODBC) API in Microsoft-based applications.

> **NOTE** Microsoft has newer approaches, such as the ActiveX Data Object
> (ADO) and Microsoft Data Access Component (MDAC) libraries, that
> encapsulate and extend ODBC. Other environments, such as COBOL or Ruby,
> have their own native APIs that often take advantage of existing ODBC or JDBC
> database drivers.

Figure 13.5 depicts a UML sequence diagram showing the basic logic for reading a single object from the database. Upon receiving a request to read itself, the business object creates an SQL Select statement (or the equivalent in whatever access language you're using) and submits it to the database. The database processes the statement and returns a result set. The object then marshals the data by removing it from the result set and updating its own attributes with the read-in values.

There is an underlying assumption that the business object already contains sufficient information to identify itself. This information will exist if the object was previously read in from the database, perhaps as the result of a search query. When the object has a surrogate key, one that has no business meaning, the attributes of that key will be maintained as "shadow data" in the object so that you have sufficient information to identify that object. If you are reading the object in for the first time, one possible technique is to create a new instance, assign it sufficient information to uniquely identify it in the database, and then use that data to formulate the query. In the case of a *Customer* object, this might be the customer number or a combination of the name and telephone number.

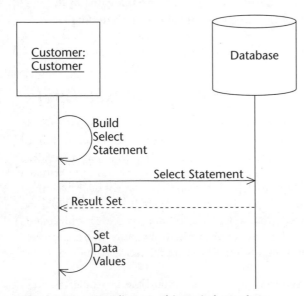

Figure 13.5   Reading an object via brute force.

The brute-force approach can be reasonably straightforward, although time-consuming, for an agile DBA to support. You may have to mentor application programmers in the basics of query languages such as SQL and OQL, database access APIs such as JDBC andODBC, and error handling. Remember, because it's brute force the application programmers are writing all of the database access code. Because you'll be helping with testing and performance tuning of the database access code, you'll need to become intimately familiar with the development environment (likely something that will happen anyway). You'll also want to help develop a standard way to do things — such as having *read()*, *delete()*, and *save()* operations in each business object — and help to set query-language coding standards.

Data Access Objects

Data access objects (DAOs) encapsulate the database access logic required of business objects. The typical approach is for there to be one data access object for each business object, for example the *Customer* class would have a *Customer_Data* class. The *Customer_Data* class implements the SQL/OQL/ . . . code required to access the database, similarly to the brute-force approach. The main advantage of data access objects over the brute-force approach is that your business classes are no longer directly coupled to the database; instead, the data access classes are. It is quite common to simply develop your own data access objects, although you may also choose to follow industry-standard approaches such as Java Data Object (JDO, see www.jdocentral.com) and ActiveX Data Object (ADO, see www.microsoft.com .

> **NOTE** ADO is, arguably, more of an implementation platform on which to build DAOs within the Microsoft environment; it's also arguable that ADO is clearly not as sophisticated as the newer JDO because it does not abstract access to the database as fully.

Figure 13.6 depicts the logic for a *Customer* object to read itself from the database. You can see that the *Customer_Data* has hidden the details of the database access from the business object.

1. The first step is for the business object to pass itself as a parameter to the DAO.

2. The DAO then obtains the value(s) for the primary key within the database; if this information is not known, the DAO needs to obtain sufficient information from the business object to identify it in the database.

3. The DAO then builds the query, invokes it on the database, and marshals the data in the resulting set by updating the business object.

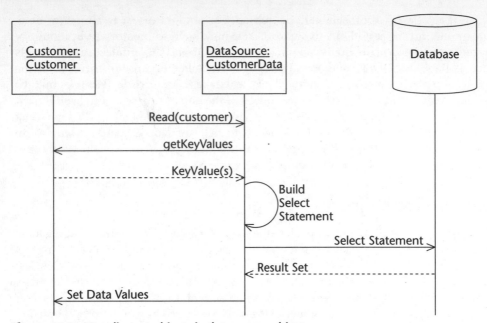

Figure 13.6   Reading an object via data access objects.

DAOs are slightly easier for an agile DBA to support than the brute-force approach because the database access logic is concentrated in one place. The application programmers will still need similar levels of mentoring, and you'll still need to help set coding standards.

Persistence Frameworks

A *persistence framework*, often referred to as a persistence layer, fully encapsulates database access from your business objects. Instead of writing code to implement the logic required to access the database, you instead define meta data that represents the mappings. So, if the *Customer* class maps to the *T_Customer* table, then part of the meta data would represent this mapping. Meta data representing the mappings of all business objects, as well as the associations between them, also needs to exist. Based on this meta data, the persistence framework generates the database access code it requires to persist the business objects. Depending on the framework, several of which are listed in Table 13.1, this code is either generated dynamically at run time or generated statically in the form of data access objects, which are then compiled into the application. The first approach provides greater flexibility, whereas the second provides greater performance.

Persistence frameworks will have a variety of features. Simple ones will support basic create, read, update, delete (CRUD) functionality for objects as well as basic transaction and concurrency control. Advanced features include robust error handling, database connection pooling, caching, XML support, schema and mapping generation capabilities, and support for industry-standard technology such as EJB.

Figure 13.7 depicts a high-level architecture for persistence frameworks. When you buy or download a persistence framework, it should include an administration facility that enables you to maintain the mapping metadata. This facility typically uses the persistence framework itself, when you install the application it will write out the metadata that it requires to describe the mapping between the metadata repository and the administration facility. The mapping meta data repository is typically a relational database, although in less-sophisticated tools this "repository" can be something as simple as an XML document or even a simple text file (when this is the case the "administration facility" is often a text editor). One easy-to-use administration facility is an important tool for an agile DBA who is responsible for maintaining the mapping meta data (more on this in a moment). Luckily, most commercial and OSS frameworks come with a GUI or HTML-based administration facility.

The persistence framework reads the mapping meta data into memory and creates a collection of "map objects" from it. It uses these map objects to create the code required to access the database. These map objects often form something referred to as a *SQL generation engine* within the persistence framework. In the case of dynamic generation, the persistence framework caches the map objects and collaborates with them each time the database is to be accessed (advanced frameworks will cache common portions of SQL code). For static generation of data access objects, the persistence framework only requires the map objects at code-generation time, although it will obviously need the data access objects at application run time.

An important issue with the design of persistence frameworks is whether persistence is *implicit* or *explicit*. With an implicit approach, the framework automatically persists the business objects without their knowledge; that is, they don't need to request to be saved, read, or whatever; it just happens. A perfect example is the Enterprise JavaBean (EJB) concept of persistence containers: to be automatically persisted, an entity bean needs to implement a standard interface (a collection of operations) and be described in the deployment descriptor (an XML document containing meta data).

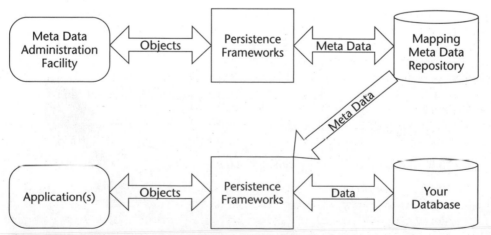

Figure 13.7   Architecture of a persistence framework.

With an explicit approach, which is by far the most common, objects need to indicate (or have something else indicate) when they should be saved. An example of an explicit and dynamic approach is depicted in Figure 13.8.

As you can see from the figure:

1. The customer object tells the persistence framework to read itself.

2. The framework collaborates with its collection of map objects to dynamically generate the SQL statement to be invoked on the database.

The important thing to notice is that the business object only needs to interact with the framework, most frameworks typically have a class called *Database*, *Persistence-Framework*, or *PeristenceBroker* that implements its public interface.

The persistence framework approach makes the job of an agile DBA a little more complex but a lot less onerous. You will be expected to install, if necessary, the persistence framework. You will also need to work with the administration facility to define and maintain the mapping meta data. In the case of explicitly controlled persistence frameworks, application programmers will need mentoring in the use of the framework, often a very simple task.

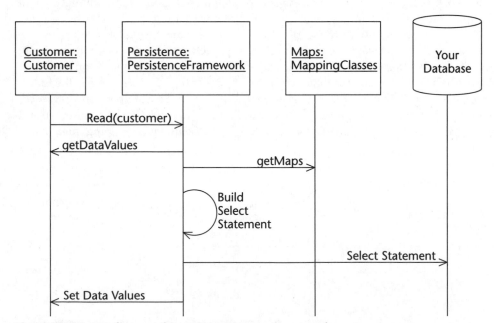

Figure 13.8   Reading an object via persistence frameworks.

Table 13.1 Sample Products

PRODUCT	PLATFORM	DESCRIPTION	URL
Castor	Java	OSS persistence framework with support for XML, JDO, DSML (Directory Service Markup Language), caching, two-phase commit, OQL to SQL mappings, ability to create base mapping, support for EJB containers, and the ability to create an XML schema.	http://castor.exolab.org
CocoBase Enterprise O/R	Java	Commercial persistence framework that creates maps from objects to tables, tables to objects, existing objects with existing tables, existing object models using transparent persistence, and UML/XMI object models. Generates Java code a variety of approaches data objects, EJB CMP/BMP (container-managed persistence/bean-managed persistence) entity beans, EJB session beans, JSPs, and servlets.	www.thoughtinc.com
Deklarit	.NET	Commercial development environment that allows you to describe business objects and rules in a declarative way, with no programming, and it generates the database schema and the ADO.NET strongly typed DataSets and DataAdapters necessary to support them.	www.deklarit.com

(continued)

Table 13.1 *(continued)*

PRODUCT	PLATFORM	DESCRIPTION	URL
Hibernate	Java	OSS persistence framework that generates code dynamically at system startup time. Supports an ODMG 3 interface as well as a custom API.	http://hibernate .bluemars.net
JC Persistent Framework	Visual Basic 6	OSS persistence framework that manages transactions in a transparent manner to most relational databases.	http://sourceforge.net/ projects/jcframework/
Osage Persistence Plus XML	Java	OSS persistence framework that features JDBC-based object-relational mapping that allows experienced Java developers to quickly implement database access in their applications. It generates SQL for retrieving, saving, and deleting objects. Supports object relationships and can automatically generate keys.	http://osage .sourceforge.net
Pragmatier	Visual Basic 6, .NET	Commercial persistence framework/code generator that generates the code for DAO objects with full CRUD + filter/sort capabilities on the MS platforms. Includes development environment that enables you to map data access objects that you create to your existing database, or you can let the framework create the database for you (or a mix thereof). Support for distributed transactions and object caching, XML serialization, and traversable data model.	www.pragmatier.com

Table 13.1 *(continued)*

PRODUCT	PLATFORM	DESCRIPTION	URL
Versant Enjin	Java	Commercial persistence framework that provides transparent persistence for Java objects within the application server and web server tiers. EnJin stores objects transactionally in the middle tier and distributes these objects on demand to local caches in the application and Web servers.	www.versant.com
Webware for Python	Python	OSS suite of software components for developing object-oriented, Web-based applications including an object to relational mapper.	http://webware .sourceforge.net

As you can see in Table 13.1, there are many persistence frameworks available for download or purchase, and a much longer list is maintained at: www.ambysoft.com/ persistenceLayer.html.

This URL also includes a white paper describing the design of a persistence layer. If you discover that a persistence framework does not exist on your platform, or that the ones available do not meet your needs, then you might decide to build your own. If you do decide to build, then you might find the design ideas presented in the afore-mentioned white paper useful. Furthermore, Fowler et al. (Fowler, Rice, Foemmel, Hieatt, Mee, and Stafford 2003) describe several patterns — Active Record, Data Mapper, Identity Map, Inheritance Mappers, Repository, and Unit of Work — that may be useful.

TIP If at all possible, avoid building your own persistence framework. Having built several myself, I highly recommend against building yet another framework. Although I have to admit that it's a great learning experience, it's also a heck of a lot of work.

Services

For the sake of discussion, a service is an operation offered by a computing entity that can be invoked by other computing entities. At the time of this writing, the most popular architectural strategy is Web services (McGovern et al. 2003); however, as you see in the following list, it is only one of several common strategies available to you. Services are typically used to encapsulate access to legacy functionality and data, and there is a clear preference within the industry to build new applications following a Web-services-based architecture to facilitate reuse via system integration.

Common Object Request Broker Architecture (CORBA). CORBA (www.corba.org) was popularized in the early 1990s as the preferred approach for implementing distributed objects on non-Microsoft platforms. Today CORBA is used, for the most part, as a wrapping technology around legacy computing assets (it is even used to wrap access to DCOM applications).

Customer Information Control System (CICS) Transaction. CICS (www-3.ibm.com/software/ts/cics/) was a transaction processor (TP) monitor popularized by IBM in the 1970s. Today, it is still a growing technology platform for mission-critical business applications.

Distributed Component Object Model (DCOM). DCOM (www.microsoft.com/com/tech/DCOM.asp) was popularized in the early 1990s as the preferred approach for implementing distributed components within Microsoft environments. DCOM is a protocol that enables software components to communicate directly over a network in a reliable, secure, and efficient manner. DCOM is still an important part of the Microsoft platform.

Electronic data interchange (EDI). EDI is the standardized exchange of electronic documents between organizations, in an automated manner, directly from a computer application to another. EDI was popularized in the mid-1980s by large manufacturers, and their suppliers, and still forms the basis of many mission-critical applications today. It appears that EDI is slowly being replaced by Web services.

Stored procedures. Stored procedures implement functionality, typically a collection of SQL statements, within a database. Stored procedures were popularized in the mid-1980s and are still a valid implementation technology today.

Web Services. Web services (www.w3.org/2002/ws/) are self-contained business functions, written to strict specifications, which operate over the Internet using XML (see Chapter 22). Common Web-service platforms are Microsoft .NET (www.gotdotnet.com) and Sun ONE (www.sun.com/software/sunone/) technology.

Figure 13.9 depicts how a service could provide access to customer data, as follows:

1. The customer object invokes the read customer service, passing the customer ID to identify which customer to retrieve.

2. The service uses this data to invoke a wrapped legacy application.

3. The legacy application, in turn, reads the data from the database.

4. The customer data is returned to the service.

5. The service creates an XML document and returns it to the object.

6. The object unmarshals the data from the XML document and updates itself.

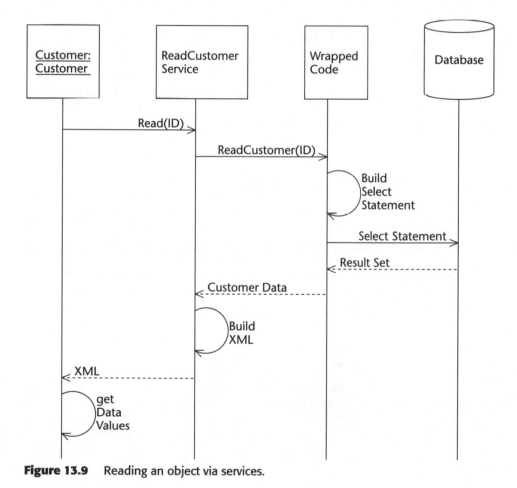

Figure 13.9   Reading an object via services.

NOTE Notice that the service didn't have to access a wrapped legacy application, it could just as easily accessed the database directly or other functionality as required. Also note that the use of XML was simply a design choice, that other ways to transport the information could have been used.

Services will likely require agile DBAs to have an understanding of what services are available. This information should be available from your enterprise administrators and/or enterprise architects, and better yet should be freely available through a reuse repository (such as Flashline's www.flashline.com). For services that encapsulate data access, an agile DBA will likely be expected to work with application developers to write code to invoke that service.

When to Use Each Strategy

In this section, you have seen that there are several common architectural strategies for encapsulating access to a database. As you see in Table 13.2, each one has its advantages and disadvantages, and as a result there are times when one approach is more appropriate than the others. The implication is that both agile DBAs and application programmers need to understand each strategy and be prepared to work with each. One size does not fit all.

Transitioning between Strategies

As your application grows, you often discover that the simpler encapsulation strategies need to be replaced with more sophisticated approaches. How do you ensure that this transition is relatively easy to accomplish? A good start is to follow common strategies such as applying coding standards, writing classes that are highly cohesive and loosely coupled, and applying common architectural and design patterns. Table 13.3 summarizes design strategies that can be used to improve the quality of each type of encapsulation strategy.

Table 13.2 Comparing the Strategies

STRATEGY	ADVANTAGES	DISADVANTAGES	WHEN TO USE
Brute force	• Very simple approach. • Can develop code very quickly. • Can support access to very bad data designs (although performance may suffer).	• Directly couples your object schema to your data schema. • Application developers need to learn database access language (for example, SQL). • Database refactoring (Chapter 12) impeded due to high coupling. • Difficult to reuse database access code.	• At beginning of a project when your persistence approach is still in flux. • For small applications (less than 20 business classes) and/or prototypes.
Data access objects	• Database access code encapsulated into its own set of classes. • Business classes no longer coupled to database. • Database refactoring easier due to lowered coupling. • Can support access to very bad data designs (although performance may suffer). • Possible to reuse data access objects.	• Object schema still coupled to your data schema, via the data access objects. • Application developers need to learn SQL. • Often platform-specific.	• Medium-sized application (20 to 100 business classes).

(continued)

Table 13.2 *(continued)*

STRATEGY	ADVANTAGES	DISADVANTAGES	WHEN TO USE
Persistence framework	• Application programmers do not need to know the data schema. • Application programmers don't even need to know where the data is stored. • Frameworks reflect performance expertise of its builders (unless you're an expert, your "brute-force" code likely isn't as good as the framework's generated code). • Administration facility can ease database refactoring because it simplifies impact analysis by tracing columns to object attributes. • Administration facility aids performance tuning because it makes it easy to change mappings. • Possible to reuse framework and mapping meta data between applications.	• Perceived performance impact on your applications (if the framework is poorly built). • Requires reasonably clean data designs because the framework may not support the overly complex mappings. • Often platform-specific.	• Medium-sized and large applications. • When it is common practice within your organization to use a persistence framework.
Services	• Potential to create platform independent services. • Web services quickly becoming an industry standard. • Supports reuse between applications.	• Web services standards and tools still evolving. • Performance becomes a problem when combining several services in serial or simply when services are invoked across a network.	• Medium to large sized applications. • Whenever an appropriate service already exists that you can reuse.

Table 13.3 Design Approaches for Each Encapsulation Strategy

ENCAPSULATION STRATEGY	COMMON TRANSITIONS	DESIGN STRATEGIES
Brute Force	• To Data Access Objects • To Persistence Framework • To Services	• Implement a common persistence interface across business objects. For example, each object implements retrieve(), save(), and delete() operations. • Refactor common database access functionality, such as session pooling and marshaling code, into common classes. • Copy and paste database access code examples between classes to help implement a common approach.
Data Access Objects (DAOs)	• To Persistence Framework • To Services	• Implement a common interface across all data access objects. • Use existing, standard approaches such as JDO and ADO. • Each DAO should persist a single business class. • Refactor common database access functionality, such as session pooling and marshaling code, into common classes. • Copy and paste database access code examples between DAOs to help implement a common approach.
Persistence Framework	• To Services	• Include the ability to access a wide variety of data sources, including relational databases, XML data sources, and nonrelational databases. • Implement wrappers to legacy data sources (see Chapter 8) to make them appear similar. • Support both synchronous and asynchronous invocation. • Support ability to manage complex transactions (discussed in Chapter 15).
Services	• To Persistence Framework	• Implement a common approach to passing data to, and receiving responses from, each service. • Implement database access code in a common manner, ideally using one of the other encapsulation strategies.

Marshaling and Data Validation

Marshaling is the conversion of an object into a data structure such as an XML document or a data set. *Unmarshaling* is the corresponding conversion of data to objects. However, it is common to refer to both types of conversion simply as *marshaling*.

Because unmarshaling occurs at boundary points within your system, you need to consider validating the data. You want to ensure that your data is in a valid state, that individual values conform to business rules (for example, someone's age is less than 150) and to referential integrity rules (which I discuss in Chapter 19). In Chapter 8, I described many common data-quality problems that you may want to try to detect. There are several data-validation issues that you need to consider:

Do you validate the data at all?   You don't always need to validate data. Perhaps you know that the data comes from a clean source. Perhaps there are no applicable validation rules against which to check the data. Perhaps the performance characteristics of your application simply don't allow for validation to occur.

Where is validation performed?   Do your business objects validate the data? Does your database validate the data, perhaps through constraints, triggers, and stored procedures? If you're working with XML documents, do you use your parser to check its document type definition (DTD) or schema definition? A specialized data validation facility? A combination thereof?

Do you validate data automatically?   XML parsers, as well as some persistence frameworks, offer the ability to automatically validate data as it is being unmarshaled. The advantage is that this is very easy and convenient for developers; the problem is that performance is affected because you're always validating the data.

What do you do when you find a problem?   You will need to define an effective error-handling strategy (see the next section).

Error Handling

An important feature of a database-encapsulation layer is its ability to handle database errors appropriately. Whenever the encapsulation layer interacts with a data source there is a potential for an error to occur. Common types of database-oriented errors include:

- The database is not available.
- The network is not available.
- The request you made to the database is not correct (for example, it is improperly formulated SQL code, or you're trying to invoke a stored procedure that doesn't exist).

- You are trying to work with data that doesn't exist (for example, trying to update a deleted record).

- You are trying to insert existing data.

- The data you want to access is locked (for example, you want to update a record that another user has write-locked).

The list described above is nowhere near complete, you only have to look at the list of error codes in the manuals for your database to see this, but it is a good start. The point is that errors happen, and you need to be prepared to act on them. A good encapsulation layer should be able to:

- Detect database-oriented errors and continue processing.

- Log the details pertaining to the error (error information returned by the database, date and time of the error, user ID, application/service affected, and so on). This should be at the option of the invoking application.

- Report the error to the invoking application in an intelligible manner, converting DB vendor's error code 1701 to a more generic "Cannot Update Deleted Record" error message.

You will want a common approach to these error messages, something that your enterprise administrators may even set corporate standards for.

Summary

By encapsulating access to your database(s), you improve your overall architecture through the reduction of coupling. This makes your system easy to develop and to maintain, supporting agile development techniques such as evolutionary design through database refactoring. An effective database-encapsulation layer becomes an enabler for agile database development.

You also discovered that there are several fundamental strategies for implementing access to a database, including brute-force, data access objects, persistence frameworks, and services. Although the brute-force approach really isn't a database encapsulation strategy, it is still an architectural consideration for many project teams. Regardless of your database encapsulation strategy, you will still need to set marshaling and error-handling strategies for your application.

CHAPTER 14

Mapping Objects to Relational Databases

*You are playing a losing game if you need to "use a stick"
to motivate someone to do things your way.*

Most modern business application development projects use object technology, such as Java or C#, to build the application software and relational databases to store the data. This isn't to say that you don't have other options; there are many applications built with procedural languages such as COBOL, and many systems will use object databases or XML databases to store data. However, because object and relational technologies are by far the norm that's what I assume you're working with in this chapter. If you're working with different storage technologies then many of the concepts are still applicable, albeit with modification (Chapter 22 provides an overview of mapping issues pertaining to objects and XML).

In Chapter 7, I discussed the impedance mismatch between object and relational technology, both of which are technologies that project teams commonly use to build software-based systems. It is quite easy to overcome this impedance mismatch; the secret to doing so is twofold: you need to understand the process of mapping objects to relational databases, and you need to understand how to implement those mappings. In this chapter, the term *mapping* will be used to refer to how objects and their relationships are mapped to the tables, and the relationships between them in a database. As you'll soon find out, it isn't quite as straightforward as it sounds — although it isn't too bad either.

This chapter focuses on mapping and touches on implementation issues. Specific implementation details are addressed in following chapters. The topics covered in this chapter are:

- The role of the agile DBA
- Basic mapping concepts

- Mapping inheritance structures
- Mapping associations
- Mapping class-scope properties
- The implementation impact on your objects
- Implications for the Model Driven Architecture (MDA)
- Patternizing the mappings

The Role of the Agile DBA

Figure 14.1 shows the role that an agile DBA plays when it comes to mapping objects to relational databases. There are three primary activities that we are interested in:

Mapping.   The basic goal is to determine an effective strategy for persisting object data. This includes saving both the data attributes of individual objects and the relationships between objects, while respecting the inheritance structures between classes.

Implementing mappings.   Once a mapping is defined, you need to implement it within your system, something often referred to as performing data bindings. Chapter 13 presents several basic strategies for doing this, including embedding Structure Query Language (SQL) statements in your objects (brute force), using data access objects, using persistence frameworks, and using services.

Performance tuning.   Because mappings define how your objects interact with the database, they become a significant factor in the performance tuning of your system. Agile DBAs recognize this and work closely with application developers to tune all three aspects of a system — objects, mappings, and the database — involved with database access. Database tuning is only one aspect of data access performance tuning (Chapter 15 discusses performance tuning in detail).

As you can see from Figure 14.1, agile DBAs and application developers work together on all three of these activities; although the agile DBA may be responsible for ensuring that the mappings are effective, he or she is not solely responsible for the actual effort. Working with others, not working alone, is the secret to success in agile software development.

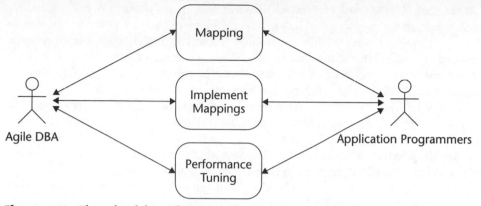

Figure 14.1   The role of the agile DBA in mapping.

Basic Mapping Concepts

When you are learning how to map objects to relational databases, the place to start is with the data attributes of a class. An attribute will map to zero or more columns in a relational database. Remember, not all attributes are persistent; some are used for temporary calculations. For example, a *Student* object may have an *averageMark* attribute that is needed within your application but isn't saved to the database because it is calculated by the application. Because some attributes of an object are objects in their own right — for example, a *Customer* object likely has an *Address* object as an attribute — this really reflects an association between the two classes that would likely need to be mapped, and the attributes of the *Address* class itself will need to be mapped. The important thing is that this is a recursive definition: At some point, the attribute will be mapped to zero or more columns.

First off, let's get some basic mapping terminology out of the way:

Mapping.   (v) The act of determining how objects and their relationships are persisted in permanent data storage, in this case relational databases. (n) The definition of how an object's property or a relationship is persisted in permanent storage.

Property.   A data attribute, either implemented as a physical attribute, such as the string *firstName*, or implemented as a virtual attribute via an operation, such as *getTotal()*, which returns the total of an order.

Property mapping.   A mapping that describes how to persist an object's property.

Relationship mapping.   A mapping that describes how to persist a relationship (association, aggregation, or composition) between two or more objects.

It may help you to think that classes map to tables; in a way they do, but not always directly. Except for very simple databases, you will never have a 100 percent pure one-to-one mapping of classes to tables, something you will see in the "Mapping Inheritance Structures" section later in this chapter. However, a common theme that you will see throughout this chapter is that a one-class-to-one-table mapping is preferable for your initial mapping (performance tuning may motivate you to refactor your mappings).

For now, let's keep things simple. Figure 14.2 depicts two models: a UML class diagram and a physical data model that follows the UML data-modeling profile described in Chapter 2. Both diagrams depict a portion of a simple schema for an order system. You can see how the attributes of the classes could be mapped to the columns of the database. For example, it appears that the *dateFulfilled* attribute of the *Order* class maps to the *DateFulfilled* column of the *Order* table and that the *numberOrdered* attribute of the *OrderItem* class maps to the *NumberOrdered* column of the *OrderItem* table.

TIP The easiest mapping you will ever have is a property mapping of a single attribute to a single column. It is even simpler when each have the same basic types, for example, they're both dates, the attribute is a string and the column is a char, or the attribute is a number and the column is a float.

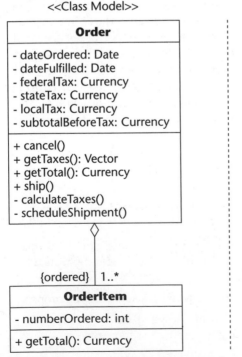
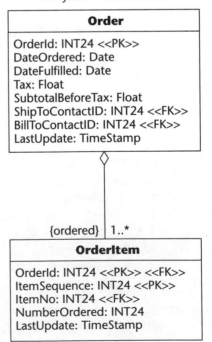

Figure 14.2   A simple mapping example.

Note that these initial property mappings were easy to determine for several reasons:

- Similar naming standards were used in both models, an aspect of the Agile Modeling (AM) *Apply Modeling Standards* practice.

- It is very likely that the same people created both models. When people work in separate teams it is quite common for their solutions to vary, even when the teams do a very good job, because they make different design decisions along the way.

- One model very likely drove the development of the other model. In Chapter 9, I argued that when you are building a new object-oriented system your object schema should drive the development of your database schema, a practice that I discuss later in this chapter.

Even though the two schemas depicted in Figure 14.2 are very similar, there are differences. These differences mean that the mapping isn't going to be perfect. The differences between the two schemas are:

- There are several attributes for tax in the object schema yet only one in the data schema. The three attributes for tax in the *Order* class presumably should be added up and stored in the *tax* column of the *Order* table when the object is saved. When the object is read into memory, however, the three attributes would need to be calculated (or a lazy initialization approach would need to be taken, and each attribute would be calculated when it is first accessed). A schema difference such as this is a good indication that the database schema needs to be refactored to split the tax column into three.

- The data schema indicates keys, whereas the object schema does not. Rows in tables are uniquely identified by primary keys, and relationships between rows are maintained through the use of foreign keys. Relationships to objects, on the other hand, are implemented via references to those objects not through foreign keys. The implication is that in order to fully persist the objects and their relationships, the objects need to know about the key values used in the database to identify them. This additional information is called "shadow information" and is discussed in greater detail in the next section.

- Different types are used in each schema. The *subTotalBeforeTax* attribute of *Order* is of the type *Currency*, whereas the *SubTotalBeforeTax* column of the *Order* table is a float. When you implement this mapping, you will need to be able to convert back and forth between these two representations without loss of information.

Shadow Information

Shadow information is any data that objects need to persist themselves above and beyond their normal domain data. This typically includes primary key information, particularly when the primary key is a surrogate key that has no business meaning and concurrency control markings such as timestamps or incremental counters (see Chapter 17). For example, in Figure 14.2 you can see that the *Order* table has an *OrderID* column used as a primary key and a *LastUpdate* column, which is used for optimistic concurrency control that the *Order* class does not have. To persist an order object properly, the *Order* class would need to implement shadow attributes that maintain these values.

Figure 14.3 shows a detailed design class model for the *Order* and *OrderItem* classes. There are several changes from Figure 14.2. First, the new diagram shows the shadow attributes that the classes require to properly persist themselves. Shadow attributes have an implementation visibility, there is a space in front of the name instead of a minus sign, and they are assigned the stereotype <<Persistence>> (this is not a UML standard). Second, it shows the scaffolding attributes required to implement the relationship of the two classes. Scaffolding attributes, such as the *orderItems* vector in *Order*, also have an implementation visibility. Third, a getTotalTax() operation was added to the *Order* class to calculate the value required for the *tax* column of the *Order* table. This is why I use the term *property mapping* instead of *attribute mapping* — what you really want to do is map the properties of a class, which are sometimes implemented as simple attributes and other times as one or more operations, to the columns of a database.

> **TIP** It is a common style convention in the UML community to not show shadow information, such as keys and concurrency markings, on class diagrams (Ambler 2003). Similarly, the common convention is to not model scaffolding code. The idea is that everyone knows you need to do this sort of thing, so why waste your time modeling the obvious?

One type of shadow information that I have not discussed yet is a Boolean flag to indicate whether an object currently exists in the database. The problem is that when you save data to a relational database, you need to use a SQL update statement if the object was previously retrieved from the database and a SQL insert statement if the data does not already exist. A common practice is for each class to implement an *isPersistent* Boolean flag, not shown in Figure 14.3, that is set to true when the data is read in from the database and set to false when the object is newly created.

Shadow information doesn't necessarily need to be implemented by the business objects, although your application will need to take care of it somehow. For example, with Enterprise JavaBeans (EJBs) you store primary key information outside of EJBs in primary key classes, the individual object references a corresponding primary key object. The Java Data Object (JDO) approach goes one step further and implements shadow information in the JDOs and not the business objects.

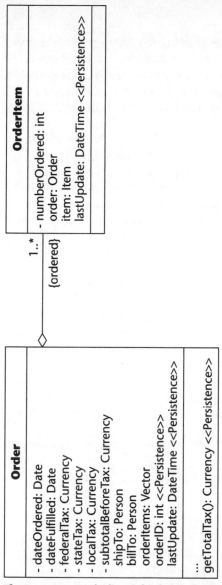

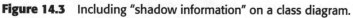

Figure 14.3   Including "shadow information" on a class diagram.

Mapping Meta Data

Figure 14.4 depicts the meta data representing the property mappings required to persist the *Order* and *OrderItem* classes of Figure 14.3. Meta data is information about data. Figure 14.4 is important for several reasons. First, we need some way to represent mappings. We could put two schemas side by side, as you see in Figure 14.2, and then draw lines between them but that gets complicated very quickly. Another option is a tabular representation that you see in Figure 14.4. Second, the concept of mapping meta data is critical to the functioning of persistence frameworks, discussed in Chapter 13, which are a database encapsulation strategy that can enable agile database techniques.

The naming convention that I'm using is reasonably straightforward: *Order.dataOrdered* refers to the *dataOrdered* attribute of the *Order* class. Similarly *Order.DataOrdered* refers to the *DataOrdered* column of the *Order* table. Order.getTotalTax() refers to the getTotalTax() operation of *Order* and *Order.billTo.personID* is the *personID* attribute of the *Person* object referenced by the *Order.billTo* attribute. Likely the most difficult property to understand is *Order.orderItems.position(orderItem)*, which refers to the position within the *Order.orderItems* vector of the instance of *OrderItem* that is being saved.

Figure 14.4 hints at an important part of the technical impedance mismatch (Chapter 7) between object technology and relational technology: classes implement both behavior and data, whereas relational database tables just implement data. The end result is that when you're mapping the properties of classes into a relational database, you end up mapping operations such as getTotalTax() and position() to columns. Although it didn't happen in this example, you often need to map two operations that represent a single property to a column — one operation to set the value, for example, setFirstName(), and one operation to retrieve the value, for example, getFirstName(). These operations are typically called *setters* and *getters*, respectively, or sometimes *mutators* and *accessors*.

Property	Column
Order.orderID	Order.OrderID
Order.dateOrdered	Order.DateOrdered
Order.dateFulfilled	Order.DateFulfilled
Order.getTotalTax()	Order.Tax
Order.subtotalBeforeTax	Order.SubtotalBeforeTax
Order.shipTo.personID	Order.ShipToContactID
Order.billTo.personID	Order.BillToContactID
Order.lastUpdate	Order.LastUpdate
OrderItem.ordered	OrderItem.OrderID
Order.orderItems.position(orderItem)	OrderItem.ItemSequence
OrderItem.item.number	OrderItem.ItemNo
OrderItem.numberOrdered	OrderItem.NumberOrdered
OrderItem.lastUpdate	OrderItem.LastUpdate

Figure 14.4　Basic mapping meta data for Order and OrderItem.

TIP Whenever a key column is mapped to a property of a class, such as the mapping between *OrderItem.ItemSequence* and *Order.orderItems .position(orderItem)*, this is really part of the effort of relationship mapping that's discussed later in this chapter. This is because keys implement relationships in relational databases.

Mapping Inheritance Structures

Relational databases do not natively support inheritance, forcing you to map the inheritance structures within your object schema to your data schema. Although there is somewhat of a backlash against inheritance within the object community, due in most part to the fragile base class problem, my experience is that this problem is mostly due more to poor encapsulation practices among object developers than with the concept of inheritance (Ambler 2001a). Put another way, the fact that you need to do a little bit of work to map an inheritance hierarchy into a relational database shouldn't dissuade you from using inheritance where appropriate.

The concept of inheritance throws in several interesting twists when you are saving objects into a relational database. How do you organize the inherited attributes within your data model? In this section, you'll see that there are three primary solutions for mapping inheritance into a relational database, and a fourth supplementary technique that goes beyond inheritance mapping. These techniques are:

- Map the entire class hierarchy to a single table.
- Map each concrete class to its own table.
- Map each class to its own table.
- Map the classes into a generic structure.

To explore each technique, I will discuss how to map the two versions of the class hierarchy presented in Figure 14.5. The first version depicts three classes: *Person*, an abstact class, and two concrete classes, *Employee* and *Customer*. You know that *Person* is abstract because its name is shown in italics. In older versions of UML, the constraint "{abstract}" would have been used instead. The second version of the hierarchy adds a fourth concrete class to the hierarchy, *Executive*. The idea is that you have implemented the first class hierarchy and are now presented with a new requirement to support giving executives, but not nonexecutive employees, fixed annual bonuses. The *Executive* class was added to support this new functionality.

For the sake of simplicity, I have not modeled all of the attributes of the classes, nor have I modeled their full signatures or any of the operations. This model is just barely good enough for my purpose; in other words, it is an agile model. Furthermore, these hierarchies could be approved by applying the *Party* analysis pattern (Fowler 1997) or the *Business Entity* (Ambler 1997) analysis pattern. I haven't done this because I need a simple example to explain mapping inheritance hiearchies, not to explain the effective application of analysis patterns — I always follow the AM principle *Model with a Purpose*.

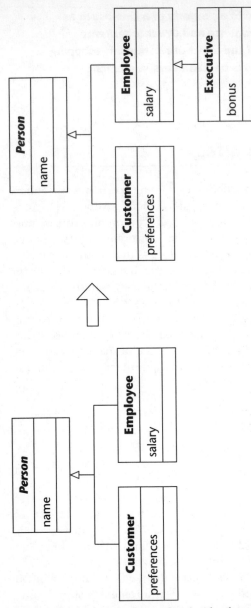

Figure 14.5 Two versions of a simple class hierarchy.

TIP Inheritance can also be a problem when it's misapplied — for example, the hierarchy in Figure 14.5 could be better modeled via the Party (Hay 1996, Fowler 1997) or the Business Entity (Ambler 1997) patterns. For instance, if someone can be both a customer and an employee, you would have two objects in memory for them, which may be problematic for your application. I've chosen this example because I needed a simple, easy-to-understand class hierarchy to map.

Map Entire Class Hierarchy to a Table

This approach is often called the "one table per hierarchy" strategy. Following this strategy, you store all the attributes of the classes in one table. Figure 14.6 depicts the data model for the class hierarchies of Figure 14.5 when this approach is taken. The attributes of each of the classes are stored in the *Person* table, a good table-naming strategy is to use the name of the hierarchy's root class in a very straightforward manner. The majority of the effort to support executives was the addition of the *Person.Bonus* column.

Two columns have been added to the table — *PersonPOID* and *PersonType* — above and beyond the business attributes of the classes. The first column is the primary key for the table (you know this because of the <<PK>> stereotype), and the second is a code indicating whether the person is a customer, an employee, or perhaps both. *PersonPOID* is a persistent object identifier (POID), often simply called an object identifier (OID), which is a surrogate key. I could have used the optional stereotype of <<Surrogate>> to indicate this but chose not to because POID implies this; thus, indicating the stereotype would only serve to complicate the diagram (follow the AM practice *Depict Models Simply*). Chapter 3 discusses surrogate keys in greater detail.

The *PersonType* column is required to identify the type of object that can be instantiated from a given row. For example, the value of *E* would indicate the person is an employee, *C* would indicate customer, and *B* would indicate both. Although this approach is straightforward, it tends to break down as the number of types and combinations begin to grow. For example, when you add the concept of executives, you need to add a code value, perhaps *X*, to represent this. Now the value of *B*, representing both, is sort of goofy. Furthermore, you might now have combinations involving executives; for example, it seems reasonable that someone can be both an executive and a customer, so you'd need a code for this. When you discover that combinations are possible, you should consider applying the *Replace Type Code with Booleans* database refactoring guideline, as you see in Figure 14.7.

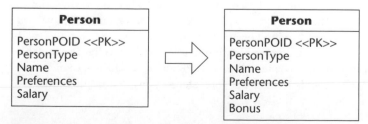

Figure 14.6   Mapping the class hierarchy to one table.

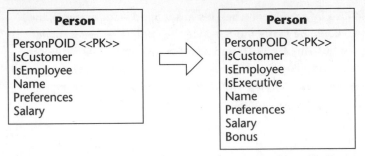

Figure 14.7   Alternate version of mapping a class hierarchy to one table.

For the sake of simplicity, I did not include columns for concurrency control, such as the time stamp column included in the tables of Figure 14.3, nor did I include columns for data versioning.

Map Each Concrete Class to Its Own Table

With this approach, a table is created for each concrete class, each table including both the attributes implemented by the class and its inherited attributes. Figure 14.8 depicts the physical data model for the class hierarchy of Figure 14.5 when this approach is taken. There are tables corresponding to each of the *Customer* and *Employee* classes because they are concrete (objects are instantiated from them), but not *Person* because it is abstract. Each table was assigned its own primary key, *customerPOID* and *employeePOID*, respectively. To support the addition of *Executive*, all I needed to do was add a corresponding table with all of the attributes required by executive objects.

Map Each Class to Its Own Table

Following this strategy, you create one table per class, with one column per business attributes and any necessary identification information (as well as other columns required for concurrency control and versioning). Figure 14.9 depicts the physical data model for the class hierarchy of Figure 14.5 when each class is mapped to a single table. The data for the *Customer* class is stored in two tables, *Customer* and *Person*; therefore, to retrieve this data you would need to join the two tables (or perform two separate reads, one to each table). To support the concept of executives, all I needed to do was add an *Executive* table that contained the new *Bonus* column and a primary key column to maintain its inheritance relationship to *Employee*.

The application of keys is interesting. Notice how *personPOID* is used as the primary key for all of the tables. For the *Customer*, *Employee*, and *Executive* tables, the *personPOID* is both a primary key and a foreign key. In the case of *Customer*, *personPOID* is its primary key and a foreign key is used to maintain the relationship to the *Person* table. This is indicated by application of two stereotypes: <<PK>> and <<FK>>. In older versions of UML, it wasn't permissible to assign several stereotypes to a single model element but this restriction was lifted in UML version 1.4.

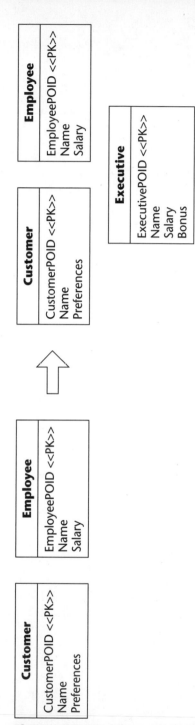

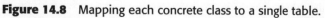

Figure 14.8   Mapping each concrete class to a single table.

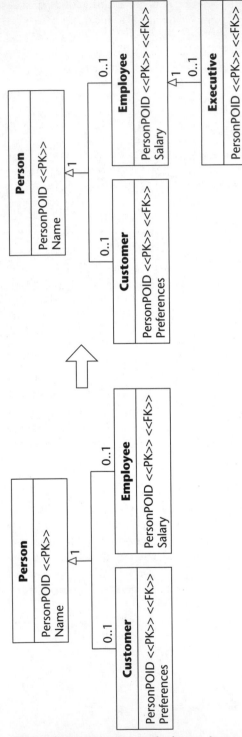

Figure 14.9 Mapping each class to its own data entity.

A common modification that you may want to consider is the addition of a type column, or Boolean columns as the case may be, in the *Person* table to indicate the applicable subtypes of the person. Although this is additional overhead, it makes some types of queries easier. The addition of views is also an option in many cases, an approach that I prefer over the addition of type or Boolean columns because views are easier to maintain.

Map Classes to a Generic Structure

A fourth option for mapping inheritance structures into a relational database is to take a generic, sometimes called metadata-driven, approach to mapping your classes. This approach isn't specific to inheritance structures; it supports all forms of mapping. In Figure 14.10, you see a data schema for storing the value of attributes and for traversing inheritance structures. The schema isn't complete; it could be extended to map associations, for example, but it's sufficient for our purposes. The value of a single attribute is stored in the *Value* table; therefore, to store an object with 10 business attributes, there would be 10 records, one for each attribute. The *Value.ObjectPOID* column stores the unique identifier for the specific object (this approach assumes a common key strategy across all objects; when this isn't the case, you'll need to extend this table appropriately). The *AttributeType* table contains rows for basic data types such as data, string, money, integer, and so on. This information is required to convert the value of the object attribute into the varchar stored in *Value.Value*.

Let's work through an example of mapping a single class to this schema. To store the *OrderItem* class in Figure 14.3, there would be three records in the *Value* table. One to store the value for the number of items ordered, one to store the value of the *OrderPOID* that this order item is part of, and one to store the value of the *ItemPOID* that describes the order item. You may decide to have a fourth row to store the value of the *lastUpdated* shadow attribute if you're taking an optimistic locking approach to concurrency control (which is discussed in Chapter 17). The *Class* table would include a row for the *OrderItem* class, and the *Attribute* table would include one row for each attribute stored in the database (in this case either three or four rows).

Now, let's map the inheritance structure between *Person* and *Customer*, shown in Figure 14.5, into this schema. The *Inheritance* table is the key to inheritance mapping. Each class would be represented by a row in the *Class* table. There would also be a row in the *Inheritance* table; the value of *Inheritance.SuperClassPOID* would refer to the row in *Class* representing *Person*, and *Inheritance.SubClassPOID* would refer to the row in *Class* representing *Customer*. To map the rest of the hierarchy, you require one row in *Inheritance* for each inheritance relationship.

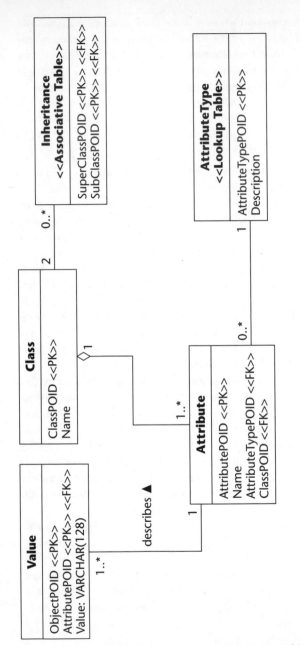

Figure 14.10   A generic data schema for storing objects.

Comparing the Mapping Strategies

None of these mapping strategies is ideal for all situations, as you can see in Table 14.1. My experience is that the easiest strategy to work with is to have one table per hierarchy at first, then refactor your schema accordingly if you need to. Sometimes, I'll start by applying the one-table-per-class strategy, whenever my team is motivated to work with a "pure design approach," I stay away from using one table per concrete class because it typically results in the need to copy data back and forth between tables, forcing me to refactor it reasonably early in the life of the project anyway. I rarely use the generic schema approach because it simply doesn't scale very well.

It is important to understand that you can combine the first three strategies — one table per hierarchy, one table per concrete class, and one table per class — in any given application. You can even combine these strategies in a single, large hierarchy.

Mapping Multiple Inheritance

Until this point, I have focused on mapping single-inheritance hierarchies. Single inheritance occurs when a subclass such as *Customer* inherits directly from a single parent class such as *Person*. Multiple inheritance occurs when a subclass has two or more direct superclasses, such as *Dragon*, directly inheriting from both *Bird* and *Lizard* in Figure 14.11. Multiple inheritance is generally seen as a questionable feature of an object-oriented language — since 1990, I have only seen one domain problem where multiple inheritance made sense — and as a result most languages choose not to support it. However, languages such as C++ and Eiffel do support it, so you may find yourself in a situation where you need to map a multiple-inheritance hierarchy to a relational database.

Figure 14.11 shows the three data schemas that would result from applying each of the three inheritance-mapping strategies. As you can see, mapping multiple inheritance is fairly straightforward; there aren't any surprises in Figure 14.11. The greatest challenge in my experience is to identify a reasonable table name when mapping the hierarchy into a single table; in this case, *Creature* made the most sense.

Table 14.1 Comparing the Inheritance Mapping Strategies

STRATEGY	ADVANTAGES	DISADVANTAGES	WHEN TO USE
One table per hierarchy	• Simple approach. It's easy to add new classes; you just need to add new columns for the additional data. • Supports polymorphism by simply changing the type of the row. • Data access is fast because the data is in one table. • Ad hoc reporting is very easy because all of the data is found in one table.	• Coupling within the class hierarchy is increased because all classes are directly coupled to the same table. A change in one class can then affect the other classes in the hierarchy. • Space is potentially wasted in the database. • Indicating the type becomes complex when significant overlap between types exists. • A table can grow quickly for large hierarchies. • The resulting table suffers from low cohesion because several concepts are stored in one table.	This is a good strategy for simple and/or shallow class hierarchies where there is little or no overlap between the types within the hierarchy.

Table 14.1   *(continued)*

STRATEGY	ADVANTAGES	DISADVANTAGES	WHEN TO USE
One table per concrete class	• Ad hoc reporting is easy because all the data you need about a single class is stored in one table. • Good performance when accessing a single object's data.	• When you modify a class, you need to modify its table and the table of any of its subclasses. For example, if you were to add height and weight to the *Person* class, you would need to add columns to the *Customer, Employee,* and *Executive* tables. • Whenever an object changes its role (say if you hire one of your customers), you need to copy the data into the appropriate table and assign it a new POID value (or perhaps you could reuse the existing POID value). • It is difficult to support multiple roles and still maintain data integrity. For example, where would you store the name of someone who is both a customer and an employee?	When changing types and/or overlap between types is rare.

(continued)

Table 14.1 *(continued)*

STRATEGY	ADVANTAGES	DISADVANTAGES	WHEN TO USE
One table per class	• Easy to understand because of the one-to-one mapping. • Supports polymorphism very well because you merely have records in the appropriate tables for each type. • Very easy to modify superclasses and add new subclasses because you merely need to modify/add one table. • Data size grows in direct proportion to growth in the number of objects. • The resulting data structure is highly denormalized, typically third normal form (3NF) or better.	• There are many tables in the database, one for every class (plus tables to maintain relationships). • Potentially takes longer to read and write data using this technique because you need to access multiple tables. This problem can be alleviated if you organize your database intelligently by putting each table within a class hierarchy on different physical disk-drive platters (this assumes that the disk-drive heads all operate independently). • Ad hoc reporting on your database is difficult, unless you add views to simulate the desired tables.	When there is significant overlap between types or when changing types is common.

Table 14.1 *(continued)*

STRATEGY	ADVANTAGES	DISADVANTAGES	WHEN TO USE
Generic schema	• Works very well when database access is encapsulated by a robust persistence framework (see Chapter 13). • It can be extended to provide meta data to support a wide range of mappings, including relationship mappings. In short, it is the start at a mapping meta data engine. • It is incredibly flexible, enabling you to quickly change the way that you store objects because you merely need to update the meta data stored in the *Class*, *Inheritance*, *Attribute*, and *AttributeType* tables accordingly.	• Very advanced technique that can be difficult to implement at first. • It only works for small amounts of data because you need to access many database rows to build a single object. • You will likely want to build a small administration application to maintain the meta data. • Reporting against this data can be very difficult due to the need to access several rows to obtain the data for a single object.	For complex applications that work with small amounts of data or for applications where your data access isn't very common or you can preload data into caches (see Chapter 15).

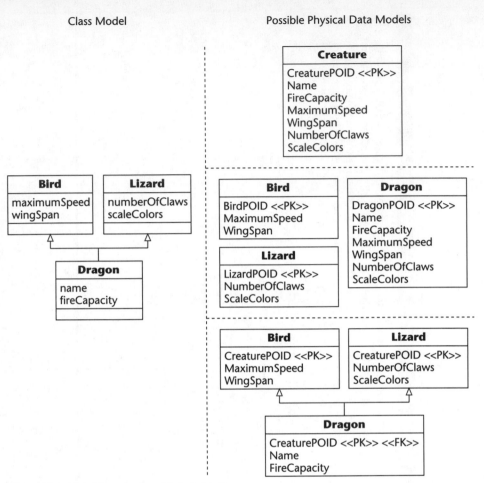

Figure 14.11   Mapping multiple inheritance.

Mapping Object Relationships

In addition to property and inheritance mapping, you need to understand the art of *relationship mapping*. There are three types of object relationships that you need to map: association, aggregation, and composition. For now, I'm going to treat these three types of relationships the same — they are mapped the same way, although in Chapter 19 you will learn that there are interesting nuances when it comes to referential integrity. In this section, I will discuss the following topics:

- Types of relationships
- How relationships are implemented between objects
- How relationships are implemented in relational databases

- Relationship mappings
- Mapping ordered collections
- Mapping reflexive/recursive associations

Types of Relationships

There are two categories of object relationships that you need to be concerned with when mapping. The first category is based on multiplicity and includes three types:

One-to-one relationships.   This is a relationship where the maximum of each of its multiplicities is one, an example of which is the *holds* relationship between *Employee* and *Position* in Figure 14.12. That is, an employee "holds" one and only one position, and a position may be "held" by only one employee (some positions go unfilled).

One-to-many relationships.   Also known as a many-to-one relationship, this occurs when the maximum of one multiplicity is one and the other is greater than one. An example is the *works in* relationship between *Employee* and *Division*. An employee works in one division, and any given division has one or more employees working in it.

Many-to-many relationships.   This is a relationship where the maximum of both multiplicities is greater than one, an example of which is the *assigned* relationship between *Employee* and *Task*. An employee is assigned one or more tasks, and each task is assigned to zero or more employees.

The second category is based on directionality, and it contains two types: unidirectional relationships and bidirectional relationships.

Unidirectional relationships.   A unidirectional relationship occurs when an object knows about the object(s) it is related to but the other object(s) do not know of the original object. An example of this is the *holds* relationship between *Employee* and *Position* in Figure 14.12, which is indicated by the line with an open arrowhead on it. *Employee* objects know about the position that they hold, but *Position* objects do not know which employee holds them (there was no requirement to do so). As you will soon see, unidirectional relationships are easier to implement than bidirectional relationships.

Bidirectional relationships.   A bidirectional relationship exists when the objects on both end of the relationship know of each other, an example of which is the *works in* relationship between *Employee* and *Division*. *Employee* objects know what division they work in, and *Division* objects know what employees work in them.

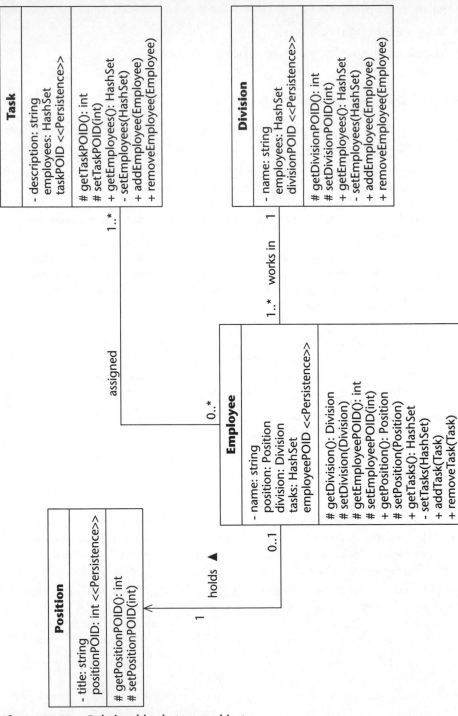

Figure 14.12   Relationships between objects.

It is possible to have all six combinations of relationship in object schemas. However one aspect of the impedance mismatch between object technology and relational technology is that relational technology does not support the concept of unidirectional relationships — in relational databases all associations are bidirectional.

How Relationships Are Implemented between Objects

Relationships in object schemas are implemented by a combination of references to objects and operations. When the multiplicity is one (for example, 0..1 or 1), the relationship is implemented with a reference to an object, a getter operation, and a setter operation. For example, in Figure 14.12, the fact that an employee works in a single division is implemented by the *Employee* class via the combination of the attribute *division*, the getDivision() operation (which returns the value of *division*), and the setDivision() operation (which sets the value of the *division* attribute). The attribute(s) and operations required to implement a relationship are often referred to as *scaffolding*.

When the multiplicity is many (for example, N, 0..*, 1..*) the relationship is implemented via a collection attribute, such as an *Array* or a *HashSet* in Java, and operations to manipulate that array. For example, the *Division* class implements a *HashSet* attribute named *employees*, getEmployees() to get the value, setEmployees() to set the value, addEmployee() to add an employee into the *HashSet*, and removeEmployee() to remove an employee from the *HashSet*.

When a relationship is unidirectional, the code is implemented only by the object that knows about the other object(s). For example, in the unidirectional relationship between *Employee* and *Position*, only the *Employee* class implements the association. Bidirectional associations, on the other hand, are implemented by both classes, as you can see with the many-to-many relationship between *Employee* and *Task*.

How Relationships Are Implemented in Relational Databases

Relationships in relational databases are maintained through the use of foreign keys. A foreign key is a data attribute(s) that appears in one table that may be part of or is coincidental with the key of another table. With a one-to-one relationship, the foreign key needs to be implemented by one of the tables. In Figure 14.13, you see that the *Position* table includes *EmployeePOID*, a foreign key to the *Employee* table, to implement the association. I could easily have implemented a *PositionPOID* column in *Employee* instead.

To implement a one-to-many relationship, you implement a foreign key from the "one table" to the "many table." For example, *Employee* includes a *DivisionPOID* column to implement the *works in* relationship to *Division*. You could also choose to overbuild your database schema and implement a one-to-many relationship via an associative table, effectively making it a many-to-many relationship.

There are two ways to implement many-to-many associations in a relational database. The first one is to implement in each table the foreign key column(s) to the other table several times. For example to implement the many-to-many relationship between *Employee* and *Task*, you could have five *TaskPOID* columns in *Employee* and the *Task*

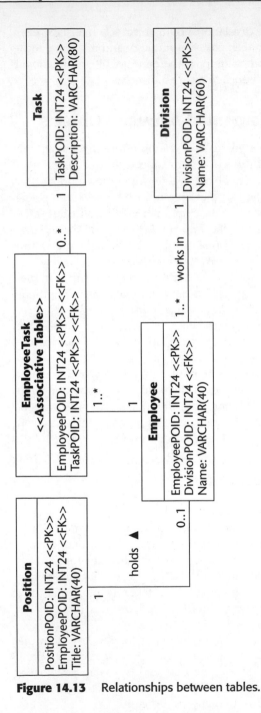

Figure 14.13   Relationships between tables.

table could include seven *EmployeePOID* columns. Unfortunately, you run into a problem with this approach when you assign more than five tasks to an employee or more than seven employees to a single task. A better approach is to implement what is called an *associative table*, an example of which is *EmployeeTask* in Figure 14.13, which includes the combination of the primary keys of the tables that it is associated with. With this approach, you could have 50 people assigned to the same task, or 20 tasks assigned to the same person, and it wouldn't matter. The basic "trick" is that the many-to-many relationship is converted into two one-to-many relationships, both of which involve the associative table.

Because foreign keys are used to join tables, all relationships in a relational database are effectively bidirectional. This is why it doesn't matter in which table you implement a one-to-one relationship, the code to join the two tables is virtually the same. For example, with the existing schema in Figure 14.13 the SQL code to join across the holds relationship would be:

```
SELECT * FROM Position, Employee
WHERE Position.EmployeePOID = Employee.EmployeePOID
```

Had the foreign key been implemented in the Employee table, the SQL code would be:

```
SELECT * FROM Position, Employee
WHERE Position.PositionPOID = Employee.PositionPOID
```

Now that you understand how to implement relationships in each technology, let's see how you map them. In the next section, I will describe the mappings from the point of view of mapping the object relationships into the relational database.

NOTE Remember that in some cases you have design choices to make. Once again, beware of the "magic CASE tool button" that supposedly automates everything for you.

Relationship Mappings

A general rule of thumb with relationship mapping is that you should keep the multiplicities the same. Therefore, a one-to-one object relationship maps to a one-to-one data relationship, a one-to-many maps to a one-to-many, and a many-to-many maps to a many-to-many. The fact is that this doesn't have to be the case; you can implement a one-to-one object relationship with a one-to-many, or even a many-to-many, data relationship. This is because a one-to-one data relationship is a subset of a one-to-many data relationship, and a one-to-many relationship is a subset of a many-to-many relationship.

Figure 14.14 depicts the property mappings between the object schema of Figure 14.12 and the data schema of Figure 14.13. Note how I have only had to map the business properties and the shadow information of the objects, but not scaffolding attributes such as *Employee.position* and *Employee.tasks*. These scaffolding attributes are represented via the shadow information that is mapped into the database. When the relationship is read into memory, the values stored in the primary key columns will be stored in the corresponding shadow attributes within the objects. At the same time, the relationship that the primary key columns represent will be defined between the corresponding objects by setting the appropriate values in their scaffolding attributes.

> **TIP** A consistent key strategy within your database can greatly simplify your relationship-mapping efforts. The first step is to preferably use single-column keys. The next step is to use a globally unique surrogate key, perhaps following the GUID or High-Low strategies described in Chapter 3, so you are always mapping to the same type of key column.

Mapping One-to-One Relationships

Consider the one-to-one object relationship between *Employee* and *Position*. Let's assume that whenever a *Position* or an *Employee* object is read into memory, the application will automatically traverse the *holds* relationship and automatically read in the corresponding object. The other option would be to manually traverse the relationship in the code, taking a lazy read approach (discussed in Chapter 19), where the second object is read at the time it is required by the application. Figure 14.15 shows how the object relationships are mapped.

Let's work through the logic of retrieving a single *Position* object one step at a time:

1. The *Position* object is read into memory.

2. The *holds* relationship is automatically traversed.

3. The value held by the *Position.EmployeePOID* column is used to identify the single employee that needs to be read into memory.

4. The *Employee* table is searched for a record with that value of *EmployeePOID*.

5. The *Employee* object (if any) is read in and instantiated.

6. The value of the *Employee.position* attribute is set to reference the *Position* object.

Property	Column
Position.title	Position.Title
Position.positionPOID	Position.PositionPOID
Employee.name	Employee.Name
Employee.employeePOID	Employee.EmployeePOID
Employee.employeePOID	EmployeeTask.EmployeePOID
Division.name	Division.Name
Division.divisionPOID	Division.DivisionPOID
Task.description	Task.Description
Task.taskPOID	Task.TaskPOID
Task.taskPOID	EmployeeTask.TaskPOID

Figure 14.14   Property mappings.

Object Relationship	From	To	Cardinality	Automatic Read	Column(s)	Scaffolding Property
holds	Employee	Position	One	Yes	Position.EmployeeOID	Employee.position
held by	Position	Employee	One	Yes	Position.EmployeePOID	Employee.position
works in	Employee	Division	One	Yes	Employee.DivisionPOID	Employee.division
has working in it	Division	Employee	Many	No	Employee.DivisionPOID	Division.employees
assigned	Employee	Task	Many	No	Employee.EmployeePOID EmployeeTask.EmployeePOID	Employee.tasks
Assigned to	Task	Employee	Many	No	Task.TaskPOID EmployeeTask.TaskPOID	Task.employees

Figure 14.15 Mapping the relationship.

Next, let's work through the logic of retrieving a single *Employee* object one step at a time:

1. The *Employee* object is read into memory.

2. The *holds* relationship is automatically traversed.

3. The value held by the *Employee.EmployeePOID* column is used to identify the single position that needs to be read into memory.

4. The *Position* table is searched for a row with that value of *EmployeePOID*.

5. The *Position* object is read in and instantiated.

6. The value of the *Employee.position* attribute is set to reference the *Position* object.

Now, let's consider how the objects would be saved to the database. Because the relationship is to be automatically traversed, and to maintain referential integrity, a transaction is created (transactions are discussed in Chapter 19). The next step is to add update statements for each object to the transaction. Each update statement includes both the business attributes and the key values mapped in Figure 14.15. Because relationships are implemented via foreign keys, and because those values are being updated, the relationship is effectively being persisted. The transaction is submitted to the database and run.

There is one annoyance with the way the *holds* relationship has been mapped into the database. Although the direction of this relationship is from *Employee* to *Position* within the object schema, it's been implemented from *Position* to *Employee* in the database. This isn't a big deal, but it is annoying. In the data schema, you can implement the foreign key in either table and it wouldn't make a difference, so from a data point of view, when everything else is equal, you could toss a coin. Had there been a potential requirement for the *holds* relationship to turn into a one-to-many relationship, something that a change case (Bennett 1997, Ambler 2001a) would indicate, then you would be motivated to implement the foreign key to reflect this potential requirement. For example, the existing data model would support an employee holding many positions. However, had the object schema been taken into account, and if there were no future requirements motivating you to model it otherwise, it would have been cleaner to implement the foreign key in the *Employee* table instead.

TIP   A common physical-data-modeling practice is to combine two tables that are related to one another via a one-to-one mapping. Although this results in a table with low cohesion, it now implements two concepts instead of one and improves performance by removing the need to join those two tables.

Mapping One-to-Many Relationships

Now, let's consider the *works in* relationship between Employee and Division in Figure 14.12. This is a one-to-many relationship — an employee works in one division, and a single division has many employees working in it. As you can see in Figure 14.15, an interesting thing about this relationship is that it should be automatically traversed from *Employee* to *Division*, something often referred to as a *cascading read*, but not in the other direction. Cascading saves and cascading deletes are also possible, something covered in the discussion of referential integrity in Chapter 19.

When an employee is read into memory, the relationship is automatically traversed to read in the division that the employee works in. Because you don't want several copies of the same division (for example, if you have 20 employee objects that all work for the IT division and you want them to refer to the same IT division object in memory). The implication is that you will need to implement a strategy for addressing this issue; one option is to implement a cache that ensures that only one copy of an object exists in memory or to simply have the *Division* class implement its own collection of instances in memory (effectively a minicache). If the application needs to, it will read the *Division* object into memory and then set the value of *Employee.division* to reference the appropriate *Division* object. Similarly, the *Division.addEmployee()* operation will be invoked to add the employee object into its collection.

Saving the relationship works similarly to the way it does for one-to-one relationships. When the objects are saved, so are their primary and foreign key values, automatically saving the relationship.

> **TIP** Every example in this chapter uses foreign keys, such as *Employee.DivisionPOID*, pointing to the primary keys of other tables, in this case *Division.DivisionPOID*. This doesn't have to be the case; sometimes a foreign key can refer to an alternate key. For example, if the *Employee* table of Figure 14.13 were to include a *SocialSecurityNumber* column, then that would be an alternate key for that table (assuming that all employees were American citizens). If this were the case, you would have the option to replace the *Position.EmployeePOID* column with *Position.SocialSecurityNumber*.

Mapping Many-to-Many Relationships

To implement many-to-many relationships, you need the concept of an *associative table*, a data entity whose sole purpose is to maintain the relationship between two or more tables in a relational database. In Figure 14.12 there is a many-to-many relationship between *Employee* and *Task*. In the data schema in Figure 14.13, I needed to introduce the associative table *EmployeeTask* to implement a many-to-many relationship between the *Employee* and *Task* tables. In relational databases, the attributes contained in an associative table are traditionally the combination of the keys in the tables involved in the relationship, in this case *EmployeePOID* and *TaskPOID*. The name of an associative table is typically either the combination of the names of the tables that it associates or the name of the association that it implements. In this case, I chose *EmployeeTask* over *Assigned*.

Notice the application of multiplicities in Figure 14.12. The rule is that the multiplicities "cross over" once the associative table is introduced, as indicated in Figure 14.13. A multiplicity of 1 is always introduced on the outside edges of the relationship within the data schema to preserve overall multiplicity of the original relationship. The original relationship indicated that an employee is assigned to one or more tasks and that a task has zero or more employees assigned to it. In the data schema, you see that this is still true even with the associative table in place to maintain the relationship.

Assume that an employee object is in memory and we need a list of all the tasks the employee has been assigned. The steps that the application would need to go through are:

1. Create a SQL Select statement that joins the *EmployeeTask* and *Task* tables together, choosing all *EmployeeTask* records with the an *EmployeePOID* value the same as the employee we are putting the task list together.

2. The Select statement is run against the database.

3. The data records representing these tasks are marshaled into *Task* objects. Part of this effort includes checking to see if the *Task* object is already in memory. If it is, then we may choose to refresh the object with the new data values (see Chapter 17 for a detailed discussion of concurrency issues).

4. The *Employee.addTask()* operation is invoked for each *Task* object to build the collection up.

A similar process would have been followed to read in the employees involved in a given task. To save the relationship, still from the point of view of the *Employee* object, the steps would be:

1. Start a transaction.

2. Add Update statements for any task objects that have changed.

3. Add Insert statements for the *Task* table for any new tasks that you have created.

4. Add Insert statements for the *EmployeeTask* table for the new tasks.

5. Add Delete statements for the *Task* table any tasks that have been deleted. This may not be necessary if the individual object deletions have already occurred.

6. Add Delete statements for the *EmployeeTask* table for any tasks that have been deleted, a step that may not be needed if the individual deletions have already occurred.

7. Add Delete statements for the *EmployeeTask* table for any tasks that are no longer assigned to the employee.

8. Run the transaction.

Many-to-many relationships are interesting because of the addition of the associative table. Two business classes are being mapped to three data tables to support this relationship, so there is extra work to do as a result.

Mapping Ordered Collections

Figure 14.2 depicted a classic *Order* and *OrderItem* model with an aggregation association between the two classes. An interesting twist is the {ordered} constraint placed on the relationship — users care about the order in which items appear on an order. When mapping this to a relational database, you need to add an addition column to track this information. The database schema, also depicted in Figure 14.2, includes the column *OrderItem.ItemSequence* to persist this information. Although this mapping seems straightforward on the surface, there are several issues that you need take into consideration. These issues become apparent when you consider basic persistence functionality for the aggregate:

Read the data in the proper sequence.   The scaffolding attribute that implements this relationship must be a collection that enables sequential ordering of references, and it must be able to grow as new *OrderItems* are added to the *Order*. In Figure 14.3, you see that a vector is used, a Java collection class that meets these requirements. As you read the order and order items into memory, the vector must be filled in the proper sequence. If the values of the *OrderItem.ItemSequence* column start from 1 and increase by 1, then you can simply use the value of the column as the position to insert order items into the collection. When this isn't the case, you must include an ORDER BY clause in the SQL statement submitted to the database to ensure that the rows appear in order in the result set.

Don't include the sequence number in the key.   You have an order with five order items in memory, and they have been saved into the database. You now insert a new order item in between the second and third order items, giving you a total of six order items. With the current data schema of Figure 14.2, you have to renumber the sequence numbers for every order item that appears after the new order item and then write out all them even though nothing has changed other than the sequence number in the other order items. Because the sequence number is part of the primary key of the *OrderItem* table, this could be problematic if other tables, not shown in Figure 14.2, refer to rows in *OrderItem* via foreign keys that include *ItemSequence*. A better approach is shown in Figure 14.16, where the *OrderItemID* column is used as the primary key.

When do you update sequence numbers after rearranging the order items?   Whenever you rearrange order items on an order (perhaps you moved the fourth order item to be the second one on the order), you need to update the sequence numbers within the database. You may decide to cache these changes in memory until you decide to write out the entire order, although you run the risk that the proper sequence won't be saved in the event of a power outage.

Do you update sequence numbers after deleting an order item?   If you delete the fifth of six order items, do you want to update the sequence number for what is now the fifth item or do you want to leave it as is? The sequence numbers still work — the values are 1, 2, 3, 4, 6 — but you can no longer use them as the position indicators within your collection without leaving a hole in the fifth position.

Consider sequence number gaps greater than one.   Instead of assigning sequence numbers along the lines of 1, 2, 3, and so on, assign numbers such as 10, 20, 30, and so on. That way you don't need to update the values of the *OrderItem.ItemSequence* column every time you rearrange order items because you can assign a sequence number of 15 when you move something between 10 and 20. You will need to change the values every so often; for example, after several rearrangements, you may find yourself in the position of trying to insert something between 17 and 18. Larger gaps help you to minimize this (for example, 50, 100, 150, and so on) but you'll never completely avoid this problem.

Mapping Recursive Relationships

A *recursive relationship*, also called a *reflexive relationship* (Reed 2002; Larman 2002), is one where the same entity (class, data entity, table, and so on) is involved with both ends of the relationship. For example, the *manages* relationship in Figure 14.17 is recursive, representing the concept that an employee may manage several other employees. The aggregate relationship that the *Team* class has with itself is recursive — a team may be a part of one or more other teams.

Figure 14.17 depicts a class model that includes two recursive relationships and the resulting data model that it would be mapped to. For the sake of simplicity the class model includes only the classes and their relationships, and the data model includes only the keys. The many-to-many recursive aggregation is mapped to the Subteams associative table in the same way that you would map a normal many-to-many relationship — the only difference is that both columns are foreign keys into the same table. Similarly, the one-to-many *manages* association is mapped in the same way that you would map a normal one-to-many relationship; the *ManagerEmployeePOID* column refers to another row in the *Employee* table where the manager's data is stored.

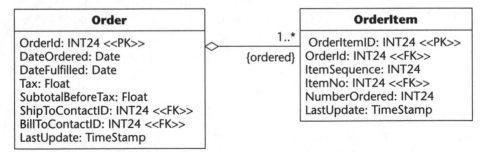

Figure 14.16 Improved data schema for persisting Order and OrderItem.

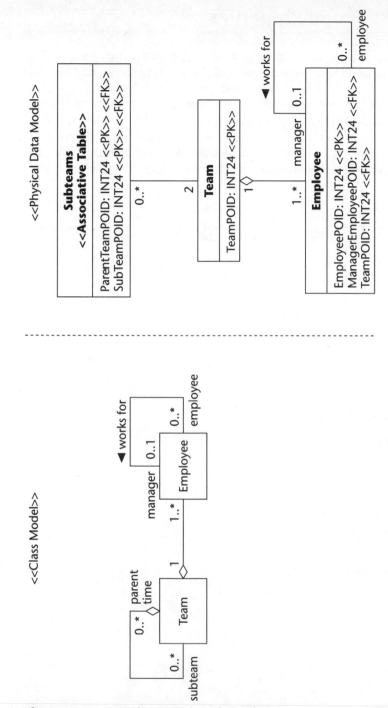

Figure 14.17 Mapping recursive relationships.

Mapping Class Scope Properties

Until now I have focused on mapping instance attributes, such as *Customer.customer-Number* in Figure 14.18, to a relational database. Sometimes a class will implement a property that is applicable to all of its instances and not just single instances. The *Customer* class in Figure 14.18 implements *nextCustomerNumber*, a class attribute (you know this because it's underlined) that stores the value of the next customer number to be assigned to a new customer object. Because there is one value for this attribute for the class, not one value per object, you need to map it in a different manner. Table 14.2 summarizes the four basic strategies for mapping class scope properties.

Table 14.2   Strategies for Mapping Class Scope Properties

STRATEGY	EXAMPLE	ADVANTAGES	DISADVANTAGES
Single-column, single-row table	The *CustomerNumber* table in Figure 14.18 implements this strategy.	• Simple • Fast access	• This could result in many small tables.
Multicolumn, single-row table for a single class	If *Customer* implemented a second class-scope attribute, then a *CustomerValues* table could be introduced with one column for each attribute.	• Simple • Fast access	• This could result in many small tables, although fewer than the single-column approach.

Table 14.2 *(continued)*

STRATEGY	EXAMPLE	ADVANTAGES	DISADVANTAGES
Multicolumn, single-row table for all classes	The topmost version of the *ClassVariables* table in Figure 14.18. This table contains one column for each class attribute within your application, so if the *Employee* class had a *next EmployeeNumber* class attribute, then there would be a column for this as well.	• Minimal number of tables introduced to your data schema	• Potential for concurrency problems if many classes need to access the data at once. One solution is to introduce a *ClassConstants* table, as shown in Figure 14.18, to separate attributes that are read-only from those that can be updated.
Multirow generic schema for all classes	The bottommost version of the *ClassVariables* and *ClassConstants* tables of Figure 14.18. The table contains one row for each class scope property in your system.	• Minimal number of tables introduced to your data schema • Reduces concurrency problems (assuming that your database supports row-based locking)	• Need to convert between types (for example, *CustomerNumber* is an integer but is stored as character data). • The data schema is coupled to the names of your classes and their class scope properties. You could avoid this with an even more generic schema along the lines of Figure 14.10.

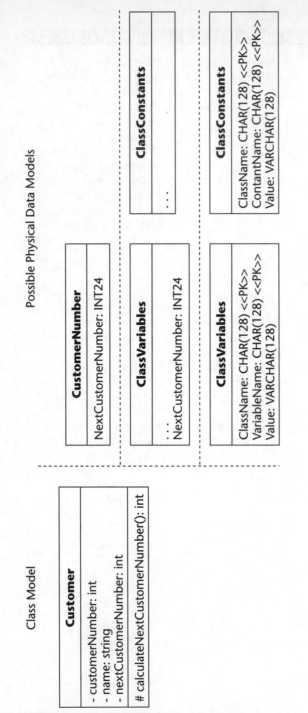

Figure 14.18 Mapping class scope attributes.

Why Data Schemas Shouldn't Drive Object Schemas

A common problem that I run into again and again is the idea that a data model should drive the development of objects. This idea comes in two flavors:

- A physical data schema should drive the development of objects.

- A conceptual/logical data model should be (almost) completely developed up front before one begins to design one's objects.

Both of these views are inappropriate for nonagile projects and clearly wrong for agile projects. Let's explore this issue in more depth.

Why do people want to base their object models on existing data schemas? First, there is very likely a desire to reuse the existing thinking that was behind the current schema. I'm a firm believer in reusing things, but I prefer to reuse the right things. As you saw in Chapter 7, there is an impedance mismatch between the object and relational paradigms, and this mismatch leads object and data practitioners to different designs. You also saw in Chapters 2 and 5 that object developers apply different design techniques and concepts than the techniques and concepts described in Chapter 3 and 4 that data modelers apply. Second, the database owner seeks to maintain or even enhance his or her political standing within your organization by forcing you to base your application on the existing design. Third, the people asking you to take this approach may not understand the implications of this decision or that there are better ways to proceed.

Why is basing your object model on an existing data schema a bad idea? First, your legacy database design likely has some significant problems, as described in Chapter 8. I'll look at existing physical data models to get an idea of what is currently going on, and to get a feel for the technical constraints that I'll have to work with, but I won't unnaturally constrain my application with a bad data design. Second, even if the existing database design is very good, there can be significant differences in the way that you map objects to relational databases. Consider Figure 14.19, which depicts three object schemas, all of which can be correctly mapped to the data schema on the right. Now, pretend you have the data schema as your starting point. Which of the three object schemas would you generate from it? Likely the top one, which may in fact be correct for your situation, but then again maybe one of the other two schemas could have been better choices. Yes, all of the models in Figure 14.19 could be improved, but I needed a simple example that showed how different object schemas map to the same data schema.

Why do people want to create (nearly) complete data models early in the project? First, this likely reflects the existing culture within your organization. This is the way it's always been done, this is the way that they like, therefore this is the way that they're going to continue to work. Second, data modeling might be the only thing they know, or at least it's what they prefer to specialize in. When all you have is a hammer, not only does every problem look like a nail, but nails appear to be the most important problem that needs to be addressed right now. Third, this reflects a serial mindset.

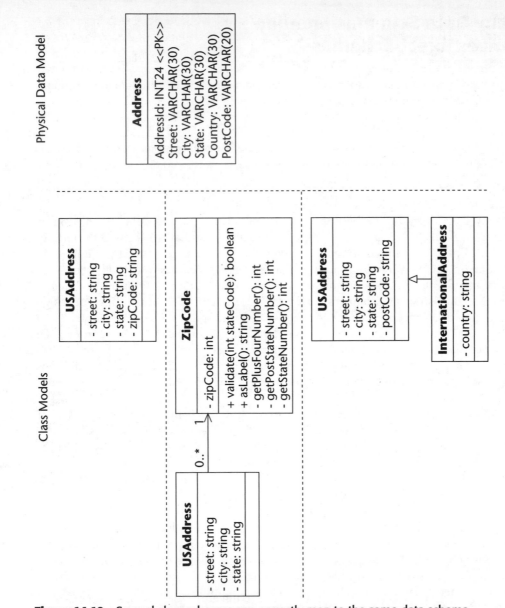

Figure 14.19 Several class schemas can correctly map to the same data schema.

Many developers have little or no experience taking an iterative and incremental approach to development, let alone taking it one step further to take an evolutionary/emergent approach. Fourth, they assume that the cost of change is high. This is completely true when you're following a nonagile approach, but with modern techniques such as AM (discussed in Chapter 10) and database refactoring (discussed in Chapter 12), the cost of change becomes much lower because these techniques support change. Fifth, they likely assume that the data group will go off and develop the database, while the application programmers go off and build the application. This may have worked for COBOL project teams but it doesn't work for agile software development teams — there is one team that works together, not several teams that work in isolation.

Why is basing your object model on a conceptual or logical data model a bad idea? Actually, it's not such a bad idea, as long as you're taking an iterative and incremental approach; the real problem is the big design up front (BDUF) approach that many data professionals seem to prefer. Flexibility in your approach is critical to success. However, there are much better options. Although the object role modeling (Halpin 2001) notation is very good, I have found that Class Responsibility Collaborator (CRC) cards (Beck & Cunningham 1989; Ambler 2001a) to be a very useful technique for domain modeling with my project stakeholders. Similarly, although logical data models can be quite useful, I personally find UML class models much more expressive due to their ability to depict behavior as well as data. Although David Hay (2003) argues in his excellent book *Requirements Analysis* that you should not use UML class diagrams for domain or analysis modeling, my experience is that you can do so quite easily if you choose to. However, I have to concede his point that many object modelers struggle with analysis, but in the end that's a separate issue.

So, should you blindly base your data schema on your object schema? No! You need a much more robust approach. You saw in Figure 14.19 that it is possible for several object schemas to map to a single data schema, and in Figure 14.11 that it is possible for a single object schema to map to several data schemas. There is a skill to successfully mapping objects to relational databases; you can't simply create one model, press the "magic CASE tool button," and come up with the right answer every time.

My advice is to:

Recognize that existing legacy databases are a technical constraint.   They aren't carved in stone; they can be refactored over time. You can even map to an imperfect schema and survive the experience.

Take an iterative and incremental approach to development, including modeling.   In Chapter 9 you saw that agile developers iterate back and forth between tasks such as data modeling, object modeling, refactoring, mapping, implementing, and performance tuning.

Adopt AM's principle of *Use Multiple Models*.   No one model, certainly not a data model nor a UML class diagram, is sufficient for real-world development. A modeler who only knows how to work with one type of model is just like a carpenter who only has a hammer in his or her toolkit — challenged at best, a significant danger to your project at worst. Although class models look at a much wider picture than data models because they take behavior into account as well as data, they still aren't sufficient by themselves.

Reconsider your approach to modeling.   Your requirements should drive your object schema, your object schema should drive your data schema and source code, and performance challenges and platform (code and DB) features should motivate evolutionary design changes to your object schema.

Work together as a single team.   It's not them and us; it's simply us. The idea that the data team will go off and create the data model for the team, or that they must bless your data model before development can proceed, is not agile, nor is it effective for nonagile efforts. The best thing that I can say about this type of approach is that it is incompetent; the worst thing is that it is purposely done to support dysfunctional political goals such as justifying the existence of a political faction or even to force a project team to fail.

Choose to succeed.   Many people feel unempowered, often because they are. If you want things within your organization to improve, you're going to have to start by improving them yourself. Start sharing new, agile ideas with other developers. They have a choice, but they have to decide for themselves to improve their situation. Sometimes, you may even decide to seek employment elsewhere.

Implementation Impact on Your Objects

The impedance mismatch between object technology and relational technology forces you to map your object schema to your data schema. To implement these mappings, you will need to add code to your business objects, code that affects your application. This impact is the primary fodder for the argument that object purists make against using object and relational technology together. Although I wish the situation were different, the reality is that we're using object and relational technology together and very likely will for many years to come. Like it or not, we need to accept this fact.

I think that there is significant value in summarizing how mapping affects your objects. Some of this material you have seen in this chapter, and some you will see in other chapters. The effects on your code include the need to:

- **Maintain shadow information.**
- **Refactor it to improve overall performance.**
- **Work with legacy data.** In Chapter 8, you saw that it is common to work with legacy databases and that there are often significant data quality, design, and architectural problems associated with them. The implication is that you often need to map your objects to legacy databases and that your objects may need to implement integration and data-cleansing code to do so.
- **Encapsulate database access.** Chapter 13 describes strategies for encapsulating database access, thus implementing your mappings. Your objects will be impacted by your chosen strategy, anywhere from including embedded SQL code to implementing a common interface that a persistence framework requires.

- **Implement concurrency control.** Because most applications are multiuser, and because most databases are accessed by several applications, you run the risk that two different processes will try to modify the same data simultaneously. Therefore your objects need to implement concurrency control strategies that overcome these challenges, the topic of Chapter 17.

- **Find objects in a relational database.** You will want to work with collections of the same types of objects at once, perhaps you want to list all of the employees in a single division. Chapter 18 explores strategies for implementing "find logic" in your business objects.

- **Implement referential integrity.** Chapter 19 describes strategies for implementing referential integrity between objects and within databases. Although referential integrity is a business issue, and therefore should be implemented within your business objects, the reality is that many if not all referential integrity rules are implemented in the database instead.

- **Implement security access control.** Different people have different access to information. As a result you need to implement security access control logic within your objects and your database, the topic of Chapter 20.

- **Implement reports.** Do your business objects implement basic reporting functionality or do you leave this effort solely to reporting tools that go directly against your database? Or do you use a combination? Chapter 21 covers reporting architectural, design, and implementation issues.

- **Implement object caches.** Object caches, discussed in Chapter 15, can be used to improve application performance and to ensure that objects are unique within memory.

Implications for the Model Driven Architecture (MDA)

The Model Driven Architecture (MDA) (Object Management Group 2001b) defines an approach to modeling that separates the specification of system functionality from the specification of its implementation on a specific technology platform. In short, it defines guidelines for structuring specifications expressed as models. The MDA promotes an approach whereby the same model that specifies system functionality can be realized on multiple platforms through auxiliary mapping standards or through point mappings to specific platforms. It also supports the concept of explicitly relating the models of different applications, enabling integration, interoperability, and supporting system evolution as platform technologies come and go.

Although the MDA is based on UML and UML does not yet officially support a data model along the lines of the profile described in Chapter 2, my expectation is that object-to-relational mapping will prove to be one of the most important features that MDA-compliant CASE tools will support. My hope is that the members of the OMG will find a way to overcome the cultural impedance mismatch (Chapter 7) and start to work with data professionals to bring issues such as UML data modeling and object-to-relational mapping into account. Time will tell.

Patternizing the Mappings

Throughout this chapter, I have described mapping techniques in common prose. Although most authors prefer these techniques (visit www.ambysoft.com/mapping Objects.html for an extensive list of links to mapping papers), some authors choose to write patterns instead. The first such effort was Brown and Whitenack's (1996) *Crossing Chasms* pattern language, and the latest effort is captured in the book *Patterns of Enterprise Application Architecture* (Fowler et. al. 2003). Table 14.3 summarizes the critical material presented in this chapter as patterns.

Table 14.3   Mapping Patterns

PATTERN	DESCRIPTION
Class Table Inheritance	Map each individual class within an inheritance hierarchy to its own table.
Concrete Table Inheritance	Map the concrete classes of an inheritance hierarchy to its own table.
Foreign Key Mapping	A relationship between objects is implemented in a relational database as foreign keys in tables.
Identity Field	Maintain the primary key of an object as an attribute. This is an example of Shadow Information.
Lazy Initialization	Read a high-overhead attribute, such as a picture, into memory when you first access it, not when you initially place the object into memory.
Lazy Read	Read an object into memory only when you require it.
Legacy Data Constraint	Legacy data sources are a constraint on your object schema but they should not drive its definition.
Map Similar Types	Use similar types in your classes and tables. For example, it is easier to map an integer to a numeric column than it is to map it to a character-based column.
Map Simple Property to Single Column	Preferentially map the property of an object, such as the total of an order or the first name of an employee, to a single database column.
Mapping-Based Performance Tuning	To improve overall data access performance, you can change your object schema, your data schema, or the mappings in between the two.
Recursive Relationships Are Nothing Special	Map a recursive relationship exactly the same way that you would map a nonrecursive relationship.

Table 14.3   *(continued)*

PATTERN	DESCRIPTION
Representing Objects as Tables	Preferentially map a single class to a single table but be prepared to evolve your design to improve performance.
Separate Tables for Class-Scope Properties	Introduce separate tables to store class scope properties.
Shadow Information	Classes will need to maintain attributes to store the values of database keys (see Identity Field) and concurrency columns to persist themselves.
Single-Column Surrogate Keys	The easiest key strategy that you can adopt within your database is to give all tables a single-column, surrogate key that has a globally unique value.
Single-Table Inheritance	Map all the classes of an inheritance hierarchy to a single table.
Table Design Time	Let your object schema form the basis from which you develop your data schema but be prepared to iterate your design in an evolutionary manner.
Unidirectional Key Choice	When a one-to-one unidirectional association exists from class A to class B, put the foreign key that maintains the relationship in the table corresponding to class A.

Summary

In this chapter, you learned the basics of mapping objects to relational databases (RDBs), including some basic implementation techniques that will be expanded on in following chapters. You saw that there are several strategies for mapping inheritance structures to RDBs and that mapping object relationships into RDBs is straightforward once you understand the differences between the two technologies. Techniques for mapping both instance attributes and class attributes were presented, providing you with strategies to complete a map class's attributes into an RDB.

This chapter also included some methodological discussions that described how mapping is one task in the iterative and incremental approach that is typical of agile software development. Related to this concept is the fact that it is a fundamental mistake to allow your existing database schemas or data models to drive the development of your object models. Look at them, treat them as constraints, but don't let them negatively affect your design if you can avoid it.

CHAPTER 15

Performance Tuning

First you make it work. Then you make it work fast if you need to.

One of the most valuable tasks that an agile DBA can be involved with is performance tuning. This chapter explores the following topics:

- The role of the agile DBA
- Identifying a performance problem
- Profiling a performance problem
- Tuning the problem away

An Overview of Performance Tuning

When you work with structured technology, your performance tuning efforts generally fell into one of three categories:

System tuning.   Ensuring your hardware and middleware are configured properly.

Database performance tuning.   Modifying the database schema.

Data access performance tuning.   Modifying the way that applications interact with the database.

Although these categories are still applicable when you're working with object technology, things have changed a little. Figure 15.1 implies the situation is a little more complicated. It's important to remember that your object schema also has structure to it. In Chapter 14, you saw that your object schema was coupled to your data schema via mappings. For example, assume that the *Employee* class has a *homePhoneNumber* attribute. A new feature requires you to implement phone-number-specific behavior (for example, your application can call people at home). You decide to refactor *home-PhoneNumber* into its class, an example of third normal object form (3ONF, discussed in Chapter 5), and therefore update your mappings to reflect this change. Performance degrades as a result, motivating you to change either your mappings (which are the data access paths) or the database schema itself. Therefore, a change to your object source code could motivate a change to your database schema. Sometimes the reverse happens as well. This is perfectly fine because, as an agile software developer, you are used to working in an evolutionary manner (as described in Chapter 9). The implication is that we need to add a fourth category to the ones listed above: *application tuning*.

Figure 15.1 depicts the fact that your system likely needs to access legacy assets; in fact, both your application code and your database may do so. As you saw in Chapter 8, those legacy assets are often less than perfect, the implication being that your system's overall performance may be outside your control. Therefore, you're potentially going to need to work closely with the owners of these other systems to improve them over time, perhaps via refactoring, in order for your system to achieve the performance levels that you require. Or perhaps you're simply going to have to accept these challenges and work around them. Either way, it's important to recognize that performance tuning is often an enterprise-level issue, not just a project-level issue.

TIP The books *Database Administration* (Mullins 2002) and *Database Tuning* (Shasha and Bonnet 2003) are very good resources for anyone interested in performance tuning. The sites www.javaperformancetuning.com and www.sql-server-performance.com are also worth visits.

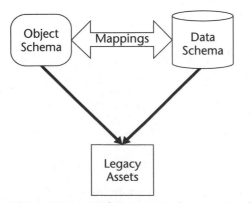

Figure 15.1   Performance-tuning opportunities.

The Role of the Agile DBA

Agile DBAs must become proficient, at least over time, at performance tuning. Whenever there is a perceived performance issue with the database, the project team will typically turn to the agile DBA for help. I use the word "perceived" because, as you can see in Figure 15.1, the performance of your system depends on far more than just your database. Agile DBAs will also find that they need to work with the owners of legacy systems, as well as enterprise administrators and enterprise architects, to deal with performance issues involving the organization's overall environment.

A critical concept is that agile DBAs need to be prepared to take an evolutionary approach to performance tuning. In the past, it was common to leave performance tuning until late in the life cycle because one often wanted to wait until most of the system was in place. Agile teams, however, produce working software in an incremental manner — at the end of each iteration, which is often as short as a week or two. The implication is that performance tuning should potentially occur throughout software development in an evolutionary manner, as Chapter 9 indicates.

Although performance tuning is an evolutionary effort, it can be helpful for agile DBAs to think of it as a three-step process:

- Identify
- Profile
- Tune

These steps are discussed in detail in the following sections.

Step One: Identify a Performance Problem

My grandfather always said "if it ain't broke, don't fix it." The obvious implication for software development is that if your system is working fast enough already, then making it faster isn't a good use of your time. Without a clear performance problem to address, you are better advised to invest your time improving your application's functionality — follow the Agile Modeling (discussed in Chapter 10) practice of *Maximize Stakeholder Investment* by focusing your efforts where they are most needed.

Overtuning a system is a waste of effort. If you're addressing a performance problem and find that you've addressed the issue then stop working on it and move on to something else.

Step Two: Profile the Problem

Don't guess where a performance problem is; instead, use profiling tools to track down the source of the problem. This is something called *root cause analysis*. Without identifying the root cause(s) of a performance problem, you can easily make the wrong guess, and then spend significant effort tuning the wrong thing to no avail. Although most database management systems (DBMSs) come with a profiling tool, as do some integrated development environments (IDEs), you will likely still find that you need to purchase or download one or more separate tools. Table 15.1 presents a sampling of such tools.

Once you have the profiling results in hand, you are in a position to identify where the performance bottleneck is. You can then apply one or more of the techniques in the next section and then profile your system again to see if you have addressed the problem. You proceed iteratively until you have fixed the problem.

Table 15.1   Some Performance-Profiling Tools

TOOL	DESCRIPTION	URL
DBFlash for Oracle	A database-profiling tool that continuously monitors Oracle databases to reveal internal bottlenecks such as library cache waits and external bottlenecks such as network or CPU problems. It also displays data contention at the row level, enabling you to detect concurrency control (see Chapter 17) issues.	www.confio.com
DevPartnerDB	A suite of tools for database and access profiling that works on several database platforms (Oracle, SQL Server, Sybase). Profiles a wide variety of elements including SQL statements, stored procedures, locks, and database objects.	www.compuware.com
JunitPerf	JUnitPerf is a collection of Junit (www.junit.org) test decorators used to measure the performance and scalability of functionality in Java applications.	www.clarkware.com
PerformaSure	PerformaSure profiles multitier J2EE applications by reconstructing the execution path of end-user transactions to highlight potential performance problems.	java.quest.com
Rational Quantify	An application-performance-profiling tool that delivers repeatable timing data for all parts of an application, not just the parts for which you have the source code. There are Windows and Unix versions.	www.rational.com

TIP Be humble. Although it would be nice to be omniscient, the reality is that you don't know everything — nor can you. The important thing is that you're willing to investigate a performance problem and then do the best that you can to address it. It's perfectly fine to say, "I don't know why the system is acting this way" as long as you're also willing to say, "Let me look into it right away and get back to you."

Step Three: Tune the Problem Away

An agile DBA understands that there are four categories of tuning that they need to consider:

- System tuning
- Database-access tuning
- Database tuning
- Application tuning

These categories are discussed in detail in the following sections.

System Tuning

Whenever you're involved with performance tuning, the very first thing you should try to determine is whether everything is set up properly. Your database not only is one part of the overall technical environment but it also relies on other components to work properly. With respect to software, are the operating systems, middleware, transaction monitors, and caches installed and configured properly? You may need to work with an enterprise administrator with expertise in these various technologies to ensure that they're not the cause of your performance problems.

Similarly, hardware can pose performance challenges. Does your database server have sufficient memory and disk space? How about your application servers? It is critical to have sufficient memory; several times I've seen the performance of a computer worth tens of thousands of dollars dramatically improved by the installation of a couple of thousand dollars worth of memory. What about your network hardware? A few years back I did an architectural review of a system that was suffering from serious performance problems. The client feared that there was a significant design flaw with the application, but the real problem was that the database server needed its network interface card (NIC) upgraded at a cost of $150.

The manner in which your system interacts with legacy systems can have a significant performance impact. Simple things like keeping a pool of connections to the legacy applications or installing a virtual private network (VPN) link between the applications can make a world of difference.

Database Access Tuning

After system tuning, the most likely candidate for performance problems is the way that your database is accessed. There are three basic strategies that you should consider:

- Choose the right access strategy.
- Tune your SQL code.
- Tune your mappings.

Choose the Right Access Strategy

When it comes to accessing data in relational databases you have choices, each of which has its strengths and weaknesses. The following list summarizes common strategies. Most applications will use a combination of these strategies, and some very complex ones may even use all of them.

Indexed access.   Supports a random-access approach to data. It is quite common to introduce an index to support a specific query. Indices are also used to avoid implicit sorts such as those caused by DISTINCT, UNION, GROUP BY, and ORDER BY clauses in SQL WHERE clauses.

Persistence framework.   A common database encapsulation strategy (see Chapter 13). One of several advantages of good persistence frameworks is that they will implement many data access performance "tricks" that novice DBAs may not be aware of.

Stored procedures.   Used to implement complex database functionality and/or to encapsulate database access. A common strategy is to introduce a stored procedure to process data in the database server to reduce the result set before transmitting it across the network. See common database refactorings (see the Appendix) such as *Encapsulate Calculation With Method, Encapsulate CRUD Access with Methods, Introduce Method to Reduce Data Transfer, Migrate Method to Database, Replace Calculated Column with a Method,* and *Replace View with Method(s)*.

Table scan.   Supports sequential data access. With this approach, you should consider data read ahead strategies where you prefetch the next data you need into a cache, while the existing data is being processed.

Views.   A database view is a representation of a table defined by SQL code. Therefore, when an SQL query accesses a view, you're effectively embedding SQL within SQL, implying that SQL tuning techniques are applicable. Views are often used to restrict access to a portion of a table (perhaps some columns or rows aren't accessible to some users) or to combine data from several tables to make it appear as one table. Consider the database refactorings *Encapsulate Common Structure with View* and *Encapsulate Table with View*.

TIP It is common practice to create sequence diagrams to model complex usage scenarios. As a result, sequence diagrams often explore critical collaborations between business objects that in turn require interactions with the database. Reed (2002) points out that sequence diagrams often imply primary data access paths; therefore, sequence diagrams are good indicators for where you should start profiling your application to detect potential performance problems.

Tune Your SQL

Tuning your SQL code is often a very effective strategy. However, depending on your encapsulation strategy, you may not be able to directly tune your SQL code and instead will only be able to change the configuration variables. Tuning strategies that you should consider:

Choose the right type of SQL. The different types of SQL — planned or unplanned, dynamic or static, embedded or standalone — have different performance characteristics. Although you might want the flexibility of dynamically generated SQL, you may discover that the performance needs of your system require you to use static SQL instead.

Loosen your locking strategy. In general, the more restrictive your locking strategy is, the poorer the performance due to an increased number of collisions. You may discover that you need to trade off data integrity for performance. Chapter 17 provides an overview of various locking strategies.

Commit frequently. You should issue commits as soon as possible to release any locks or database objects held by your application code. This will reduce the number of collisions as well as free up memory.

Consider batch processing. You don't need to do everything online, nor do you need to do it against the most up-to-date version of your data. Mission-critical applications such as invoicing are often done in batches against a "snapshot" of the required data (which is often hours, days, or even weeks old).

Avoid joins. Joins, particularly of two large tables, can be very expensive. Avoid them if possible, perhaps by denormalizing your database schema or introducing indices to support the join.

Take advantage of specific database features. Each database vendor offers a unique collection of features, many of which can be used to enhance performance. Yes, each time you follow this strategy you run the risk of writing code that you can't port to another database at some time in the future, but most firms are locked into their current database vendor so portability really isn't much of an issue.

Retrieve only the columns you need.   Instead of writing *SELECT ** instead write *SELECT FirstName, LastName, BirthDate* to specify only the columns that you want. This way, you're working with smaller result sets that are easier to process and to transmit.

Avoid OR in WHERE clauses.   Instead of writing clauses such as *Name = 'Smith' OR Name = 'Jones'* you should instead write *Name IN ('Smith', 'Jones')*. Most databases will process the latter clause more efficiently than the former.

Avoid LIKE clauses.   Clauses such as *Name LIKE '%r'* require a table scan, which is expensive, although most databases will process *Name LIKE 'R%'* effectively as long as there is an index defined on the *Name* column.

Before making any changes to your SQL, you should first profile your code, then make the change, then profile it again to ensure that the change actually helped. The best performance tuners do their work based on solid information, not just good guesses.

TIP Get training in database performance tuning. Every database has its own unique features and development tools. To be effective at tuning your database and your access code, you will need an intimate knowledge of these things.

Tune Your Mappings

In Chapter 14, you learned that there is more than one way to map object schemas to data schemas. For example, there are four ways to map inheritance structures, two ways to map a one-to-one relationship (depending on where you put the foreign key), and four ways to map class-scope properties. Because you have mapping choices, and because each mapping choice has its advantages and disadvantages, there are opportunities to improve the data-access performance of your application by changing your choice of mapping. Perhaps you implemented the one table per class approach to mapping inheritance only to discover that it's too slow, motivating you to refactor it to use the one table per hierarchy approach.

Database Tuning

Database performance tuning focuses on changing the database schema itself. Strategies that you want to consider include:

- Denormalize your data schema.
- Rework database logs.
- Update your database configuration.
- Reorganize data storage.
- Rework your database architecture/design.

TIP Refactorings, be they code refactorings (Fowler 1999) or database refactorings (see Chapter 12 and the Appendix), improve a design without changing its semantics. When you're performance tuning, you want to make your system run faster without affecting its overall functionality (you want the same thing only faster). You'll likely discover that common code refactorings are sufficient for many of your application-tuning needs, and similarly database refactorings will often solve common database-performance issues.

Denormalize Your Data Schema

Normalized data schemas often suffer from performance problems. This makes sense — the rules of data normalization focus on reducing data redundancy, not on improving performance of data access. Denormalization should be resorted to only when one or more of the following is true:

- Performance testing shows that you have a problem with your system, subsequent profiling reveals that you need to improve database access time, and denormalization is your last option.

- You're developing a reporting database. Reports require many different views on data, views that typically require denormalized information. Reporting is discussed in detail in Chapter 21.

- Common queries require data from several tables. This includes common repeating groups of data and calculated figures based on several rows.

- Tables need to be simultaneously accessed in various ways.

For example, the data model of Figure 15.3 looks nothing like the normalized schema of Figure 15.2 (taken from Chapter 4). To understand why the differences between the schemas exist, you must consider the performance needs of the application. The primary goal of this system is to process new orders from online customers as quickly as possible. To do this, customers need to be able to search for items and add them to their order quickly, remove items from their order if need be, then have their final order totaled and recorded quickly. The secondary goal of the system is to the process, ship, and then bill customers for the orders afterwards.

TIP Not all performance problems can be solved, at least not for a reasonable amount of money. The implication is that you sometimes just need to do your best and then accept the resulting level of performance because that's as good as you're going to get it.

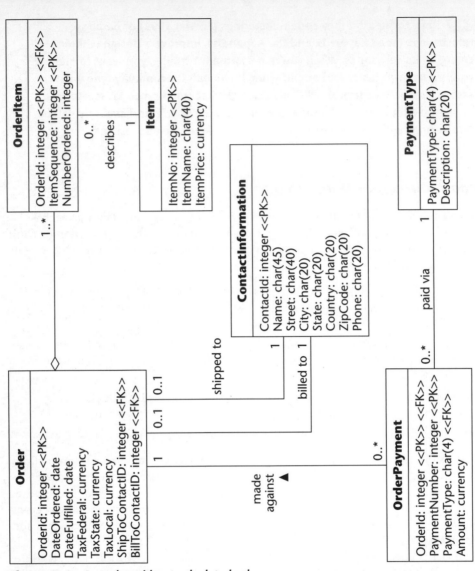

Figure 15.2   An order without calculated values.

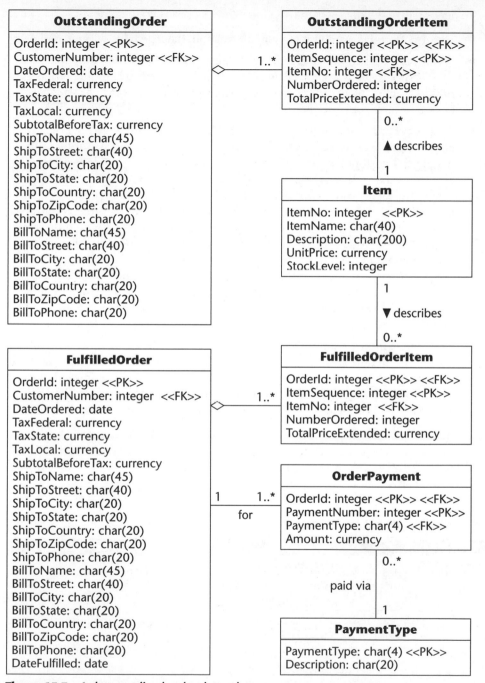

Figure 15.3   A denormalized order data schema.

To denormalize the data schema, the following decisions were made:

- To support quick searching of item information, the *Item* table was left alone.

- To support the addition and removal of order items to an order, the concept of an *OrderItem* table was kept, albeit split in two to support outstanding orders and fulfilled orders. New order items can easily be inserted into the *Outstanding-OrderItem* table, or removed from it, as needed.

- To support order processing, the *Order* and *OrderItem* tables were reworked into pairs to handle outstanding and fulfilled orders respectively. Basic order information is first stored in the *OutstandingOrder* and *OutstandingOrderItem* tables and, when the order has been shipped and paid for, the data is then removed from those tables and copied into the *FulfilledOrder* and *FulfilledOrderItem* tables, respectively. Data access time to the two tables for outstanding orders is reduced because only the active orders are being stored there. On average, an order may be outstanding for a couple of days, whereas for financial-reporting reasons may be stored in the fulfilled order tables for several years until archived. There is a performance penalty under this scheme because of the need to delete outstanding orders and then resave them as fulfilled orders, clearly something that would need to be processed as a transaction. This is an application of the *Separate Data Based on Timeliness* database refactoring.

- The contact information for the person(s) the order is being shipped and billed to was also denormalized back into the *Order* table, reducing the time it takes to write an order to the database because there is now one write instead of two or three. The retrieval and deletion times for that data would also be similarly improved. This is an application of the *Introduce Redundant Column* database refactoring.

Table 15.2 summarizes a collection of denormalization strategies suggested by Craig Mullins (2002), all of which are supported through one or more database refactorings (see the Appendix).

Table 15.2 Denormalization Strategies

STRATEGY	DESCRIPTION	DATABASE REFACTORING(S)
Combined tables	Combine tables with a one-to-one relationship to reduce the number of joins.	Combine One-to-One Tables
Derivable data	When the cost of calculating/deriving data is expensive, consider physically storing the derived data in a column. Figure 15.3 could be denormalized further in this manner by adding a GrandTotal column to the Order table.	• Encapsulate Calculation with Method • Introduce Calculated Data Column • Introduce Trigger(s) for Calculated Column

Table 15.2   *(continued)*

STRATEGY	DESCRIPTION	DATABASE REFACTORING(S)
Mirror tables	When a table is very active, create one or more copies of it so that the accesses can be spread out.	Introduce Mirror Table
Pre-joined tables	A table is created on a periodic basis to join data from two or more tables, the primary advantage being that the cost of the join is incurred only once each time the table is created.	Introduce View Table
Redundant data	Create copies of columns from other tables that are commonly accessed when this row is. For example, Figure 15.3 could be denormalized further in this manner by copying the PaymentType .Description column into the OrderPayment table.	Introduce Redundant Column
Repeating groups	You reverse a first normal form (1NF) decision and bring a repeating group back into a table. An example of this is the bill to and ship to information contained in the Order table of Figure 15.3.	Move Column
Report tables	The data for a specific report is created in batch and loaded, in the appropriate order, into a table containing the columns required for that report.	Introduce View Table
Split tables	When a table is accessed by different and distinct groups of users, consider splitting the table either horizontally or vertically in a manner that reflects the types of access by the different groups.	• Separate Data Based on Timeliness • Separate Read-Only Data

Rework Database Logs

Database logs, also known as *transaction logs*, are used to commit and roll back transactions as well as to restore databases. It is clear that database logs are important. Unfortunately, there is a performance and complexity overhead to support logs — the more information you record in the log, the worse your performance will be. Therefore, you need to be very careful what you log. At one extreme, you could choose to log "everything" but you will very likely discover that the performance impact is more than you can tolerate. At the other extreme, if you choose to log the bare minimum, you may find that you don't have sufficient information to recover from an adverse situation. Once again, the agile data (AD) method's sixth philosophy (Chapter 1) of finding the sweet spot between two extremes is critical to your success.

Update Your Database Configuration

Although the default configuration values for your database are a good start, they likely don't reflect the detailed nuances for your situation. Furthermore, even if you have configured your database appropriately, your situation changes over time — perhaps you have more transactions to process than you originally thought, perhaps your database is growing at a different rate than you expected, and so on — which will motivate changing your database configuration.

Reorganize Data Storage

Over time, data within a database becomes disorganized and as a result performance degrades. Common problems include:

Extents.   An extent is an addition to a database that is used to extend its size. The end result is that tables may not be stored contiguously or that tables required by a single query are stored in different files. Performance degrades because your DBMS needs to process several files instead of one.

Fragmentation.   Small areas of storage are scattered throughout your database but they're too small to be usable. Space is lost, resulting in other problems such as the addition of new extents.

Row chaining/migrating.   An existing row is updated but it no longer fits into the space it currently occupies, forcing your DBMS to move it. When you take a chaining approach, part of the row is moved to another physical portion of your database, whereas when you take a migration approach the entire row is moved.

Unclustered data.   Data becomes unordered over time as it's added and deleted. For example, Customer 1701 and Customer 1702 could be in completely different physical parts of your database, even though this data is accessed in order on a frequent basis.

Data reorganization utilities are common features in DBMSs and their accompanying administration tools. An agile DBA will often automate the running of database reorganization utilities, often at off-peak times, to keep the physical data storage as efficient as possible.

Rework Your Database Architecture/Design

In addition to denormalizing the data schema to improve performance, you should also consider the following issues when tuning your database:

Nested trigger calls.   Triggers are event-driven methods that are often used to enforce referential integrity constraints within relational databases. They can cascade, in other words a trigger can cause several others to run. For example, if you delete a row from the *Order* table, it causes the corresponding rows in the *OrderItem* table to be deleted and the *TotalCustomerOrder* column to be updated in another table. As your database schema is refactored over time to include new triggers, you may discover that the performance of some queries degrades due to excessive triggers, and therefore some triggers need to be removed. Chapter 19 presents alternatives to triggers that you may want to consider.

Distributed databases.   When a database is distributed across several servers, servers that may be physically located in different places, performance will be affected. You may need to rethink your distribution strategy.

Keys.   Many databases work more efficiently when an index is based on a specific type, such as an integer, prompting you to change your key strategy (discussed in Chapter 3). Similarly, some databases struggle to process indices used to implement composite keys with a large number of columns (seven is often a magic number).

Indices.   The performance of a query can often be improved by the addition of a supporting index. However, additional indices on a table degrade the performance of inserts, updates, and deletes because each index potentially needs to be updated when each of these actions occurs.

Free space.   Is there sufficient space in your database for data growth?

Archiving.   The larger a table is, the slower it is to process. Tables can be reduced in size by archiving old data that isn't needed anymore, or at least that is unlikely to be needed. Alternatives to archiving include the *Separate Data Based on Timeliness* and *Separate Read-Only Data refactorings* (see the Appendix).

Page size.   The page size used by your database can have a huge impact on its performance. For example if the size of a row is 1,500 bytes, then a 4K page size allows two records per page, whereas an 8K page size allows five. If queries often result in many rows, an 8K page size is better; if most queries result in one or two rows, then 4K may be a better option.

Security options.   The amount of security you implement in your database will affect its performance — the more security checks, the lower the performance. Chapter 20 describes several strategies for implementing security within your system, and moving it out of your database is one of them.

Application Tuning

Your application code is just as likely to be the root of performance problems as is your database. In fact, in situations where your database is a shared resource, you are likely to discover, for reasons discussed in Chapter 12, that it is much easier to change your application code than your database schema. You have several alternatives available to you:

- Share common logic.
- Implement lazy reads.
- Introduce caches.
- Combine granular functionality.

TIP Keep it simple, silly (KISS) is the order of the day when you are tuning for performance. If you have several options for solving a performance problem, choose the simplest one and move on.

Share Common Logic

An unfortunately common problem in many systems is that the same logic is implemented in several tiers. For example, you may discover that referential integrity logic is implemented both in your business objects and your database. Another culprit may be security access control logic that is implemented on each tier "just to be safe." If you're doing the same thing in two places, you're clearly doing it in one place too many. Root out and then resolve these redundant inefficiencies.

Implement Lazy Reads

An important performance consideration is whether the attribute should be automatically read in when an object is retrieved. When an attribute is very large and rarely accessed, you may want to consider taking a lazy read approach. A good candidate would be the picture of a person, perhaps on average 100K in size, data that few operations actually need. Instead of automatically bringing the attribute across the network when the object is read, you instead retrieve it only when the attribute is actually needed. This can be accomplished by a getter method, an operation whose purpose is to provide the value of a single attribute, that checks to see if the attribute has been initialized, and if not, retrieves it from the database at that point.

Other common uses for lazy reads are retrieving objects as the results of searches implementing reports (discussed in Chapter 21) within your object code. In both situations, you only need a small subset of the data of an object.

Introduce Caches

A *cache* is a location where copies of entities are temporarily kept in memory. Because database accesses often take the majority of processing time in business applications, caches can dramatically reduce the number of database accesses that your applications need to make. Examples of caches include:

Object cache.   With this approach copies of business objects are maintained in memory. Application servers may put some or all business objects into a shared cache, enabling all the users that it supports to work with the same copies of the objects. This reduces its number of interactions with the database(s) because now it can retrieve the objects once and consolidate the changes of several users before updating the database. Another approach is to have a cache for each user where updates to the database are made during off-peak times, an approach that can be taken by fat client applications as well. An object cache can be implemented easily via the *Identity Map* pattern (Fowler et. al. 2003) that advises use of a collection that supports the looking up of an object by its identity field (the attribute[s] representing the primary key within the database, one type of shadow information).

Database cache.   A database server will cache data in memory, enabling reducing the number of disk accesses.

Client data cache.   Client machines may have their own smaller copies of databases, perhaps a Microsoft Access version of the corporate Oracle database, enabling them to reduce network traffic and to run in disconnected mode. These database copies are replicated with the database of record (the corporate database) to obtain updated data.

Combine Granular Functionality

A common mistake is to implement very granular functionality within an application. For example, you may implement separate Web services to update the name of a customer, to update the customer's address, and to update the customer's phone number. Although these are cohesive services, they aren't very effective performance-wise if you commonly need to do these three things together. Instead, it would be better to have a single Web service that updated the name, address, and phone number of a customer because it would run faster than invoking three separate Web services.

Summary

In this chapter, you discovered that in agile software development, as in everything else, performance tuning can and should be approached in an evolutionary manner. I also showed that there are several aspects to performance tuning — system, database access, database, and application — each of which are important in their own way. You also learned that there are several techniques available to you in each category, providing you with multiple avenues of attack.

CHAPTER 16

Tools for Evolutionary Database Development

A fool with a tool is still a fool.
Source Unknown

Agile DBAs need to adopt, build, and/or modify a collection of tools in order to be effective. Furthermore, tools are just a start; they also need an effective technical environment in which to use them. This environment should comprise several "sandboxes" in which you will work. Finally, agile DBAs will discover that they need several different types of scripts to support their development efforts.

This chapter explores:

- Tools
- Sandboxes
- Scripts

Tools

Having an effective toolset is a critical success factor for any software development effort. Table 16.1 lists categories of tools, the target audience for the tool, how you would use the tool, and links to a representative sample of such tools. Chances are very good that you already have many of these tools in-house, although you will undoubtedly need to obtain several of them.

Table 16.2 lists tools that to my knowledge do not exist yet, at least at the time of this writing, that are needed to support the agile data method. My hope that we will see both commercial and open source tools available in the near future, particularly tools that support database refactoring (as discussed in Chapter 12).

Table 16.1   Potential Tools That Support Agile Data Efforts

TOOL CATEGORY	ROLE	PURPOSE	EXAMPLES
CASE tool — development modeling	Application developer, agile DBA	To support your application development efforts.	Artisan: www.artisansw.com Poseidon: www.gentleware.com/
CASE tool — enterprise modeling	Enterprise architect	To define and manage your enterprise models.	System Architect: www.popkin.com/
CASE tool — physical data modeling	Agile DBA	To define and manage your physical database schema. Many data-modeling tools support the generation and deployment of data definition language (DDL) code, making it easier to change your database schema. They also produce visual representations of your schema and support your documentation efforts.	ER/Studio: www.embarcadero.com ERWin Data Modeler: www3.ca.com/Solutions/Product.asp?ID=260 PowerDesigner: www.sybase.com
Configuration management	Everyone	You need to place all DDL, source code, models, scripts, documents, and so on under version control.	ChangeMan: www.serena.com CVS: www.cvshome.org IBM TeamConnection: www.ibm.com Rational ClearCase: www.rational.com
Development IDE	Application developer, agile DBA	To support your programming and testing efforts.	Borland Delphi: www.borland.com/delphi/index.html IDEA: www.intellij.com/idea/ Microsoft Visual Studio: msdn.microsoft.com

Table 16.1 *(continued)*

TOOL CATEGORY	ROLE	PURPOSE	EXAMPLES
Extract transform load (ETL)	Agile DBA, enterprise administrator	ETL tools can automate your data-cleansing and -migrating efforts as you evolve your database schema.	Ascential Software: www.ascential-software.com/etl_tool.htm Data Junction: www.datajunction.com Embarcadero DT/Studio: www.embarcadero.com Sagent: www.sagent.com
Other testing tools for load testing, user-interface testing, system testing, and so on	Application developer, agile DBA	You will need to go beyond unit testing to perform a more robust set of tests that go beyond unit testing. Chapter 9 of *The Object Primer 2/e* (Ambler 2001a) summarizes the Full Lifecycle Object-Oriented Testing (FLOOT) method, which encapsulates a wide range of testing techniques.	Empirix: www.empirix.com Mercury Interactive: www-svca.mercuryinteractive.com/ products/testing RadView: www.radview.com Rational Suite Test Studio: www.rational.com/products/systest.jsp Web Performance: www.webperformanceinc.com
Persistence frameworks	Application developer, agile DBA	Persistence frameworks/layers (discussed in Chapter 13) encapsulate your database schema, minimizing the chance that database refactorings will force code refactorings of external applications.	Castor: castor.exolab.org CocoBase: www.thoughtinc.com Prevayler: www.prevayler.org TopLink: www.objectpeople.com
Test data generator	Application developer, agile DBA	Developers need test data against which to validate their systems. Test data generators can be particularly useful when you need large amounts of data, perhaps for stress and load testing.	Datatect: www.datatect.com/ Princeton Softech: www.princetonsoftech.com/ products/relationaltools.htm

(continued)

Table 16.1   *(continued)*

TOOL CATEGORY	ROLE	PURPOSE	EXAMPLES
Traceability management/ repository	Everyone	Traceability-management and meta data-repository tools enable you to track the relationships between systems. Maintaining such traceability meta-data is unfortunately problematic when many systems are involved because it requires a precise change-control process. However, it is possible.	CA Advantage: www3.ca.com Caliber RM: www.borland.com DOORS: www.telelogic.com/index.cfm Rochade: http://www.asg.com RTM: www.chipware.com
Unit testing tools for your applications	Application developer	Developers must be able to unit test their work, and to support iterative development they must be able to easily regression test their work.	Check for C: check.sourceforge.net JUnit: www.junit.org VBUnit: www.vbunit.org
Unit testing tools for your database	Agile DBA	Whenever you change your database schema, perhaps as the result of a database refactoring, you must be able to regression test your database to ensure that it still works.	UTPLSQL for Oracle: oracle.oreilly.com/utplsql

Table 16.2   Future Tools

TOOL CATEGORY	DISCUSSION
Automated schema traceability management tools	Although Table 16.1 includes traceability management tools, the reality is that most tools are geared either toward requirements traceability or data-access traceability (as in the case of repositories such as Rochade and Advantage). Neither type is suited for the fine-grained traceability required for database refactoring (discussed in Chapter 12). Ideally, you need a tool that can trace a wide range of application features, such as COBOL procedures and Java operations, to database features such as stored procedures and table columns. Because of the complexity of this task, the less manual intervention the better — ideally, it should be able to parse your application and database code and create the traceability matrix automatically.
Database refactoring browser	This tool should work in a similar manner to existing code-refactoring browsers, with the target environment being your database instead of your application source code.

Sandboxes

A *sandbox* is basically a technical environment whose scope is well defined and respected. The following list describes the four different types of sandboxes:

Development.   This is the working environment of individual developers, programming pairs, or individual feature teams. The purpose of this environment is for the developer team to work in seclusion from the rest of the project team, enabling him or her to make and validate changes without having to worry about adversely affecting the rest of the project team. These environments are likely to have their own databases.

Project integration.   Each project team should have its own integration environment, often referred to as a build environment or simply a build box. Developers will promote their changed code to this environment, test it, and commit it to their team's configuration-management system. The goal of this environment is to combine and validate the work of your entire project team so it can be tested before being promoted into your test/QA sandbox.

Test/QA.   This sandbox is shared by several project teams and is often controlled by a separate team, typically your testing/QA group. This environment is often referred to as a *preproduction sandbox*, a *system testing area*, or simply a *staging area*. Its purpose is to provide an environment that simulates your actual production environment as closely as possible so you can test your application in conjunction with other applications. This sandbox is crucial for complex environments where several applications access your database, although even if your database is only accessed by a standalone application, you will still be required to test within this sandbox before deploying your application in production.

Production. This is the actual environment in which your system will run once it is deployed.

Figure 16.1 depicts the nature of the work performed within each sandbox, the deployment effort between them, and the flow of bug reports. You can see the following things from the figure:

- The effort within development sandboxes is highly iterative, and you will frequently deploy your work in your project integration sandbox.

- Deployment in the test/QA sandbox is less frequent, typically at the end of an iteration and often only at the end of some iterations. There is greater control over whether you deploy in this sandbox because it is typically a shared resource that other teams are deploying in as well; therefore, someone needs to verify that your system appears to have been sufficiently tested in isolation and is ready for system integration testing. It should be even harder to deploy in production than test/QA because you need to be able to show that your application has been thoroughly tested and appears to integrate into your organizational infrastructure.

- Bug reports are always fed back to the development environment, and not to the previous sandbox, to be fixed.

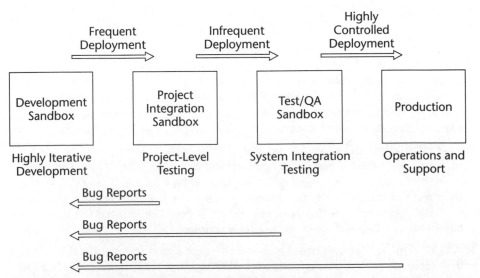

Figure 16.1 Sandboxes within your technical environment.

Scripts

Pramod Sadalage and Peter Schuh (2002) suggest that agile DBAs maintain what they call a *database change log* and an *update log*, the minimum that you require for simple stovepipe projects, where a single application accesses your database. However, to support more complex environments where many applications access your database, you also require a *data migration log*. Let's explore how you use each log:

Database change log.   This log contains the DDL source code that implements all database schema changes in the order that they were applied throughout the course of a project. This includes structural changes such as adding, dropping, renaming, or modifying things such as tables, views, columns, and indices.

Update log.   This log contains the source code for future changes to the database schema that are to be run after the deprecation period for database changes. Chapter 12 argues that refactoring your database schema is inherently more difficult than refactoring application source code — other developers on your project team need time to update their own code and worse yet, other applications may access your database and therefore need to be modified and deployed as well. Thus, you will find that you need to maintain both the original and changed portions of your schema, as well as any scaffolding code to keep your data in sync, for a period of time called the *deprecation period*.

Data migration log.   This log contains the data manipulation language (DML) to reformat or cleanse the source data throughout the course of your project. You may choose to implement these changes using data cleansing utilities, often the heart of extract-transform-load (ETL) tools, examples of which are listed in Table 16.1.

You may choose to implement each logical script as a collection of physical scripts, perhaps one for each development iteration or even one for each individual database refactoring or data migration, or you may choose to implement as a single script that includes the ability to run only a portion of the changes. You must be able to apply subsets of your changes to be able to put your database schemas into known states. For example, you may find yourself in development iteration 10 to discover that you want to roll back your schema to the way it was at the beginning of iteration 8.

It's important to recognize that scripts are a simple way to achieve these goals. However, in the coming years, I fully expect to see development tools that support database refactoring, and I expect them to use a more sophisticated approach. Having said that, scripts work well for now.

TIP Agile Modeling (discussed in Chapter 10) advises you to follow the practice *Use the Simplest Tools* and pick the simplest tool that gets the job done. Although many vendors would like to sell you complicated development environments, the reality is that there are many open source tools available to you as well as very simple tools such as whiteboards and text files that work perfectly fine.

Summary

Agile DBAs are no different from application developers — they need more than just techniques to be effective, they also need technologies. In this chapter, I reviewed common technologies that support the activities of agile DBAs. These include development tools, an effective technical environment that supports controlled change, and database scripts. These are all basic technologies, but they are still critical to success.

Three

Practical Data-Oriented Development Techniques

This part focuses on implementation techniques and strategies that agile developers require to effectively apply object and data-oriented technologies together. An important observation is that many of these topics are traditionally thought of as data issues, but as you'll see, there is far more to them than this — it isn't a black-and-white world. I suggest that you skim these chapters at first to make yourself aware of their contents, then use them as reference as you need to when these issues occur on your projects.

Chapter 17: Implementing Concurrency Control. Concurrency control deals with the issues involved with allowing multiple people simultaneous access to shared entities, be they objects, data records, or some other representation.

Chapter 18: Finding Objects in Relational Databases. A common programming task is to retrieve one or more objects from a database, perhaps to display a list of people that work in a department, to list available inventory items that meet user-defined search criteria, or simply to implement a report.

Chapter 19: Implementing Referential Integrity and Shared Business Logic. When one entity references another, the referenced entity should exist. Referential integrity is an issue when one row references another row, an object references another object, or an object represents a data within a database (or vice versa).

Chapter 20: Implementing Security Access Control.   Your system must ensure that authenticated users access only what they are authorized to. The complexities of modern development require developers to understand a wide range of options to do exactly this.

Chapter 21: Implementing Reports.   There are several common strategies to support reporting functionality within your system and/or to integrate your system with a common reporting application that crosses a variety of systems.

Chapter 22: Realistic XML.   XML is a robust and growing set of technologies. Unfortunately, many people seem to have forgotten the data community's hard-earned lessons and seem to think that XML is the panacea that will solve all of their problems. This is hardly the case. XML has a very bright future but you need to look beyond the hype and use it for its true strengths.

CHAPTER 17

Implementing Concurrency Control

There is no I in agile. ;-)

Assume that you and I both read the same row from the *Customer* table, we both change the data, and then we both try to write our new versions to the database. Whose changes should be saved? Yours? Mine? Neither? A combination? Similarly, if we both work with the same Customer object stored in a shared object cache and try to make changes to it, what should happen? Concurrency control deals with the issues involved with allowing multiple people simultaneous access to shared entities, be they objects, data records, or some other representation. To understand how to implement concurrency control within your system you must start by understanding the basics of collisions — you can either avoid them or detect and resolve them. The next step is to understand transactions, which are collections of actions that potentially modify one or more entities. Examples of transactions include the transfer of funds between two bank accounts, the updating of all employee salaries to give them a 5 percent cost of living adjustment, and the updating of a customer's home phone number. In the case of the transfer, the transaction consists of debiting the source account, crediting the target account, and recording the fact that this occurred.

As you can see, modern software-development projects demand that concurrency control and transactions be not simply the domain of databases, but rather be issues that are potentially pertinent to all of your architectural tiers.

This chapter explores:

- The role of the agile DBA
- Collisions
- Understanding transactions

The Role of the Agile DBA

When it comes to concurrency control, the role of agile DBAs is straightforward. They will:

- Work with enterprise administrators and enterprise architects to learn about and potentially evolve any pertinent enterprise standards.
- Mentor application developers in concurrency control strategies.
- Work with rest of team to choose approach(es) to concurrency control.
- Work with application developers to implement concurrency control strategies.

Collisions

Chapter 19 discusses the referential integrity challenges that result from there being an object schema that is mapped to a data schema, something called *cross-schema referential integrity problems*. With respect to collisions, things are a little simpler; we only need to worry about ensuring the consistency of entities within the system of record. The system of record is the location where the official version of an entity is located. This is often data stored within a relational database, although other representations, such as an XML structure or an object, are also viable.

A *collision* is said to occur when two activities, which may or may not be full-fledged transactions, attempt to change entities within a system of record. There are three fundamental ways (Celko 1999) that two activities can interfere with one another:

Dirty read.   Activity 1 (A1) reads an entity from the system of record and then updates the system of record but does not commit the change (for example, the change hasn't been finalized). Activity 2 (A2) reads the entity, unknowingly making a copy of the uncommitted version. A1 rolls back (aborts) the changes, restoring the entity to the original state that A1 found it in. A2 now has a version of the entity that was never committed and therefore is not considered to have actually existed.

Nonrepeatable read.   A1 reads an entity from the system of record, making a copy of it. A2 deletes the entity from the system of record. A1 now has a copy of an entity that does not officially exist.

Phantom read.   A1 retrieves a collection of entities from the system of record, making copies of them, based on some sort of search criteria such as "all customers with first name Bill."A2 then creates new entities, which would have met the search criteria (for example, inserts "Bill Klassen" into the database), saving them to the system of record. If A1 reapplies the search criteria it gets a different result set.

So what can you do? The data needs to be locked somehow. The following section describes the various types of locking available to you.

Types of Locking

You have several options when choosing how to lock your files, including:

- Take a *pessimistic locking* approach that avoids collisions but reduces system performance.

- Use an *optimistic locking* strategy that enables you to detect collisions so you can later resolve them.

- Take an *overly optimistic locking* strategy that ignores the issue completely.

In the following sections, I assume that the system of record is a relational database and that objects form the copies of entities.

Pessimistic Locking

Pessimistic locking is an approach whereby an entity is locked in the database for the entire time that it is in application memory (often in the form of an object). A lock either limits or prevents other users from working with the entity in the database. There are two types of locks: *read locks* and *write locks*; both are discussed in the following sections.

Write Locks

A write lock indicates that the holder of the lock intends to update the entity and disallows anyone from reading, updating, or deleting the entity.

As an example of write locking, say that you want to update the values of a *Customer* object representing Doug Emerson. You retrieve the object into memory, placing a write lock on the row(s) that the *Customer* class is mapped to. You work with the object and eventually decide to save it. The attribute values are written to the appropriate columns in the locked rows, and the rows are unlocked. Once the rows are unlocked, other users are free to work with them.

Read Locks

A read lock indicates that the holder of the lock does not want the entity to change while it's holding the lock, allowing others to read the entity but not update or delete it. The scope of a lock might be the entire database, a table, a collection of rows, or a single row. These types of locks are called database locks, table locks, page locks, and row locks, respectively.

Read locks are often used by processes that require a consistent view of the data, such as a report summarizing sales for a given period of time or a batch job that transforms the data into another format (such as an extract to a data mart).

One problem with read locks is deadlocks. A deadlock occurs when one activity holds a lock on an entity, another activity holds a lock on another activity, and each activity needs to lock the entity held by the other activity before it can proceed. A real-world example of a deadlock would occur if:

- I have the keys to the car but need money to go shopping.

- My girlfriend has money but needs the keys to the car to go to work.

- I refuse to give her the keys until she gives me the money I need.

- She refuses to give up the money without first getting the keys.

That is, each of us has a resource the other needs, but neither of us is willing to give it up, and neither of us can proceed as a result.

One way to get around deadlocks is to introduce *priorities* and *timeouts*. Each process has a different priority, allowing the system to determine which one should get access to the entity next, and locks time out so that entities are eventually made available. With this approach comes the problem of *livelocks*, in which case low-priority processes never get access to the entities that they require because higher-priority processes keep bumping them.

The advantages of pessimistic locking are that it:

- Is easy to implement.

- Guarantees that your changes to the database are made consistently and safely

The primary disadvantage is that this approach isn't scalable. When a system has many users, or when the transactions involve a greater number of entities, or when transactions are long lived, the chance of having to wait for a lock to be released increases, limiting the practical number of simultaneous users that your system can support.

Optimistic Locking

With multiuser systems, it is quite common to be in a situation where collisions are infrequent. Say that you and I are working with Customer objects; you're working with the Wayne Miller object, while I work with the John Berg object, and therefore we won't collide. When this is the case, optimistic locking becomes a viable concurrency control strategy. The idea is that you accept the fact that collisions occur infrequently, and instead of trying to prevent them you simply choose to detect them and resolve the collisions when they do occur.

Figure 17.1 depicts the logic for updating an object when optimistic locking is used. The application reads the object into memory. To do this, a read lock is obtained on the data, the data is read into memory, and the lock is released. At this point in time, the row(s) may be marked to facilitate detection of a collision. The application then manipulates the object until the point that it needs to be updated. The application then obtains a write lock on the data and reads the original source back to determine if there's been a collision. The application either:

- Determines that there has not been a collision so it updates the data and unlocks it.

- Recognizes a collision has occurred that will need to be resolved.

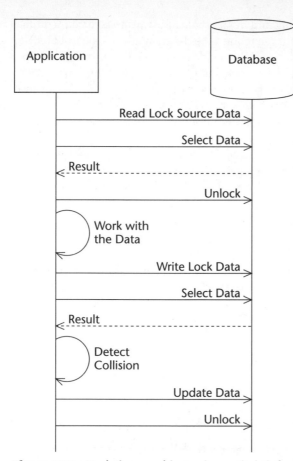

Figure 17.1   Updating an object using optimistic locking.

There are two basic strategies for determining if a collision has occurred:

Mark the source with a unique identifier.   The source data row is marked with a unique value each time it is updated. At the point of update, the mark is checked, and if there is a different value than what you originally read in, then you know that there has been an update to the source. There are different types of concurrency marks — datetimestamps (the database server should assign this value because you can't count on the time clocks of all machines to be in sync), incremental counters, user IDs (this only works if everyone has a unique ID *and* you're logged into only one machine *and* the applications ensure that only one copy of an object exists in memory), and even values generated by a globally unique surrogate key generator.

Retain a copy of the original.   The source data is retrieved at the point of updating and compared with the values that were originally retrieved. If the values have changed, then a collision has occurred. This strategy may be your only option if you are unable to add sufficient columns to your database schema to maintain the concurrency marks.

Figure 17.1 depicts a naive approach, and in fact there are ways to reduce the number of database interactions. The first three requests to the database — the initial lock, marking (if appropriate) the source data, and unlocking — can be performed as a single transaction. The next two interactions, to lock and obtain a copy of the source data, can easily be combined in a single trip to the database. Furthermore, the updating and unlocking can similarly be combined. Another way to improve this approach is to combine the last four interactions into a single transaction and simply perform collision detection on the database server instead of the application server.

The advantage of optimistic locking is that it scales well because it enables you to support far more concurrent users than does pessimistic locking. The disadvantage is the increased complexity over pessimistic locking due to the need to detect and then resolve collisions.

Overly Optimistic Locking

With this strategy, you neither try to avoid nor detect collisions, assuming that they will never occur. This strategy is appropriate for single-user systems, where the system of record is guaranteed to be accessed by only one user or system process at a time. These systems are rare but do occur. It is important to recognize that this strategy is completely inappropriate for multiuser systems.

Resolving Collisions

You have five basic strategies that you can apply to resolve collisions:

Give up. This is the simplest solution. You detect that a collision has occurred and throw an exception (or return an error) to inform the calling application. That's it. The changes are lost.

Display the problem and let the user decide. The collision is reported and the problem is presented to the user for resolution. At a minimum, a description of the problem, such as "Another user has updated this customer information while you were working with it," is displayed along with an option to either continue the update or to cancel it.

Merge the changes. You can try to determine which data attributes have been changed and then attempt to merge the two changes together. If you have kept a copy of the original data, and now have a copy of the changed source data as well, then you can analyze the two to determine which attributes have changed. You then display these differences to your user, who can then make an informed decision. A riskier approach is to simply let the system automatically "do the right thing."

Log the problem so someone else can decide later. This strategy is similar to displaying the problem, the only difference is that the calling application is running unattended, perhaps in batch, so no one is there to address the problem. You'll likely require an administration application to work with the logged collisions; they might be simple database scripts or something with a more sophisticated UI. This approach suffers from the problem that additional changes to the source data may occur during the period that the collision is initially logged and someone attempts to resolve it. One way around this problem is to read lock the source data until the collision is resolved (or timeout occurs).

Ignore the collision and overwriting.   With this approach you have basically incurred the additional overhead of optimistic locking, yet in reality you are taking an overly optimistic locking approach. This strategy isn't advisable.

TIP Assume that you and someone else are both working with a copy of the same Customer entity. If you update a customer's name and I update their shopping preferences, then we can still recover from this collision. In effect, the collision occurred at the entity level; we updated the same customer, but not at the attribute level. It is very common to detect potential collisions at the entity level, then get smart about resolving them at the attribute level.

Understanding Transactions

A *business transaction* is an interaction in the real world, usually between an enterprise and a person, where something is exchanged. An *online transaction* is the execution of a program that performs an administrative or real-time function, often by accessing shared data sources, usually on behalf of an online user (although some transactions are run offline in batches). This transaction program contains the steps involved in the business transaction. This definition of an online transaction is important because it makes it clear that there is far more to this topic than database transactions.

A transaction-processing (TP) system is the hardware and software that implements the transaction programs. A TP monitor is a portion of a TP system that acts as a kind of funnel or concentrator for transaction programs, connecting multiple clients to multiple server programs (potentially accessing multiple data sources). In a distributed system, a TP monitor will also optimize the use of the network and hardware resources. Examples of TP monitors include:

- IBM's Customer Information Control System (CICS): www-3.ibm.com/ software/ts/cics/
- IBM's Information Management System (IMS): www-3.ibm.com/software/ data/ims/
- BEA's Tuxedo: www.bea.com/products/tuxedo/index.shtml
- Microsoft Transaction Server (MTS): www.microsoft.com/com/tech/mts.asp

The leading standards efforts for TP monitors include:

- X/OPEN: www.opengroup.org/products/publications/catalog/tp.htm
- Object Management Group's (OMG) Common Object Request Broker Architecture (CORBA) Object Transaction Service (OTS): www.omg.org/technology/documents/corba_spec_catalog.htm
- The Enterprise JavaBean (EJB) specification: java.sun.com/products/ejb/docs.html

TIP **If you are interested in learning more about transaction processing, I highly recommend *Principles of Transaction Processing* by Phillip A. Bernstein and Eric Newcomer (1997). It is well written and covers the topic thoroughly.**

The Basics of Transactions

This section covers the basics of transactions, primarily providing an overview for application developers who may be new to the concept. The critical concepts, which are discussed in detail in the following sections, are as follows:

- ACID properties
- Two-phase commits
- Nested transactions

ACID Properties

An important fundamental of transactions is the four properties that they must exhibit. These properties are:

Atomicity.   The whole transaction occurs or nothing in the transaction occurs; there is no in between. In SQL, the changes become permanent when a COMMIT statement is issued, and they are aborted when a ROLLBACK statement is issued. For example, the transfer of funds between two accounts is a transaction. If we transfer $20 from account A to account B, then at the end of the transaction A's balance will be $20 lower and B's balance will be $20 higher (if the transaction is completed) *or* neither balance will have changed (if the transaction is aborted).

Consistency.   When the transaction starts the entities are in a consistent state, and when the transaction ends the entities are once again in a consistent, albeit different, state. The implication is that the referential integrity rules and applicable business rules still apply after the transaction is completed.

Isolation.   All transactions work as if they alone were operating on the entities. For example, assume that a bank account contains $200 and each of us is trying to withdraw $50. Regardless of the order of the two transactions, at the end of them the account balance will be $100, assuming that both transactions work. This is true even if both transactions occur simultaneously. Without the isolation property two simultaneous withdrawals of $50 could result in a balance of $150 (both transactions saw a balance of $200 at the same time, so both wrote a new balance of $150). Isolation is often referred to as *serializability*.

Durability.   The entities are stored in a persistent media, such as a relational database or file, so that if the system crashes the transactions are still permanent.

Two-Phase Commits

Transactions are fairly straightforward when there is a single system of record. But what happens in a distributed environment where several systems of record, perhaps two relational databases and a prevalence server, are involved? In this situation, you can find yourself in trouble when a transaction crosses several systems and one or more of those systems fails during the transaction. For a transaction to work, you still need to ensure that the four ACID properties hold, in particularly atomicity. The most common way to do this is to implement the two-phase commit (2PC) protocol.

As the name suggests, there are two phases to the 2PC protocol: the attempt phase, where each system tries its part of the transaction, and the commit phase, where the systems are told to persist the transaction. The 2PC protocol requires the existence of a *transaction manager* to coordinate the transaction. The transaction manager will assign a unique transaction ID to the transaction to identify it. The transaction manager then sends the various transaction steps to each system of record, so they may attempt them, each system responding back to the transaction manager with the result of the attempt. If an attempted step succeeds, then at this point the system of record must lock the appropriate entities and persist the potential changes in some manner (to ensure durability) until the commit phase. Once the transaction manager hears back from all systems of record that the steps succeeded, or once it hears back that a step failed, then it sends out either a commit request or an abort request to every system involved.

The 2PC protocol isn't foolproof; for example, what happens if one of the systems of record goes down after confirming the result of the attempt but before receiving the commit? To get around issues like this, timeout rules, or additional rounds of messages, need to be introduced.

The advantage of the 2PC protocol is that it enables you to scale your systems into distributed environments. The disadvantage is the overhead imposed by the additional round of messages.

Nested Transactions

So far I have discussed flat transactions, transactions whose steps are individual activities. A *nested transaction* is a transaction in which some of the steps are other transactions, referred to as *subtransactions*. Nested transactions have several important features:

- When a program starts a new transaction, if it is already inside of an existing transaction then a subtransaction is started. Otherwise, a new top-level transaction is started.

- There does not need to be a limit on the depth of transaction nesting.

- When a subtransaction aborts, all of its steps are undone, including any of its subtransactions. However, this does not cause the abortion of the parent transaction, instead the parent transaction is simply notified of the abort.

- When a subtransaction is executing, the entities that it is updating are not visible to other transactions or subtransactions (as per the isolation property).

- When a subtransaction commits then the updated entities are made visible to other transactions and subtransactions.

Implementing Transactions

Although transactions are often thought of as a database issue, the reality could be further from the truth. From the introduction of TP monitors, such as CICS and Tuxedo, in the 1970s and 1980s to the CORBA-based object request brokers (ORBs) of the early 1990s to the EJB application servers of the early 2000s, transactions have clearly been far more than a database issue. This section explores three approaches to implementing transactions that involve both object and relational technology. The material here is aimed at application developers as well as agile DBAs who need to explore strategies that they may not have run across in traditional data-oriented literature.

Database Transactions

The simplest way for an application to implement transactions is to use the features supplied by the database. Transactions can be started, attempted, and then committed or aborted via SQL code. Better yet, database APIs such as Java Database Connectivity (JDBC) and Open Database Connectivity (ODBC) provide classes that support basic transactional functionality.

In SQL, it is possible to define the isolation level of transaction. There are four isolation levels:

Serializable.   This is the strictest level of isolation because it does not allow any collisions.

Repeatable read.   This allows phantom reads but not dirty or nonrepeatable reads.

Read committed.   This allows phantom reads and nonrepeatable reads but not dirty reads.

Read uncommitted.   This is the weakest isolation level because it allows all three types of collisions.

The stricter the isolation level, the greater the chance that a collision will be detected and therefore force you to abort the transaction. This is an important design trade-off — you need to understand what potential collisions will occur with the data you are working with *and* determine which types of collisions you'd be willing to accept if they do occur.

The advantages of this approach are that it is architecturally simple and that it works in a vast majority of technical situations. There are several disadvantages. First, this strategy requires you to define transactions in terms of data, something that you will discover in the next two sections may not be sufficient for your needs. Second, in order to support transactions across several databases, you either need to write a significant amount of code, effectively implementing a transaction manager, or work with a full-fledged TP monitor.

Object Transactions

At the time of this writing, support for transaction control is one of the most pressing issues in the Web services community, and full support for nested transactions is under discussion within the EJB community as well. As you see in Figure 17.2, databases aren't the only things that can be involved in transactions. The fact is that objects, services, components, legacy applications, and nonrelational data sources can all be included in transactions.

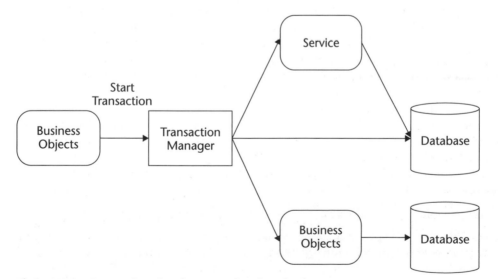

Figure 17.2   Transactions involve more than just databases.

So what? The implication is that not only do you need to consider data issues in transactions, but you may also find that you also need to consider behavioral ones as well. For example, consider the undo/redo functionality in your favorite drawing program. Although it isn't labeled as such, when you think about it this application treats drawing as a series of transactions. You decide to add a square to your picture, so you click on the square button on the drawing palette. This starts a "square transaction." You drag a square onto your picture, decide that you don't like it, and click on the undo button. This effectively aborts the square transaction. You drag another square onto the picture and decide that you do like it. You then click on the drawing palette again, perhaps to draw another square, and at that point you effectively commit the square transaction to the picture (in this drawing application you can no longer undo this action). The point is that this application works in transactional manner and a database wasn't involved at all.

When objects are involved in transactions, it is possible to have both data-oriented and behavioral-oriented steps within a transaction. For example, the following code snippet could represent a valid object transaction:

```
transaction := Transaction.new();
transaction.addStep(customer, "setFirstName", "John");
transaction.addStep(customer, "setLastName", "Smith");
transaction.addStep(screen, "drawSquare", Square.new(10,12,2));
result := transaction.run();
```

In the code, a transaction is created, the steps of changing the first and last name of a customer are added to the transaction, and a square is drawn on the screen. The transaction is run. Because it follows the 2PC protocol, it first attempts the steps, retrieves the responses (every step works), and then commits the transaction. If the transaction hadn't worked, then the steps would have been rolled back and an error code returned.

This code is interesting because it provides an example of one way that transactions can be implemented within your code. The Transaction class would likely be one part of a persistence framework, one option for encapsulating access to a relational database. You can still work with transactions in your application code even if you're not using a persistence framework. For example, JDBC and ODBC both include database transaction functionality, and you can simply code the additional logic required to include behavioral steps in transactions.

The advantage of adding behaviors implemented by objects (and similarly services, components, and so on) to transactions is that they become far more robust. Can you imagine using a code editor, word processor, or drawing program without an undo function? If not, then it becomes reasonable to expect both behavior invocation and data transformations as steps of a transaction. Unfortunately, this strategy comes with a significant disadvantage — increased complexity. For this to work, your business objects need to be *transactionally aware*. Any behavior that can be invoked as a step in a transaction requires supporting attempt, commit, and abort/rollback operations. Adding support for object-based transactions is a nontrivial endeavor.

TIP In addition to the granularity of a collision being important, the fact that systems of record may be implemented using different technologies becomes an issue. To determine if two transactions have collided, do you look at the object level or the table row level? Do you look at the attributes of an object or the column values of a row? Or combinations thereof? Although transaction processing can become quite complex, always remember to strive to keep things as simple as possible.

Distributed Object Transactions

Just as it is possible to have distributed data transactions, it is possible to have distributed object transactions as well. To be more accurate, as you see in Figure 17.2, it's just distributed transactions period — it's not just about databases any more, but rather databases plus objects plus services plus components, and so on.

In this environment, you require a transaction manager, perhaps a CORBA ORB such as Orbix (www.iona.com/products/corba_technology.htm) and the open source Fnorb (www.fnorb.org), which is able to work with a wide range of transaction sources. Each transaction source, such as a service or object server, must be transactionally aware. Ideally, each transaction source should implement the same transaction protocols.

The advantage of this approach is that it provides a very robust approach to distributed software development. There are several disadvantages:

- The concept of distributed objects never really went anywhere. Although CORBA has been around for over a decade, and in the beginning enjoyed great fanfare and industry support, the reality is that the most common application of CORBA-based technologies is system integration. Yes, some organizations are building very interesting applications via a distributed object approach but they are definitely in the minority.

- The development of distributed applications is hard and few developers have the requisite skills.

- Distributed object development has been overshadowed by application-server-based approaches such as J2EE or Web-services-based approaches such as .NET (www.gotdotnet.com) and sun one (www.sun.com/software/sunone/).

Including Nontransactional Sources in a Transaction

Sometimes you find that you need to include a nontransactional source within a transaction. A perfect example is an update to information contained in an LDAP (Lightweight Directory Access Protocol) directory or the invocation of a Web service, neither of which at the time of this writing support transactions. The problem is that as soon as a step within a transaction is nontransactional the transaction really isn't a transaction any more. You have four basic strategies available to you for dealing with this situation:

Remove the nontransactional step from your transaction. This is the easiest solution; simply invoke the step before or after the rest of the transaction.

Implement commit. This strategy, which could be thought of as the "hope the parent transaction doesn't abort" strategy, enables you to include a nontransactional step within your transaction. You will need to simulate the attempt, commit, and abort protocol used by the transaction manager. The attempt and abort behaviors are simply stubs that do nothing other than implement the requisite protocol logic. The one behavior that you do implement, the commit, will invoke the nontransactional functionality that you want. A different flavor of this approach, which I've never seen used in practice, would put the logic in the attempt phase instead of the commit phase.

Implement attempt and abort. This is an extension to the previous technique whereby you basically implement the "do" and "undo" logic but not the commit. In this case, the work is done in the attempt phase; the assumption is that the rest of the transaction will work, but if it doesn't, you still support the ability to roll back the work. This is an "almost transaction" because it doesn't avoid the problems with collisions described earlier.

Make it transactional. With this approach, you fully implement the requisite attempt, commit, and abort behaviors. The implication is that you will need to implement all the logic to lock the affected resources and to recover from any collisions. An example of this approach is supported via the J2EE Connector Architecture (JCA) (java.sun.com/j2ee/connector/), in particular by the Local-Transaction interface.

Which approach should you take? A major issue to consider is that the *Make it transactional* strategy is the only one that passes the ACID test. I prefer the first and last strategies listed above — when it comes to transactions, I want to do it right or not do it at all. The problem with implementing full transactional logic is that it can be a lot of work. I'll consider the Implement attempt and abort strategy when it is possible to live with the results of a collision, and consider the Implement commit strategy only as a last resort.

Summary

Understanding the basics of concurrency control, as well as strategies for ensuring it, are fundamental skills that all software developers should have. In this chapter, you learned that collisions occur in multiuser systems. Pessimistic locking can be used to avoid collisions, although this approach doesn't scale well. An optimistic locking strategy can instead be applied to detect collisions, a strategy that requires you to then resolve the collision.

You also learned about the fundamentals of transaction control, learning about the ACID properties, two phase commits (2PC), and nested transactions. You saw that transactions go beyond the database and can possibly include both data and behavior.

Agile software developers will approach concurrency control with an open mind, realizing that it is an important aspect of their system and that they have several choices as to the approach that they take to implement it.

CHAPTER 18

Finding Objects in Relational Databases

Would you rather be a whiteboard warrior or a paper pusher?

A common programming task is to find one or more objects that are currently stored in the database and bring them into memory. Perhaps you need to display a list of people who work in a department, enable your users to define search criteria used to list available inventory items, or implement a report. Although these sound like easy tasks, there are many interesting implementation options and issues that you need to be aware of.

This chapter describes:

- The role of the agile DBA
- Find strategies
- Implementation techniques
- Representing find results

The Role of the Agile DBA

The role of agile DBAs is fairly straightforward: they will work with, and mentor, application developers in the techniques and issues involved with finding the data stored in RDBs.

Find Strategies

For the sake on convenience, I use the term *find strategy* to refer to your implementation strategy for finding the data representing objects within relational databases. The deciding factor in choosing a find strategy is the level of database encapsulation that you wish to have. In Chapter 13, we discussed four basic approaches for implementing database access, namely brute force, data access objects (DAOs), persistence frameworks, and services. Similarly, there are different find strategies that you may choose from: brute force, query objects, and meta data-driven.

Brute Force (Embedded SQL)

With the brute-force find strategy, you simply embed database access code, such as Structured Query Language (SQL) statements or Enterprise JavaBean (EJB) Query Language (EJB QL), in your business objects. The typical strategy is to write a single operation for each way you want to find objects. For example, in Figure 18.1 you see two versions of a Customer class, one as a standard business object and one as an EJB. Each version implements five different finder operations — one to find by the value of the primary key, one to search by name, one to search by Social Security number (SSN), one to search by a combination of name and phone number, and one to search by various criteria. Each finder takes the parameter(s) passed to it, builds a SELECT statement using those values, submits the statement to the database, and then works with the results.

Customer
+ <u>find(poid: int)</u> : Customer + <u>find(name :String)</u> : Array + <u>find(ssn :int)</u> : Array + <u>find(name :String, phone: String)</u> : Array + <u>findcriteria :Vector)</u> : Array

Customer <<EJBEntityBean>>
+ ejbFindByPrimaryKey(key :CustomerPK)　: CustomerPK + ejbFindByName(name :String)　: Collection + ejbFindBySSN(ssn :int)　: Collection + ejbFindByNamePhone(name :String, phone: String)　: Collection + ejbFindByCriteria(criteria :Vector)　: Collection

Figure 18.1　Operation signatures for brute force finders.

The reason why two versions are shown is to depict two common approaches to implementing brute-force finders. The top version shows how the finder operations are implemented as static operations because they potentially work on multiple instances of the class. As you can see, four of the five operations return an array of objects. The only one that returns a single object is the one that searches based on the value of the primary key. From a theoretical point of view, it makes sense that this is a static operation because conceptually it is searching through all of the instances of Customer and selecting the one with the given key value. From a practical point of view, it's better to have a consistent approach. Another example of consistency is the fact that I've named all of the operations find() — this is allowable in Java because the entire operation signature, including the parameters and return values, must be unique, not just the operation name. Consistent naming conventions make your code easier to read. The EJB version of Customer in Figure 18.1 conforms to the EJB specification (java.sun.com/products/ejb/) and therefore implements the finders as instance-scope operations that conform to the ejbFindBy... naming convention. The internal implementation of the finders is still the same.

In each version, the finder that is based on the primary key returns a single object. The find() version returns the customer object with the primary key value, although if the customer doesn't exist in the database you will need to either return an empty customer object with the primary key value set or throw an appropriate exception/error. Approaches for handling situations like this are discussed later in this chapter. The ejbFindByPrimaryKey() version returns an instance of the primary key object that uniquely identifies the customer and must throw a Java exception if it doesn't exist in the database.

In each version, there is also a finder that takes a *vector* of criteria (a vector is a Java collection) presumably to support a search screen or report. In this case, the finder would need to parse each criteria, such as *name=S** and *hireDate>Jan 26 1972*, and convert it to SQL search clauses such as *Customer.Name= 'S%'* and *Customer.HireDate > '26-01-1972'*. With a brute-force approach, this conversion would be hard-coded within the operation.

Query Objects

Query objects (Brant & Yoder 2000) are the find strategy version of DAOs. Instead of embedding SQL code in your business objects, you encapsulate it in separate classes. Figure 18.2 depicts how the Customer class of Figure 18.1, the non-EJB version, would be implemented using this strategy. There is one query object for each finder, each of which would implement the same type of logic described for the brute-force approach. The Customer class would implement the same operations shown in Figure 18.1 and simply delegate them to the appropriate query object.

A simple approach would implement a single public operation that accepted the criteria and returned a collection of zero or more objects representing the result set. A more sophisticated approach would enable you to work with the query result in a number of different ways, such as collections of objects, as XML documents, or as simple data sets. The various ways that query results can be represented are discussed later in the chapter.

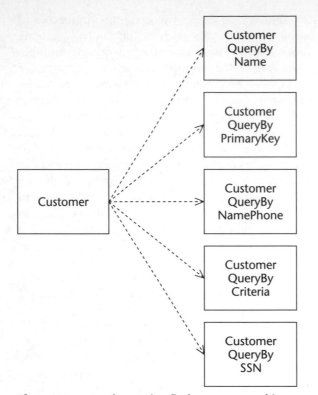

Figure 18.2 Implementing finders as query objects.

Meta Data-Driven

A meta data-driven approach is the most sophisticated strategy available to you and is typically implemented as part of a persistence framework. The basic idea is that you want to decouple your object schema from your data schema, and the only way to do this is to describe the mappings (Chapter 14) between them in meta data instead of in hard-coded SQL. Instead of defining a SQL SELECT statement that specifies the search in terms of database columns, your application must define the search in terms of the object's attributes.

Figure 18.3 illustrates an overview of how this would work. The business object submits the meta data for a query, perhaps represented as an XML document or as a full-fledged object (Ambler 2001d), to a query processor. This meta data would represent concepts to perform tasks such as return all customers whose name looks like 'Sc* A*', return the account with account number 1701-1234, and return all employees whose hire date is between January 1 1987 and June 14 1995 that work in the Marketing Department. The query processor passes the query to a query builder that uses the mapping meta data to build a SELECT statement, which can then be submitted to the database. The results come back from the database and are converted into the appropriate representation (such as an XML structure, a collection of objects, and so on). The representation is then returned to the business object.

Building the SELECT statement is obviously the lynchpin in this entire approach, so let's work through an example. The following XML structure represents the meta data for a "Return all orders placed on January 27, 2003 where the subtotal before tax is at least $1000" query.

```
<Query>
<Search For>Order</Search For>
<Clause>
<Attribute> "dateOrdered" </Attribute>
<Comparison> "=" </Comparison>
<Value> "27-Jan-2003" </Value>
</Clause>
<Clause>
<Attribute> "subtotalBeforeTax" </Attribute>
<Comparison> ">=" </Comparison>
<Value> "1000.00" </Value>
</Clause>
</Query>
```

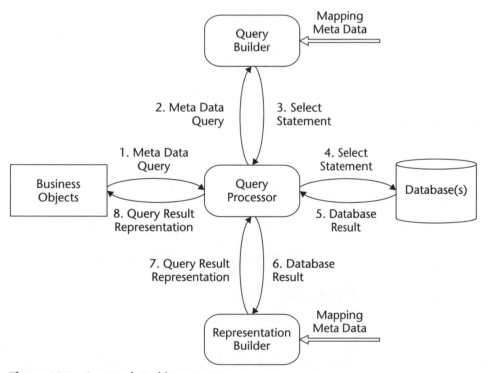

Figure 18.3 A meta data-driven strategy.

Notice how the XML refers to the attributes of the *Order* class, not to the database columns. By combining this meta data with the property mappings (depicted in Figure 18.4 and originally presented in Chapter 14) between the *Order* class and the *Order* table, the query builder can create the following SQL SELECT statement:

```
SELECT *
FROM Order
WHERE Order.DateOrdered = '2003-01-27'
AND Order.SubtotalBeforeTax >= 1000.00
```

The primary advantage of this approach is that it enables you to keep your object schema and data schema decoupled from one another. As long as the query meta data reflects the structure of the current object schema and the mapping meta data is current, you do not need to embed SQL within your object schema to find objects stored in relational databases.

When to Apply Each Strategy

Your choice of database encapsulation strategy (Chapter 13) is the major determinant of when you can apply each find strategy, as you see in Table 18.1. My advice is to choose your database encapsulation strategy first then choose the find strategy that best fits it.

Property	Column
Order.orderID	Order.OrderID
Order.dateOrdered	Order.DateOrdered
Order.dateFulfilled	Order.DateFulfilled
Order.getTotalTax()	Order.Tax
Order.subtotalBeforeTax	Order.SubtotalBeforeTax
Order.shipTo.personID	Order.ShipToContactID
Order.billTo.personID	Order.BillToContactID
Order.lastUpdate	Order.LastUpdate
OrderItem.ordered	OrderItem.OrderID
Order.orderItems.position(orderItem)	OrderItem.ItemSequence
OrderItem.item.number	OrderItem.ItemNo
OrderItem.numberOrdered	OrderItem.NumberOrdered
OrderItem.lastUpdate	OrderItem.LastUpdate

Figure 18.4   Basic mapping meta data for Order.

Table 18.1   When to Apply Each Strategy

STRATEGY	APPLICATION
Brute force	• Works well with the brute-force, DAO, and services database encapsulation strategies • Very simple and straightforward, although it results in high coupling between your object and data schemas
Query objects	• Work well with the DAO and services database encapsulation strategies • Very simple and straightforward, resulting in slightly less coupling than the brute-force strategy • Good strategy for implementing reports in your operational application (discussed in Chapter 21)
Meta data-driven	• Really a portion of a persistence framework encapsulation strategy • Greater complexity, but it results in very low coupling between your object and data schemas

Implementation Techniques

Deciding on and then implementing your find strategy is just the first step. You also need to resolve basic issues such as how to handle errors, how many objects you expect to come back as the result of a find query, when to bring the result across the network, and how to accept search criteria from users. In the following sections, I describe several techniques that I have found useful over the years to address these issues.

Use the Native Error-Handling Strategy

Things don't always go right and therefore you need to handle error conditions properly. Languages offer two basic facilities for indicating error: exceptions and return codes. Languages such as Java and C# support the ability to throw exceptions from operations. The idea is that the invoking code catches the thrown exception and handles it accordingly. You should use exceptions to indicate serious problems, such as the network or database being unavailable. You should handle logic problems, such as an empty result set or a result set that contains too many records, via the return value. When languages, such as C++ and Smalltalk, don't support exceptions, you should indicate the error in the return value. The point is that you should use the best error-handling approach provided by the development language and do so in a consistent manner.

Expect "Logic" Errors

When many users can access the database simultaneously, the norm for most applications, logic errors (likely referential integrity errors) will occur. For example, you may read a customer into memory and work with it for a bit. In parallel, another user deletes that customer from the database. Later on you attempt to refresh the customer object, only to discover that nothing is returned as the result of your query. You'll need a strategy to deal with this problem. Another example would be that you may discover that you search on an attribute that you believe is unique, such as the Social Security number (SSN) of an employee, only to discover that two people have been assigned the same SSN in your database (perhaps due to input error or because the same fake SSN was assigned to two non-Americans). You will want to detect these problems and act accordingly, such as displaying an error message in the user interface.

Always Return a Collection

Although Figure 18.1 breaks this rule with the find() operation, your should always return a collection, such as a vector or array, as the result of a finder. This is a good strategy because:

- It's a single, consistent approach.
- You can easily determine the size of a collection. This simplifies logic error detection because you can determine if there are no objects as the result of your query or several objects when you only expected one.
- In languages that don't support exceptions, you can simply use the first element in the collection as the location for the error code/message/object.

A more sophisticated approach is to develop a *FindResult* class that includes a collection containing the result set and the error (if any). This class would have the ability to iterate over the collection, to answer basic queries such as isEmpty() and isSingleResult().

Use Proxies and Lazy Initialization for Search Lists

Lazy initialization is an object-level technique for improving system performance via an object proxy. An object proxy contains just enough information to identify the object within the system, very likely the primary key attributes, and enough information for users to identify the object. The columns that are displayed on a search result screen often determine the latter information. The basic idea is that instead of bringing all of the data for every object in the result set you only bring across the identifying information. This information is displayed to the user, who then selects one of the proxies from the list to work with it. The system then retrieves all of the information for the selected business object and enables the user to work with that object.

Let's work through an example:

1. A user inputs criteria into an employee search screen. The search is performed and the results, 43 employees, are displayed on the screen. The list only displays the employee name, department, and telephone number because this is sufficient information for the user to identify the individual.

2. The user then selects Sally Jones from the list. Because this is a proxy object, the system uses the *employeePOID* attribute to identify the employee information within the database, retrieving the 27 properties required by the employee editing screen.

The advantage of this approach is that you transmit a minimum amount of information across your network. When you are implementing search screens, it is quite common that your user only wants to work with a small subset of the search results. It doesn't make sense in this situation to bring data across the network that you don't need. The disadvantage is the additional complexity required to work with the object proxies.

Use Lazy Reads for High-Overhead Attributes

Lazy reading is an attribute-level technique for improving system performance. The basic idea that the attribute's value is read from the database, or calculated as the case may be, the first time it is needed, instead of setting the value when the object is first retrieved into memory. A lazy read is a good option when an object's attribute is high-overhead, say if it is very large and would be slow to transmit over the network or if it requires intensive calculations to compute, and when it is rarely accessed.

The advantage of this approach is that the read/calculation of the attribute is put off for as long as possible and potentially even avoided. There are two disadvantages. First, it requires you to work with attributes via getters and setters, also known as accessors and mutators, respectively. This is actually a good programming practice (Ambler 2001a) and so is arguably an advantage. Second, the getter operation for any attribute that is lazily read must check to see if it has been read/calculated, and if not then do so before returning the current value.

Program for People

When you're building a search screen, your users need some way to indicate their search criteria. The important thing to remember is that your users very likely aren't computer professionals; they might be struggling with basic computer literacy and may not even be comfortable using computers. Have you told someone that you were a software architect for a large and impressive firm, and the only question they have for you is how much memory they should get when they buy a home computer next month? This person is very likely not one of your more advanced users, and they clearly don't understand what it is that you do for a living.

The point is that your search facility will need to be user-friendly. It should follow accepted user interface standards, which your organization should have in place — if it doesn't, then your team should follow industry standards. There are published user interface guidelines for Java (Sun Microsystems 2001), Microsoft (msdn.microsoft .com), and the Macintosh (Apple Computer 2002). Most user interface standards discuss common wildcard symbols, such as an asterisk to indicate zero or more characters. This is different from the percentage sign that SQL databases use for LIKE clauses. The point is that your user interface should conform to the user interface guidelines, not the database standards, and therefore you should support search clauses that use asterisks. If there are no applicable user interface guidelines (more likely the real problem is that nobody has looked into this), then you should talk with your users and discover what their expectations are.

The advantage of this approach is that your application is easier to work with. The disadvantage is that you will likely need to write a simple conversion utility to take the user's search clause and convert it to a suitable database search clause. Luckily, this is straightforward code that you should be able to find on the Internet.

Representing Find Results

Although this may sound like blasphemy to object purists, you don't always need nor want objects as the result of a search. The fact is that there are several ways that the results of a find can be represented, as you see in Table 18.2, which describes the various ways to represent customers. You don't need to support all of these representations in your application but you will likely find that you need several.

Table 18.2 Various Ways to Represent the Results of a Find

APPROACH	DESCRIPTION	ADVANTAGES	DISADVANTAGES
Business objects	The result set is marshaled into a collection of *Customer* objects.	• You can directly work with the business objects. • Supports a "pure object" approach. • Receiver is decoupled from database schema.	• Marshaling overhead to create the objects can be significant. • You may need other business objects, perhaps representing orders, to obtain all the information required by a process or application.
Comma-separated value (CSV) file	The result set is marshaled into a text file with one row in the file for each customer. Commas separate the column values (for example, Scott, William, Ambler).	• Platform-independent approach to representation. • Easy to archive or version the data. • Easy to include additional, noncustomer data specific to the needs of a process or application. • Receiver decoupled from database schema.	• File needs to be parsed to obtain individual customer information. • File needs to be created from the database result set. • Being superceded by XML documents.
Data structure	The result set is marshaled into a collection of data structures. Each customer data structure is typically just a collection of data values.	• Customer data is represented in a relatively accessible manner. • Easy to include additional, noncustomer data specific to the needs of a process or application. • Receiver decoupled from database schema.	• You need to parse the structure to obtain individual customer information. • File needs to be created from the database result set. • Being superceded by XML documents.

(continued)

Table 18.2 (continued)

APPROACH	DESCRIPTION	ADVANTAGES	DISADVANTAGES
Data transfer objects	The result set is marshaled into a collection of objects that just contain the data and the getters and setters to access the data. These objects are serializable. See Marinescu (2002) and Fowler et. al. (2003) for detailed discussions.	• Supports low-overhead transfer of customer objects across a network. • Easy to include additional, noncustomer data specific to the needs of a process or application. • Receiver decoupled from database schema.	• Marshaling overhead to create the objects can be significant. • Being superceded by XML documents.
Dataset	The result set from the database as it is returned by your database access library (for example, JDBC or ADO.NET).	• No marshalling overhead. • Easy to include additional, noncustomer data specific to the needs of a process or application.	• Receiver must be able to work with the dataset, coupling it to the database access library. • Receiver is now coupled to the database schema.
Flat File	The result set is marshaled into a text file, with one row in the file for each customer. The data values are written into known positions (for example, the first name is written into positions 21 through 40).	• Platform-independent approach to representation. • Easy to include additional, noncustomer data specific to the needs of a process or application. • Receiver decoupled from database schema. • Easy to archive or version the data.	• File needs to be parsed to obtain individual customer information. • File needs to be created from the database result set. • Being superceded by XML documents.

Table 18.2 (continued)

APPROACH	DESCRIPTION	ADVANTAGES	DISADVANTAGES
Proxies	The result set is marshaled into a collection of proxy objects that contain just enough information for both the system and your users to identify the object.	• Receiver decoupled from database schema. • Reduced network traffic.	• Marshaling overhead to create the proxies can be significant, although less than for business objects. • Receiver requires additional code to appropriately replace proxy objects with actual business objects.
Serialized business objects	The result set is marshaled into a collection of business objects. This collection is, in turn, converted into a single binary large object (BLOB), or another similar format, which can be transmitted across the network as a single entity and then converted back into the original collection of objects by the receiver.	• Receiver decoupled from database schema. • Easy to archive or version the data. • Works well with prevalence layers (Chapter 13).	• Marshaling overhead to create the objects can be significant.
XML document	The result set is converted into a single XML document, which will contain zero or more customer structures.	• Platform-independent approach to representation. • Significant market support for XML exists. • Easy to include additional, noncustomer data specific to the needs of a process or application. • Receiver decoupled from database schema. • Easy to archive or version the data.	• Marshaling overhead to create the XML document can be significant.

Summary

In this chapter, I've shown that finding objects in a relational database can be as simple as submitting a SQL SELECT statement and marshaling the results into business objects, or that it could be as complex as a meta data-driven approach where a persistence framework defines the appropriate database query based on object-based criteria. Furthermore, the return value doesn't have to be just business objects; it can be as simple as the raw data set or as complex as a detailed XML document. You saw that there are several implementation strategies for you to consider that can improve both the performance of your application as well as its usability.

The critical lesson is that you have alternatives to select from. Choose wisely.

Implementing Referential Integrity and Shared Business Logic

It's not just a black and white issue; there are also shades of gray. Furthermore, last time I looked there's a whole spectrum of colors out there as well.

Referential integrity (RI) refers to the concept that if one entity references another, then that other entity actually exists. For example, if I claim to live in a house at 123 Main Street, then that house must actually be there, otherwise I have an RI error. In relational database design, the referential integrity rule (Halpin 2001) states that each non-null value of a foreign key must match the value of some primary key.

In the 1970s, when relational databases first came on the scene, the standard implementation technology was procedural languages such as PL/1, Fortran, and COBOL. Because these languages didn't implement anything similar to data entities and because the relational database did, it made sense that relational databases were responsible for ensuring RI. Furthermore, relational databases back then were relatively simple: they stored data and supported the ability to implement basic RI constraints. The end result was that business logic was implemented in the application code, and RI was implemented in the database.

Modern software development isn't like that anymore. We now work with implementation languages such as C# and Java that implement entities called classes. As a result, RI also becomes an issue for your application code as well as your database. Relational database technology has also improved dramatically, supporting native programming languages to write stored procedures, triggers, and even standard object programming languages such as Java. It is now viable to implement business logic in your database as well as in your application code. The best way to look at it is that you have options as to where RI and business logic are implemented, making it an important architectural decision for your team.

This chapter explores the implications of this observation by discussing the following topics:

- The role of the agile DBA
- How object technology complicates RI
- Where you should implement RI

The Role of the Agile DBA

When it comes to ensuring RI and implementing business rules, the role of the agile DBA is to:

- Be fluent in the technical issues described in this chapter.
- Work alongside application programmers to implement the necessary code.
- Be prepared to mentor application programmers and enterprise professionals, including both architects and administrators, in the technical issues.

How Object Technology Complicates Referential Integrity

Modern deployment architectures are complex. The components of a new application may be deployed across several types of machines, including various client machines, Web servers, application servers, and databases. Figure 19.1 depicts a simplified deployment architecture diagram to provide an overview of the situation that developers face on a daily basis. Note that you may not have all of these platforms, or they might be connected in slightly different ways. The important point is that business logic could be deployed to a wide number of platforms, to any of the boxes shown in Figure 19.1, as could entities. For example, a new browser-based application could have JavaScript embedded in the HTML code that simply performs data validation. The primary business objects could reside on the application servers, which in turn invoke several Web services that wrap access to procedures deployed on the mainframe. These stored procedures encapsulate shared functions that are implemented in the three relational databases accessed by the objects.

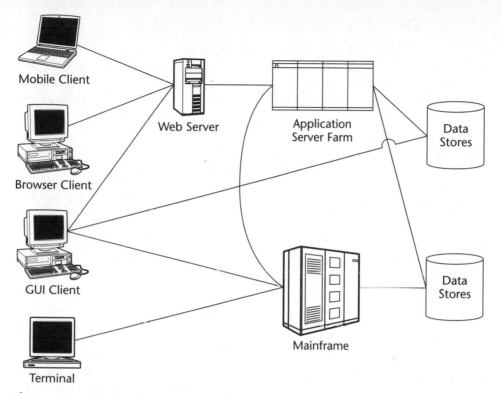

Figure 19.1   Modern deployment architectures.

It is important to recognize that software development has become more complex over the years. One of the main reasons why the object-oriented paradigm was embraced so ardently by software developers is that it helped them to deal with this growing complexity. Unfortunately, the solution, in this case the common use of object technology within an *n*-tiered environment, has added a few complications with respect to ensuring RI. In particular, there are several aspects of object technology that you need to come to terms with, as discussed in the following sections:

- Multiple entity representation
- Object relationship management
- Lazy reads
- Caches
- Aggregation, composition, and association
- Architectural layering
- Removal from memory vs. persistent deletions

Multiple Entity/Relationship Representation

Figure 19.1 makes it clear that an entity can be represented in different ways. For example, the concept of a customer is represented as data displayed on an HTML page, as a customer object that resides on an application server, and as a table in a database. Keeping these various representations in sync is a concurrency-control issue (the topic of Chapter 17). Concurrency control is nothing new; it is something that you need to deal with in a multiuser system regardless of the implementation technology being used. However, when you are using object technology and relational technology together, you are in a situation where you are implementing structure in two places: in your object schema as classes that have interrelationships and in your data schema as tables with interrelationships. You will implement similar structures in each place. For example, you will have an *Order* object that has a collection of *OrderItem* objects in your object schema and an *Order* table that is related to the *OrderItem* table. It should be obvious that you need to deal with RI issues within each schema. What isn't so obvious is that because the same entities are represented in multiple schemas, you have "cross-schema" RI issues to deal with as well.

Let's work through an example using orders and order items. To keep things simple, assume that there is a straight one-to-one mapping between the object and data schemas. Also assume that you're working with a fat-client architecture, built in Java, and a single database. You would have the same issues that I'm about to describe with an *n*-tier architecture that involves a farm of application servers, but let's keep things simple. I read an existing order and its order items into memory on my computer. There are currently two order items, A and B. Shortly thereafter you read the exact same order and order items into memory on your computer. You decide to add a new order item, C, to the order and save it to the database. The order-order item structure is perfectly fine on each individual machine — my order object references two order item objects that exist in its memory space; your order object references three order item objects that exist in its memory space, and the three rows in the *OrderItem* table all include a foreign key to the row in the *Order* table representing the order. When you look at it from the point of view of the entities, the order, and its order items, however, there is an RI problem because my order object doesn't refer to order item C.

A similar situation would occur if you had deleted order item B — now my order object would refer to an order item that no longer exists. This assumes of course that the database is the system of record for these entities. When something is changed in the system of record, it's considered an "official" change. Without a defined system of record, it becomes difficult to determine what changes are official and which are not (perhaps the deletion of B should be backed out).

This concept is nothing new. When the same entities are stored in several databases, you have the exact same RI issues to deal with. The fundamental issue is that whenever the same entities are represented in several schemas, regardless of whether they are data schemas or object schemas, you have the potential for cross-schema RI problems.

Object Relationship Management

A common technique to ensure RI is to use triggers to implement cascades. A *cascade* occurs when an action on one table fires a trigger that in turn creates a similar action in another table, which could in turn fire another trigger, and so on recursively. Assuming that the triggers are implemented correctly according to the applicable businesses, cascades effectively support automatic relationship management.

Database Cascades

There are three common types of database cascades:

Cascading deletes.   The deletion of a row in the *Customer* table results in the deletion of all rows referring to the row in the *CustomerHistory* table. Each deletion from this table causes the deletion of a corresponding row, if any, in the *CustomerHistoryNotes* table.

Cascading inserts.   The insertion of a new row into the *Customer* table results in the insertion of a row into the *CustomerHistory* table to record the creation.

Cascading updates.   The updating of a row in the *OrderItem* table results in an update to the corresponding row in the *Item* table to record a change, if any, in the current inventory level. This change could in turn trigger an update to the row in the *DailyInventoryReorder* table representing today's reorder statistics, which in turn triggers an update to the *MonthlyInventoryReorder* table.

Most reasonably sophisticated data-modeling tools, such as Computer Associate's ERWin and Oracle's Designer, will automatically generate the stubs for triggers based on your physical data models. All you need to do is write the code that makes the appropriate change(s) to the target rows. Development tools are discussed in greater detail in Chapter 16.

Object Relationship Cascades

The concept of cascades is applicable to object relationships, and once again there are three types:

Cascading deletes.   The deletion of a *Customer* object results in the deletion of its corresponding *Address* object and its *ZipCode* object. In languages, such as Java and Smalltalk, that support automatic garbage collection, cascading deletes, at least of the object in memory, is handled automatically. However, you will also want to delete the corresponding rows in the database that these objects are mapped to.

Cascading reads.   When an *Order* object is retrieved from the database, you also want to automatically retrieve its *OrderItem* objects and any corresponding *Item* objects that describe the order items.

Cascading saves.   When an *Order* object is saved, the corresponding *OrderItem* objects should also be saved automatically. This may translate into either inserts or updates into the database as the case may be.

You have several implementation options for object cascades, the choice of which should be driven by your database encapsulation strategy (discussed in Chapter 13). First, you can code the cascades. As with database triggers, sophisticated object-modeling CASE tools, such as TogetherCC and Poseidon, will automatically generate operation stubs that you can later write code for. This approach works well with a brute-force, data-access-object, or service approach to database encapsulation. Second, your persistence framework may be sophisticated enough to support automatic cascades based on your relationship-mapping meta data.

Implications of Cascades

There are several important implications of cascades:

You have an implementation choice.   First, for a given relationship, you need to decide if there are any cascades that are application and if so where you intend to implement them: in the database, within your objects, or both. You may find that you take different implementation strategies with different relationships. Perhaps the cascades between customers and addresses are implemented via objects, whereas the cascades originating from order items are implemented in the database.

Beware of cycles.   A cycle occurs when a cascade cycles back to the starting point. For example a change to A cascades to B, which cascades to C, which in turn cascades back to A.

Beware of cascades getting out of control.   Although cascades sound great, and they are, there is a significant potential for trouble. If you define too many object read cascades you may find that the retrieval of a single object could result in the cascaded retrieval of thousands of objects. For example, if you were to define a read cascade from *Division* to *Employee* you could bring several thousand employees into memory when you read the object representing the Manufacturing Division in memory.

Cascading Strategies

Table 19.1 summarizes strategies to consider when defining object cascades on a relationship. For aggregation and composition, the whole typically determines the persistence life cycle of the parts and thus drives your choice of cascades. For associations, the primary determining factor is the multiplicity of the association. There are several activities, such as reading in a composition hierarchy, you almost always want to always do. For other activities, such as deleting a composition hierarchy, there is a good chance that you want to implement a cascade, and therefore I indicate that you should "consider" it. In the cases where you should consider adding a cascade, you need to think through the business rules pertaining to the entities and their interrelationship(s) as well as how the entities are used in practice by your application.

Table 19.1   Strategies for Defining Object Cascades

RELATIONSHIP TYPE	CASCADING DELETE	CASCADING READ	CASCADING SAVE
Aggregation	Consider deleting the parts automatically when the whole is deleted.	Consider reading the parts automatically when the whole is read.	Consider saving the parts automatically when the whole is saved.
Association (one to one)	Consider deleting the corresponding entity when the multiplicity is 0..1. Delete the entity when the multiplicity is exactly one.	Consider reading the corresponding entity.	Consider saving the corresponding entity.
Association (one to many)	Consider deleting the many entities.	Consider reading the many entities.	Consider saving the many entities.
Association (many to one)	Avoid this. Deleting the one entity is likely not an option because other objects (the many) still refer to it.	Consider reading in the one entity.	Consider saving the one entity.
Association (many to many)	Avoid this. Deleting the many objects likely isn't an option because there may be other references to them, and because of the danger of the cascade getting out of control.	Avoid this because the cascade is likely to get out of control.	Avoid this because the cascade is likely to get out of control.
Composition	Consider deleting the parts automatically when the whole is deleted.	Read in the parts automatically when the whole is read.	Save the parts automatically when the whole is saved.

In addition to cascades, you also have the issue of ensuring that objects reference each other appropriately. For example, assume that there is a bidirectional association between *Customer* and *Order*. Also assume that the object representing Sally Jones is in memory but that you haven't read in all of the orders that she has made. Now, you retrieve an order that she made last month. When you retrieve this *Order* object, it must reference the Sally Jones *Customer* object, which in turn must reference this *Order* object. This is called the *corresponding properties principle* — the values of the properties used to implement a relationship must be maintained appropriately.

Lazy Reads

Lazy reads (discussed in Chapter 15) are a performance-enhancing technique common in object-oriented applications whereby the values of high-overhead attributes are defined at the time they are needed. An example of a high-overhead attribute is a reference to another object, or a collection of references to other objects, used to implement an object relationship. In this situation, a lazy read effectively becomes a just in time (JIT) traversal of an object relationship to read in the corresponding object(s).

What are the trade-offs between a JIT read and a cascading read? A JIT read provides greater performance because there is the potential that you never need to traverse the relationship. A JIT read is a good strategy when a relationship isn't traversed very often but a bad strategy for relationships that result from the additional round trip to the database. A cascading read is easier to implement because you don't need to check to see if the relationship has been initialized (it happens automatically).

Caches

As I discussed in Chapter 15, a cache is a location where copies of entities are temporarily kept. The principle advantage of caches is performance improvement. Database accesses often prove to take the majority of processing time in business application, and caches can dramatically reduce the number of database accesses that your applications need to make.

Unfortunately, there are several disadvantages of caches:

- They add complexity to your application because of the additional logic required to manage the objects and data in your cache. This additional logic includes the need to refresh the cache with the database of record on a regular basis and to handle collisions between the cache and database (Chapter 17 discusses strategies for doing so).

- You run the risk of not committing changes to your database if the machine on which a memory-based cache resides crashes.

- Caches exacerbate cross-schema RI problems discussed earlier. This happens because caches increase the time that copies of an entity exist in multiple locations and thus increase the likelihood of a problem occurring.

> **TIP** How you use caches is important. If a cache is read-only, then chances are good that you don't need to refresh it as often as you would an updateable cache. You may want to only cache data that is unlikely to change very often, such as a list of countries, not data that is likely to change, such as customer data.

Aggregation, Composition, and Association

There are three types of object relationships — aggregation, composition, and association — that we are interested in. *Aggregation* represents the concept that an object may be made up of other objects. For example, in Figure 19.2 you see that a flight segment is part of a flight plan. *Composition* is a stronger form of aggregation, typically applied to objects representing physical items such as an engine being part of an airplane. *Association* is used to model other types of object relationships, such as the fact that a pilot flies an airplane and follows a flight plan.

From a RI perspective, the only difference between association and aggregation/composition relationships is how tightly the objects are bound to each other. With aggregation and composition, anything that you do to the whole you almost always need to do to the parts, whereas with association that is often not the case — something that is apparent in Table 19.1. For example, if you fly an airplane from New York to San Francisco, you also fly the engine there as well. More importantly, if you retrieve an airplane object from the database, then you likely also want to retrieve its engines (airplanes without engines make little sense). Similarly, a flight plan without its flight segments offer little value. You almost always want to delete the parts when you delete the whole; for example, a flight segment doesn't make much sense outside the scope of a flight plan. Association is different. A pilot object without the airplane objects that it flies makes sense, and if you delete an airplane, then the pilot objects that flew it at one point shouldn't be affected.

Clearly the type of relationship between two classes will provide guidance as to their applicable RI rules. Composition relationships typically result in more RI rules than does aggregation, which in turn typically results in more rules than does association.

TIP Although inheritance is a type of object relationship, it isn't a factor when it comes to RI between objects. This is the result of inheritance being natively implemented by the object-oriented languages. When inheritance structures are mapped into a relational database (discussed in Chapter 14), you may end up with several tables and therefore have the normal database RI issues to deal with.

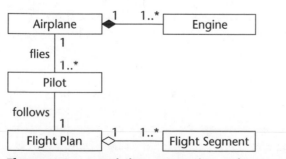

Figure 19.2 Association, aggregation, and composition.

Architectural Layering

Layering is the concept of organizing your software design into layers/collections of classes or components that fulfill a common purpose. Figure 19.3 depicts a five-layer class-type architecture (Ambler 2001a) for the design of object-oriented software. These layers are:

User interface (UI) layer.   A UI class implements a major UI element of your system such as a Java ServerPage (JSP), an Active Server Page (ASP), a report (see Chapter 21), or a graphical user interface (GUI) screen.

Domain layer.   Domain classes implement the concepts pertinent to your business domain, such as customer or order, focusing on the data aspects of the business objects plus behaviors specific to individual objects.

Controller layer.   Controller classes implement business logic that involves collaborating with several domain classes or even other controller classes. In Enterprise JavaBeans (EJB) (Roman et. al. 2002), entity beans are domain classes and session beans are controller classes.

Persistence layer.   Persistence classes encapsulate the ability to permanently store, retrieve, and delete objects without revealing details of the underlying storage technology (database-encapsulation strategies are discussed in Chapter 13).

System layer.   System classes provide operating-system-specific functionality for your applications, isolating your software from the operating system (OS) by wrapping OS-specific features and increasing the portability of your application.

Architectural layering is a common design approach because it improves the modularity, and thus the maintainability, of your system. Furthermore, it is an approach that is commonly accepted within the object community, and it is one of the reasons why object developers take offense to the idea of implementing business logic and RI within your database.

Removal from Memory versus Persistent Deletion

A straightforward but important issue is the distinction between removing an object from memory and permanently deleting it from the database. You will often remove an object from memory, an act referred to as garbage collection, when you no longer require it, yet you won't delete it from the database because you'll need it later.

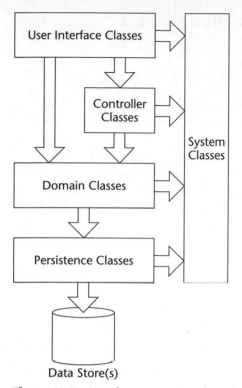

Figure 19.3   Layering your system based on class types.

Where Should You Implement Referential Integrity?

As Figure 19.1 demonstrates, you have a choice as to where you implement business logic, including your RI strategy. Anyone who tells you that this logic *must* be implemented in the database or *must* be implemented in business objects is clearly showing his or her prejudices — this isn't a black-and-white issue. You have architectural options for how you implement RI as well as other types of business logic. Although it may be painful to admit, there isn't a perfect solution. Implementing everything in business objects sounds nice in theory, but in Chapter 13 you saw that it is common for some applications to either not use your business objects or simply be unable to do so due to platform incompatibilities. Implementing everything in your database also sounds nice in theory, but in Chapter 13 you saw that it is common to have several databases within your organization, the implication being that your database really isn't the centralized location that you want it to be. Instead of following strategies that are nice in theory, you need to determine an approach that will actually work for you in practice. That's the topic of the following sections.

Referential Integrity Implementation Options

There are two basic philosophies as to where RI rules should be implemented:

- The largest camp, the "traditionalists," maintain that RI rules should be implemented within the database. Their argument is that modern databases include sophisticated mechanisms to support RI and that the database provides an ideal location to centralize RI enforcement that all applications can take advantage of.

- A smaller camp, the "object purists," maintain that RI rules should be implemented within the application logic, either the business objects themselves or within your database-encapsulation layer. Their argument is that RI is a business issue and therefore should be implemented within your business layer, not the database. They also argue that the RI enforcement features of relational databases reflect the development realities of the 1970s and 1980s, not the *n*-tier environment of the 1990s and 2000s.

My belief is that both camps are right and that both camps are also wrong. The traditionalists' approach breaks down in a multidatabase environment because the database is no longer a centralized resource in this situation. It also ignores the need to ensure RI across tiers — RI is no longer just a database issue. The object-purist approach breaks down when applications exist that cannot use the business layer. This includes nonobject applications, perhaps written in COBOL or C, as well as object applications that simply weren't built to reuse the "standard" business objects. The reality of modern software development, apparent even in the simplified deployment diagram of Figure 19.1, is that you need to find the sweet spot between these two extremes.

An agile software developer realizes that there are several options available when it comes to implementing RI. Table 19.2 compares and contrasts these options from the point of view of each strategy being used in isolation. The important thing to realize is that no option is perfect; each has its trade-offs. For example, within the database community the "declarative vs. programmatic RI" debate rages on and likely will never be resolved (and that's exactly how it should be). A second important observation is that you can mix and match these techniques and thereby avoid some problems. Today within your organization, you are likely using all of them, and you may even have individual applications that apply each one. Once again, it isn't a black-and-white world.

Table 19.2   Referential Integrity Implementation Options

OPTION	DESCRIPTION	ADVANTAGES	DISADVANTAGES	WHEN TO USE
Business objects	Programmatic approach where RI is enforced by operations implemented by business objects within your application. For example, as part of deletion an *Order* object will automatically delete its associated *OrderItem* objects.	• Supports a "pure object" approach. • Testing is simplified because all business logic is implemented in one place.	• Every application must be architected to reuse the same business objects. • Extra programming required to support functionality that is natively supported by your database.	• For complex, object-oriented RI rules. • When all applications are built using the same business object, or better yet domain component (Ambler 2001a), framework.
Database constraints	This approach, also called declarative RI (DRI), uses data definition language (DDL) defined constraints to enforce RI. For example, adding a NOT NULL constraint to a foreign key column.	• Ensures RI within the database. • Constraints can be generated and reverse engineered by data-modeling tools.	• Every application must be architected to use the same database or all constraints must be implemented in each database. • Proves to be a performance inhibitor with large tables.	• When the database is a shared by several applications. • For simple, data-oriented RI. • Use in conjunction with database triggers and possibly updatable views. • For large databases, use during development to help you identify RI bugs, but remove the constraints once you deploy the code in production.

(continued)

Table 19.2 *(continued)*

OPTION	DESCRIPTION	ADVANTAGES	DISADVANTAGES	WHEN TO USE
Database triggers	Programmatic approach whereby a procedure is "triggered" by an event, such as a deletion of a row, to perform required actions to ensure that other RI is maintained.	• Ensures RI within the database. • Triggers can be generated, and reverse engineered, by data-modeling tools.	• Every application must be architected to use the same database or all triggers must be implemented in each database. • Proves to be a performance inhibitor in tables with large numbers of transactions.	• When the database is shared by several applications. • For complex, data-oriented RI. • Use in conjunction with database constraints and possibly updatable views. • Use during development to discover RI bugs, then remove once you deploy the code in production.
Persistence framework	RI rules are defined as part of the relationship mappings. The multiplicity (cardinality and optionality) of relationships is defined in the meta data along with rules indicating the need for cascading reads, updates, or deletions.	• RI implemented as part of overall object persistence strategy. • RI rules can be centralized into a single meta data repository.	• Every application must be architected to use the same persistence framework, or at least work from the same relationship mappings. • Can be difficult to test meta data-driven rules.	• For simple, object-oriented RI rules. • When all applications are built using the same persistence framework.

Table 19.2 (continued)

OPTION	DESCRIPTION	ADVANTAGES	DISADVANTAGES	WHEN TO USE
Updatable Views	RI rules are reflected in the definition of the view.	• RI is enforced within the database.	• Updatable views are often problematic within relational databases due to RI problems. • Updatable views that update several tables may not be an option within your database. • All applications must use the views, not the source tables.	• When the database is shared by several applications. • When your RI needs are simple. • Use in conjunction with database constraints and database triggers.

Business Logic Implementation Options

You also have choices when it comes to implementing non-RI business logic, and once again you can apply a combination of technologies. Luckily, this idea does seem to be contentious; the only real issue is deciding when to use each option. Table 19.3 describes each implementation option and provides guidance as to the effective application of each.

> **NOTE** For years, I have advised developers to avoid using stored procedures because they aren't portable between databases. During the 1990s, I was involved with several projects that ran into serious trouble because they needed to port to a new database in order to scale their application, and as a result they needed to redevelop all of their stored procedures. Ports such as this were common back then because the database market hadn't stabilized yet. It wasn't clear what products were going to survive, and as a result organizations hadn't committed yet to a single vendor. Times have changed. Most database vendors have solved the scalability issue, making it unlikely that you need to port. Furthermore, most organizations have chosen a primary database vendor — it is quite common for an organization to be an "Oracle shop," a "DB2 shop," or a "MySQL shop" — making it unlikely that you will be allowed to port anyway. Therefore stored procedures, assuming that they are well written and implemented according to the guidelines described below, are now a viable implementation option in my opinion. Use them wisely.

General Implementation Strategies

In the previous sections, you have seen that you have several technical alternatives for implementing RI and other business logic. You have also seen that each alternative has its strengths and weaknesses. This section provides an overview of several strategies that you should consider when deciding where to implement this logic. These strategies are:

Recognize that it isn't a black and white decision.   I simply can't say this enough: Your technical environment is likely too complex to support a "one size fits all" strategy.

Implement logic on commonly shared tier(s).   The best place to implement commonly used logic is on commonly used tiers. If your database is the only common denominator between applications (this is particularly true when applications are built on different platforms or with different technologies), then your database may be your only viable option to implement reusable functionality.

Table 19.3 Business Logic Implementation Options

OPTION	DESCRIPTION	ADVANTAGES	DISADVANTAGES	WHEN TO USE
Business objects	Business objects, both domain and controller objects, implement the business logic as a collection of operations.	• Reflects standard layering practices within the development community. • Business functionality is easily accessible by other object applications. • Very good development tools exist to build business objects.	• Significant performance problems for data-intensive functions. • Nonobject applications may have significant difficulty accessing functionality.	• With complex business functionality that does not require significant amounts of data.
Services	An individual service, such as a Web service or CICS transaction, implements a cohesive business transaction such as transferring funds between accounts.	• Services can be accessed in a standard, platform-independent manner. • Promotes reuse.	• Web services standards are still evolving. • Developers are still learning to think in terms of services. • Need tools to manage, find, and maintain services.	• As a wrapper around new or existing business logic implemented by legacy systems, stored procedures, and business objects. • With new functionality that needs to be reused by multiple platforms.
Stored procedures	Functionality is implemented in the database.	• Accessible by wide range of applications.	• Potential for database to become a processing bottleneck. • Requires application programmers to have significant database development experience in addition to "normal" application development experience. • Very difficult to port between database vendors.	• With data-intensive functions that produce small result sets.

Implement unique logic in the most appropriate place.   If business logic is unique to an application, implement it in the most appropriate place. If this happens to be in the same place that you're implementing shared logic, then implement it in such a way as to distinguish it and, better yet, keep it separate so that it doesn't get in the way of everyone else.

Implement logic where it's easiest.   Another factor you need to consider is ease of implementation. You may have better development tools, or more experience, on one tier than another. All things being equal, if it's easier for you to develop and deploy logic to your application server than it is into your database server, then do so.

Be prepared to implement the same logic in several places.   You should always strive to implement logic once, but sometimes this isn't realistic. In a multidatabase environment, you may discover that you are implementing the same logic in each database to ensure consistency. In a multitier environment, you may discover that you need to implement most, if not all, of your RI rules in both your business layer (so that RI rules are reflected in your object schema) and your database.

Be prepared to evolve your strategy over time.   Some database refactorings include moving functionality into or out of your database. A long-term architectural direction might be to eventually stop implementing business logic in some places.

However, having said all this the reality is that databases are often the best choice for implementing RI. The growing importance of Web services and XML point to a trend where application logic is becoming less object-oriented and more data-processing oriented, even though object technology is the primary underlying implementation technology for both. Nevertheless, your team still needs to work through this critical architectural issue.

Summary

This chapter explored the concept of referential integrity (RI), arguing that it is an issue for both your objects and your database(s). You learned that object technology adds some interesting twists to RI, in part because it adds cross-schema issues into the mix and because common object implementation strategies, such as layering and lazy reads, complicate matters.

More importantly, this chapter compared and contrasted strategies for implementing RI and non-RI business rules. You learned that there are several ways to implement this logic in your database, strategies preferred by data purists. You also learned that there are several ways to implement it in your business objects, strategies preferred by object purists. Unfortunately, it isn't a "pure" world. As the sixth philosophy of the agile data method advises, you are better off to look for the sweet spot somewhere in between these two extremes. RI is an important architectural decision that your team must make, one that isn't black and white.

CHAPTER 20

Implementing Security
Access Control

If you're not agile, you're fragile.

Security access control, or simply access control, is an important aspect of any system. Security access control is the act of ensuring that an authenticated user accesses only what they are authorized to and no more. The bad news is that security is rarely at the top of people's lists, although mention terms such as data confidentiality, sensitivity, and ownership and they quickly become interested. The good news is that there is a wide range of techniques that you can apply to help secure access to your system. The bad news is that as Mitnick and Simon (2002) point out "...the human factor is the weakest link. Security is too often merely an illusion, an illusion sometimes made even worse when gullibility, naivette, or ignorance come into play." They go on to say that "security is not a technology problem — it's a people and management problem." My experience is that the "technology factor" and the "people factor" go hand in hand; you need to address both issues to succeed.

This chapter overviews the issues associated with security access control within your system. As with other critical implementation issues, such as concurrency control and referential integrity, it isn't a black and white world. A "pure object" approach will likely prove to be insufficient as will a "pure database" approach, instead you will need to mix and match techniques.

This chapter addresses:

- The role of the agile DBA
- Authentication
- Authorization
- Effective security strategies

The Role of the Agile DBA

When it comes to security access control, the role of agile DBAs is straightforward. They will:

- Mentor application programmers in security access control strategies.

- Work with enterprise administrators responsible for security administration to identify viable security strategies that conform to your corporate security policy.

- Work with rest of team to choose approach(es) to security access control.

- Work with application programmers to implement security access control strategies.

- Temper database security approaches with potential restrictions imposed by your database-encapsulation schema and object-to-data mappings.

Authentication

Authentication is the act of determining the identity of a user and of the host that he or she is using. The goal of authentication is to first verify that the user who is attempting to interact with your system, whether it be a person or system, is allowed to do so. The second goal of authentication is to gather information regarding the way that the user is accessing your system. For example, a stock broker should not be able to make financial transactions during off hours from an Internet cafe, although he or she should be able to do so from a secured workstation at the office. Therefore, gathering basic host information, such as location and the security aspects of its connection (is it encrypted? is it via a physical line? is the connection private? and so on), is critical.

There are several strategies that you can follow to identify a client:

User ID and password. This is the most common, and typically the simplest, approach to identifying someone because it is fully software-based.

Physical security device. A physical device, such as a bank card, a smart card, or a computer chip (such as the "Speed Pass" key chains used by gas stations) is used to identify a person. Sometimes a password or personal identification number (PIN) is also required to ensure that it is the right person.

Biometric identification. Biometrics is the science of identifying someone from physical characteristics. This includes technologies such as voice verification, a retinal scan, palm identification, and thumbprints (Nanavati, Thieme, and Nanavati 2002).

Because there are many ways that you can authenticate a user, and very likely more will be developed in the future, you may discover that your application needs to support several authentication techniques. This is particularly true if your application runs on several platforms and/or has to support clients implemented on various platforms.

If this is the case, you may want to consider Pluggable Authentication Modules (or PAMs, see www.kernel.org/pub/linux/libs/pam/FAQ) that provide a way to develop programs that are independent of authentication technique.

TIP Lightweight Directory Access Protocol (LDAP) is an industry standard for organizing data of all kinds for easy and flexible retrieval in what is typically referred to as the LDAP Directory. LDAP is often used as a central password database and even for access control lists (ACLs) that define which services/operations a user or application is allowed to access. An advantage of LDAP directories is that they are hierarchical in nature, making it easy to develop cascading permissions.

Authorization

Authorization is the act of determining the level of access that a user has to perform behaviors and obtain or alter data. The following sections explore the issues surrounding authorization and then discusses various database and object-oriented implementation strategies and their implications.

Issues

Fundamentally, to set an effective approach to authorization, the first question that you need to address is, "What will I control access to?" My experience is that you can secure access to both data and functionality, such as access to quarterly sales figures and the ability to fire another employee, respectively. Your stakeholder's requirements will drive the answer to this question. However, the granularity of access and your ability to implement it effectively are significant constraints. For example, although you may be asked to control access to specific columns of specific rows within a database based on complex business rules, you may not be able to implement this in a cost-effective manner that also conforms to performance constraints. Table 20.1 lists various levels of access granularity that are often combined within systems that you need to consider.

Table 20.1 Granularity of Access

GRANULARITY LEVEL	EXAMPLE
Attribute/column	A human resources (HR) manager may update the salary of an employee, and an HR employee may look at the salary, but an employee may not.
Row/object	You are allowed to withdraw money from your bank accounts, whereas I am not.

(continued)

Table 20.1   *(continued)*

GRANULARITY LEVEL	EXAMPLE
Table/class	A database administrator has full update access to system tables within a database that application programmers may not even know exist.
Application	Senior managers within your organization have access to an executive information system (EIS) that provides them with critical summary about the departments they manage. This system is not available to nonmanagement employees.
Database	Sally Jones in manufacturing has access to the inventory database that John Smith in accounting does not have access to.
Host	Sally Jones can work with the machine-control application from her workstation on the shop floor but does not have access to it from her home PC. This is often called host permissions or geographic entitlement.

The second question that you need to answer is, "What rules are applicable?" The answer to this question is also driven by your stakeholder's requirements, although you may need to explore various security factors that they may not be aware of (they're not security experts after all). These factors, which are often combined, include:

Connection type.   Should your access vary based on your connection to the system? For example, should you have different access from a tablet PC with a Wi-Fi wireless connection than from a desktop machine that is connected via an Ethernet cable even though both machines are in the same room?

Update access.   Is it possible for some users to only have read access but not update or deleted access? For example, can a system administrator update tables that users can only read?

Time of day.   Should access levels vary based on time of day? For example, should John Smith in accounting have the ability to post debits and credits during normal office hours but not on the weekends?

Existence.   Should someone even be allowed to know that something exists? For example, your bank may decide to track the amount and frequency of purchases made in liquor stores and bars for each of their customers. This information could be made available to mortgage and car loan officers even though you don't know that it exists.

Cascading authorization.   Do authorization rules reflect your organizational structure? For example, if John Smith can run a batch job to balance all accounts within your organization should his manager automatically be allowed to do it too? Or, if you can input your time into a weekly timesheet, can your manager (or their manager, for that matter) update it?

Global permissions.   Are there certain things that everyone can do, regardless of all other issues?

Combination of privileges.   When several levels of authorization apply, do you take the intersection or union of those authorizations? For example, what should happen if a user has update authority on a table but the host he or she is working at does not? With an intersection approach the user would not have authority because both roles must have authority, with the union approach the user would have the authority because only one role is required to have authority.

Database Implementation Strategies

Let's start by reviewing the concepts of roles and security contexts. A role is a named collection of privileges (permissions) that can be associated to a user. So, instead of managing the authorization rights of each individual user you instead define roles such as *HR_Manager*, *HR_User*, *Manufacturing_Engineer*, *Accountant*, and so on and define what each role can access. You then assign users to the roles, so Sally Jones and her coworkers would be associated with the role of *Manufacturing_Engineer*. Someone else could be assigned the roles of *HR_Manager* and *HR_User* if appropriate. The use of roles is a generic concept that is implemented by a wide range of technologies — not just by databases — to simplify the security administration effort.

A security context is the collection of roles that a user is associated with. The security context is often defined as part of the authentication process. Depending on the technology used, a security context is maintained by the system (this is very common in GUI applications) or must be passed around by the system (this is common with browser-based *n*-tiered system). A combination of the two strategies is also common.

Authorization can be enforced within your database by a variety of means (which can be combined). These techniques, compared in Table 20.2, include:

Permissions.   A permission is a privilege, or authorization right, that a user or role has regarding an element (such as a column, table, or even the database itself). A permission defines the type of access that is permitted, such as the ability to update a table or to run a stored procedure. In SQL, permissions are given via the GRANT command and removed via the REVOKE command. When a user attempts to interact with a database his or her permissions are checked, and if the user is not authorized to perform part of the interaction, which could be a transaction, the interaction fails and an error is returned.

Views.   You can control, often to a very fine level, the data that a user can access via the use of views. This is a two-step process. First, you define views that restrict the tables, columns, and rows within the tables that a role can access. Second, you define permissions on those views.

Stored procedures.   Code within the stored procedure can be written to programmatically check security access rules.

Proprietary approaches.   A new option being offered by some database vendors is proprietary security tools. One example is Oracle Label Security (www.oracle. com), an add-on that enables you to define and enforce row-level permissions. Over time, my expectation is that database vendors will begin to implement security strategies similar to those described in Table 20.2 for object technology.

TIP Many organizations choose to disallow ad hoc queries to production databases to help minimize the chance of unauthorized access (as well as to avoid the associated performance problems). As Chapter 21 describes, many organizations introduce reporting databases, such as data marts, to support ad hoc queries.

TIP A common approach to implementing database connections is to implement a pool of generic connections obtained by logging into the database with application user IDs. For standalone GUI applications, the pool size is typically one, for application servers the pool size could easily be in the hundreds or even thousands. The thinking is that the users have already been authenticated via your login process; therefore, because they've overcome a basic security hurdle already you don't need to worry about security anymore. In many situations this is a fair assumption. This is a good strategy because the alternative — logging individual users into the database — requires extra work and resources and can adversely affect performance. The disadvantage is that if the database doesn't know who the user is then audit logging of database changes can only be traced to the application and not the individual. Contact your enterprise administrator for applicable development guidelines regarding this issue.

Security Design Patterns

Yoder and Barcalow (2000) have developed a pattern language for enabling application security, the patterns of which are presented in Table 20.3. Although these patterns are straightforward, which is a good thing, the interesting ones are the two that deal with user interface (UI) issues — Full View With Errors and Limited View. These patterns address the existence issue discussed earlier and commingle it with usability issues.

Table 20.2   Comparing Database-Oriented Implementation Strategies

STRATEGY	ADVANTAGES	DISADVANTAGES	ADVICE
Permissions	Simple and effective technique.	Easy to get around with generic application user IDs.	• This is a very common approach. It is hard to imagine a situation where you wouldn't use permissions in a database. • Development teams should be aware of enterprise security guidelines pertaining to permissions and potential use of generic IDs.
Proprietary approaches	• You can code very complex authorization rules. • Potentially easier than coding stored procedures.	• Not portable between vendors. • Can become a bottleneck.	Consider proprietary approaches when there is a clear architectural decision within your organization to stick with that vendor and you truly require complex authorization.
Stored procedures	You can code very complex authorization rules.	• Not portable between vendors. • Can become a bottleneck. • Requires you to block access via other means, such as simply reading the raw data from the source tables.	• Use stored procedures as for situations where a combination of views and permissions is insufficient. • Programmatic approaches might be better left to the business tier.
Views	Provides detailed authorization down to the row and column level.	• Can increase the complexities of mapping and your database encapsulation strategy if multiple updatable views need to be supported/used by a single application because there are effectively multiple sources for the same data now. • Complex views requiring multiple joins can degrade performance.	• Use views when you need finer control than what permissions will provide. • Because views are often used to encapsulate access to deprecated data structures (perhaps because of a database refactoring) as well as denormalized reporting structures, you may need a strategy to differentiate between views used for security and views used for other purposes.

Table 20.3 Security Design Patterns

PATTERN	DESCRIPTION
Check Point	This is the place to validate users and to make appropriate decisions when dealing with security breaches. Also known as Access Verification, Validation and Penalization, and Holding off Hackers.
Full View with Errors	Users are presented with all functionality, but when they attempt to use functionality that they are not authorized to use, an appropriate error-handling procedure is followed. The advantage is that this approach is easy to implement, but it puts you at risk because it reveals functionality to people that they may then decide to try and gain unauthorized access to.
Limited View	Users are presented with what they are allowed to run. This approach is generally harder to implement but is considered user-friendly and more secure than a Full View with Errors approach.
Roles	Users should be assigned to one or more roles, such as *HR_Manager*, and security rules should be defined in terms of those roles.
Secure Access Layer	Because an application is only as secure as its components and interactions with them, you need a secure access layer (or framework) for communicating with external systems in a secure manner. Furthermore, all components of an application should provide a secure way to interact with them.
Session	Captures basic authentication information (ID and host) as well as the user's security privileges. Also known as Session Context or Security Context.
Single Access Point	Entry into a system should be through a single point. It should not be possible to get into a system via a back door. Also known as Login Window, Guard Door, and One Way In.

Object-Oriented Implementation Strategies

Because objects encapsulate both data and behavior, an object-oriented (OO) authorization strategy needs to include the ability to secure both. This can be problematic because common object-oriented programming languages (OOPLs), such as Java, C#, C++, and Visual Basic, do not natively include security features. Instead you must adopt a strategy, perhaps a combination of the ones listed in the following list, and then follow that strategy. The implication is that you need to verify, through testing and inspections, that your organizational security strategy is being followed.

Authorization can be implemented with your objects by following a variety of strategies. These strategies, which are compared in Table 20.4, include:

Brute force.   Any operation that requires authorization must implement all of the logic itself.

Business rules engine.   Authorization logic is passed via invocations to a business rules engine, such as Blaze (www.blaze-advisor.net/business_rules_engine.htm), the Versata Transaction Logic Engine (www.versata.com), or QuickRules (www.yasutech.com/products/quickrules/features.htm). Each operation that requires authorization simply needs to invoke the appropriate rule(s) in the business engine and act accordingly.

Permissions.   This is the same strategy as using permissions within a database, the only difference is that permissions are applied to the operations of classes instead of to database elements. This approach is taken by Enterprise JavaBean (EJB) servers (Roman et. al. 2002), where the EJB container automatically compares the access rights of an operation with that of the user invoking it. When no permissions are set, the container will still check the defaults and perform the same type of check.

Security framework/component.   Authorization functionality is encapsulated within a security framework. Examples of commercial security frameworks include the security aspects of the .NET framework (www.gotdotnet.com/team/clr/about_security.aspx) and the Java Authentication and Authorization Service (JAAS) (java.sun.com/products/jaas/). You may need to build your own security framework for other environments (Ambler 1998b, Ambler 1998c). Security frameworks/components can be deployed to client, application server, or even database server machines.

Security server.   A specialized, external server(s) implements the security access control rules that are invoked as required. Commercial products include Cisco Secure Access Control Server (www.cisco.com) and RSA Cleartrust Authorization Server (www.rsasecurity.com).

Aspect-oriented programming (AOP).   Aspect-oriented software development is an emerging collection of technologies and techniques for separation of concerns in software development. The techniques of AOSD make it possible to modularize crosscutting aspects of a system. A good resource is the Aspect Oriented Software Development home page (aosd.net/). Examples of aspect-oriented tools include AspectJ (www.eclipse.org/aspectj/) for Java, AspectR (aspectr.sourceforge.net/) for Ruby, and Java Access Components (JAC) (jac.aopsys.com/) for distributed Java programming.

TIP *Security Engineering* **by Ron Anderson (2001) gives a comprehensive look at how to develop secure systems.** *Writing Secure Code*, **Second Edition (Howard and LeBlanc 2003) is also a good reference for any programmer who is serious about developing secure systems.**

Table 20.4 Comparing Object-Oriented Implementation Strategies

STRATEGY	ADVANTAGES	DISADVANTAGES	WHEN TO USE
Aspect-oriented programming (AOP)	• Potential to easily add security access control to an existing application. • Wide range of AOP tools for Java.	• Few people understand AOP. • AOP is still an emerging technology. • Non-Java AOP tools are not as common.	• When you are retrofitting security into an existing application. • When you are able to tolerate (radically) new technologies.
Brute Force	Simple to implement.	The code maintenance burden increases as number and complexity of security requirements increase.	When very few authorization rules are required.
Business Rules Engine	You can code very complex authorization rules.	• Business objects become tightly coupled to the business rule engine. • Programmers need to learn how to work with the engine. • Potential performance overhead when invoking the engine, particularly if it is located on a separate machine. • Potential single point of failure.	• When the engine is already needed for something else (such as the implementation of business rules). • When you have many complex authorization rules.

Table 20.4 *(continued)*

STRATEGY	ADVANTAGES	DISADVANTAGES	WHEN TO USE
Permissions	• Simple to implement. • Potential to integrate with other permissions-based approaches.	• Often vendor-specific. • Requires an administration system to work manage permissions. • Can be difficult to authorize access to specific objects (for example, you can only withdraw money from your bank accounts, not from your neighbor's accounts).	When your application server or object environment natively supports permissions.
Security framework/ component	You can code very complex authorization rules.	• Often language- and even vendor-specific. • Programmers must learn the framework.	When you have many complex authorization rules.
Security server	• Security logic is encapsulated in one place. • Potential to implement very complex authorization rules.	• Performance is impacted by invocation across network. • Potential single point of failure.	• When you require a sophisticated approach to authorization. • When you want to encapsulate security rules in one place.

Implications

In the previous sections, you have seen that you have several technical alternatives for implementing authorization rules and that each alternative has its strengths and weaknesses. Similarly to referential integrity (discussed in Chapter 19), there are some important implications for agile software developers:

Recognize that it isn't a black-and white-decision.   You clearly have implementation choices.

Implement security access control on commonly shared tier(s).   In other words, consider applying the *Secure Access Layer* pattern described in Table 20.3.

Be prepared to combine strategies.   For example, although a security framework such as JAAS works well for basic security access control, it doesn't work well for object-level access, implying that you need to follow another strategy at that point.

Be prepared to implement security access control logic in several places.   In complex environments, you are likely to discover that you need to implement security access control on several tiers, including your database(s) and objects. In these situations, you should consider security management products such as Control/SA (www.bmc.com) and Tivoli (www-3.ibm.com/software/tivoli/). These products have their own preferred way of working that will drive some of your implementation choices.

Keep performance in mind.   A good rule of thumb is to keep security checks as close to the user as possible. For example, in a three-tiered system don't rely on the database to determine authorization; if the client or application server can do it, you thereby eliminate one or two potentially slow interactions across the network.

Take advantage of existing database authorization practices.   Many organizations have an effective data security strategy in place but struggle with object-oriented and application-based authorization. Consider evolving your existing data security strategy, but do so with the realization that the security needs of objects differ from those of data.

Be prepared to evolve your strategy over time.   Your security needs will change over time; therefore, your security strategy will need to as well.

Effective Security Strategies

Before closing this chapter, I'd like to share a few words of advice that have worked well for me over the years:

Base your security approach on actual requirements.   The implementation of security within a system is one of those things that can easily spin out of control, resulting in a "really cool" framework that no one needs or uses. Let your project stakeholders, which can include people with an enterprise-level vision as well as a project-level vision, help identify security requirements. Walk them through security issues if you need to but make sure they understand the implications of what they're asking for. Everybody wants high levels of security, but they can often live with much less when they discover how much it will cost to build and how long it will take to do so.

Strive for an enterprise security strategy, but be realistic.   Your organization may already have an existing security strategy in place, something that your enterprise architects and enterprise administrators should advise you on. Or the organization may be in the process of developing one. A single security strategy may be difficult to adopt because each application may have its own specific definition of roles; for example, John Smith might qualify for the role of *Accounting_Manager* in one application but not in another. Basic system integration issues can be a problem — what good is a Java-based security server if your mainframe applications can't easily connect to it?

Don't overdo security.   Your software still needs to be usable, and a security access control strategy that makes your system difficult to work with will quickly undermine your efforts.

No security approach is foolproof.   As Mitnick and Simon (2002) point out, the real challenge is the people, not the technology. Your technical solutions are just a start; the secret is to make sure that people are aware of security issues and act accordingly.

Give people only the access that they need.   This is the entire point of security access control! Global privileges and potentially destructive activities, such as running data definition language (DDL) code in a relational database, are best assigned to a small group of responsible administrators.

Limit permissions to a small set of hosts.   An effective strategy for preventing external "crackers" from harming your systems is to limit access to a defined group of secure hosts. Unfortunately, this approach is problematic when you consider the growing number of potential hosts — personal digital assistants (PDAs), personal computers, and farms of application servers.

Remember performance.   There is a security/performance trade-off — the greater the granularity of security access control and the greater the number of rules to be checked, the slower your security scheme becomes.

Don't forget other security issues.   In addition to authentication and authorization, you need to consider the security issues summarized in Table 20.5. It doesn't make much sense to implement a security access control scheme if people can easily get around it because you haven't addressed other basic security issues.

Adopt industry standards.   Emerging standards include Security Assertion Markup Language (SAML) (www.oasis-open.org/committees/security/) and Securely Available Credentials (SACRED) (www.ietf.org/html.charters/sacred-charter.html). Your organization isn't the only one dealing with security issues, so why reinvent the wheel when a perfectly good standard already exists?

Table 20.5 Additional Security Issues

ISSUE	DESCRIPTION
Audit logging	Recording of activities of users. Activities potentially include changes made to the data and perhaps nondata actions (such as drawing a square).
Cryptography	Cryptography is the act of ensuring that only the intended recipient can read a message. Approaches include public key encryption strategies such as Pretty Good Privacy (PGP) (www.pgpi.org) and secure connections such as HTTPS and SSL.
Digital certificates	The digital certificate is a common credential, assigned by a trusted entity (typically another organization), that provides a means to verify identity of an external user. The use of digital certificates is common when your system needs to interact with other, external systems.
Non-repudiation	The ability to identify exactly who/what made data changes or performed actions. This information may aid your efforts to recover from security breaches after the fact.

Summary

Security is an important concern for any system, one that you should take seriously. This chapter focused on implementation strategies for security access control using both database and object-oriented technologies. Data-oriented security is a very good start but may not prove sufficient for the needs of modern software development. Luckily, there are several options for implementing authorization rules within your object-oriented code that enable you to secure access to both data and behavior. None of these approaches are perfect for every situation, which is why you need to be aware of the options and their strengths and weaknesses, so you can chose the approach(es) that are best suited for your situation.

CHAPTER 21

Implementing Reports

Coupling is the enemy.

Reporting is a necessity within every organization and within virtually every business application. Your project stakeholders will define some requirements that are best implemented as operational functionality, such as the definition and maintenance of customer information, and other requirements that are best implemented as reports. This chapter explores critical report-implementation issues. For example, should you build reports within your application or separately within another specialized reporting facility? Should you implement using object technology or with reporting tools?

For our purposes, a report is the read-only output of information, potentially including both "raw" base data and calculated/summarized values. Reports can be rendered in a variety of manners — printed, displayed on a screen, or saved as an electronic file. Reports can be created in batch or in real time. A customer invoice is a report and so is a quarterly sales summary by division.

This chapter explores the following topics:

- The role of the agile DBA
- Database deployment architecture
- Reporting within your application
- Reporting outside your application

- Database design strategies
- Implementation strategies
- Challenges that make reporting hard

The Role of the Agile DBA

Agile DBAs take an active role in the report implementation. Figure 21.1 shows the primary tasks that agile DBAs will be involved with, including:

Develop database architecture.   The development team, including the agile DBA, will develop an architecture for their application. This architecture should reflect the overall enterprise architectural vision as well as the evolving needs of their project stakeholders.

Develop data extracts.   When reporting is performed from another database(s), such as a data mart or data warehouse, some sort of data extract/replication strategy will need to be put in place to copy data from your operational database to the other databases as required. The agile DBA will work with both the application programmers and with the external database owners, often acting as an intermediary.

Develop reports.   The agile DBA will work with the other members of the team, including both application programmers and project stakeholders, to develop and evolve reports.

Evolve corporate data definitions.   When you extract data into a database that is required to conform to corporate data standards, which is often the case with corporate data warehouses, you will often discover new data elements not yet covered by your standards. When this occurs, the agile DBA will work with the enterprise administrators to evolve the standards.

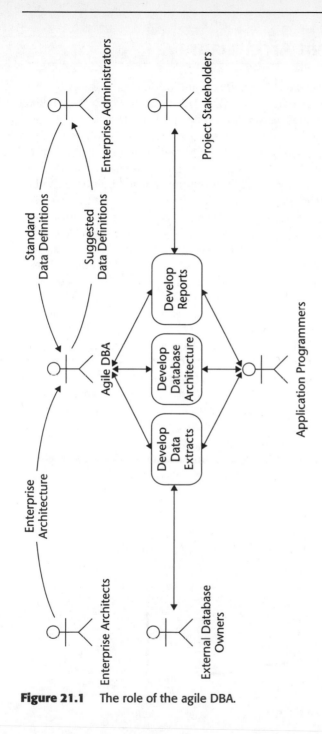

Figure 21.1   The role of the agile DBA.

Database Deployment Architecture

Most business applications, particularly those that edit and update data contained in a relational database, require relatively normalized data. This basic manipulation of data is often referred to as the operational features of an application. In Chapter 4, you learned that data normalization is a design process where the goal is to ensure that data is stored in one and one place only. This results in cohesive tables and a database schema that is very flexible. Because reports often require a wide range of data, resulting in the need to join many normalized tables, a highly normalized database can be difficult to report from. This problem is exacerbated when a report needs to "crunch" a large amount of data. The implication is that you need a database architecture that supports the operational needs of your application as well as its reporting needs.

My experience is that because the operational needs of an application are best served by a highly normalized schema, and that because reporting needs are best served by a denormalized data schema, you should consider implementing two separate schemas. So far the focus of this book has been on the operational needs of an application, not on its reporting needs, and therefore I have not discussed the idea of separate data schemas. Figure 21.2 shows a logical database deployment architecture, depicting the idea that your application will read and update information from an operational database. This architecture is a subset of your overall enterprise technical architecture, which includes hardware, middleware, software, and data. Data from the operational database will be used to load data marts, if any, as well as your corporate data warehouse. An operational database, also called an operational data store (ODS), supports online transaction processing and analytical reporting. A data mart is a department/application-specific database used for reporting. A data warehouse is a collection of subject-oriented databases where each unit of data is relevant to a given moment in time. Table 21.1 compares and contrasts these types of databases.

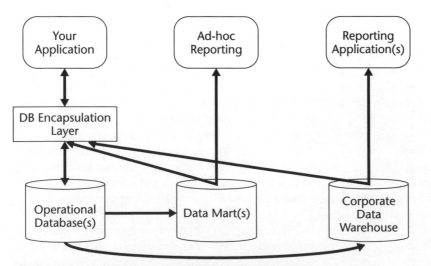

Figure 21.2   Logical database deployment architecture.

Table 21.1   Comparing Databases

OPERATIONAL DATABASE	DATA MART	DATA WAREHOUSE
• Highly normalized • Some summary data for online reporting • Requirements driven • Supports read/write access by applications • Specific to one or more applications • Operational applications typically work with this type of database	• Highly denormalized • Requirements driven • Specific to a single department and/or collection of application reports • Contains a snapshot of near-term information, typically less than a year old • Supports read-only access by applications • Often uses multi-dimensional database management system • Supports very flexible and unpredictable access to data • Ad hoc reporting facilities typically work with this type of database	• Highly normalized • May have some summary data • Flexible design which stores granular data • Supports read-only access by applications • Not specific to any application or department • Driven by enterprise-level requirements • Contains massive amounts of data, typically an order of magnitude greater than a data mart or operational database • Often includes several (upward of 10) years worth of data • "Standard" reports are developed and run on a regular basis against this type of database

Figure 21.2 depicts a logical architecture because a large organization is likely to have many physical operational databases, many physical data marts, and even several physical warehouses. A small company may have a single database that is used for all three purposes. Regardless of your physical implementation of this architecture, the basics still hold.

Inmon (2002) describes a process where the data from operational databases, including legacy databases (see Chapter 8), is denormalized and fed into the appropriate data marts. This data is loaded on a regular basis into the data marts, typically on a daily basis, although periods of a few hours or even a few minutes is common. The data is also removed on a regular basis from the database to keep the data marts at a relatively stable size. Data is also loaded into your corporate data warehouse, although now this data will be highly denormalized and may need to be transformed to fit corporate data standards.

An advantage of separating operational databases from data marts and data warehouses is that it provides your team with the option to decouple your application from reporting-based data schemas. Although Figure 21.2 shows your application, via your encapsulation layer, accessing all three types of databases, you could choose to only interact directly with the operational database. This works when your application implements reports that are based only on data contained in the operational database. A better strategy is to externalize reports from your application and implement them via data-mart or data-warehouse-based reporting tools.

> **TIP** Agile DBAs need to be aware of enterprise data standards. When an agile DBA evolves the data schema of an operational database, perhaps through database refactoring, he or she should always strive to ensure that the schema follows the enterprise data standards. This means the agile DBA will need access to the standards, perhaps stored online in a meta data repository, and will need to work with the enterprise administrators to evolve the standards over time.

Reporting within Your Application

Like any other functionality within your application, a report needs to be based on requirements. This is why Figure 21.1 shows project stakeholders working with application programmers and agile DBAs to develop reports; the project stakeholders provide the requirements for and feedback on the work of the developers.

My implementation strategy for including reports in an application changes according to the development platform. When I'm building a fat-client application, perhaps building it with a Java Swing user interface or with Visual Basic, my preferred approach is to separate most if not all reports into their own application. In other words, I build two applications, one that implements the operational logic and one that implements the reports. The operational application is typically implemented with an object-oriented language such as Java, C#, or Visual Basic, and the reporting application is developed using a reporting tool (see Table 21.2). The reason for this is simple — I prefer to use the right development environment for the job. Sometimes I will invoke the reporting tool from the operational application so I can deploy a single, integrated application. Other times, my stakeholders already have an existing reporting facility and they want the new reports to be added to it. Larry Greenfield presents a comprehensive list of reporting and query tools at www.dwinfocenter.org/query.html.

When I'm building a browser-based application, I typically prefer to include reports in the operational application, although, once again, if my stakeholders want the reports to appear in a separate reporting application, then that's what I'll do. My experience is that users of browser applications tend to want links to all related functionality within the application, whereas users of fat-client applications don't mind having a separate reporting application. I'll implement a report as an HTML page that displays read-only information, or, better yet, as an XML data structure that is then converted to HTML via XSLT (Extensible Stylesheet Language Transformation).

Table 21.2 Representative Reporting Frameworks

FRAMEWORK	DESCRIPTION	URL
ActiveReports	ActiveReports includes a report wizard that steps you through creating simple reports without writing any code. Visual Basic and .NET versions are available.	www.datadynamics.com
Crystal Reports	A reporting facility that can be integrated into Visual Studio .NET to create reports that can be invoked by .NET platform applications. It can also be integrated into Java applications via its Java reporting SDK (software development kit), or use JavaBeans as data sources for reports.	www.crystaldecisions.com
Jasper Reports	A Java-based, open source report-generating tool that can deliver content onto the screen or printer, or into PDF, HTML, XLS, CSV, and XML file formats.	jasperreports.sourceforge.net
Microsoft Access and Excel	A common approach to implementing reports within Microsoft applications is to simply invoke either Access or Excel.	www.microsoft.com
Oracle Reports	A reporting tool for Oracle databases. A Java framework exists so that reports can be included in operation applications.	www.oracle.com
Report Builder Pro	A report-building IDE for Borland Delphi.	www.digital-metaphors.com

The logic to implement a report within your application code is fairly straightforward. You identify the selection rules for the information to appear in the report, for example, "all employees with five or more years seniority that work in a Canadian subsidiary." You then obtain the data using one of the strategies described in Chapter 18 (brute force, query objects, or persistent search criteria). This data is then converted into a format that your report-generation strategy can work with. If you are not using a reporting framework, then you will need to code the report yourself. A good strategy is to use the Report Objects design pattern (Brant & Yoder 2000), which implements a report with objects that obtain the data, known as query objects, and with objects that output the data, known as viewing objects. Figure 21.3 depicts a UML sequence diagram that provides an overview of this strategy. The report object collaborates with the query object to obtain the data, marshaling the results into the format required by the viewing object. The viewing object works with the marshaled results to produce the output report.

A design rule of thumb is that reports that appear as part of your operational application should be based on your operational data and should answer a "What is happening right now?" type of question. Examples of this type of question include "What is the current inventory level of Blink 182 CDs?", "Who is currently on call to answer Level 4 customer questions?", and "When is customer X's order scheduled to be shipped?" When these two factors aren't true, you should consider building the report as part of an external reporting application.

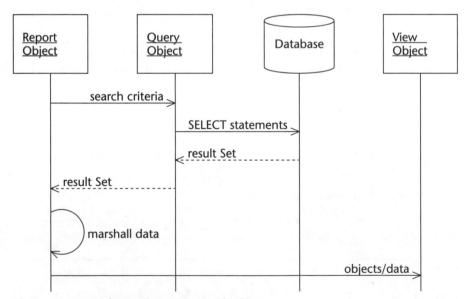

Figure 21.3 Implementing reports with objects.

Reporting outside Your Application

A common strategy is to implement reports outside your application, typically using a reporting facility designed for exactly that purpose. This strategy is often referred to as business intelligence or analytical reporting. Figure 21.2 depicts this concept, showing how an ad hoc reporting facility is often used against data marts, whereas predefined reports are often run against data warehouses. Ad hoc reporting is typically performed for the specific purposes of a small group of users where it is common that the users write the report(s) themselves. Predefined reports are typically developed by the IT department in response to a user's request, sometimes within the scope of an application and sometimes as a small project in its own right.

Why separate ad hoc reports from predefined reports? As you saw in Table 21.1, data marts are designed to support flexible, unpredictable access to data, whereas data warehouses are not designed this way. So, we don't really need to separate the reports per se, just the databases. Representative vendors in the business intelligence reporting tool market include Cognos (www.cognos.com), Hummingbird (www.hummingbird.com), Information Builders (www.informationbuilders.com), and Sagent (www.sagent.com).

The implication is that your organization may already have a reporting strategy in place. This strategy will be reflected in your enterprise's technical architecture and will encompass standard reporting tools, frameworks, and database technologies.

Database Design Strategies

How do you design a database to be "performance friendly" to reports? In an ideal world, you would like to have a perfectly normalized database, but it isn't an ideal world. To support reports, you often need to consider the following changes to your database design:

Take advantage of database features. Each database implements joins, indices, SQL Select statement execution, and access paths in slightly different ways. All of these things influence the performance of your queries and thus your reports. This sort of basic knowledge is taught in database-certification courses, and I highly recommend that all agile DBAs become certified on the database technologies that they work with. The disadvantage is that this approach helps to lock you into your database vendor because you come to rely on the unique features that they provide.

Introduce aggregate tables. An aggregate table stores denormalized copies of data. For example, a *CustomerOrders* aggregate table would store summary totals of the orders for customers. There would be one row for each customer that records the number of orders placed, the number of shipments made, the grand total of the orders for that customer, and so on. The primary disadvantage is that you need to maintain the aggregate table.

Remove unnecessary data.   The smaller the amount of data to process, the faster your queries will run. By removing unnecessary data, either by archiving it or simply deleting it, you can improve the performance of your reports. The disadvantages are that you need to develop an archiving/deletion strategy and in the case of archiving you also need to develop a date recovery process to support retrieval of archived data.

Caching.   In Chapter 19, you learned that caches, either of data or of objects, can dramatically improve your system performance by replacing relatively slow disk accesses with memory accesses. The disadvantages are the increased complexity and the increased chances of cross-schema referential integrity problems introduced by caches.

Partition a table.   The goal is to take a large table, which results in poor performance, and reorganize it into several smaller tables. Tables can be partitioned vertically by storing different columns in each table as well as horizontally by storing collections of rows in different tables. Combinations are also possible. The primary disadvantages are that partitioning will complicate your mapping efforts (mapping is discussed in Chapter 14) and queries can become more complex because you need to work with several tables to support a single concept.

Disallow real-time reports.   Many organizations choose to only support batch reporting against databases to ensure that report queries do not interfere with operational applications, to guarantee consistent performance levels within data marts and data warehouses, and to reserve update windows for those databases.

Introduce indices.   If a report needs to obtain data in a different order than that in which it is stored, a common way to support this is to introduce an index that accesses the data in the required order. The disadvantage is that this slows down runtime performance due to the need to update the additional index.

There are other strategies that a good DBA can implement to improve reporting performance, strategies that Larry Greenfield nicely summarizes at www.dwinfocenter.org/fstquery.html.

Implementation Strategies

When you implement reports, and the data extracts to support them, there are several implementation strategies you should adopt:

Follow report design guidelines.   Your organization likely has report design guidelines, either formally documented ones that should be available from your enterprise administrators or informal ones that you will need to derive from existing reports. These design guidelines will describe issues from the mundane, such as standard headers and footers, to critical report-layout conventions. Although it may seem boring and your "creative juices" may motivate you to take your own approach, if you do in fact have a reasonable set of guidelines in place, you should follow them. If all reports within your organization follow the same set of conventions, they will be easier for your stakeholders to work with.

Follow data design standards for extracted data.   A primary goal of your enterprise administrators is to maintain and support common data definitions and standards for your organization's data. Although you should be applying these conventions when you are designing your database schema, it is critical that extracted data does so because it will be shared throughout your organization.

Add database views to support common reporting needs.   Reporting data can be easier to extract with the addition of database views that perform common joins and projections within your database.

Be prepared to work with imperfect data.   As you saw in Chapter 8, there are many potential data-quality problems, an issue that is exacerbated by the fact that the data in data marts and data warehouses comes from many sources. Even if all of the data conforms to corporate standards, there are very likely differences in the timeliness of data. Some extractions may run daily, whereas others run hourly, and some daily extractions may run several hours after others. These timing issues will have an impact on your reports.

Treat data extraction requests as new requirements.   Agile software developers typically work from a prioritized stack of requirements. When a new requirement is proposed by project stakeholders, the developers estimate it and ask the stakeholders to prioritize it, and if the stakeholders don't like the estimate ("What do you mean this will cost $50,000?!"), rework and resubmit the requirement. The requirements are pulled off the stack and implemented in order of priority. When an external database owner requests data elements from you, perhaps to fulfill the requirements of other project teams, the request should be treated exactly like any other requirement — it should be estimated, prioritized, put on the stack, and eventually implemented.

Investigate printing facilities and supplies.   Your organization may have a printing framework, or perhaps a standard approach to printing, that your team can take advantage of. This is particularly true for any reports that are sent to your customers, such as invoices. The type of paper and envelopes will affect your report design. For example, does your organization have a standard envelope that requires you to print the address in a specific spot so that it lines up with the envelope window? Folding and envelope capacity are issues that you may need to be aware of as well. The point is that you need to work closely with your operations staff, people who are also considered to be project stakeholders.

Challenges That Make Reporting Hard

Object technology doesn't readily lend itself to reporting. Although you have several implementation strategies available to you, none of them are ideal. A "pure" object-oriented approach would be solely based on objects, but because many reports require information from thousands and sometimes millions of objects, the database access and marshaling alone can be performance-inhibitive. Luckily "impure" solutions exist, such as developing report objects or integrating reporting tools, but they will most likely require you to break your encapsulation strategy.

When reports are printed, physical issues are brought into your design. Simple things, such as aligning your output with the fields on preprinted forms, can be tedious when you don't have printer drivers specifically designed for those forms.

A more difficult issue to address is the fact that the owners of the data marts and your corporate data warehouse likely do not work in an agile manner. You will need to find ways to work with them, perhaps a combination of helping them to become more agile and with learning to tolerate a little bit of bureaucracy. They may not be able to tolerate your team's refactoring the layout of the data extract schema on a rapid basis and may, in fact, require you to release code on a much slower basis (quarterly instead of weekly). Furthermore, they may not be able to respond quickly to your requests for schema changes within their databases. You'll need to find ways to work together effectively, something that can be particularly hard if your project is the first one in your organization to take an agile approach to development.

Similarly, your Operations Department, which likely controls access to your corporate printing facilities, may not work in an agile manner. Once again, you'll need to find ways to work together.

Summary

This chapter focused on a basic but critical aspect of software-based systems — reporting. Your organization likely has a database architecture that takes reporting into consideration. This architecture may involve separate reporting databases, such as data marts and data warehouses, which you will need to export data to and then report from. You learned that existing reporting tools and frameworks may exist for you to reuse on your project.

A fundamental decision that you need to make is whether reports are included as part of your application, are to be implemented in a separate reporting application/facility, or are to be produced as a combination of these approaches. When you are building reports into your application, you may choose to code them yourself or to use an integrated reporting tool.

My final word of advice is this: Don't underestimate the difficulties of implementing reports. The technical issues are straightforward to overcome but the people-oriented issues can prove to be your downfall. Work closely with all of your project stakeholders, not just the business stakeholders.

CHAPTER 22

Realistic XML

XML is just a commonly accepted representation of data and technologies to work with it. Not really all that much to get excited about when you stop and think about it.

XML is a subset of Standard Generalized Markup Language (SGML), the same parent of Hypertext Markup Language (HTML). At the time of this writing, XML is a robust and growing technology. However, in everyone's zeal to work with these new technologies, many people have forgotten some of the data community's hard-earned lessons. Although XML has been clearly overhyped, it still has a very bright future. As a result, the primary goal of this chapter is to do some level setting with respect to XML.

This chapter briefly provides an overview of Extensible Markup Language (XML) techniques and technologies and discusses potential issues that project teams face when working with XML, including:

- The role of the agile DBA
- An XML primer
- Practical applications for XML
- Vocabularies
- How to model XML
- XML mapping and data binding
- How to persist XML in relational databases
- How to persist XML in XML databases
- XML development strategies

The Role of the Agile DBA

The role of the agile DBA is to ensure that the transmission and sharing of data involving the systems they work on occur in accordance to the needs of your organization. Because XML is the most commonly used technology for performing these functions, agile DBAs must understand XML technologies and be prepared to work with application developers in order to use XML effectively.

An XML Primer

What is XML? From the data point of view, XML is simply a standardized approach to storing text-based data in a hierarchical manner and to defining meta data about said data. The data is stored in structures called XML documents, a simple example of which follows:

```
<locations
  xmlns:offc = "http://www.ronin-intl.com/names/office"
  xmlns:st = "http://www.ronin-intl.com/names/state"
  xmlns:ctry = "http://www.ronin-intl.com/names/country">
  <offc:office>
    <offc:name>Ronin International, Inc. HQ</office:name>
    <st:state>
      <st:name>Colorado</state:name>
      <st:area>North West</state:area>
    </st:state>
    <ctry:country>
      <country:name>United States of America</country:name>
    </ctry:country>
  </offc:office>
  <offc:office>
    <offc:name>Ronin Canada</office:name>
    <st:state>
      <st:name>Ontario</state:name>
    <st:area>Great White North</state:area>
    </st:state>
    <ctry:country>
      <country:name>Canada</country:name>
    </ctry:country>
  </offc:office>
</locations>
```

The meta data in an XML document is contained in document type definitions (DTDs) or the newer XML Schema definitions (XML Schema definitions will likely replace DTDs within the next few years). From an object-oriented point of view, XML is a data representation, backed by meta data, plus a collection of standardized (or at least in the process of being standardized) technologies. An overview of the critical standards is provided in Table 22.1, and details are posted at www.w3c.org.

Table 22.1   XML Standards

STANDARD	DESCRIPTION
Extensible Stylesheet Language (XSL)	XSL enables you to present data in a paginated format. XSL supports the ability to apply formatting rules to elements (for example to display Model with Others as *Model with Others*), to apply formatting rules to pages to add things like headers and footers, and to render XML documents on various display technologies. XSL is typically used to publish documents, often for printing, whereas XSL-T is used to generate markup-oriented presentations such as HTML or VoiceXML.
Extensible Stylesheet Language Transformations (XSL-T)	XSL-T enables you to transform data from one format to another. XSL-T is often used to rearrange the order of the content within an XML document so that it makes the most sense for display. XSL-T is effectively used to transform data documents into presentation documents, and then a user interface technology such as XSL or a Cascading Style Sheets (CSS) is used to publish or display the data. It is important to recognize that XSL-T suffers from performance issues when compared to traditional programming languages.
XML Linking Language (XLink)	XLink enables you to link data between elements. A link can be a simple link that references a single document (similar to a link in an HTML document) or a complex extended link that references multiple target documents. In other words, simple links implement one-to-one associations between XML documents, and extended links implement one-to-many associations. By combining XLink with XPointer, you can reference specific portions of other XML documents.
XML Namespaces	Namespaces enable you to use the same XML tag, such as *name* in the XML document example, in several places within the same or different XML documents. This prevents name collisions, just as packages within Java prevent name collisions between classes (for example, you could have an *Address* class in the *Customer* package and an *Address* class in the *Communication* package). Namespaces are indicated by the *xmlns* keyword associated to the XML element tag, as you see with the three namespaces assigned to *locations* in the XML document example.
XML Path Language (XPath)	XPath enables you to refer to data elements within an XML document. The XPath statement /locations/office[Name= "Ronin Canada"] refers to the second office listed in the XML document example. XPath statements are typically passed to operations in order to reference a location within an XML document.

(continued)

Table 22.1 *(continued)*

STANDARD	DESCRIPTION
XML Pointer Language (XPointer)	XPointer enables you to specify locations within an XML document, extending XPath to include the notion of ranges and points. This enables you to both specify elements within a specific node and to cross node boundaries. XPointer is useful for hypertext applications.
XML Query Language (XQuery)	XQuery enables you to search for data within an XML document, the XML equivalent of an SQL SELECT statement. XQuery uses XPath statements to build a complex, multiple-criteria expressions. XQuery is best used to find multiple XML documents in an XML database.
XML Schema	XML Schema enables you to define the structure and definition rules of an XML document. DTDs can only be used to define the structure. XML Schema provides the ability to specify data types to the level of precision that you see in programming languages and simple data-modeling CASE tools. You can specify simple types such as strings or create your own "complex types" (data structures). You can also specify the cardinality and optionality (what UML combines into the single concept of multiplicity) for an attribute. Simple validation rules can be defined as well. The greatest drawback of XML Schema is its complexity because it has a large feature set.

TIP *XML: A Manager's Guide,* **Second Edition by Kevin Dick (2003) is a great starting point to learn about XML, and it really is a good book for anyone, not just managers, who want to learn the basics of XML. A more advanced book is Mark Graves' (2002)** *Designing XML Databases,* **particularly if you are using XML for persistent storage.**

Strengths of XML

XML has several advantages over previous data sharing and integration technologies such as common-separated value (CSV) files and Common Object Request Broker Architecture (CORBA) objects:

XML is cross-platform.   XML is used in Java, Microsoft, Linux, and mainframe-based environments and is in fact one of the few similarities between them. XML is an enabling technology for system integration.

XML is standards based. The World Wide Web Consortium (www.w3c.org) is doing a very good job at defining and promoting technical standards for XML. XML.org (www.xml.org) helps to promote vertical XML standards within specific industries such as insurance, defense, and retailing.

XML enjoys wide industry acceptance. Developers, tool vendors, and industry standards bodies are clearly working with and on XML.

XML documents are human-readable. As you can see in the sample XML document earlier in this chapter, XML documents are fairly easy to read.

XML separates content from presentation. XML technologies such as XSL and XSL-T enable you to store data in a common format yet render it in many different manners.

XML is a middle-of-the-road approach. XML is more then just data but it is far less than shared objects. XML is supported by a wide range of processing technologies that CSV files never enjoyed. XML doesn't suffer from the complexities that CORBA suffered from in trying to define a cross-platform, distributed objects environment.

Weaknesses of XML

XML isn't perfect, nothing is, and as a result suffers from several weaknesses. These weaknesses are:

XML documents are bulky. When the last name of a customer is represented as *<lastName>Smith</lastName>*, you can quickly see how there can be performance challenges arising from additional network traffic.

XML requires marshaling. There can be significant (un)marshaling activities when objects, XML, and relational databases are used together. For example, assume that an XML document is passed as a parameter to an application. The data from the document would be extracted and converted into an object, an activity called unmarshaling. The objects would then collaborate with one another to implement the business logic. The objects would either then be marshaled back into XML documents or into your database. Even if the XML document wasn't unmarshaled into objects — perhaps the application simply processed the data — you still might need to write the XML elements out to individual table columns, a process called shredding (assuming that you're not working with an XML database). All of this conversion activity represents processing overhead.

XML standards are still evolving. Many of the critical XML standards are still evolving, particularly those addressing more advanced issues such schema, transactions, and security. Although time will resolve this issue, you need to be patient.

XML business standards will prove elusive. Although industry organizations such as the ACORD (www.acord.org) insurance standards and the OASIS (www.oasis-open.org) Financial Services standards are valiant efforts, I just don't see them succeeding. On the surface, industry standards seem like a good idea, and they most definitely are; it's just that this is not a very realistic goal. Every insurance company works a different way, they maintain variations of data, and even for the data they have in common, they each define different semantics and ontologies for that data. Furthermore, although every insurance company would love to steal business away from their competitors, they really don't want to share their valuable data with others. Worse yet, standards bodies are political exercises that spread competitive misinformation more than anything else. The best situation for business standards is when a large organization is able to force a standard on everyone else. We saw this in the late 1980s when General Motors forced electronic data interchange (EDI) standards on their suppliers. However, we've also seen organizations fail at this approach too — remember Microsoft's "Hailstorm" XML business standards? Another situation is where organizations are truly motivated to cooperate with one another via a common data standard. The securities field is such an example, with ISO 15022 (www.iso15022.org) as the standard. Security traders make money on a per transaction basis, so if there is a standard in place, it is easier for everyone to process more transactions and thus everyone succeeds.

Practical Applications for XML

I'd like to start by cutting through the XML hype to describe what I believe are real-world, effective uses of XML. In order of importance, these include:

Data transfer within an "application." XML is being used as the primary information format to transfer data between two software components deployed on different hardware nodes. The data is marshaled into XML document(s), transmitted from one component to the other component, and then unmarshalled by the receiver. Web services are commonly used for this because of the plethora of development tools that make it easy to do so — why create your own strategy when a well-supported standard exists?

Application integration. Some organizations are using XML along with some fairly sophisticated middleware to integrate their applications. Note the use of the word "some." It's easy to say that all you need to do is write some wrapper code around a legacy application, but it's much harder to do in practice (Ambler 1997). Legacy systems, like legacy data sources, often prove to be highly coupled, low-cohesion kludges — it simply isn't possible to turn them into a collection of services that are loosely coupled and highly cohesive without a major rewrite.

Data storage (files). Applications use XML documents to maintain configuration information and even use XML as their primary file formats (for example, the latest version of Microsoft Office does this). This makes sense for several reasons. First, there are some great XML parsing tools out there that make it really easy to work with XML files. Second, it becomes easier for other applications to use the generated files — no more proprietary file formats (okay, this is probably hype because we're seeing proprietary XML documents already).

Data storage (databases).   XML is now being stored in databases, either natively in XML databases (see the "Working with XML Databases" section later in this chapter) or as large columns (for example, as character largeobjects) in non-XML databases. This is motivated in large part because of the growing use of XML and not because of any particular advantage that XML has over relational data.

The important thing to understand is that XML is being used for practical purposes. However, the "world-changing" uses — such as easy and full integration of legacy systems, domination of e-commerce with the retail market, and the emergence of widely available Web services — have not come about — nor will they any time soon — if ever. My point is that if you remain realistic about XML, you'll find some interesting uses for it because it is quite useful.

Vocabularies

When I was first introduced to XML in 1997, I wasn't impressed. As far as I was concerned, XML was just another file format, and at that time it was. Although DTDs (document type definitions) were interesting, all you could do was define the structure of the document. It was nice but there's far more to data than structure; you really need to understand its vocabulary.

A vocabulary goes beyond structure to address the semantics of the data captured within the structure, including the pertinent taxonomical and ontological relationships of the data. Whew, what a mouthful. Let's explore this definition a piece at a time.

When we say that we're defining the semantics of data, what we're really doing is defining its meaning. For our purposes, to define the semantics of data you need to identify the allowable values for data attributes and the relationships between those values. Consider the inventory catalog for a grocery store chain. One of the items they carry is ice cream. According to the industry standard, ice cream DTD, a type of ice cream is described by two tags — Volume and Flavor. You look at several existing XML documents and see value pairs of {3, Chocolate}, {2.5, Rocky Road}, and {400, Vanilla}. 400 what? Litres? Ounces? Isn't Rocky Road a type of chocolate ice cream? In other words, knowing the structure isn't sufficient; you also need to know the semantics.

Now, let's assume that we each work for different grocery chains and we're trying to share ice cream information with one another via XML. My chain carries chocolate, strawberry, and vanilla ice cream. Your chain carries Chocolate, Rocky Road, Mocha Fudge, Swiss Fudge, Strawberry Classic, Ultra Strawberry, Royal Vanilla, Exquisite Vanilla, and Tiger Tail. Although we both sell ice cream, and you sell all the flavors that I do, it's very difficult for me to process your data because I need to map your flavors to the ones that I understand. I would need to know that the Rocky Road, Mocha Fudge, and Swiss Fudge are all types of chocolate, that Ultra Strawberry is a type of strawberry, and so on. The end result would be a taxonomy, or classification, of flavors.

Then, we decide to start selling groceries online. We quickly realize that our users search on a wide variety of terms. For example, if someone searches for desserts, then ice creams, candies, and fresh fruit should appear in the list. If someone else searches on frozen goods, then ice creams, frozen dinners, and frozen vegetables should appear in the list. We need to relate the fact that ice cream is both a dessert and a frozen good, among other things. In other words, we need to define the ontology for our product line that relates these concepts together.

Ontology goes beyond taxonomy. Where taxonomy addresses classification hierarchies, ontology will represent and communicate knowledge about a topic as well as a set of relationships and properties that hold for the entities included within that topic.

Why is this important? First, I hope that it's clear that you need to be worried about more than just the structure of XML documents in order to succeed. Second, if you can't agree to the semantics of the data that you're sharing, then integration is little more than a fantasy. This is one of the reasons why I hold out little hope for XML Meta data Interchange (XMI), the standard approach via which development tools are supposed to share models. It's arguable whether XMI defines the proper data structure; it certainly doesn't contain the rich semantics of the data that vendors are supposedly sharing, and even if it did it is very unlikely the vendors will ever agree to the semantics. To prove my point, although many tools currently claim to support XMI, to my knowledge there isn't a single combination where you can model in one tool, export that model to another, update the model, then export it back to the original tool without any loss of information.

TIP The site www.ontology.org is a good resource for anyone interested in ontology. Tim Berners-Lee, one of the people behind the World Wide Web, wrote an essay entitled Semantic Web Road Map (www.w3.org/DesignIssues/Semantic.html) that argues for the importance of a standard approach to representing meta data describing the semantics of data.

How to Model XML

To tell you the truth, I don't invest a lot of time modeling XML documents. I prefer to keep my documents small and simple and as a result I can typically code the DTDs or Schema definitions by hand. Of course, if someone was to build a really slick XML modeling tool I'd be tempted to change my approach. Having said this it is valuable to understand the fundamentals of XML modeling because it's going to help you even if you're coding everything by hand.

TIP David Carlson's Web site, http://xmlmodeling.com, and his book *Modeling XML Applications With UML* (2001) are two good references for XML modeling. In *Designing XML Databases*, Mark Graves (2002) shares important design insights for modeling effective XML structures.

First some terminology. Up until now, I've been talking about XML elements as opposed to XML attributes. Table 22.2 compares and contrasts the two approaches, which can be combined as needed. For the sake of simplicity, I will use the term "field" to refer to either elements or attributes. Furthermore, I'll use the data-modeling term "entity type" to refer to substructures within an XML document. An entity type contains one or more fields and/or other entity types. For example, in the XML document in the "An XML Primer" section earlier in this chapter, *locations*, *office*, *state*, and *country* are all entity types.

Figure 22.1 depicts an XML model, using UML notation, for an XML document representing *Customer* information. A class box is used to represent an entity type; *Customer* is the root of the XML document, and both *Address* and *Phone* are substructures within the document.

NOTE I could have assigned a stereotype to *Customer* to indicate that it's the root — <<root>> would be a good choice, but that's implied by the fact that *Customer* isn't a part of another entity type, so I chose not to clutter up the diagram.

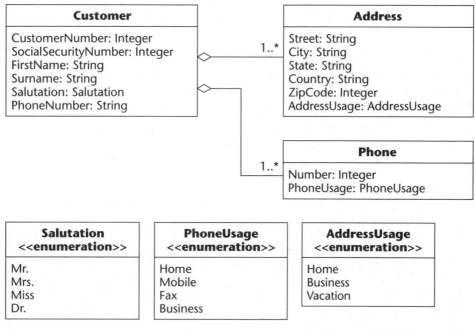

Figure 22.1   Modeling Customer information as an XML data structure.

Table 22.2 Comparing Attributes and Elements

APPROACH	EXAMPLE	APPLICATION	ADVANTAGES	DISADVANTAGES
Attribute	\<name= "John Smith" phone = 4165551212\>	Can be used to contain control information, such as names or unique identifiers, that you don't want to have to iterate over the embedding elements in order to find.	• Easier to understand. • Improves application efficiency. • Simpler. • Uses less space.	• Provides minimal data type validation.
Element	\<name\>John Smith \</name\> \<phone\>4165551212 \</phone\>	Use to structure the business information within your documents.	• Defines constraints for structure content. • Provides embedded structure. • Can have multiple values (for example, must use for collections). • Can be referenced via a link (thus, you can share information). • Preserves white space. • Can have default values (when using a DTD or schema). • More convenient for large values or binary entities. • Can contain quotes easily.	• Slower to process and to transmit due to wordiness.

Figure 22.1 includes three classes assigned the <<enumeration>> stereotype. Carlson (2001), in his unofficial UML profile for XML modeling, suggests using this stereotype to indicate that the class represents a collection of allowable values (an enumeration) for a field. For example, the *Salutation* enumeration lists the allowable values for the *Customer.Saluation* field. Although enumerations help to define the semantics of your XML documents, they can also clutter your diagrams, motivating you instead to capture this information in an XML schema definition.

Notice how all of the relationships in Figure 22.1 are aggregations. I use aggregations to model the relationships between entity types within a single XML document. My style is to draw aggregation hierarchies from left to right, with the root being the leftmost entity type. In Figure 22.2, I'm using a dependency with a stereotype of <<references>> to model the fact that *Order* includes a reference to the *Customer* XML document. This could be implemented via XPointer, for example.

Figure 22.2 is interesting because it depicts two ways to model Order, either as an XML document that includes a reference to another XML document or as a single, larger document. The advantage of having two documents is that it's easier to share and manage customer information — John Smith's data can be stored in a single XML document and referenced by many orders. However, it increases the complexity to work with the documents because you need to be able to traverse the reference. Not a big problem, but not as easy as having the information all in one place.

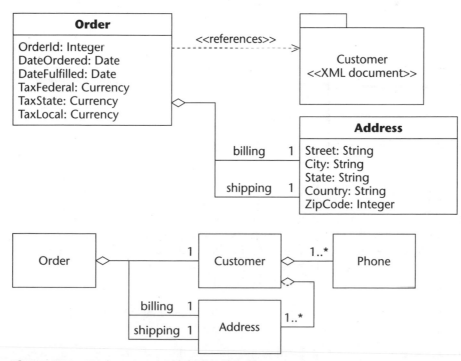

Figure 22.2 Two ways to model an Order document.

The first version of *Order* models *Customer* as a UML package. Carlson (2001) suggests using packages to delineate XML namespaces, a very good idea. Common modeling practice (Ambler 2003) is to use packages to represent a cohesive collection of modeling elements, in this case the model depicted in Figure 22.1.

The second version of *Order* depicts abbreviated versions of the entity types; only the names are shown within the class boxes. Notice how the Address entity type appears at two different levels within the XML document — as a substructure to *Order* as well as to *Customer*.

TIP **Whenever you're designing an XML document, you should keep several issues in mind:**

- **A good industry standard may already exist that you can reuse.**

- **Although size is not an issue with XML elements, it is with RDB columns. Therefore, if you intend to shred the XML document into an RDB, then you may need to make its attributes more finely grained than XML technology would normally motivate you to.**

- **When you follow common data-modeling practices, things should usually work out for you. The rules of data normalization (discussed in Chapter 4) can and should be applied.**

- **Existing object and RDB schemas are a serious constraint that you need to consider.**

- **Use short, but meaningful names to improve transmission performance.**

XML Mapping and Data Binding

When you use objects and XML documents together, you need to map your object schema to your XML schema just as you need to map your object schema to your relational data schema. The implementations of those mappings are often referred to as data bindings. As with relational databases, there is an impedance mismatch between objects and XML documents. As you saw in Figures 22.1 and 22.2, XML documents have a single root, *Customer* and *Order*, respectively, but class models do not. This is so because XML documents represent a hierarchical structure, whereas object schemas are usually a network structure.

These tips and techniques work well for me when mapping objects to XML documents:

Let usage drive the design.   The fundamental question that you need to answer is how will the XML document be used? Focusing on usage tells you how the XML document will be traversed, which in turn provides insight into the entity types and the fields that are required as well as the overall structure to support the intended usage.

Major business concepts usually imply the need for corresponding XML documents.   I've found that the handful of major business concepts implemented by a system — such as order, customer, shipment, and inventory item — will almost always require one or more XML representations.

Keep it simple.   I prefer one-to-one mappings wherever possible. I'll map an attribute to an XML field. I'll map the attributes of a class to an entity type with an XML document, so if the class has four attributes then the entity type includes the corresponding four fields.

Realize it isn't always simple.   Any given class can map to several XML documents, and vice versa. Furthermore some XML documents may not require all of the attributes of a class, or they may include fields that the class doesn't need. For example, in Figure 22.2 the *Address* entity type appears in two places within the XML document — as a part of an order and as a part of a customer (which in turn is part of an order).

Realize that XML documents need to be flexible.   Objects are often implemented as part of a single, specific application. XML documents are often used by several applications and sometimes even by several different organizations. Each application or each organization may choose to use the same XML document in different ways, often because they apply their own unique semantic or ontological rules to the document.

Modify object to relational mapping techniques.   Many of the techniques described for mapping objects to RDBs in Chapter 14 are applicable to mapping objects to XML structures. For example, inheritance hierarchies can be mapped to XML documents following the strategies of *one document per class*, *one document per concrete class*, and *one document per inheritance hierarchy*.

Do some reading.   Ron Bourret's site (www.rpbourret.com) is a great starting point. Ron has done, and continues to do, significant work in XML and databases.

Use consistent names.   I prefer to use business terminology, such as *Customer* and *Order*, whenever I name classes. I follow the same strategy for attribute names, for example *firstName* and *zipCode*. Similarly I prefer to use business names for my XML tags as well, such as *Customer*, *Order*, *FirstName*, and *ZipCode*. Depending on your capitalization standards, for example *ZipCode* versus *zipCode*, for each technology you may find that you need to make some minor modifications. Carlson (2001) also points out that XML names are limited to alphanumeric characters, cannot begin with the letters XML regardless of case, and only allows the special characters of underline "_", period ".", and hyphen "-".

The role names on an association are good tag names.   For example, Figure 22.2 includes roles of *billing* and *shipping* for *Address*. Therefore, I would consider the names *BillingAddress* and *ShippingAddress* for the corresponding XML tags.

The type of association can indicate potential document boundaries.   A common question that you will be constantly asking yourself is "should this entity type be part of this XML document or a separate XML document that this one references?" For example, Figure 22.2 presents two versions of the *Order* document — one where *Order* contains the *Customer* structure and one where it references it as a separate document. A good rule of thumb is that if there is an aggregation or a composition association between the two entities on your class diagram, then you likely want to keep them in the same document.

Model a namespace using packages.   Carlson (2001) suggests the use of packages to identify XML namespaces.

How to Persist XML in Relational Databases

There are three fundamental strategies for persisting an XML document in a relational database (RDB):

"Shred" the document and store each element in a separate column.   The advantage of this approach is that the data elements are easily accessible to standard SQL queries. The primary disadvantage is that it can be difficult to implement; not only do you need to map the XML structure to your database, but you also need to implement the mappings. Worse yet, the marshaling activities required for converting between XML and your RDB can significantly affect system performance.

Store each entity within the document as a separate column.   With this approach individual sections, such as the office entity in the XML example presented earlier in the chapter, are stored in their own columns. The granularity of the entities becomes an important issue for you — should the state and country subentities of the office entities also be stored in their own columns? The answer depends on your situation.

Store the entire document in a single column.   With this approach, the document is stored in a text field (this works well for small documents), as a character large object (CLOB), or as a binary large object (BLOB). One advantage of this approach is that it's very easy to implement. Another potential advantage is that it's a flexible approach; if you need to change your data structure, you can do so easily, although this can clearly be problematic if the changes aren't thought out properly. The primary disadvantages are that the individual data elements contained in the XML document aren't readily accessible via SQL queries and that you forgo many of the advantages of RDBs such as constraint checking and integrity control.

My advice is that if you're going to use an RDB to store XML documents, then you should take the first approach and shred the document. If you don't want to incur this overhead, then I would advise you to not use an RDB and either store the XML documents as individual files or use an XML database. In short, if you're going to use an RDB then use the RDB.

So how do you make shredding work? The secret is in how you map your XML documents to your relational data schema. The following heuristics should help guide you:

- Map a single XML element to a single database column.

- Keep the types the same — character data in the XML document should be character data in the database and so on.

- Base both schemas on the same conceptual model, and therefore use the same data element definitions for both.

- Be flexible when you map (you can likely use XSL-T to overcome any mismatches between the schemas).

NOTE Many of the technical issues of storing objects in RDBs are applicable to storing XML documents in RDBs. There is an impedance mismatch between the two technologies, so you need to map between the two. You need to worry about concurrency control, finding XML documents, referential integrity, and security access control. There is no free ride.

TIP Log XML structure. If you choose to shred your XML structures, you might want to consider saving the XML structure in a log for auditing purposes. It's simple and it works.

How to Persist XML in XML Databases

XML databases are a new option for persisting your data. The *XML:DB Project* (www.xmldb.org) indicates that a native XML database (NXD) should define a logical model for XML documents, natively support XML documents, but is not required to have any particular underlying technology. An XML database (XEDB) is a database that has an XML mapping layer added on to it. Data manipulation in an XEDB happens with either XML technologies (for example, XPath) or database technologies (for example, SQL). Finally, a Hybrid XML Database (HXD) is one that can be treated as either a NXD or a XEDB, depending on the requirements of the application. Table 22.3 describes several of the leading options available to you.

Table 22.3 XML and XML-Enabled Databases

TOOL	DESCRIPTION	URL
Birdstep RDM XML	A NXD that works on PDAs and other small-footprint devices, enabling you to bind XML to data to C++ and Java objects. A server-side component supports transaction logging and data-integrity functions required to support wireless operation.	www.birdstep.com
Exelon's Extensible Information Server (XIS)	An NXD built on top of ObjectStore. Supports XQuery, XPath, and full-text searching as well as a proprietary updating language.	www.exln.com
NeoCore XML Management System (XMS)	A high-performance NXD that indexes all content in the XML store. Supports ACID transactions. Includes C, C++, Java, and J2EE APIs.	www.neocore.com
Oracle 9i	An XEDB that manipulates data regardless of whether it's stored as XML or in tables. Supports an XMLType, enabling you to store documents in tables as well as an XML repository that mimics an XML database.	www.oracle.com
Ozone	An open source object-oriented HXD written in Java.	www.ozone-db.org
Sybase Adaptive Server Enterprise 12.5	An XEDB that stores XML data natively instead of shredding it into tables.	www.sybase.com
Xindice	An open source NXD that supports both XPath and XUpdate. Xindice supports the XML:DB interface, a Java API, and an XML-RPC plug in.	http://xml.apache.org/xindice/

Although I prefer to work with RDBs on the back end, and realistically most organizations use relational databases as the primary means of storage, I do recognize that sometimes an XML database may be a valid option for you. Important issues you should consider include:

Concurrency.   In XML databases, locking is often at the level of entire documents; the implication is that XML databases are a good option if it is very unlikely that two or more users will need to access the same XML document concurrently.

Consistency.   XML documents become very large (for example, they are highly denormalized) and not only contain data from several logical entity types but can also contain copies of data. This can make data sharing difficult, although not impossible. It can also make it difficult to ensure that data remains consistent. In Figure 22.2, you saw that there were two ways to represent *Order* information — one that referenced *Customer* information and one that contained it. The method that references *Customer* information is more normalized, thus enabling you to store the information for a single customer in one place (assuming that you code this into your application) and increasing the chance that your customer data will remain consistent.

Manipulation.   You don't store information in a database just so you have somewhere to keep it; you also want to be able to manipulate that information in various ways. Relational databases are incredibly good at that because they're flexible. Although many data professionals dislike XML databases because "they're just like hierarchical databases from the 1970s, and they failed," the real issue is lack of flexibility. If you can find an XML database that is easy to work with that enables you to manipulate data in a flexible manner, then consider working with it.

You don't need to be pure.   An XEDB, such as Oracle 9i, or an HXD, such as Ozone, may be a viable option for you. Both types of XML databases enable you to work with your data via traditional SQL, although there may be a performance price to pay. Because major RDB vendors are extending their databases into XEDBs, many developers are finding that their corporate standard database offers the modern XML features that they're looking for. If you're smart about the way you work with your XEDB, you can get the best of both worlds.

Administrative functions.   Many XML databases, because they're new products, lack the comprehensive administration tools that you're used to with RDBs.

XML Development Strategies

When working with XML, the following strategies have worked very well for me in practice:

Remember that XML isn't your only option.   Although XML might be the latest "shiny new toy" for you to play with, and a very popular one at that, just remember that you have other choices. There are many very successful systems out there that don't use XML at all. Furthermore, many new systems are being built right now that don't use XML.

Adopt XML Schema.   Vocabularies are critical to the success of XML, and at the time of this writing your best option for implementing the required supporting meta data is XML Schemas. Over the next few years this standard will evolve, but that's no reason not to start using them now.

Design your XML documents.   The XML documents that you create today will become part of tomorrow's legacy landscape. Small and reasonably cohesive documents are the order of the day.

Use namespaces.   Dick (2003) says it best — the need for namespaces increases in direct proportion to the number of different groups that will use a document format.

Use a real XML editor.   Use the best tool for the job. Although simple code editors can be used to manipulate XML documents, I would much rather use a tool such as Altova's XML Spy (www.xmlspy.com) or XML Mind (www.xmlmind.com).

Your deployment environment determines your validation strategy.   Although DTDs and XML schemas offer the potential for some sophisticated runtime validation, there are some deployment issues you need to consider. First, do you need to validate the XML documents at run time? If not, then don't. Second, can you count on the DTD or schema being available? If not, you need to programmatically implement the validation. Third, how much validation is required? If it's simple, then a DTD is sufficient; if it's complex, then a schema is required; if it's incredibly complex, you will need to code some validation logic.

Summary

This chapter described XML technologies and their effective application in practice. You learned that XML data structures can be modeled via the UML and how to map these structures to your business objects. You also discovered that you have several strategies available to you for persisting XML documents, including various ways to store them in relational databases.

As you've seen, there is significant hype around XML and its usage. XML won't likely replace other technologies, but it will enhance them. Every developer should understand the basics of XML, and this chapter provides a good start at doing exactly that.

Adopting Agile Database Techniques

This part describes strategies for both individuals and organizations to effectively adopt agile database techniques. Everyone should read Chapter 23 because it gives advice that you can put into practice immediately on an individual level. If you're trying to motivate your manager to try an agile approach, or if you're formally responsible for introducing agility into your organization, Chapter 24 provides relevant advice.

Chapter 23: How You Can Become Agile. As an individual, you need to decide to become more agile in the way that you work. First, you need to adopt "the agile attitude," and then you need to actively work towards gaining the skills to make you a valued member on an agile project team.

Chapter 24: Bringing Agility into Your Organization. People, and therefore organizations, resist change. To adopt agile database techniques, you need to overcome this resistance to change.

CHAPTER 23

How You Can Become Agile

Ouch! My paradigm just shifted.

If you're still reading this far in the book, chances are excellent that you think that there is something to the philosophies and techniques I describe. If so, good. Unfortunately, there is a big difference between reading about agility and actually becoming agile. You've already taken the most important step: you've decided to consider new ways to do things. Now, you need to follow through and actually internalize them.

I have three critical insights for becoming an agile software developer:

- You don't have to be superhuman.
- Agility is really just a mindset.
- Become a generalizing specialist.

You Don't Have to Be Superhuman

This book describes a wide range of skills that agile software developers, in particular agile DBAs, should have. These include an understanding of:

- Agile software development, Agile Modeling (AM), and agile documentation.
- The basics of object orientation, relational databases, data modelling, and the object-relational impedance mismatch.
- Evolutionary database techniques, including Agile Model Driven Development (AMDD), test-driven development (TDD), and database refactoring.

- Development techniques such as mapping objects to relational databases, database encapsulation, concurrency control, security access control, referential integrity, and the effective use of XML.

This is a formidable list. Am I asking too much of you? It clearly isn't realistic to expect you to become adept at all of these things overnight, but it would be reasonable to expect you to pick up these skills over time. After reading this book, which provides a very good overview of all of these issues, how long do you think it would take you to become reasonably adept? My experience is that many professionals can become adept at agile database techniques, when given the opportunity, in several months. The secret is that you need to be actively involved with a project and working with others who already have some of these skills (or at least skills closely resembling them). For example, many Java programmers are familiar with some if not most of the techniques listed for working with relational databases, although they might not be aware of all of their options or the implications of each alternative. Many DBAs are already quite adept at evolving a database schema, although they may not have taken it to the next level encompassed by database refactoring. The point is that it isn't as hard to pick up these new skills as you may think; you just need to get started.

Agility Is Really Just a Mindset

So what does it mean to be agile? Agility is more of an attitude than a skillset. In my experience, the common characteristics of agile software developers are:

- They're open-minded and therefore willing to learn new techniques.
- They're responsible and therefore willing to seek the help of the right person(s) for the task at hand.
- They're willing to work closely with others, via pair programming or in small teams as appropriate.
- They're willing to work iteratively and incrementally.

Notice that I didn't say that they program in a specific language, or that they have a minimum number of years experience with JUnit, or that they are certified DBAs. Technical skills are definitely important, but they aren't what determines your agility. It's your mindset that is the determining factor. To help you grow into each of the four roles defined by the agile data method Table 23.1 provides some specific suggestions that you should consider.

TIP The books *Who Moved My Cheese?* by Dr. Spencer Johnson (London: Vermilion 1998) and *Navigating the Winds of Change* by Andy Kaufman (Zurich Press 2003) are both short, well-written resources for anyone struggling with change. The first book will help you to identify four common personality types and their ability to handle change, and both books provide advice for accepting and embracing change in your day-to-day working life.

Table 23.1   Recommendations for Becoming More Agile

ROLE	RECOMMENDATIONS
Agile DBA	• Gain some experience as an application developer so you understand the issues that they face. • Gain basic DBA skills, reading *Database Administration* (Mullins 2002) is a good start, and enhance them with the techniques described in this book.
Application developer	• Recognize that there is more to agile software development than Extreme Programming (XP). • Gain some database experience, often by working closely with your team's agile DBA.
Enterprise architect	• Recognize that you're in a support role to agile project teams. • Recognize that you must be prepared to work in an iterative and incremental manner. • Gain some experience as an agile developer and/or agile DBA to learn the tools, techniques, and technologies that they work with on a regular basis. • Become actively involved with agile development projects.
Enterprise Administrator	• Recognize that you're in a support role to agile project teams. • Recognize that you must be prepared to work in an iterative and incremental manner. • Favor mentoring, and getting actively involved with, people on projects as opposed to simply reviewing their work.

Become a Generalizing Specialist

A critical concept is that you need to move away from being a narrowly focused specialist to become more of what I like to call a generalizing specialist. A generalizing specialist is someone with one or more technical specialties who actively seeks to gain new skills in both his or her existing specialties and other areas. When you get your first job as an IT professional, it is often in the role of a junior programmer or junior DBA. You will initially focus on becoming good at that role, and if you're lucky your organization will send you on training courses to pick up advanced skills in your specialty. Once you're adept at that specialty, or even when you've just reached the point of being comfortable at it, it is time to expand your horizons and learn new skills in different aspects of the software life cycle. When you do this, you evolve from being a specialist to being a generalizing specialist.

The problem with specialists is that they have difficulty working together effectively with others, who are often specialists themselves, because they don't have the background to understand the issues that others are trying to deal with. Furthermore, they are often motivated to create far more documentation than is required — when all you can do is write use cases, then those use cases will end up including information that could be better recorded elsewhere — and very likely require reviews of said documentation when they provide it to other specialists. The implication is that the same piece of information will often be captured by several specialists because they're afraid that they'll lose that information. It's quite common on projects dominated by specialists to see a business rule captured in a user interface specification, in a business rule specification, in a logical data model (LDM), in a UML class diagram, in acceptance tests, and in source code. Clearly, there's a chance that the business rule will be described inconsistently, not to mention the obvious overhead involved with reviewing and maintaining each version of it.

A generalizing specialist will write less documentation than a specialist because he or she has a greater range of options available. Instead of having a user-interface specialist capture the rule in a screen specification, the data specialist capture it in an LDM, and so on, the generalizing specialist will instead capture it in the most appropriate place(s). In this case, that could be in the form of one or more acceptance tests as well as in the source code. In short, a generalizing specialist can choose the right artifact to get the job done and will be able to capture the information in one and only one place. The implication is that generalizing specialists are more effective than specialists because they can do significantly less work yet still achieve the goal of building an existing system that meets the needs of their stakeholders.

Because a generalizing specialist is someone with a good grasp of how everything fits together, he or she will typically have a greater understanding and appreciation of what their teammates are working on. They at least are willing to listen to and work with their teammates because they know that they'll likely learn something new. Specialists, on the other hand, often don't have the background to appreciate what other specialists are doing, often look down on that other work, and often aren't as willing to cooperate.

A generalizing specialist is more than just a generalist. A generalist is a jack-of-all-trades but a master of none, whereas a generalizing specialist is a jack-of-all-trades and master of a few. Big difference. A team of generalists can easily flounder because none of them have the skills to get anything done.

In many ways, a generalizing specialist is simply a software craftsperson (McBreen 2001). The reason I don't use the term "software craftsperson" is that it is a loaded term, one that will immediately turn off a large number of traditional developers. I believe that "generalizing specialist" is more palatable.

In short, my experience is that generalizing specialists are much more effective than specialists or generalists. My experience is that the best developers are generalizing specialists, or are at least actively trying to become so. There is still room for specialists within your IT departments, they can often act as internal consultants to your development teams, but as IT departments become more agile we will see fewer specialists surviving over time.

Summary

The decision to become agile really is a personal one because you're the only one responsible for your career. I suspect that if you're reading this book, and others like it, that you're already well down the path. My best advice is to do everything that you can to stay on the path.

CHAPTER 24

Bringing Agility into Your Organization

United we stand, divided we fall. It's impossible to work together effectively when we're still fighting turf battles.

This book has presented a wide range of philosophies, proven techniques, and one or two considered theories about effective ways to go about the data-oriented aspects of software development. What it hasn't done is discussed what you need to do to succeed at them. Until now. In this chapter, I describe how your organization can adopt the agile database techniques described in this book. My expectation is that it will be difficult for many organizations to adopt agile database techniques. It's not because there is anything inherently complex about them; the problem is due, for the most part, to cultural inertia within your organization. To successfully adopt these philosophies and techniques you must:

- Change the way you look at software development
- Understand the challenges you face
- Actually try it
- Block nonagile coworkers
- Be realistic

Change the Way You Look at Software Development

The philosophies and techniques described in this book have several significant implications for your organization. My experience is that you must accept the following things:

Everyone needs to work closely together.   Software development is a communication game, and as Cockburn (2002) argues documentation is the worst form of communication available to you whereas face-to-face communication standing around a whiteboard is the best. Simple things such as co-locating the team in a single workspace, using simple tools such as whiteboards and paper, and having project stakeholders as active members of your team will improve your productivity by at least an order of magnitude.

The models and documents are finished when the software ships.   It's an iterative and incremental world now, not a serial one. The requirements are fully defined for the release of a system, if at all, only until the software is ready to go to final acceptance testing. Until then they might change. The same thing can be said of your logical data model, if you even create one, and your physical data. These artifacts evolve as work progresses on the system and may even change just hours before the production baseline of your system is finalized.

Power within your department will shift.   Changes in process always entail shifts within the power structure of an organization, and agile data is no exception. Agile database techniques shift the way that enterprise concerns, particularly those pertaining to data, are considered. Architectural model reviews are a thing of the past because your models evolve over time and because reviews are a "process smell" in the agile development, indicating that you've made an organizational mistake earlier in your project. One way to look at it is that if someone is qualified to review an artifact why didn't you involve that person in its initial development? Existing organizational structures, particularly those based on specialized skills or a "command-and-control" structure, need to be reworked in favor of a more organic structure.

Everyone needs to become actively involved.   The day of the specialist who attends reviews, or has artifacts submitted to him or her for review and feedback, is over. The day of the bureaucrat who merely pushes paper and has no direct influence on the creation, maintenance, operation, or support of a system should never have come about in the first place. Bureaucrats can't hide behind their onerous and prescriptive processes anymore, instead they must roll up their sleeves, work closely with project teams, and actually add value to your efforts. People who fight this concept are likely good candidates for reeducation, and in extreme cases may need to be made aware of opportunities in other organizations (if you get my meaning).

Everyone needs to rethink their approach and beliefs.   There are many thought-provoking ideas presented in this book. It is possible to take an evolutionary approach to database design. There is more to modeling than UML, or data for that matter. There are many different ways that you can approach development; one size does not fit all. Many technical issues often thought to be the domain of databases, including both referential integrity and transaction control, are also pertinent within your objects. You have many technical options available to you, and they all have their strengths and weaknesses. The point is that these ideas are likely to go against what you currently believe, or how you currently prefer to work. Change isn't easy.

Understand the Challenges You Face

You also need to understand the challenges that you are likely to face when introducing agile data techniques into your organization. My experience is that the most difficult challenges that you will need to overcome are not technical in nature but instead are people-oriented. At the risk of promoting stereotypes, I have found that experienced IT professionals, novice developers, and managers all seem to have their own unique challenges that need to be overcome. Let's look at each group one at a time.

Experienced IT professionals, often people with 20 or more years in the industry, likely:

- Haven't invested the time to understand agile software development.
- Haven't taken, or been allowed, the time to try the techniques and philosophies described in this book.
- Aren't comfortable with change, particularly change that dramatically shifts the political power structure within the IT department.
- Are convinced that their existing approaches work (which they do in some situations), so don't see the need to change their ways.
- Have had bad experiences in the past with "code-and-fix" (CAF) approaches. Because they don't understand agile software development, they often equate it with CAF and therefore assume that agile techniques are a bad idea.
- Have some very good points that aren't well addressed by the agile community, such as data-oriented and enterprise issues, and therefore they feel that agile techniques aren't sufficient for their needs.
- Believe that their situation is unique; perhaps they work in a Fortune 50 company (although 49 other organizations are also in this situation) or a government agency, and therefore they feel that agile techniques won't work for them.
- Focus on symptoms, and not the root causes of problems within their IT organization, and therefore they haven't questioned their preferred approach to development.
- Haven't coded in years and don't realize the implications of the new techniques and tools currently being used by developers.

- Have listened to other experienced IT professionals whom they respect, unfortunately people who are also struggling with agile concepts and who are likely to tell them what they want to hear, and as a result these IT professionals feel that they don't need to continue looking into agility.

- Are narrowly focused specialists, often with years, if not decades, of experience, and therefore have difficulty understanding the big development picture.

- Are likely scared that they don't fit into agile development (and very likely don't given their current skillset).

Novice IT professionals are also struggling with learning agile techniques, although they face different challenges. They likely:

- Perceive agility as meaning that they don't have to model and they don't have to write documentation.

- Have very narrow experience, if any, as programmers.

- Don't have the experience to appreciate the bigger picture, or at least to appreciate its nuances.

- Are focused on a single technology or programming language.

Managers within your organization have their own unique issues regarding agility. They often:

- Don't want to, or can't, provide adequate resources for your team.

- Have had bad experiences in the past with new techniques and are unwilling to try yet another one.

- Believe that agile software development is another fad and will go away after a few years.

- Don't realize that an agile development team requires other parts of the organization, including IT groups such as enterprise architects and data management/administration, to work in an agile manner as well when they interact with the team.

Everyone needs to approach agility with an open mind, ideally without any preconceptions. They need to look at the big picture, recognize that they have serious problems that aren't going to go away unless they act. Ideally everyone needs to work with, and be mentored by, experienced agile developers in order to learn these new approaches. Although it is possible to bootstrap your project team, and even your entire organization, into agile software development, you are much better advised to seek the help of people who have gone before you. Education and training in agile software development are also important, although not as critical as good mentoring.

Experienced developers and managers need the opportunity to try these new approaches, and more importantly be given the time it takes to break themselves of their "bad" nonagile habits. Novice developers need to focus on education/mentoring as well as simply gaining experience. Novice developers will likely learn agile techniques more easily than experienced developers will because they have less baggage to discard along the way.

Actually Try It

There is a significant difference between theory and practice. You can read about something all you want, but until you try something you truly won't understand it and its implications. At some point, you're going to have to get your feet wet and try this stuff out on a real project.

A really good start is to decide to adopt the concept of delivering working software at the end of short iterations. "Short" is relative, I would question anything over 8 weeks, although for organizations that are new to evolutionary development 4-week iterations is a reasonable goal. If you're experienced with evolutionary development, or something close to it, then iterations of 1 or 2 weeks is a reasonable goal. By agreeing to work in this manner, you very quickly realize that you need to discard much of the pomp and circumstance of traditional techniques.

Block Nonagile Coworkers

A common strategy is to start with a pilot project that tries the new techniques in practice, so you can gain some insight into how they'll work within your organization. Although this enables the individual team to be agile the challenge is that the rest of your organization is still following your existing, nonagile approach. The implication is that they may expect certain models or deliverables to be delivered at specific times in specific formats, or they may require status reports or other management artifacts, or they may require you to follow their nonagile procedures. Ideally, you should negotiate away the need to venture into this bureaucratic morass; realistically, you often can't and therefore you put your pilot project at risk of failure (exactly what many of the bureaucrats are hoping for).

One way to overcome this problem is to assign one or two people on your team to be blockers. In North American football the primary goal of a blocker is to prevent the other team from sacking your quarterback or tackling your receivers, either of which would cause your play to fail. In software development, a blocker attends the meetings of the bureaucrats and produces the artifacts that they require, freeing up the rest of the team to focus on the activities that actually lead to building your system. The blockers effectively implement a "process facade" around your team that makes it appear to the rest of the organization that your team is following their existing procedures. This satisfies the bureaucrats, yet prevents them from meddling with the people who are doing the real work. Although it sounds like wasted overhead, and it is because it would be far more effective to divert both the blockers and bureaucrats to efforts that produce something of value, the advantage is that it enables the rest of the team to get the job done. The role of blocker is often taken on by your team's project manager or coach, although in the past I have let this be a revolving role on the project, so as to spread out the pain of dealing with the paper pushers.

Be Realistic

The following list describes several important factors that you need to consider when bringing agile database techniques into your organization.

Be patient, it will take a generation.   I believe that the adoption curve for agile software development, including agile database techniques, will be similar to that of object technology. Object technology was first being considered within the business community in the late 1980s, and at the time of this writing many organizations, often referred to as the late majority or laggards on the technology adoption curve (Moore 2002), are still struggling with adopting object orientation (OO). That's 15 years by my count, and I expect no different for agile software development (the implication is that it may be 2020 before your organization finally catches up).

Don't be too fervent.   The surest way to turn someone off agile techniques is to try to convince him or her that agile is the only way. Remember the sixth philosophy of agile data — recognize that you should strive to find the appropriate sweet spot between extremes. The implication is that you might not become as agile as you'd like right away, but you very likely could become more agile than you currently are.

Don't go in blind.   Reading this book is a good first step toward becoming more agile in your data-oriented activities, but it's only the first step. Do some more reading before you try to adopt the techniques and philosophies described in this book; www.agilealliance.org and www.agilemodeling.com are great resources that you should take advantage of. Talk with people who are following agile techniques on their own projects to discover what they've experienced. Get involved with the agile data community; www.agiledata.org lists good online resources, and share your own experiences.

Don't underestimate the politics.   Process is politics, and when you change the process as radically as I describe in this book, many people will obviously take issue with the necessary changes.

Be prepared to find work elsewhere.   Your organization may not be ready for agility, and worse yet may not be for some time. The implication is that you have a very difficult decision to make — do you continue to wait and hope that an opportunity arises within your organization, do you try to create such an opportunity, or do you update your resume and start looking for work elsewhere. (As Ron Jeffries likes to say, "Change your organization or change your organization.") It's your life; take control of it.

Parting Thoughts

My hope is that you have found this book to be full of illuminating philosophies and useful techniques. Although you may not agree with everything that I have written, the fact is that I truly do believe that agile software development is real and here to stay. If this is true, then we clearly need to find ways that enable everyone to work together effectively within an agile environment — this includes object, data, and enterprise professionals. My experience is that it's a lot more enjoyable to work in environments where everyone respects one another, strives to work together effectively, and works toward the common goal of delivering and supporting systems that meet the needs of their stakeholders. I've worked in many environments where this wasn't the case and hated it. Life is too short to not enjoy what you do for a living.

How you utilize the advice presented in this book is up to you. I've described a wide range of techniques, some of which may be completely new to you and others of which may be presented in a significantly different light from what you're used to. Start by adopting these techniques a few at a time, apply them in practice, and discover how to make them work in your environment. Over time, both you and your coworkers will become significantly more effective at developing systems, making you significantly more employable. I can't help but think that being able to write "Proficient at agile database techniques such as database refactoring, Agile Model Driven Development (AMDD), and object to relational mapping" is good to have on your resume. Choose to succeed.

Database Refactoring Catalog

This appendix summarizes the database refactorings that I have discovered over the years as well as some refactorings identified by others (Sadalage 2003). It is important to have a catalog of refactorings such as this to provide a common language that agile DBAs and application developers can use when working together to evolve database schemas. I maintain an updated list of database refactorings at www.agiledata.org/essays/databaseRefactoringCatalog.html that includes all of the ones described here. Please feel free to provide suggestions for new ones that you run across.

Table A.1 presents a catalog of common database refactorings. For the sake of simplicity, I will use the following terms in Table A.1:

- *Application* refers to anything that is coupled to your database schema, such as another database, system, data extract, and so on.

- *Deprecate*, as in deprecate the column, implies that the item in question has been targeted for removal (a removal date is negotiated, documented, and communicated to interested parties) and will be removed on or after the agreed upon time.

- *Develop*, as in develop a stored procedure, infers that the stored procedure is designed, written, tested, and deployed appropriately.

- *Method* refers to a stored procedure, trigger, or object operation (such as a Java operation) within the database.

Table A.1   Summary of Common Database Refactorings

NAME	CATEGORY	MOTIVATION	MECHANICS	EXAMPLE
Apply Standard Codes	Data Quality	Different columns store the same kind of data using different codes.	• Identify a common representation and use it consistently.	One table indicates colors using codes "C01," "C02," and "C03," whereas another uses "RE," "GR," and "BL."
Apply Standard Types to Similar Data	Data Quality	Similar data is stored using different types within your database.	• Identify a standard approach for storing this kind of data and apply that approach consistently.	A phone number is stored as a string in one table and an integer in another.
Combine Columns Representing a Single Concept	Structural	A concept has been factored too finely.	• Introduce a single column for the concept. • Combine the existing data values appropriately and store the value in the new column. • Deprecate each of the original columns.	A North American phone number is stored in three columns (one for each part of (905) 555-1212)
Combine One-to-One Tables	Performance	Two tables with a one-to-one relationship between them are joined on a regular basis.	• Create the new table. • Introduce an update scheme to keep the original tables in sync with the new table (either introduce updatable views with the same names as the original two tables or introduce triggers between the three tables). • Copy the data from the original tables to the new table. • Deprecate the original tables.	Employee information is stored in two tables, *Employee* and *EmployeeDetails*. There is a row in each table for each employee within your organization.

Table A.1 *(continued)*

NAME	CATEGORY	MOTIVATION	MECHANICS	EXAMPLE
Consolidate Key Strategy for Entity	Data Quality	Various tables use a different primary key strategy for the same type of entity.	• Identify one primary key strategy for the entity. • For each entity not using the chosen key strategy: • Deprecate the index implementing the primary key (if any). • Introduce columns required by the chosen strategy. • Assign values to the new columns as appropriate. Implement the column. • Deprecate the columns of the original primary key that are no longer required in that table.	To identify customers one table uses customer IDs, another uses Social Security numbers, and another a surrogate key. The surrogate key strategy is chosen and applied to the two tables not currently using it.
Encapsulate Calculation with a Method	Architectural	Several data records are required to calculate a simple figure.	• Develop a method, likely a stored procedure or object operation, to perform the calculation.	To calculate the subtotal of an order, you must subtotal individual line items and then sum those subtotals.
Encapsulate Common Structure with View	Architectural	Applications join several tables to obtain a denormalized view of a common data structure.	• Develop a view in the database for the structure.	To obtain the data for a line item on an order, the *OrderItem* and *Item* tables are joined to get the number of items ordered (from *OrderItem*), the price (from *Item*), and the description (from *Item*).

(continued)

Table A.1 *(continued)*

NAME	CATEGORY	MOTIVATION	MECHANICS	EXAMPLE
Encapsulate CRUD Access with Methods	Architectural	Data structures (potentially stored in several tables) are accessed by systems via submission of SQL insert, select, update, and delete statements by applications. The table schema(s) are now intimately coupled to the applications that access them.	• Develop methods (likely stored procedures or object operations) to read, write, and delete data structures.	To access Customer data you introduce stored procedures named *CustomerRead*, *CustomerWrite*, *CustomerDelete*.
Encapsulate Table with View	Architectural	Data structures (potentially stored in several tables) are accessed by systems via submission of SQL insert, select, update, and delete statements by applications. The table schema(s) are now intimately coupled to the applications that access them.	• Develop one or more views, updatable views where appropriate, to encapsulate access to the data structure. • For databases that do not support updates to multitables through views several views may need to be introduced.	To access Customer data you introduce a view named *VCustomer*.
Introduce Not Null Constraint (also known as *Make Column Non-Nullable* [Sadalage 2003])	Data Quality	A change to your requirements requires that every row have a value for a given column.	• Replace NULL values in the column with a default value. • Update the column constraint to NOT NULL.	The default value for a *Hobbies* column now needs to be "None."

Table A.1 *(continued)*

NAME	CATEGORY	MOTIVATION	MECHANICS	EXAMPLE
Introduce Column Constraint	Data Quality	The data values within a column are well defined.	• Identify the values that you wish to constrain the column to. • Ensure that each row within the table actually contains one of these values for this column, updating the rows as needed. • Develop a constraint for that column defining the values.	The day of the week column may only contain the values "Su," "Mo," and "Sa."
Introduce Alternate Index (see also *Add Unique Index* [Sadalage 2003])	Performance	An entity needs to be accessed in several common ways.	• Develop an alternate index for each common access strategy that is not based on the primary key to increase performance.	Customers are accessed by Social Security number, by customer ID, and by name.
Introduce Calculated Data Column	Performance	A calculation is made often on relatively static data.	• Introduce a column for the calculated value. • To keep the column value up to date: refactor all applications accessing the data *or* Introduce Trigger(s) for Calculated Columns.	A *GrandTotal* column is introduced to the *Order* table.
Introduce Cascading Delete	Referential Integrity	The persistence life cycle between two tables is highly related.	• Develop a delete trigger to cascade the delete from the original table to the newly introduced one.	When a row from the *Order* table is deleted, the appropriate rows are similarly deleted from the *OrderItem* table.

(continued)

Table A.1 (continued)

NAME	CATEGORY	MOTIVATION	MECHANICS	EXAMPLE
Introduce Common Format	Data Quality	Data within a string-based column is stored in several formats.	• Define a common format. • Reformat all of the data within that column to conform to the formatting conventions. • Note that the common format should already be in use within the column; otherwise, existing applications will not be able to work with the new format.	Phone numbers are stored in "(905) 555-1212" and "416 967-1111" formats within a single colum.
Introduce Default Value (also called *Add Default Value* [Sadalage 2003])	Data Quality	Different applications have different default values for the same column.	• Identify a standard default value for that column. • Add the default value to the column. • Refactor any applications to set their own default value before an insert into the database is performed, or better yet, to simply not set it and to simply accept the value set by the database.	One application uses "Green" as a default value whereas another uses "Red" and as a result they act differently on each other's data (even though they share it).
Introduce Lookup Table	Data Quality	A column indicates a code that is interpreted within an application.	• Introduce a lookup table with the code value as the primary key. • Introduce a foreign key constraint to the original code column relating it to the primary key of the code lookup table.	A two-letter State code, such as "CA" or "ON," is converted programmatically to California or Ontario, respectively.

Table A.1 *(continued)*

NAME	CATEGORY	MOTIVATION	MECHANICS	EXAMPLE
Introduce Method to Reduce Data Transfer	Performance	One or more applications read a large amount of data from the database and then "crunch" that data to produce a much smaller result.	• Develop a stored procedure or object operation within the database to crunch the data. • Refactor the application(s) to invoke the method.	The Sales Department needs summary information for the order totals in a given month. This information is broken down by country and then by region (for exampe, state, province, canton) within that country.
Introduce Mirror Table	Performance	A table is very active, so a copy of it is introduced to spread out access overhead.	• Create the mirror table. • Introduce a replication scheme between the original and the mirror table (this could be something as simple as several triggers). • Copy data from the original table into the mirror table.	The *Item* table is accessed by thousands of users a second as they do online searches and purchases from your catalog.
Introduce Redundant Column	Performance	A column from a source table is copied into a "target" table because the source column is commonly accessed whenever a row from the target table is. This prevents the overhead of a join.	• Add the column to the target table. • Initially populate the new column with existing values from the source table. • Identify if you only need the source value at the time of creation or whether you need to keep the values in sync. • Introduce trigger(s) to copy the value of the column that reflects your synchronization needs.	The *Description* column from the *Item* table is copied into the *OrderItem* table.

(continued)

Table A.1 *(continued)*

NAME	CATEGORY	MOTIVATION	MECHANICS	EXAMPLE
Introduce Trigger(s) for Calculated Columns	Referential Integrity	Calculated values need to be updated when their source data changes.	• Develop insert trigger(s) on the appropriate table(s) to update the calculated value. • Develop update trigger(s) on the appropriate table(s) to update the calculated value. • In the case of a calculated value based on data in other table(s), introduce delete trigger(s) on those columns to recalculate the column.	When the subtotal for an order item changes (for example, when you purchase four items now instead of five, the grand total for the order must automatically be updated.

Introduce Update Trigger to Maintain History	Referential Integrity	You need to maintain a historical record of the value for the rows of a table.	• Develop an update trigger for the table.
			• This trigger will do one of two things:
			  ○ Copy the original record to a separate historical table, set a foreign key back to the original, set an applicability date to the new record, and then update to the original record overwriting the previous data.
			  ○ Make a copy of the current record in the original table assigning it a new key value, set an applicability date for the copy, mark the copy as historical, update the original record with the new values.
				A customer service application needs to maintain a record of the various addresses of a customer so that an accurate legal record is kept.

Table A.1   (continued)

NAME	CATEGORY	MOTIVATION	MECHANICS	EXAMPLE
Introduce View Table	Performance	A "view table" contains columns from other tables, that are commonly needed by an application.	• Create the view table. • Introduce a strategy to populate the view table with data. This could be done in batch, resulting in stale data within the view table, or in real-time via triggers.	The *Customer* and *Order* tables are joined, an expensive activity, by several reports. A *CustomerOrderReport* table is introduced to contain the joined data.
Migrate Database Method to Application	Performance	An existing method has been shown to be a bottleneck within your database; it is accessed by applications on similar (for example, connected) platforms, and is not accessed within your database itself.	• Develop the method within the application (potentially a shared library). • Deprecate the original method within the database.	Tax calculations are currently performed by a library of stored procedures within your database. These were originally implemented in the database because they require a small number of read-only lookup tables, tables that could easily be cached in memory by your application.
Migrate Method to Database	Performance	An existing application method is required by several other applications. The other applications are on incompatible platforms.	• Develop a stored procedure or object operation to implement the behavior within the database. • Refactor the original application(s) that implemented the method to access the database method.	The ability to determine the total amount of business that a customer has done with your organization during a given period of time is required by your discounting application, your market analysis application, and two sales applications.

(continued)

Table A.1   (continued)

NAME	CATEGORY	MOTIVATION	MECHANICS	EXAMPLE
Move Column	Structural	An existing column is moved from a source table to a target table.	• Introduce the column in the target table. • Copy data into the new column from the source column. • Introduce a replication strategy (for example, triggers). • Deprecate the source column. • Deprecate the replication strategy.	The *Hobbies* column in the *Employee* table is seldom used, so it should be moved to the *EmployeeDetails* table.
Move Data (Sadalage 2003)	Data Quality	You often need to move data values from one column to another.	• Develop data-migration scripts to move the data. • Copy the data to the new location. • Introduce a replication strategy (for example, triggers). • Refactor affected applications to work with the data in the new location. • Deprecate the replication strategy.	The *Customer.Notes* column contains description information, among other things, in the format "Eye Color: Blue" for many customers. This data needs to be extracted into its own columns.
Remove Application-Specific Constraint	Performance	The business rules for a new application differ from those of existing applications even though they share the same database.	• The applications must be reworked to implement the constraint themselves. • Deprecate the constraint.	A constraint exists limiting color choices to red, green, and blue but a new application requires a myriad of color choices.

Table A.1 *(continued)*

NAME	CATEGORY	MOTIVATION	MECHANICS	EXAMPLE
Remove Default Value	Data Quality	Your environment has changed sufficiently so that a single default value is no longer applicable for a given column.	• Individual applications must be reworked to set their own default values where applicable. • Deprecate the default value definition for the column.	The default value of Monday for day of week is not applicable for several new applications that schedule weekend events.
Remove Not Null Constraint (see also *Make Column Non-Nullable* [Sadalage 2003])	Data Quality	An existing column includes a not-null constraint but you have discovered that you need to store null values in it after all. Consider Introduce Default Value first.	• Make the column nullable. • Refactor all applications to accept null values. Any joins based on this column will need to be converted to outer joins, and source code working with this column will need to convert nulls to zeros, blanks, and so on as appropriate.	A new application is being developed that adds new records to the *Customer* table. This application will not collect the information required to fill the *Preferences* column.
Remove Redundant Column	Data Quality	Primary data that is not used as a key is stored in several places.	• Identify the primary location for the data. • Deprecate the column. • Refactor each application accessing the redundant column refactor so that it accesses the primary location.	A person's birth date is stored in two locations: the *Customer* table and the *BankAccount* table. It should only be in the *Customer* table.
Remove Table	Structural	A table is no longer required.	• Deprecate the table. • Rework any application that still accesses the table to no longer do so.	The *Y2KStatus* table, which was used to record the conversion status of other tables within your database, is no longer required.

(continued)

Table A.1 *(continued)*

NAME	CATEGORY	MOTIVATION	MECHANICS	EXAMPLE
Remove Unused Column	Structural	A column isn't used any more.	• Deprecate the unused column. • Rework any application to no longer access that column.	The *WatchesSeinfeld* column of the *TVViewingHabit* table is no longer used because the Seinfeld TV show has gone off the air.
Remove View	Structural	A view is no longer required.	• Deprecate the view. • Rework any application so that it no longer accesses that view.	The view *VCustomerDetails* has been superceded by *VCustomerInformation* as the official source of customer data.
Rename Column	Structural	A column is inappropriately or inconsistently named.	• The name of the column is changed to the new name. • Introduce a new column with the new name. • Copy data from the original column to the new column. • Deprecate the original column. • Introduce triggers to keep the two columns in sync during the deprecation period. • Remove the triggers along with the original column once it is eventually removed. • Refactor applications and your database (views, stored procs, and so on may be affected) to access the new column. • Note that if this column is used in other tables as (part of) a foreign key, then you may want to rename those columns similarly.	The column *Cust_B_Date* is to be renamed *BirthDate* to reflect your new, people-oriented naming conventions.

Table A.1 *(continued)*

NAME	CATEGORY	MOTIVATION	MECHANICS	EXAMPLE
Rename Table	Structural	A table is inappropriately or inconsistently named.	• Create a new table with the new name. • Copy data from the original table to the new table. • Delete the original table. • Create a new view with the old table name. • Deprecate the new view. • Refactor applications and your database (views, stored procs, and so on may be affected) to access the new table.	The table *T_CUST_XAE* is to be renamed *Customer* to reflect your new people-oriented naming conventions.
Replace BLOB with Table	Structural	A structure is stored as a BLOB in your database.	• Introduce a table representing the structure so that it is easily accessible to other applications. • Deprecate the column in which the BLOB is currently stored.	An XML structure that contains data about a training course is stored as a single column in your database.
Replace Calculated Data Column with a Method	Data Quality	A calculated column is inconsistently updated within the database. The value is needed by several applications.	• Develop the method, likely a stored procedure or object operation. • Deprecate the column. • Refactor the applications to access the method.	The *AverageMark* column within the *Student* table is not being updated consistently by the applications.

(continued)

Table A.1 (continued)

NAME	CATEGORY	MOTIVATION	MECHANICS	EXAMPLE
Replace Column	Structural	An existing column needs to be replaced with a new definition. Perhaps the type of the column has changed or perhaps the usage has changed.	• Introduce the new column to the table. • Copy values from the original column into the new column, transforming the data as appropriate. • Deprecate the original column. • Introduce triggers to keep the two columns up to date during the deprecation period. • Refactor applications and your database (views, stored procs, and so on may be affected) to access the new column. • Remove the triggers once the original column is eventually removed.	Customer IDs are currently stored as integer numbers. The business definition of customer IDs has changed to include a three-character alphabetic code indicating the type of customer (for example, COR for corporate customers).
Replace Natural Key with Surrogate	Structural	You want to apply a consistent surrogate key strategy within your database.	• Introduce the new column for your surrogate key. • Apply values to the surrogate key column in the same order as the existing primary key. • Introduce a new index to implement the key as a secondary index.	The *Customer* table is currently keyed on the *CustomerNumber* column. A new surrogate key *CustomerOID* will be introduced.

Table A.1   *(continued)*

NAME	CATEGORY	MOTIVATION	MECHANICS	EXAMPLE
			• Introduce a secondary index for the natural key (for applications still working with it). • Refactor existing applications to work with the new surrogate key. • Note that the natural key column(s) are not removed because they are still fundamental data elements for that table.	
Replace One-to-Many with Associative Table	Structural	You want to position yourself to be able to easily support a many-to-many association between two tables.	• Introduce the associative table. This table will contain the primary key columns from the two business tables. • From the original table implementing the relationship, copy the value of its primary key column(s) and the foreign key column(s) that implement the relationship. • Deprecate the foreign key column(s) from the original table. • Refactor the applications to work with the new associative table.	The relationship between *Customer* and *Address* is currently implemented with a foreign key column within *Customer*. This column is *AddressOID*.

(continued)

Table A.1   *(continued)*

NAME	CATEGORY	MOTIVATION	MECHANICS	EXAMPLE
Replace Repeating Groups with New Table	Structural	Data columns within a table are repeated.	• Introduce a new table representing the repeating group. • Copy the data from the columns used for repeating groups into the new table. • Deprecate the columns of the repeating groups. • The column(s) of the primary key of the original table must be included in this new table to maintain the association. • You likely need to Introduce a Cascading Delete.	The Customer table includes columns named *Account_ID1*, *Account_ID2*,.... *Account_ID10*.
Replace Type Code with Booleans	Data Quality	A column contains values for a type code, and some base types overlap.	• Introduce a Boolean column for each base type. • Deprecate the original column. • Introduce triggers to keep the columns in sync with each other or introduce views if possible. • Set the initial values of the Boolean columns based on the current values of the type code column. • Refactor the applications to work with the Boolean columns.	If the *EmployeeTypeCode* is *AI*, then the person is a line worker; if it is *B*, the person is a manager; if it is *C*, then the person is both a line worker and a manager. The column is replaced with two Boolean columns *IsWorker* and *IsManager*.

Table A.1   *(continued)*

NAME	CATEGORY	MOTIVATION	MECHANICS	EXAMPLE
Replace *View* with Method(s)	Structural	A view exists to access a common data structure within the database.	• Deprecate the view. • Develop the method(s). • Note that an updatable view will likely require method(s) to update, read, and delete the data. • Rework any application to use the method(s).	Security considerations require complex logging that isn't possible to automate. The *VCustomerInformation* view needs to be replaced with methods that can fulfill these new requirements for critical data associated with some customers.
Separate Data Based on Timeliness	Structural	A table contains sets of columns that are updated at different times. The timeliness of update is a very good indication that different applications, or portions thereof, are responsible for the update of each set.	• Introduce separate tables for each set of data. • Copy the data from the original columns into the new tables. • Introduce a view representing the former table that uses the new tables. • Deprecate the view. • Refactor applications and your database that access the original data to access the new structure.	An *Employee* table contains some columns that are updated on an ad hoc basis, some that are updated quarterly, and others that are updated annually.

(continued)

Table A.1 *(continued)*

NAME	CATEGORY	MOTIVATION	MECHANICS	EXAMPLE
Separate Read-Only Data	Structural	Some nonkey columns within a table are read-only, whereas others are updatable.	• Introduce a new table for the read-only data. • Copy the data from the original columns into the new table. • Introduce a view representing the original table. See Encapsulate Common Structure with View. • Deprecate the view. • Refactor applications and your database that access the original data so that they access the new structure.	You purchase information about your customers from a third-party vendor, such as their income. This information can be read by your applications but not updated.
Split Column	Structural	A single column is being used for several purposes or the column contains several data elements.	• Analyze how the column is being used and introduce one column for each type of usage. • Copy the data from the original column to the new columns. • Introduce triggers to keep the data up to date. • Deprecate the original column. • Remove the triggers when you remove the original column.	The *Name* column is replaced with *FirstName, MiddleName, LastName.* Unfortunately, several data formats exist. For example, names are stored as Scott William Ambler, Scott W. Ambler, Scott William Alexander Ambler, and Ambler Scott.

References and Suggested Reading

Agile Alliance (2001a) "Manifesto for Agile Software Development." www.agilealliance.org.

Agile Alliance (2001b) "Principles: The Agile Alliance." www.agilealliance.org/principles.html.

Ambler, S. W. (1995) *The Object Primer: Application Developer's Guide to Object Orientation*. New York: Cambridge University Press.

Ambler, S. W. (1997) *Building Object Applications That Work: Your Step-By-Step Handbook for Developing Robust Systems with Object Technology*. New York: Cambridge University Press. www.ambysoft.com/buildingObjectApplications.html.

Ambler, S. W. (1997b) "What's Missing from the UML?" *Object Magazine* 7(8). pp. 28–37.

Ambler, S. W. (1998a) *Process Patterns — Building Large-Scale Systems Using Object Technology*. New York: Cambridge University Press, www.ambysoft.com/processPatterns.html.

Ambler, S. W. (1998b) "Object-Oriented Security (Part 1 of 2)." *Software Development*, November 1998, 6(11), pp. 69–71.

Ambler, S. W. (1998c) "Object-Oriented Security (Part 2 of 2)." *Software Development*, December 1998, 6(12), pp. 65–67.

Ambler, S. W. (1999) *More Process Patterns — Delivering Large-Scale Systems Using Object Technology*. New York: Cambridge University Press, www.ambysoft.com /moreProcessPatterns.html.

Ambler, S. W. (2000a) "Crossing the Object-Data Divide." *Software Development*, March 2000. www.sdmagazine.com/documents/s=746/sdm0003j/0003j.htm.

Ambler, S. W. (2000b) "Crossing the Object-Data Divide, Part 2." *Software Development*, April 2000, www.sdmagazine.com/documents/s=745/sdm0004k/0004k.htm.

Ambler, S. W. (2001a) *The Object Primer 2nd Edition: The Application Developer's Guide to Object Orientation*. New York: Cambridge University Press. www.ambysoft.com/theObjectPrimer.html.

Ambler, S. W. (2001b) Enterprise Unified Process Home Page, www.enterprise unifiedprocess.info.

Ambler, S. W. (2001c) Agile Modeling Home Page. www.agilemodeling.com.

Ambler, S. W. (2001d) "The Design of a Robust Persistence Layer." www.ambysoft.com/persistenceLayer.html.

Ambler, S. W. (2001e) *Mapping Objects to a Relational Database*. www.ambysoft.com/mappingObjects.html.

Ambler, S. W. (2002a) *Agile Modeling: Best Practices for the Unified Process and Extreme Programming*. New York: Wiley Publishing, Inc., www.ambysoft.com/agileModeling.html.

Ambler, S. W. (2002c) "The Agile Data Home Page. www.agiledata.org.

Ambler, S. W. (2002d) "Refactoring for Fitness." *Software Development*, February 2002, www.sdmagazine.com.

Ambler, S. W. (2003) *The Elements of UML Style*. New York: Cambridge University Press, www.ambysoft.com/elementsUMLStyle.html.

Ambler, S. W. (2003b) "Isn't That Special?" *Software Development*, January 2003, 11(1), pp. 43 –54.

Ambler, S. W. and Constantine, L. L. (2000a) *The Unified Process Inception Phase*. Gilroy, CA: CMP Books. www.ambysoft.com/inceptionPhase.html.

Ambler, S. W. and Constantine, L. L. (2000b) *The Unified Process Elaboration Phase*. Gilroy, CA: CMP Books, www.ambysoft.com/elaborationPhase.html.

Ambler, S. W. and Constantine, L. L. (2000c) *The Unified Process Construction Phase*. Gilroy, CA: CMP Books, www.ambysoft.com/constructionPhase.html.

Ambler, S. W. and Constantine, L. L. (2002) *The Unified Process Transition and Production Phases*. Gilroy, CA: CMP Books, www.ambysoft.com/transitionProductionPhase.html.

Anderson, R. J. (2001) *Security Engineering: A Guide to Building Dependable Distributed Systems*. New York: Wiley Publishing, Inc.

Apple Computer, Inc. (2002) "Aqua Human Interface Guidelines." developer.apple.com/techpubs/macosx/Essentials/AquaHIGuidelines/index.html.

Astels, D. (2003) *Test Driven Development: A Practical Guide*. Upper Saddle River, NJ: Prentice Hall.

Atkinson, C., Bayer, J., Bunse, C., Kamsties, E., Laitenberger, O., Laqua, R., Muthig, D., Paech, B., Wust, J., and Zettel, J. (2002) *Component-Based Product Line Engineering With UML*. Upper Saddle River, NJ: Pearson Education.

Barker, R. (1990) *CASE*Method: Entity Relationship Modeling*. Reading, MA: Addison-Wesley.

Bass, L., Clements, P., and Kazman, R. (1998) *Software Architecture in Practice*. Reading, MA: Addison-Wesley Longman, Inc.

Beck, K. and Cunningham, W. (1989) "A Laboratory for Teaching Object-Oriented Thinking." *Proceedings of OOPSLA'89*, pp. 1–6.

Beck, K. (2000) *Extreme Programming Explained — Embrace Change*. Reading, MA: Addison-Wesley Longman, Inc.

Beck, K. (2003) *Test Driven Development: By Example*. Reading, MA: Addison-Wesley.

Beedle, M. and Schwaber, K. (2001) *Agile Software Development With SCRUM*. Upper Saddle River, NJ: Prentice Hall, Inc.

Bennett, D. (1997) *Designing Hard Software: The Essential Tasks*. Greenwich, CT: Manning Publications Co.

Bernstein, P.A. and Newcomer, E. (1997) *Principles of Transaction Processing: For the Systems Professional*. San Francisco: Morgan Kaufmann.

Brant, J. and Yoder, J. (2000) "Creating Reports with Query Objects". *Pattern Languages of Program Design 4*, pp. 375–390. Reading, MA: Addison-Wesley.

Brooks, F. P. (1995) *The Mythical Man Month: Essays on Software Engineering Anniversary Edition*. Reading, MA: Addison-Wesley.

Brown, K. and Whitenack, B. G. (1996) "Crossing Chasms: A Pattern Language for Object-RDBMS Integration: The Static Patterns." *Pattern Languages of Program Design 2*, pp. 227–238. Reading, MA: Addison-Wesley.

Carlson, D. (2001) *Modeling XML Applications with UML: Practical E-Business Applications*. Reading, MA: Addison-Wesley.

Celko, J. (1999) *Joe Celko's Data & Databases: Concepts in Practice*. San Francisco: Morgan Kaufmann.

Cockburn, A. (2001a) *Writing Effective Use Cases*. Reading, MA: Addison-Wesley.

Cockburn, A. (2001b) "Crystal Clear: A Human-Powered Software Development Methodology for Small Teams." members.aol.com/humansandt/crystal/clear/.

Cockburn, A. (2002) *Agile Software Development*. Reading, MA: Addison-Wesley Longman, Inc.

Constantine, L. L. and Lockwood, L. A. D. (1999) *Software for Use: A Practical Guide to the Models and Methods of Usage-Centered Design*. New York: ACM Press.

Coplien, J. and Harrison, N. (2001) Organizational Patterns Site. www.bell-labs.com/cgi-user/OrgPatterns/OrgPatterns.

Date, C. J. (2001) *An Introduction to Database System,* Seventh Edition. Reading, MA: Addison-Wesley Longman, Inc.

Dick, K. (2003) *XML: A Manager's Guide*, Second Edition. Reading, MA: Addison-Wesley Longman, Inc.

Feathers, M. (2002) "Working Effectively with Legacy Code." www.objectmentor .com/resources/articles/WorkingEffectivelyWithLegacyCode.pdf.

Finkelstein, C. (1989) *An Introduction to Information Engineering: From Strategic Planning to Information Systems*. Reading, MA: Addison-Wesley.

Fowler, M. (1997) *Analysis Patterns: Reusable Object Models*. Reading, MA: Addison-Wesley Longman, Inc.

Fowler, M. (1999) *Refactoring: Improving the Design of Existing Code*. Reading, MA: Addison-Wesley Longman, Inc.

Fowler, M. (2001a) "The New Methodology." www.martinfowler.com/articles /newMethodology.html.

Fowler, M. (2001b) "Is Design Dead?" www.martinfowler.com/articles /designDead.html.

Fowler, M., Rice, D., Foemmel, M., Hieatt, E., Mee, R., and Stafford, R. (2003) *Patterns of Enterprise Application Architecture*. Reading, MA: Addison-Wesley Longman, Inc.

Fowler, M. and Sadalage, P. (2003) "Evolutionary Database Design." www .martinfowler.com/articles/evodb.html.

Fowler, M. and Scott, K. (1999) *UML Distilled: A Brief Guide to the Standard Object Modeling Language*, Second Edition. Reading, MA: Addison-Wesley Longman, Inc.

Gamma, E., Helm, R., Johnson, R., and Vlissides, J. (1995) *Design Patterns: Elements of Reusable Object-Oriented Software*. Reading, MA: Addison-Wesley.

Gane, C. and Sarson, T. (1979) *Structured Systems Analysis: Tools and Techniques*. Upper Saddle River, NJ: Prentice Hall, Inc.

Graham, I., Henderson-Sellers, B., and Younessi, H. (1997) *The OPEN Process Specification*. New York: ACM Press.

Graves, M. (2002) *Designing XML Databases*. Upper Saddle River, NJ: Prentice Hall.

Halpin, T. A. (2001) *Information Modeling and Relational Databases: From Conceptual Analysis to Logical Design*. San Francisco: Morgan Kaufmann.

Hay, D. C. (1996) *Data Model Patterns: Conventions of Thought*. New York: Dorset House Publishing.

Hay, D. C. (1999) "A Comparison of Data Modeling Techniques." www .essentialstrategies.com/publications/modeling/compare.htm.

Hay, D. C. (2003) *Requirements Analysis: From Business Views to Architecture*. Upper Saddle River, NJ: Prentice Hall, Inc.

Hernandez, M. J. and Viescas, J. L. (2000) *SQL Queries for Mere Mortals: A Hands-on Guide to Data Manipulation in SQL*. Reading, MA: Addison-Wesley.

Herzum, P. and Sims, O. (2000) *Business Component Factory: A Comprehensive Overview of Component-Based Development for the Enterprise*. New York: Wiley Publishing, Inc.

Highsmith, J. A., III (2000) *Adaptive Software Development: A Collaborative Approach to Managing Complex Systems*. New York: Dorset House Publishing.

Hock, D. W. (2000) *Birth of the Chaordic Age*. San Francisco: Berrett-Koehler Publishers, Inc.

Hohmann, L. (1996) *Journey of the Software Professional: The Sociology of Computer Programming*. Upper Saddle River, NJ: Prentice Hall PTR.

Howard, M. and LeBlanc, D. (2003) *Writing Secure Code*, Second Edition. Redmond WA: Microsoft Press.

Hunt, A. and Thomas, D. (2000) *The Pragmatic Programmer: From Journeyman to Master*. Reading, MA: Addison-Wesley Longman, Inc.

Inmon, W. H. (2002) *Building the Data Warehouse*, Third Edition. New York: Wiley Publishing, Inc.

Jacobson, I., Booch, G., and Rumbaugh, J., (1999) *The Unified Software Development Process*. Reading, MA: Addison-Wesley Longman, Inc.

Jacobson, I., Griss, M., and Jonsson, P. (1997) *Software Reuse: Architecture, Process, and Organization for Business Success*. New York: ACM Press.

Jeffries, R., Anderson, A., and Hendrickson, C. (2001) *Extreme Programming Installed*. Reading, MA: Addison-Wesley.

Jones, C. (2000) *Software Assessments, Benchmarks, and Best Practices*. Boston: Addison-Wesley Longman, Inc.

Kerievsky, J. (2001) "Patterns and XP." In: *Extreme Programming Examined.*, Succi, G. and Marchesi, M. (eds.), Reading, MA: Addison-Wesley.

Kerth, N. (2001) *Project Retrospectives: A Handbook for Team Reviews*. New York: Dorset House Publishing.

Kleppe, A., Warmer, J., and Bast, W. (2003) *MDA Explained: The Model Driven Architecture, Practice and Promise*. Upper Saddle River, NJ: Pearson Education, Inc.

Kruchten, P. (1995) "The 4+1 View Model of Architecture." *IEEE Software*. 12(6), November 1995. pp. 42–50.

Kruchten, P. (2000) *The Rational Unified Process: An Introduction*, Second Edition. Reading, MA: Addison-Wesley Longman, Inc.

Larman, C. (2002) *Applying UML and Patterns: An Introduction to Object-Oriented Analysis and Design and the Unified Process*. Upper Saddle River, NJ: Prentice Hall PTR.

Linthicum, D. S. (2000) *Enterprise Application Integration*. Reading, MA: Addison-Wesley Longman, Inc.

Marick, B. (2002) Agile Testing Home Page. www.testing.com/agile/.

Marinescu, F. (2002) *EJB Design Patterns*. New York: Wiley Publishing, Inc.

Martin, R. C., Newkirk, J. W., and Koss, R. S. (2003) *Agile Software Development: Principles, Patterns, and Practices*. Upper Saddle River, NJ: Prentice Hall.

McBreen, P. (2001) *Software Craftsmanship: The New Imperative*. Reading, MA: Addison-Wesley Longman, Inc.

McGovern, J., Tyagi, S., Stevens, M. E., & Mathew, S. (2003) *Java Web Services Architecture*. San Francisco: Morgan Kaufmann.

Mitnick, K. D. and Simon W. L. (2002) *The Art of Deception: Controlling the Human Element of Security*. New York: Wiley Publishing, Inc.

Moore, G. A. (2002) *Crossing The Chasm: Revised Edition*. New York: HarperCollins Publishing.

Moriarty, T. (2001) "To Unify Architecture With Methodology: The Rational Unified Process Meets the Zachman Information Systems Architecture." *Intelligent Enterprise*. April 16, 2001. www.intelligententerprise.com/010416/metaprise1_2.shtml.

Muller, R. J. (1999) *Database Design for Smarties: Using UML for Data Modeling*. San Francisco: Morgan Kaufmann.

Mullins, C. S. (2002) *Database Administration: The Complete Guide to Practices and Procedures*. Reading, MA: Addison-Wesley Longman, Inc.

Naiburg, E. J. and Maksimchuk, R. A. (2001) *UML for Database Design*. Reading, MA: Addison-Wesley.

Nanavati, S., Thieme, M., and Nanavati, R. (2002) *Biometrics: Identity Verification in a Networked World*. New York: Wiley Publishing, Inc.

Object Management Group (2001a) "The Unified Modeling Language (UML) Specification." www.omg.org/technology/documents/formal/uml.htm.

Object Management Group (2001b) "Model Driven Architecture (MDA)." ftp://ftp.omg.org/pub/docs/ormsc/01-07-01.pdf.

Object Management Group (2001c) "Software Process Engineering Metamodel Specification." www.omg.org.

Palmer, S. R. and Felsing, J. M. (2002) *A Practical Guide to Feature-Driven Development*. Upper Saddle River, NJ: Prentice Hall PTR.

Pender, T. (2003) *UML Bible*. New York: Wiley Publishing, Inc.

Rational Corporation (2001) Rational Unified Process Home Page. www.rational.com/products/rup/index.jsp.

Reed, P. R. (2002) *Developing Applications with Java and UML*. New York: Addison-Wesley Longman, Inc.

Reingruber, M. C. and Gregory, W. W. (1994) *The Data Modeling Handbook: A Best-Practice Approach to Building Quality Data Models*. New York: Wiley Publishing, Inc.

Roman, E., Ambler, S. W., and Jewell, T., (2002) *Mastering Enterprise Java Beans*, Second Edition. New York: Wiley Publishing, Inc.

Rosenberg, D and Scott, K. (1999) *Use Case Driven Object Modeling With UML: A Practical Approach*. Reading, MA: Addison-Wesley Longman, Inc.

Ross, R. G. (1997) *The Business Rule Book*, Second Edition. Houston TX: Business Rules Solutions, Inc.

Rumbaugh, J., Blaha, M., Premerlani, W., Eddy, F., Lorensen, W. (1991) *Object-Oriented Modeling and Design.* Upper Saddle River, NJ: Prentice Hall.

Sadalage, P. (2003) "List of Database Refactorings." martinfowler.com/dbrefact/.

Sadalage, P. and Schuh, P. (2002) "The Agile Database: Tutorial Notes." Presented at XP/Agile Universe 2002, www.xpuniverse.com.

Schmidt, R. (1998) *Data Modeling for Information Professionals.* Upper Saddle River, NJ: Prentice Hall PTR.

Schuh, P. (2001) "Agile DBA." Presentation at Software Development East 2001, www.sdexpo.com.

Schuh, P. (2002) "Agility and the Database." *XP 2002 Conference Proceedings,* pp. 125–129.

Shasha, D. and Bonnet, P. (2003) Database Tuning: Principles, Experiments, and Troubleshooting Techniques. San Francisco: Morgan Kaufman.

Stapleton, J. (1997) *DSDM: Dynamic Systems Development Method.* Reading, MA: Addison-Wesley.

Stapleton, J. (2003) *DSDM: Business Focused Development,* Second Edition. Reading, MA: Addison-Wesley.

Sun Microsystems (2001) *Java Look and Feel Design Guidelines.* Reading, MA: Addison-Wesley.

Ulrich, W. M. (2002) *Legacy Systems: Transformation Strategies.* Upper Saddle River, NJ: Prentice Hall.

Vermeulen, A., Ambler, S.W., Bumgardner, G., Metz, E., Misfeldt, T., Shur, J., and Thompson, P. (2000) *The Elements of Java Style.* New York: Cambridge University Press.

Williams, L. and Kessler, R. (2002) *Pair Programming Illuminated.* Reading, MA: Addison-Wesley.

Wood, J. and Silver, D. (1995) *Joint Application Development,* Second Edition. New York: Wiley Publishing, Inc.

Yoder, J. and Barcalow, J. (2000) "Architectural Patterns for Enabling Application Security." *Pattern Languages of Program Design 4,* pp. 301–336. Reading, MA: Addison-Wesley.

Yourdon, E. (1989) *Modern Structured Analysis.* Upper Saddle River, NJ: Prentice Hall.

Yourdon, E. (1997) *Death March: The Complete Software Developer's Guide to Surviving "Mission Impossible" Projects.* Upper Saddle River, NJ: Prentice Hall.

ZIFA (2002) The Zachman Institute for Framework Advancement. www.zifa.com.

Index